PRAISE FOR MAJOR (RET.)

"Jason Howk has spent a career working with people from the Middle East and the greater Islamic world. His deep interactions with those of the Islamic faith have helped shape his extensive understanding of the people of the region in a way that few in the West ever come to understand."

— Dr. Ahmed Qureshi, Adjunct Professor of Middle East Studies, US Air Force Special Operations School

"Jason Howk's . . . impressive and easy to understand interpretation of Muslim orthodoxy allows the Western world an education in beliefs that are difficult to put into perspective."

—Michael Franckowiak, NFL football player; Wall Street finance trader; veteran supporter

"Jason's work across the globe has led him literally to being in the trenches to develop Muslim coalitions and being at the most senior levels of government. His experience and expertise is truly fascinating and one of a kind; not a better man for this task than Jason Howk."

—Lieutenant Colonel Jim, Army officer with years of operational experience inside foreign cultures

"Now, more than perhaps ever before, efforts are needed to improve cross-cultural and religious understanding. Opening up and explaining the key Islamic text to non-Muslims is so important when sound bites and prejudice are dominating the dialogue. . . . His work is timely and necessary."

—Evan Fuery, former U.K. Military and Joint Operations colleague; energy company executive

"While the Qur'an is open to wide interpretation, Jason does an outstanding job of providing an unbiased and easily understood translation. . . . from the beginner student to the most experienced regional expert."

—Alan Van Saun, Special Operations Professional

"This groundbreaking presentation of the Qur'an will fortify our understanding and facilitate exploration of a major dilemma of our time."

—Gloria F. Hartley, former school psychologist

"Major (ret.) Jason C. Howk is a well-prepared, well-spoken writer and lecturer. His knowledge about the Islamic faith and of the Qur'an is the result not of only his scholarship and research, but from his first-hand experience in Afghanistan, where he successfully befriended leaders and local citizens. Jason is able to help close the information and understanding gaps which exist between the Muslim and non-Muslim worlds."

—John C. Strickland, Retired banker, former Councilman in Pinehurst, N.C.

"In his presentations and classes, Jason discusses the complex history and contemporary issues of the Middle East in educated, clear, unbiased terms. Providing factual information in a non-judgmental way, Jason helps listeners understand complicated material and process current events. He utilizes his educational, professional, military, and personal experiences to describe and humanize material that typical Americans read only in newspapers."

—Martha A. Wolfe, Social Worker

"An exceptional rendition of the Qur'an written for the layman and theologian alike. This is by far the most understandable English rendition of the Qur'an to date, bringing a common understanding of Islam to historians, academia, and all people of faith. A must read for followers of the Christian and Jewish faith to allow for an educated conversation with the Muslim community."

—Brett Feddersen, U.S. National Security and Defense Professional

"Jason readily shares his in-depth knowledge of Islam, the Qur'an and the Middle East in a clear and understandable way. To seek a deeper understanding on complicated subjects, this book is the place to begin."

—Gina Brown, Retired Real Estate Company President & Owner

"Jason Howk has been studying the Middle East for over twenty years. Both in service to our nation and as an academic, he is uniquely qualified from both his academic study and the time that he has spent in the Arab world to undertake this project. . . . This translation will help all of us Westerners better understand the challenges the world faces in the Middle East."

—Lieutenant Colonel Gabe Barton, U.S. Army

"I wish every American could attend one of his talks. The truth needs to be told. An uninformed opinion leads to bias and hate. This has led me to want to learn more about Islam."

—Wanda Tubbs, Retired office manager and secretary, Pinehurst Rotary Club, N.C.

THE QUR'AN

A CHRONOLOGICAL MODERN ENGLISH INTERPRETATION

by Major (Retired)
JASON CRISS HOWK

The Qur'an: A Chronological Modern English Interpretation

Published by Old Stone Press
an imprint of J. H. Clark & Associates, Inc.
Louisville, Kentucky 40207 USA
www.oldstonepress.com

For information about special discounts for bulk purchases or autographed copies of this book, please contact Old Stone Press at john@oldstonepress.com or the author, Jason Howk at first.mentor14@gmail.com.

The Qur'an: A Chronological Modern English Interpretation
includes maps, illustrations, bibliographical references, and index

Library of Congress Control Number: 2017904866
ISBN: 978-1-938462-28-3 (Paperback: $27.95)
ISBN: 978-1-938462-30-6 (Hardcover: $39.95)
ISBN: 978-1-938462-31-3 (Ebook: $14.99)

Published in the United States

Contents

SECTION 1. TEXT OF THE QUR'AN

Meccan Period [MC] 610–622 AD (12 Years/86 Chapters)

CHRONOLOGICAL CHAPTER TITLES		TRADITIONAL SURA NUMBERS		
24	Abasa (He Frowned)	80	(42 verses)	22
25	Al-Qadr (The [night of] Fate/Ordainment)	97	(5 verses)	23
26	Al-Shams (The Sun)	91	(15 verses)	23
27	Al-Burooj (The Constellations of Stars)	85	(22 verses)	24
28	Al-Tin (The Fig)	95	(8 verses)	25
29	Quraish (The Quraish or Quraysh Tribe)	106	(4 verses)	25
30	Al-Qariah (The Catastrophe)	101	(11 verses)	26
31	Al-Qiyama (Resurrection Day)	75	(40 verses)	26
32	Al-Humaza (The Slanderer)	104	(9 verses)	28
33	Al-Mursalat (The Emissaries)	77	(50 verses)	28
34	Al-Qaf (The Arabic letter Qaf/the *Q* sound)	50	(45 verses)	30
35	Al-Balad (The Town/City)	90	(20 verses)	33
36	Al-Tariq (The Nightly Visitor/Bright Star)	86	(17 verses)	34
37	Al-Qamar (The Moon)	54	(55 verses)	35
38	Saad (The Arabic Letter Saad)	38	(88 verses)	38
39	Al-Araf (The Heights)	7	(206 verses)	44
40	Al-Jinn (The Genies)	72	(28 verses)	66
41	Ya Seen (one of the prophet's names)	36	(83 verses)	68
42	Al-Furqan (The Criterion)	25	(77 verses)	74
43	Fatir (The Originator or the Angels)	35	(45 verses)	80
44	Maryam (Mary)	19	(98 verses)	85
45	Ta Ha (Arabic letters with *T* and *H* sounds)	20	(135 verses)	93
46	Al-Waqia (Imminent Hour—Judgment Day)	56	(96 verses)	103
47	Al-Shuara (The Poets)	26	(227 verses)	106
48	Al-Naml (The Ants)	27	(93 verses)	116
49	Al-Qasas (The Story)	28	(88 verses)	125
50	Al-Isra/Bani Israel (Night Journey or Israelis)	17	(111 verses)	135
51	Yunus (Jonah)	10	(109 verses)	148
52	Hud (Hud)	11	(123 verses)	161
53	Yusuf (Joseph)	12	(111 verses)	175
54	Al-Hijr (Rock City)	15	(99 verses)	188
55	Al-Anam (The Cattle or Livestock)	6	(165 verses)	194
56	Al-Saffat (Those Arranged in Ranks)	37	(182 verses)	217
57	Al-Luqman (the account of Luqman)	31	(34 verses)	225
58	Saba (Sheba)	34	(54 verses)	229
59	Al-Zumar (The Throngs)	39	(75 verses)	235

Medina Period [MD] and Later, 622–632 AD (10 Years/28 Chapters or Sections)

SECTION 2.

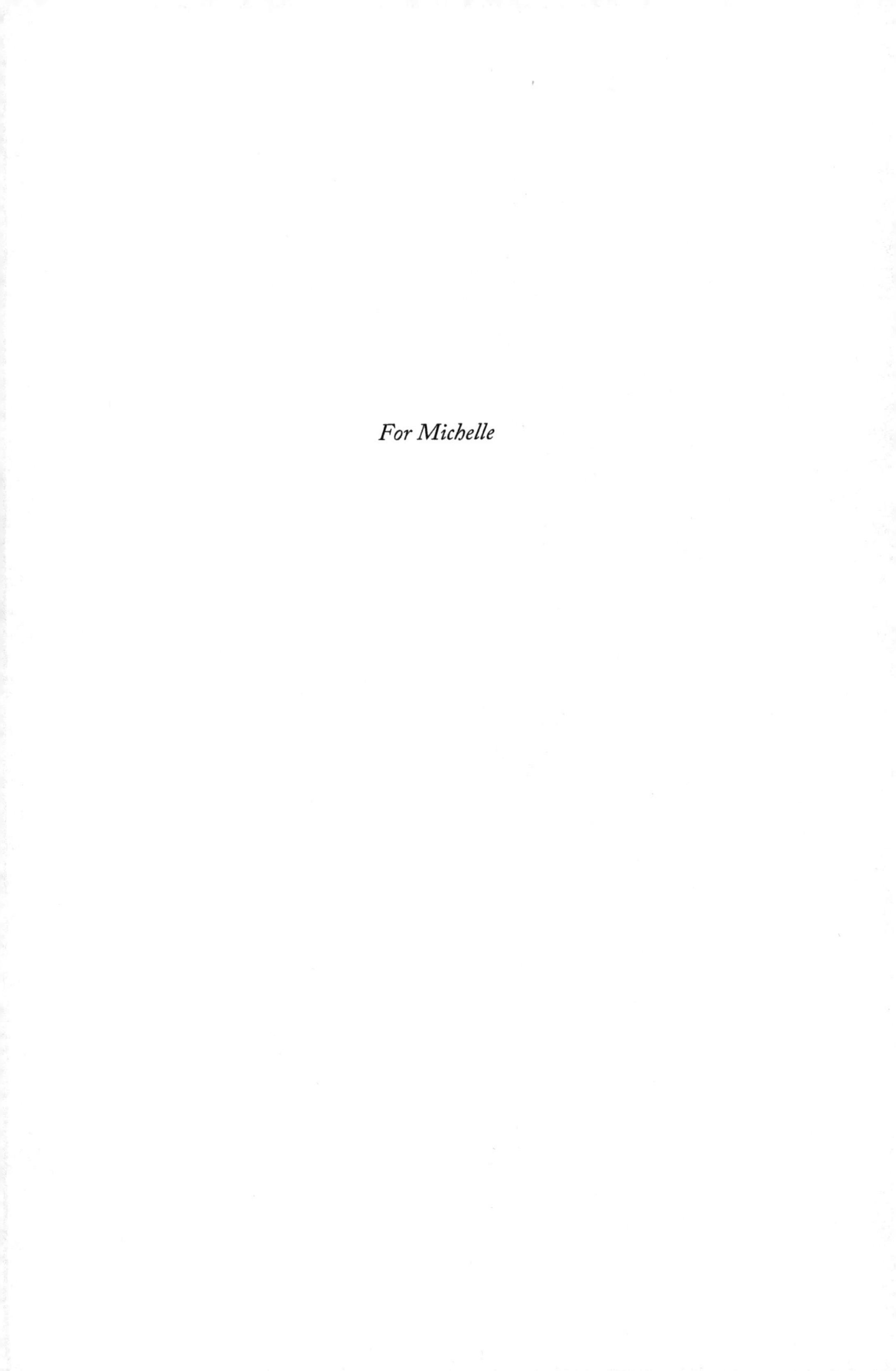

For Michelle

Jason, the Qur'an doesn't just belong to Muslims. It's a gift to humankind from God, and it invites all people to read it, think about it, interpret it, and share it. You are answering God's call. If people don't accept that, then they don't understand Islam and should read the Qur'an again.

—Dr. Abbas Kadhim, Islamic scholar and trusted friend

The two most important days in your life are the day you are born and the day you find out why.

—Mark Twain, American author and humorist

The best way to find out if you can trust somebody is to trust them.

—Ernest Hemingway, American author and lover of life

Acknowledgments

I pause here to remember my many Muslim friends that taught me what the true teachings of Islam are: kindness, charity, hospitality, forgiveness, and respect for elders. Some of my Muslim acquaintances died too young, while others continue today to live loving and peaceful lives of tolerance. May we forever be united against hateful and violent people of any religious faith.

I also pause to remember my brothers and sisters, around the globe, that have fallen in the "Great War" of our time. A toast of Balvenie to you. Whether in or out of uniform, you served honorably trying to protect the innocent and to end the intolerance of violent radical Islamists and other murderers that prey on the innocent.

My friend once told me, "Islam is not a religion of peace or war. Islam is a religion, just like any other. Peace and war depend on one's interpretation and ends." His thought provides us the answer to our current troubles. We must learn more about each other's religions and cultures and build on our similarities, not fight over our differences. I would further add that I don't want a war between all Muslims and the rest of humanity, because that is exactly what groups like ISIS seek. Only through education can the world undermine the twisted ideology that violent radical Islamist movements are spreading. Almost every religion can be, and at some point, has been, used to cloak hatred and bigotry, something which we must stand against whenever it occurs.

Thank you to my good friends and Islamic culture mentors Dr. Najibullah Sahak, MD and Dr. Abbas Kadhim, PhD. Your tireless efforts to help me understand your cultures and religion have driven me to share this topic with others. Your support over the years has been instrumental to my career.

I must thank the Weymouth Center for the Arts and Humanities for hosting me while I worked on this book. The James Boyd House is one of the most inspiring and beautiful places to write. I am proud to be one of North Carolina's writers-in-residence and to follow in the footsteps of Wolfe, Green, Fitzgerald, and Boyd, who were similarly inspired by this place. It is truly an artist's retreat.

Thanks to the Sandhills Community College for bringing me on board as a teacher, where I could further refine my understanding of Islam and the broader Middle East. That opportunity would not have been possible without the dozens of interested citizens in middle North Carolina that attended my public presentations and asked me hundreds of questions that sharpened my ideas about Islam. Thanks especially to my kind benefactors and proper southern gentlepeople Bert and Parker Hall for putting me in touch with President Dempsey at the college.

Thanks to Blair Academy for inviting me to talk to your "renaissance students" and amazing teachers. Their interest and questions about Islam continue to drive me to explain this religion.

Thanks to the wonderful and generous Rob and Julie Neff of the Sandhills. When I needed another hideaway to work on this book, you offered the perfect solution. Thanks for your never-ending enthusiasm and support. Also, thank you to the A., A., and Gus team of Northern Virginia for letting me write in a home seemingly designed to inspire writers like Ernest Hemingway and Theodore Roosevelt.

Thank you to the following people for their generosity and advice during the writing and publishing process. It meant a lot and provided me with motivation to complete this project.

Julie Neff, Robert Neff, Bill Callison, Gail Rossier, Wanda Tubbs, Reg Howk, Erin Stroyan-Peduzzi, Austin, Gina, Emily Lamb, Amy Iadarola, Charles Deleot, Jud, Lamarr "Recon" Cox, the Matchison family, Michael Franckowiak, Ben Banner, Christine, Tasha Prados, Donovan and Laura Bachtell, David Fielder, The Evans family, The Reed family, John Culpepper, Mike, the Waddell family, Jack Owens, Arthur Tills, Peanut Lamb, Richard Derby, the Brannon family, Amie Fraley, Gerald Richardson, Ghaidaa Hetou, Brian Williamson, Abbas Kadhim, David J. Katz, Bill Cosby, Brett J. Feddersen, Ian Hartin, Ahmed Qureshi, Syed Hussain, Alan Van Saun, Steve Leonard, Phil Walter, Ben Buchholz, Gabe Barton, George, and Ringo John-Paul.

Thanks to everyone who helped me with this book but, as with any book, in the end all mistakes are mine alone.

Finally, I have to extend heartfelt thanks to my muse and wife Michelle Lee Howk. You have endured more library book purchases, untimely writing sessions, and expensive research trips than most. Through it all you were supportive of my efforts; this is doubly incredible because you have watched me go through this before and knew what you were getting this time around. You are the best, and you are braver than many Soldiers I served beside when faced with insurmountable obstacles.

Introduction

Purpose

I wrote this book because I want to help people understand Islam. This is not an attempt to spread a religion or to denigrate it. I offer it as a gift to anyone seeking to bridge the gap in their understanding of Islam. In the end, education and understanding—and acceptance of other cultures—will unite the world against hatred. Let this be a part of that education.

This book is intended for audiences that have very little familiarity with Islam, the Qur'an, or Muslim culture. It also may be beneficial for Muslims that cannot read Arabic but find the current English versions difficult to read.

As a student of Islam and frequent wanderer in the broader Middle East region for over twenty years I have had many an occasion to read the Qur'an, visit mosques, and talk with my acquaintances about Islam. I took advantage of every opportunity in my studies to learn about Islam from many different points of view. I also focused on the little-known "Ibadhi Muslims" of Oman in my postgraduate thesis. While many interpretations of the Qur'an have been written by Muslims (whose first language is usually not English), those translations are often difficult to read. I attempt here to make an easy-to-read version in an unbiased way using modern English.

There are people that feel threatened by Islam as a religion. Some people assume that a Muslim translating the Qur'an into English softens the language to make it more pleasant and less threatening, so they can spread the religion. Other interpreters are even suspected of making the passages sound like God is condoning unlawful violence. On the other side of the equation, many translations or analyses of the Qur'an are done by non-Muslims that seek to find fault in the messages of the Qur'an or vilify the entire religion of Islam.

I seek a middle ground here. My sole intent is to show people what is and is not in the Qur'an and thereby, strictly speaking, what could be expected from a Muslim that adheres to the majority of the teachings of the Qur'an. I think most readers will find that, like all religious people, not all Muslims follow the teachings of the entire Qur'an.

Aims

- Not perfect English but easily readable for those with no Arabic language background or understanding of Islamic traditions
- Not a word-for-word translation but retaining all key ideas and preserving critical phrases or sentences

- A chronological rendering that provides some key historical information and provides context about the timing of particular revelations from God
- Fair to as many people as possible, knowing that not everyone can be pleased
- Helpful to those interested in studying Islam and the Qur'an
- Hopefully clarifies some myths about the Qur'an and the Islamic culture extracted from it

Structure and Style

Why modern English? I have studied Arabic and Farsi (Persian) and am an avid reader, but I still find the English interpretations that are readily available hard to read. I understand the basic Arabic grammar rules and understand why various translators attempt to create a word-for-word or phrase-for-phrase interpretation, but it makes for a very unreadable text unless you move the phrases to adhere to English grammar. I place present interpretations of the Qur'an on a readability scale between the King James Bible and Shakespeare, although some are closer to *Beowulf* or hieroglyphs. In this version words like "concatenated," "decorous," "propitiate," "tidings," "recompense," "oft," "penury," "percipient," "vicinage," "lightsome," "leave-off," and "forsooth" have been replaced with words that won't make you feel like you are studying for the SAT or the GRE, or for entrance into a monastery. Current interpretations are usually translated correctly into English but often cannot convey the thoughts quickly to a new student of Islam. I grew up in Baptist churches with the King James version of the Bible, so I am intimately familiar with Hebrew Bible (referred to by most Christians as the Old Testament) and New Testament terminology and the many biblical stories that are being retold in the Qur'an. That background certainly eased my writing of this book.

The Arabic language used in the Qur'an is centuries old. Some of the words in the Qur'an are now out of use. This helps to explain why it's difficult to translate straight from the ancient Arabic of the Qur'an into modern English. Hopefully, my attempt to replace challenging vocabulary and simplify and restructure the verses was accomplished without losing the primary meaning of the passages. In grouping together related verses, I aim to make a readable interpretation of the Qur'an.

The Qur'an becomes an interpretation once it's taken out of Arabic and translated into any other language and the interpreter takes license that assumes knowledge of what the passage is supposed to mean. In Arabic, the Qur'an is believed to be the precise word of God. I hope I am on friendly terms with God but surely don't know what He is trying to say all the time; so, this is my best effort, and I expect some passages will leave both me and the readers clueless as to their meaning. The Qur'an makes clear that some metaphors are only truly known to God.

This Qur'an interpretation varies from the dozens of English versions available in a few ways. An obvious major way is that the chapters/sections (*suras*) are placed approximately in the chronological order that they were revealed to Muhammad by God. This isn't done to claim any mistake in the Qur'an's current chapter ordering. This is simply to aid the reader that isn't familiar with Islam, as it allows the reader to see how revelations changed over the 23 years that God was communicating with Muhammad. It also aids in some of the apparent contradictions that appear because some of the revelations in the earlier verses seem to have been replaced by God with more updated verses over time.

It also differs with others because far from just attempting a word-for-word interpretation that falls back on ancient English translations, I attempted to retain the thoughts of the verses but use modern language and different sentence structure. I seldom changed the order of the verses inside the chapters—again, they are arranged by God—but if a phrase makes more sense at the beginning of a sentence, I moved it. I grouped certain verses together into larger paragraphs where connected verses make more sense read together. Many verses are merely phrases (and often out of logical English sentence sequence), so my effort was to make groups of verses into at least sentences and sometimes a paragraph. This was done to facilitate reading and comprehension. Where verses are often quoted or often sought out, I left them as individual numbered verses.

I have read all or parts of dozens of English translations and have found one common and frustrating theme. As most translators were more well-versed in Arabic than English, where a challenging Arabic word or concept was hard to convey in English, such translators just used a previous translation. That has led to sentences containing some archaic English words that have fallen out of modern usage. I am trying to use the best English word or phrase that is in common usage. I want the reader to be able to read it easily and understand it without spending hours researching each verse and chapter.

One concept that helps me read the Qur'an is thinking of each chapter as a religious sermon: a story meant to teach some lessons about morality and the power of God. As this book tries to follow chronological order, it is a bit easier to see the unfolding of the main idea of the book as each chapter builds on earlier ones. You will find lots of repetition in the chapters, but read carefully as each retelling of a story, especially biblical ones, may include new details. If you choose to read a nonchronological Qur'an, let me warn you it's like watching a 48-hour movie, with subtitles, and in which all the scenes are shot out of sequence. It can be hard for you to get the whole picture, because human brains are not exactly wired that way.

Since the Qur'an was first translated into English in the 1640s, dozens of Muslims and non-Muslims have taken on this task. No interpretations are of course exactly alike, because Arabic is a very poetic language that does not easily translate directly into English. A bit of the author is in every translation. Besides reading the Arabic text and using many translation tools to ensure I understood the intent of Arabic phrases, I also relied on the many English translations that have been published over the last century. When verifying my interpretations, I always compared at least five translations from Sunni and Shi'a Islamic scholars to see if I needed to study the Arabic source again.

In this translation, all verses are written as spoken by God or as retold by Muhammad as he recited the words he was given from God. Often you will notice the words "He," "Us," "Our," "They," or "Him" capitalized to show that the word refers to God. The word "Allah" is translated into the English word "God" in this text. When referring to gods besides the one God that the Qur'an focuses on, I use the lower-cased "god" to represent them. Quotations are used when they are most helpful to reading the entire passage as an oration. Only proper nouns are capitalized, to avoid confusing the reader. So terms that include the words "prophet" or "mosque" or adjectives describing God's attributes are not capitalized.

I do not use the commonly written or spoken term "peace and blessings be upon him" after the use of a prophet's name in this text. There are many reasons why Muslims do use it, but it is not critical to the content of this book. Nor do I begin every chapter with the recitation "In the name of Allah, the all-beneficent, the all-merciful." Occasionally a chapter begins with a letter or series of letters. The scribes that captured the text of Muhammad's recitations note that the meaning of these letters is known only to God. I include those letters but offer no answer to their meaning.

I provide limited notes in the text of the Qur'an. My additions are in keeping with earlier translations where it eases the reading. My additional text is found inside square brackets. Italics identify any Arabic word in the verses that has been transliterated into English. Those Arabic words remaining in the text can help make passages or major Islamic themes less confusing.

The dominant method of organization of the chapters of the Qur'an is to roughly place the longest chapter at the beginning of the text, followed by other chapters according to their length. Many of the longer chapters were revealed in Medina at a later part of Muhammad's life. There is basic agreement among Islamic scholars as to the chronological sequence of chapters/suras.

Remember that the Qur'an was all given orally, and the revelations occurred over many years and were not written down in one complete book until after Muhammad's death. Please approach this book with an open mind. You will find concepts and statements in this text that you vehemently disagree with. You also may find that you and the Muslims of the world actually share a lot in common, when it comes to nonreligious life values and beliefs in a higher power.

Brief History of Islam

While there are many disagreements about the exact history of Islam, a brief summary will make this interpretation of the Islamic religion's holy book more useful. This short section outlines the time, place, and circumstances of its revelation, giving the context needed to better understand the Qur'an and the prophet of Islam, Muhammad.

In 571 AD on April 22nd the Prophet Muhammad was born Ahmad, the name given by his mother, in Mecca; today it is western Saudi Arabia. His parents were Abdullah and Aminah; his father would not live to see him born. On his father's side, he was from the family of Hashim. Hashim was one part of the larger Quraysh tribe along with the Umayyad clan. Muhammad's father and family were well respected in Mecca. His mother's family was from the Najjar clan of the Khazraj tribe in Yathrib, a city north of Mecca, that plays a key role in Islam.

Muhammad was born during a time of trade between great empires that brought men to Mecca to conduct business and worship. It was a time when many gods were worshipped and the Kaaba (a building) stored idols for the travelers. This was Arabia, a land that was not very important to the ruling Persian or Byzantine kings. Zoroastrianism, Christianity, Judaism, paganism, and many other faiths were present.

Muhammad became an orphan at the age of six when his mother died. His grandfather on his father's side, Abdul al-Muttalib, chief of the Bani Hashim clan, would rename him Muhammad and begin to care for him. Within two years he would lose his grandfather, and his care at eight years old fell to his paternal uncle Abu Talib, the father of his younger cousin Ali. Ali was a future Islamic leader.

These early days of Arabia were characterized by numerous clans of various religions traveling and trading across the deserts and settlements. By age 12 Muhammad found himself in Syria with his uncle Abu Talib. Years later, as a young man, Muhammad married an older wealthy Meccan merchant named Khadijah, also from the Quraysh tribe. Muhammad was her third husband. She was his only wife until her death, although multiple wives and slaves were typical at this time in history.

Muhammad had a good reputation among the other families in Arabia and was known for his truthfulness and honor. He did not acquire formal education and would remain illiterate while being a good oral communicator. He was part of an important family in Mecca, and that would serve to his advantage for a time, but family members would also be some of his fiercest critics. The power his relatives had amassed in Mecca was at risk from the teachings of Muhammad.

By age forty, Muhammad gained a reputation as being concerned about conditions in Mecca. One day, as he sat in the Cave of Hira, he believed he was commanded by God (in Arabic God is called *Allah*) to give the message of one God to the people of his era. The word of God was first transmitted to Muhammad via the angel Gabriel in August 610 AD.

Muhammad started to recite the words that were passed to him among his friends and family. He was taking up the mantle that Moses and Jesus had previously worn as they spread the message of one God to the Jewish people. He would soon have many enemies speak and take action against him and his followers (the first Muslims). The message of one God was at odds with merchants who made a living from the pilgrims that traveled to the area.

During his life, his fellow Muslims spread the message he spoke and converted others to Islamic beliefs. Not all of Muhammad's friends and relatives took on his belief in one God.

The new converts to Islam were soon persecuted by family, friends, and Meccan authorities. The messages that Muhammad was reciting were seen as dangerous to the status quo. These recitations could equalize power among the various families in Mecca. The most powerful families would not stand for that.

Muhammad belonged to one of the poorer eight clans of Quraysh that were on the outskirts of Mecca physically and economically. His clan was called the Banu Hashim. This inequality provided an angry and poorer population ready to hear religious messages about social equality.

Map of today's Middle East with a few key cities

Map © 2017 by Michelle Lee Howk

He and his small group of followers were eventually forced to move to the city of Yathrib (which became Medina). The migration (*hijra*) of the budding Muslim populace from Mecca to Medina roughly marks the beginning of the Islamic calendar in the year 622.

Yathrib and other key settlements around Mecca contained monotheistic religions at this time. As the Romans pushed into the Holy Lands and its surrounding areas, many Jewish tribes moved into the desert and spread Judaism. Yathrib itself is believed to have been nearly half-Jewish in population by the time Muhammad made his trek to seek refuge there. Christians also had settlements throughout Arabia at the time, extending from Syria and Iraq to Yemen and even Mecca.

Besides physically moving and openly uniting the earliest Muslims in a society in Yathrib, this migration also marks for current readers some shifts in the recitations of Muhammad. The messages he shared started to change once he arrived in Medina and moved into a political and military leadership position.

During his years in Medina, Muhammad continued to pass on revelations of God, and his followers grew. The period is marked with violence and battles between the new Muslim community in Medina and the old order in Mecca. They traded raids and combat for a number of years until a treaty was signed declaring that Mecca would no longer fight against the Muslims. Though the treaty was signed in 628, it did not bring a permanent peace, so Muhammad and his followers invaded Mecca in 630 and put down all rebellions to Islam.

In 631 with a secure base in the heart of Arabia, Muhammad sent emissaries throughout the region to convince people to accept

Islam as their religion. Likewise, emissaries were sent to the new Arabian leader pledging their allegiance to his political power.

Muhammad became one of the most powerful men in Arabia by 632, but his life was short, and he died 8 June 632. Two critical issues remained unresolved. First, for the religion there was no complete and approved written record of all the revelations of God that Muhammad had recited. It took another twenty years and two caliphs (regents of the Islamic empire) for all recitations to be gathered and organized into the Qur'an that the world knows today. Second and most impactful for the future of the Islamic empire, Muhammad left no useful plan for the peaceful transfer of power. The first three leaders to act as caliphs for Islam were Abu Bakr, Umar, and Uthman. These men were colleagues of Muhammad, and some were related though marriage.

During the next handover of power, Islam as a community was changed forever. This is when the first sectarian split occurred. Ali, Muhammad's cousin and also later his son-in-law, was finally selected to take the role of caliph in Islam. This resulted in a battle between his partisans (Shi'a) and the followers of a rival family claimant from the Umayyad tribal clan. After an attempt at finding a peaceful solution and resolving all claims on the title of caliph, the Islamic empire split, with Ali and his family becoming imams (religious leaders of Shi'a Muslims) of the Shi'a followers and Muawiya leading the other followers, who would be called Sunnis. Over time the Sunni sect became the most numerous. Today the Shi'a make up about 13-16 percent of the approximately 1.8 billion

Muslims worldwide.

Over the centuries many Islamic empires rose, competed, and fell. The last Islamic caliphate ended (1924) with the collapse of the Ottoman Empire and the rise of the state of Turkey after World War I.

Muhammad is the revered prophet of Islam for all Muslims.

Other Sources of Islamic Thought

When you have finished reading this book, you will likely ask yourself where some Muslims get some of the ideas that they put forth that are not in the Qur'an. It will be obvious to you that many of the myths and distortions of Islam that you see every day on the news are clearly not in the Qur'an. This book does not aim to delve deeply into other Islamic scholarship and deviations outside of the Qur'an, but there are a few key concepts you should be aware of.

Hadiths:

These are the words attributed to Muhammad by people that were alive during his lifetime but that aren't revelations from God. The phrases and sentences are supposed to have been carefully recorded and passed down through history by a careful chain of custody. There is much controversy surrounding which hadiths are words Muhammad actually spoke and which are invented. Of course, there can be no agreement on which hadiths must be followed by the various sects of Islam.

Sunna:

The Sunni sect of Islam takes its name from this term. Sunna basically means the conduct of Muhammad that was witnessed by his followers. Again, there is much debate about which actions and activities, attributed to Muhammad, should be used as a model for how to live a righteous life.

Caliphs:

The caliphs who followed Muhammad also put forth ideas about how Muslims should live and act.

Scholars and religious leaders:

Islamic scholars and religious leaders of every stripe and sect around the world also influence adherents to Islam. Some are very knowledgeable about the Qur'an and think deeply about the meanings of the verses and how to apply them in the modern world. Others take every verse at face value and directly interpret and apply them to the world around them. Finally, some people claiming to be Islamic religious leaders can't even read Arabic and have no idea what the verses or the larger context of the Qur'an mean. That final group—the same in every religion—can influence large bodies of Muslims who are equally ignorant of the contents of the Qur'an.

What Is Islamic and What Is Muslim?

As you study the Qur'an and Islam, it is useful to think of the two key terms "Muslim" and "Islamic" as my mentor once described them. "Islamic" means that something has roots in Islam the religion.

"Muslim" refers to things that followers of Islam do and is not necessarily purely Islamic.

Brief History of the Qur'an

The history of how the verses in the Qur'an were collected and published into the modern text is not completely agreed on, but it's another useful insight for those interested in Islam.

The Qur'an is the word of God as relayed to the Prophet Muhammad by the angel Gabriel over a period of 23 years. Muhammad then recited the verses aloud, and his companions throughout his life committed them to memory or wrote them down. After his death in 632, the verses continued to be recited, collected, written down, and eventually published into 114 chapters containing over six thousand verses as a complete Qur'an by the prophet's own personal secretary Zayd ibn Thabit. Between 650 and 656 AD, nearly two decades after the death of Muhammad, Zayd tracked down verses of the Qur'an from the memories of the men who knew Muhammad and all the physical writings that existed on papyrus, stones, palm leaves, bones, leather, and wood. They were edited and published during the reign of Islamic leader Uthman. At the end of Caliph Uthman's reign in 656 AD, before the split of Shi'a and Sunni Muslims, the final version of the official Qur'an was distributed to key cities across the Middle East, and it was ordered that all previous editions and collections of verses be destroyed. The final version, which is still in use today, has 114 chapters of varying lengths. Among Muslims there is no debate that the current Qur'an as written in Arabic matches the revelations that Muhammad told to his followers during his life.

Chronology

571 AD	Muhammad is born
610	**Muhammad is inspired with first revelation near Mecca** (age 40)
622	**Muhammad leads followers to Medina** (migration or Hijra)
622	The Islamic calendar begins
624	Battle of the wells of Badr (Ali kills three of Muawiya's close family)
625	Battle of Uhud, Meccan victory over Muslims (Muhammad wounded)
627	Battle of the Ditch (leads to a peace process)
628	Muslims allowed participation in the pilgrimage to Mecca
630	Occupation of Mecca by Muhammad
630–632	Initial expansion of Islamic empire (caliphate)
632	**Muhammad receives last revelation**
632 (June)	**Muhammad's death**
632–634	Reign of Caliph Abu Bakr (died)
634–644	Reign of Caliph Umar (assassinated by a slave)
644–656	Reign of Caliph Uthman (assassinated by a mob)
650–656	Muhammad's secretary Zayd ibn Thabit ordered to collect all the verses, verify their authenticity, and compile them into an official Qur'an
656	**Official Qur'ans distributed to major cities and all old versions ordered destroyed (114 chapters containing over six thousand verses)**
656	Reign of Caliph and Imam Ali begins
658	A botched arbitration leads to Muawiya also calling himself caliph and causing division in Ali's ranks, and the Khawarij are created.
661	Caliph Ali assassinated (by Khawarij) in Kufa over religious and political power schism
661–680	Official reign of Umayyad Caliph Muawiya (heir of Caliph Uthman)
661–670	Reign of Muhammad's grandson, Imam Hasan (Caliph Ali's Shi'a son)
670–680	Reign of Muhammad's grandson, Imam Husayn (Caliph Ali's son)
1640s	**First English interpretation of the Qur'an is published**
1924	End of last official caliph by the Turkish president

Why Do I Care about Islam and the Qur'an?

I have traveled around my country talking about Islam since retiring from the United States Army and have realized how little people in America understand about Islam and the Qur'an. This book is my attempt to describe the Qur'an's contents and themes. Along the way, it can dispel some myths about Islam held by non-Muslims. Maybe it can also dispel some myths about the Qur'an and Islam for English-speaking Muslims that cannot understand the Arabic text and have never read all the words of the Qur'an before—those who have simply believed the explanations about Islam they have been told by their religious leaders without analyzing the verses for themselves.

Maybe this book can also serve as a tool for people who are willing to counteract the ideology of violent radical Islamist ideologues that attribute twisted ideas to Islamic texts. Such radicals create flimsy excuses for their heinous violence as somehow being sanctioned by a verse in the Qur'an or from a book of hadiths.

These violent people that follow a radical Islamist ideology are the descendants of the Khawarij that segregated themselves from all other Muslims during the fight for power between Ali and Muawiya while the Islamic empire (caliphate) was still young. Violent radical Islamist ideologues think they are superior to every human, especially every Muslim that doesn't agree with their extreme views. They think they best understand God's words. In their twisted view, murdering without a trial is allowed. They think crucifixions, beheadings, burnings, and drownings are acceptable punishments for disagreeing with them. They allow child sex slaves, both boys and girls, to be passed around like animals for the pleasure of their followers. They dare to hand a pistol to a tiny child and demand he commit a summary murder. These beasts do this and more and claim to believe in the Qur'an; they claim to be Muslims. They are a cancer inside the Muslim world and are spreading. They have declared war on the entire world because of their twisted beliefs, and they spread their radical Islamist ideology around the globe. They are not practicing Islam. They are evil and must be exposed so their ideology can be discredited.

From my twenty years studying or living in Islamic cultures, I have drawn some conclusions about what lessons could be taken from the Qur'an. These are the Islamic traditions I saw the best people along my travels exhibit or explain:

Forgiveness is honorable, and only God may judge others.
Kindness to strangers is never wasted.
Share your food and drink with guests, even when it is all the food you have.
Fairness at all times in business and disputes.
Care for all children, especially orphans.
Pure love and respect for God.
You can be sober but still joyful for life.
Say hello to everyone and wish them peace, happiness, and safety.
Never be prideful, extravagant, or wasteful.
Prayer should be humble and private and never for spectacle (i.e., scaring people by praying loudly before you get on a plane does not show piety, but instead selfishness).
Give freely to charity without expectation of reward.

Be protective of family and friends, and even guests you hardly know.
Religious people can coexist with others in secular countries.
Hard work is honorable.
Education is valuable.
Leaders should earn respect not demand it.
Cleanliness is desired.
Human laws should be followed, if they are just.
Stopping evil activities is expected.
Parents and elders should be respected.
Women should be respected by men.
Praying to God should not be for selfish reasons.
Loyalty is a virtue.
Other religions should be respected, but it's OK to tell people about Islam, because becoming Muslim cannot be demanded or forced.
Do good deeds daily for selfless reasons.
Violence only creates more violence.

It will take a real unity of all peace-seeking people to discredit the ideology of violent radical Islamism and replace it with a belief in human rights for all people, which includes the right to practice any religion or none at all.

Very Respectfully Yours,
JASON CRISS HOWK
An oasis amid the Sahara of the Old North State
15 June 2017 AD/1438 AH

Foreword

Few Americans possess even rudimentary knowledge of Islam and its guiding principles, even though Muslims now constitute about one quarter of the world's population, and they increasingly impact our domestic culture. The first step in addressing our deficiency is gaining basic understanding of the history and teachings set forth in the 14-centuries-old Qur'an (or "Koran"), and author Jason Howk has provided an unpoliticized guidebook, written in readable English, to take readers through the Qur'an's 114 *suras,* or chapters. This meticulous author has arranged those chapters into their chronological order, enabling readers to navigate through the 23-year period during which the Qur'an was revealed with the necessary understanding of the *suras*' contemporary history.

Mr. Howk's credentials to lead this exploration are both unique and impeccable. After his initial military service in the Middle East, where he trained in parallel with the United Arab Emirates Special Forces, the author returned repeatedly to work in the Middle East and also to academe, where he earned a master's degree in Middle Eastern and South Asian Security Studies. He studied both Arabic and the Afghan dialect of Persian/Farsi languages, facilitating interaction with Muslim colleagues and friends and further validating his interpretation of the Qur'an. His expertise was rewarded by assignment to key policy and political positions in the Middle East; he was a primary aide to the ISAF (International Security Assistance Force) commander of all forces in Afghanistan and was an assistant and advisor to two other senior ISAF leaders. He interacted regularly with Afghanistan's senior leadership. As a decorated officer, after two tours of duty, Jason Howk returned to Washington, where he led teams who provided briefings on the broader Middle East to senior defense and White House decision makers.

During my own military and business careers, I have lived and worked abroad much of the time and have usually had no difficulty accommodating the cultural differences I have encountered. However, as a young JAG (Judge Advocate General) officer resolving legal issues in Libya, as a maturing businessman attending Middle Eastern industrial-development meetings in Beirut, and as a seasoned airline executive moving Hajj pilgrims to Saudi Arabia, I frequently lamented that, "I just don't get it." Jason Howk has resolved many of these complexities for me through his respectful, honest, and learned explanations of Islam and the Qur'an. I am pleased that the same road map to understanding is now available to all interested people through this book, which I recommend to schools and individual readers alike.

ROBERT ARTHUR NEFF
Attorney, international executive,
and author (*Über Alles,* 2016)

Section 1.
Text of the Qur'an

Meccan Period [MC], 610–622 AD

(12 Years/86 Chapters)

Opening invocation (chapter 5 chronologically)

Chapter/sura 1 (7 verses/ayat), Al-Fatihah (The Opening)

[*Sura,* the Arabic word for chapter or section. *Ayat,* the Arabic word for verses.]

[Chapter 5, chronologically, is the first chapter used in every nonchronological or standard Qur'an as the opening statement of God. I will also place it first in this text for continuity and to provide context to the book.]

[Say unto me]

1. In the name of the most gracious and merciful God.

2–4. All praise should be to God, the Lord and judge of the all that exists.

5. We worship only You and ask You for help.

6–7. Guide us on the righteous path. The path of those You approve of, and not the path of those You are displeased with.

Chapter 1 (first chapter chronologically)

Sura 96 (19 verses), Al-Alaq (The Clot)

In the name of Allah, the all-beneficent, the all-merciful. [I will omit the repeated opening to every chapter for the remainder of the book, but be aware this is a phrase often used by Muslims in many situations including outside of prayer. Anglicized it sounds like bis-mil-lah-al-rah-man-al-ra-heem.]

1–2. Recite! In the name of the Lord who made man from a clot of blood.

3–5. Proclaim! That your God is most generous, and He taught man to write. Indeed, He taught man everything, all the things he didn't know.

6–7. Man is being rebellious when he thinks he doesn't need God and can depend on himself.

8. The path back to heaven is through the Lord [or You owe all you have to God].

9–16. The man who forbids others to pray should be following God's guidance and asking others to pray as well. He should not call the faithful liars; he doesn't know God is watching. If he doesn't stop interfering with the faithful, We shall seize the lying sinner by the hair.

17–19. Let him call out to his fellow man at judgment time, and We shall call the keepers of hell for him. Don't listen to unbelievers; instead pray and bring yourself closer to God.

Chapter 2 (chronologically)

Sura 68 (52 verses), Al-Qalam (The Pen)

1–4. The Arabic letter *noon* [*N* sound]. Muhammad, by the grace of God, they will record by the pen that you are not crazy, and indeed you possess great character. You will be and you have an everlasting reward.

5–7. You and the other will see who is crazy. God knows who has followed the righteous path and who has not.

8–9. Don't listen to the deniers [of Islam/monotheism]. They want you to compromise your beliefs so they can continue their evil ways.

10–14. Those men are liars, slanderers, and sinners. They are greedy, violent bastards. They hinder goodness and think they can get away with it because they are wealthy and have many sons.

15–16. When they hear the revelations [Qur'an], they say it's just the myths of the old times. When the time comes, they will be marked on their noses.

17–27. [MD: Given in Medina] God will test them like He tested the people of the garden. They had vowed to collect their fruits at dawn but failed to invoke God's blessings. The Lord destroyed their crop while they slept. When they went to gather their fruits early so the poor people couldn't take it first, they found it empty. They then uttered that they must have gone astray from the righteous path to have lost the fruits of their labor.

28–32. [MD] One of the best among them asked why they hadn't invoked God's blessings. They replied, "We have been following the wrong path. Glory be to God." Next they started to blame each other. They wondered if God would replace the garden with a better one if they begged Him, and they began to worship Him more earnestly.

33. [MD] That was how God punished them on earth; if they had only known the punishment would even be worse after they left earth.

34. Those who are righteous will enjoy a garden paradise near their Lord in the hereafter.

35. "Should We treat the righteous like We treat the sinners after death?

36–39. "What is wrong with you? How would you judge them? Have you read a book that tells you that you can choose what you like in the hereafter? Did you receive a covenant that on the day of judgment you will have all your demands met?

40-41. Ask them, "Which of you has someone who can vouch for your demands in the hereafter? Do you have some other gods? If you are not a liar, show me your gods."

42–43. On the day of judgment when those people are called to prostrate themselves, they won't be able to. With their eyes downcast and covered in shame, they will realize they should have bowed down before this when they were healthy.

44-45. Let Me deal with the ones who reject the message. They will not even be aware that We are drawing them into ruin. They will have a long immunity, but My scheme for them is strong.

46. Is it that you ask them for a reward for your message that they are so burdened with debt?

47. Do they have access to the unknown so that they can write it down?

48–50. [MD] Be patient and wait for the Lord's judgment. Don't be like [Jonah] who cried out in distress. He owes all to God for choosing him to be a prophet. He would have surely ended up on an empty shore as a sinner.

51–52. Those who don't believe My message look at you with resentment and say you must be crazy for speaking it. You are sending a reminder to the entire world.

Chapter 3 (chronologically)

Sura 73 (20 verses), Al-Muzzammil

(The Enshrouded One bundled up)

1–4. You, who are wrapped in your garments, pray through most of the night reciting the Qur'an.

5. Soon the Lord will send you a weighty message.

6–7. The night is the best time for prayer and praise and understanding the word of God. For in the day you are busy with daily duties.

8–9. Celebrate and remember the Lord and completely devote yourself to Him, for He is the only God of the world. Accept Him as your protector and salvation.

10–11. [MD] Be patient and noble Muhammad when dealing with detractors. In time I will handle those wealthy and comfortable people who deny the truth you speak.

12–14. When the day of judgment comes and the mountains shake and become like sand dunes, I have a painful punishment for the unbelievers. They will be bound and burned and choke on their food.

15–16. God sent Muhammad to mankind as a messenger, just as He sent one to the Pharaoh. Remember that Pharaoh was punished heavily for denying God's messenger.

17–19. If you deny God, then you won't be able to protect yourself from His judgment at the end of times, when His promise is fulfilled. This is a reminder to choose the righteous path to God.

20. [MD] Remember, the Lord knows when you pray, recite, and worship correctly at night and is merciful if you are unable to keep track of time. Recite as much of the Qur'an as you can. God knows that you may not be able to worship fully when you get sick, or go on long travels, or even go into battle for God's cause. Always recite as much of the Qur'an as you can, pray regularly, pay your tithes to help those in need. Whatever good deeds and forms of worship you can do will be rewarded by God. Always seek God's forgiveness as He is all-forgiving and all-merciful.

Chapter 4 (chronologically)

Sura 74 (56 verses), Al-Muddaththir (The Cloaked One)

1–5. You, wrapped in your cloak! Rise and deliver God's warning. Magnify your Lord, keep your cloak pure, and avoid the unclean.

6–7. Do not show favor to others seeking worldly gains for yourself, and be patient for the Lord's sake.

8–10. For when the trumpet is sounded, it will be a day of hardship for the unbelievers.

11–14. I will deal with the creatures whom I alone created. Whom I gave vast riches and sons to be by his side. Whom I made a smooth and comfortable life for.

15–17. Because after all I gave him, he wanted more. And with all I gave him, he opposed the signs you revealed about God. So I will overwhelm him with hardships and punishments.

18–25. He had time to reflect on God's message and chose how he would perish. He listened and scowled and, full of pride, said that My revelations through Muhammad were nothing but old traditions and magic handed down by a human being and not a message from God.

26. So I will cast him into hell.

27–31. How should I explain hell? Hell spares no one as it burns the skin, and it is guarded by angels. Know that God can lead astray whoever He wishes and can guide others on a righteous path. Only God knows who the angels are that guard hell.

32–37. The moon in the sky visible at night and dawn is one of the greatest signs of God to humans that they should accept the prophet's messages and warnings, for God is all-powerful.

38–42. Every person's soul must receive what they have earned in life [in hell], except those who have followed the righteous path shown by God. The righteous people in the Gardens [heavens] will ask of the sinners, what did you do to deserve hell?

43–47. The sinners will answer: We did not pray. We did not feed the poor. We gossiped and lied. We called the day of judgment a lie and a myth; until we died and the hour of judgment arrived.

48. No one will intervene on behalf of the sinners to keep them from hell.

49–52. Why didn't these sinners listen to the prophets? Why did they run from the messengers like a terrified ass from a lion? They all wanted to be handed an unrolled scripture straight from God in order to believe the message.

53. Those who don't want to hear the message do not fear not the hereafter.

54–55. This is a reminder of what is to come. Let whoever wants to accept the message and heed the warning.

56. But God is all-powerful, righteous, and merciful; He must will you to accept this message.

Chapter 5 (chronologically, but also listed above as the opening invocation)

Surah 1 (7 verses), Al-Fatihah (The Opening)

Say unto me:

1. In the name of the most gracious and merciful God.

2–4. All praise should be to God, the Lord and judge of the all that exists.

5. We worship only You and ask You for help.

6–7. Guide us on the righteous path. The path of those You approve and not the path of those You are displeased with.

Chapter 6 (chronologically)

Sura 111 (5 verses), Al-Masad (Rope of Palm Fiber)

[After a man left Muhammad's company]

1–5. The power of Abu Lahab will perish; he will perish, and all his wealth and earnings can't save him. He will burn in the fires of hell, and his wife, who acted as he did, shall enter too with a twisted rope of palm fiber around her neck.

Chapter 7 (chronologically)

Sura 81 (29 verses), Al-Takwir (The Darkening [of all life])

1–9. When the end is near, when the sun is covered, when the stars have scattered, when the mountains are moved, when the pregnant camels are left untended, when the wild beasts are herded together, when the oceans boil over with fire, when all souls are reunited with their bodies, and when the female [infant] buried alive [by earlier pagans] is asked for what sin she was killed?

10–14. When the scrolls [accounting good and bad deeds] are laid open, when heaven has its covering removed, when the hell fires are lit, and when paradise is brought near, then every soul shall know what it has done in life.

15–21. So I swear by the stars that rise and set, by the night as it departs, and by the dawn as it brightens the darkness that these are God's words from a most honorable messenger who is trusted by the Lord. He is to be obeyed and trusted.

22–25. Muhammad is not possessed or crazy. He saw the angel Gabriel clearly. He does not conceal any truths from you about what has been revealed to him. He is not controlled by, or speaking for, Satan.

26-29. Which way will you go mankind? This is a Message to everyone in the world. Those among you who wish to live a righteous life cannot do so without the support of the will of God, the Lord of all worlds.

Chapter 8 (chronologically)

Sura 87 (19 verses), Al-A'la (The Most Exalted, the Lord on High)

1–5. Praise the name of your Lord, the most exalted one. He who created all things and ordained all laws. He who guides us. He who brings about our harvest and causes it to fail.

6–8. God will make you [Prophet] recite the Qur'an so you won't forget it. You will know it except what God withholds from you, as He knows what is hidden from man. Muhammad, we will make it easy for you to follow the righteous path.

9–15. Go forth Muhammad and give this message to mankind. He who fears God will listen to you, and those who are most despicable will not. Those despicable people will burn in hell eternally and wish for death. Those who follow a righteous path, glorify God, and pray will find success.

16–17. Mankind, you prefer the life of this world, but the life in the hereafter is better and eternal.

18–19. This Qur'an is the same revelation as the earlier scriptures, the books of Abraham and Moses.

Chapter 9 (chronologically)

Sura 92 (21 Verses), Al-Lail (The Night)

1–4. I swear by the night when it envelops and by the day in its brightness; by Him who created man and woman; your life's efforts will achieve diverse ends.

5–7. He who gives to charity, follows his duties, and fears God will find a path made easier by God.

8–11. But he who is greedy and thinks he doesn't need God; he who rejects goodness will find God has made his life a path of misery. His wealth will not be able to help him on judgment day.

12–13. God is the only one that can give guidance to man. God controls this world and the hereafter.

14–16. I am warning you about the flames of hell, in which only the worst among you will be cast. Those wretched who deny My message and turn away.

17–21. But hell is not for those who are righteous and who give their wealth to benefit others without an expectation of reward and recognition. You are safe if you live to honor God, for He will be pleased in you.

Chapter 10 (chronologically)

Sura 89 (30 Verses), Al-Fajr (The Daybreak)

1–5. I swear by the daybreak, by the ten nights, by the even and odd, and by the night when it departs. For those who have the intellect, these oaths provide proof.

6–13. Did you not see how your Lord dealt with the tribe of Ad, of the city of Iram, with the Thamud people, and with Pharaoh? To those who rebelled against God and caused trouble in their lands? The Lord punished them with disasters and scourges.

14. God is ever watchful of man.

15–16. When God blesses men allowing them gifts and honors, they say that God honors me. But when God tests man and asks him to restrict himself to a righteous path, man says the Lord is humiliating me, that he despises me.

17–20. It's not humiliation but simply that you don't care for orphans, you don't urge one another to feed the poor, you greedily use up your inheritance, and you love wealth too much.

21–23. When the earth is leveled down to a plain, and the Lord and His angels arrive, and man is brought face-to-face with hell, then man will remember God's messages. But it will be too late to help them.

24. Man will say if only I had lived a righteous life to record the good deeds in heaven for the hereafter.

25–26. On this judgment day God will punish man like no one has ever punished. He will bind man like no one has ever bound him.

27–30. To the righteous God says return to the Lord for you have pleased me, enter as one of My servants into My paradise.

Chapter 11 (chronologically)

Sura 93 (11 Verses), Al-Duha (The Morning Brightness)

1–4. By the morning brightness and by the night calm, your Lord has not forsaken you, nor is He unhappy with you. Know that the hereafter will be better for you than the present world.

5–8. The Lord will give you what pleases you. He found you

shelter as an orphan. He saw you astray and gave you guidance. He found you needy and enriched you.

9–10. Therefore, don't mistreat orphans nor drive away beggars.

11. Proclaim your Lord's blessing.

Chapter 12 (chronologically)

Sura 94 (8 Verses), Al-Sharh (Opening)

1–4. Did God not open your heart so you could accept [Islam]? And take your heavy burdens from your back? And make your name famous?

5. For every hardship there is relief.

6. For every hardship there is relief.

7-8. Therefore when you are free from burden, turn your attention eagerly to the Lord.

Chapter 13 (chronologically)

Sura 103 (3 Verses), Al-Asr (The Time)

1–3. Throughout time man is lost, except those who are faithful and, while conducting good deeds, encouraging each other to be patient and truthful.

Chapter 14 (chronologically)

Sura 100 (11 Verses), Al-Adiyat (The Chargers)

1–7. I swear by the charging steeds snorting, by the sparks from their hooves, by the raiders at dawn raising a dust trail as they crash into the midst of the enemy; man is truly ungrateful to God, and he shows it in his deeds.

8. Man is persistent in his love of wealth.

9–11. Doesn't man know that at judgment day when his soul is laid bare for inspection, his Lord will know all about his deeds.

Chapter 15 (chronologically)

Sura 108 (3 verses), Al-Kauther (The Abundance)

1–3 God has given you abundance, so in return pray and sacrifice to the Lord. Your enemies will be without posterity.

Chapter 16 (chronologically)

Sura 102 (8 verses) Al-Takathur (The Rivalry)

1–8. Competition for worldly things distracts man until he dies. You will see soon the results of your distraction and you will understand your folly clearly when you see the fire of hell. You will be asked about your earthly actions on judgment day.

Chapter 17 (chronologically)

Sura 107 (7 verses), Al-Ma'un (The Aid or Act of Kindness)

1–3. Did you see the men that deny the final reckoning? They are the ones who failed to care for orphans and didn't urge people to feed the poor.

4–7. [MD] Woe be unto those who worship, who neglect their prayers, who do good deeds only to be publicly seen, but do not give small acts of kindness and aid.

Chapter 18 (chronologically)

Sura 109 (6 verses), Al-Kafiroon (The Faithless/Disbelievers)

1–3. Disbelievers! I don't worship what you worship; and you don't worship what I worship.

4–5. And I won't worship what you worship; and you won't worship what I worship.

6. So you worship as your religion requires, and I shall worship according to mine.

Chapter 19 (chronologically)

Sura 105 (5 verses), Al-Fil (The Elephant)

1. Remember how the Lord dealt with the force on elephants

[sent to destroy the Kaaba in Mecca]?

2–3. Didn't God upset their strategy of attack when He sent a flock of birds against them?

4–5. When He struck them with stones of baked clay and left the battlefield looking like a field with all its crops harvested.

Chapter 20 (chronologically)

Sura 113, (5 verses), Al-Falaq (The Sunrise/Dawn)

1–5. Say, I seek protection from the Lord of the dawn from the evil He has created, from the evil of the darkness of night, from those who practice witchcraft, and from the evil of those who are envious.

Chapter 21 (chronologically)

Sura 114 (the last chapter in traditional sequence; 6 verses), Al-Nas (Mankind)

1–6. Say, I seek the protection of God, the Lord of mankind, the king of man, from the evils of Satan [*Shaitan* in Arabic] who tempts the hearts of mankind and genies.

Chapter 22 (chronologically)

Sura 112 (4 verses), Al-Ikhlas (The Purity)

1–2. Say, God is the one and only, who all eternally depend upon.

3–4. God neither gave birth to anyone nor was He born. There is no being equal to God.

Chapter 23 (chronologically)

Sura 53 (62 verses), Al-Najm (The Star)

1–9. I swear by the setting star, Muhammad has not gone astray nor is he being misled. What he recites to you does not come from his own thoughts. What is being revealed to him is coming from a being of great power and wisdom. [The medium is often noted as the angel Gabriel, *Jibrael.*]

10–11. What was revealed to Muhammad was an inspiration to him, and he would not lie about it.

12–16. Do you accuse him of lying about what he saw and heard? For he certainly saw Him a second time near the farthest lote tree of the ultimate boundary near the garden of abode. [Verses describing the ascent of Muhammad to see the heavens.]

17–18. Muhammad saw what he should see and nothing more when he saw the signs of the Lord.

19–23. What about Lat, Uzza [idols], and Manat [female idol]? Do you worship the males while He worships the females? That would seem unfair. These are just names not gods, which you and your ancestors created with no authority from God. The idol worshippers follow speculation and their own desires, despite the fact that guidance from God has already come to them.

24. Should man just have whatever he wishes for?

25. This world and the hereafter belong to God.

26. No matter how many angels in heaven try to help, they cannot intercede on a human's behalf. God is the only one who can allow someone to enter heaven.

27–28. Those who don't believe in the hereafter give female names to angels. But they don't know what they are doing and follow speculation, which can never replace truth.

29–30. Avoid people who turn away from our message and only want to enjoy this life. It is all their knowledge allows them. God knows who strays from His path and who follows it.

31. God owns everything on earth and in the heavens. God may punish those who do evil deeds, as He may reward those who do good deeds.

32. [MD] God may be forgiving of those who avoid great sins but have small faults. God has known you since you were in the womb, so do not flaunt your good deeds, for He truly knows who is virtuous.

33–37. Do you see those who turn their back from [Islam], those who gave a little of themselves and then stopped? Do those who pull back have the knowledge of this message so they can see what you see? No, he is not aware of the scriptures, lessons, and actions of Moses and Abraham:

38–42. That no man has to bear the sins of another man. That man can only have things he works for. That man's efforts will be seen. That man will be rewarded for his efforts. That the final goal of man is God.

43–46. That God grants laughter and tears. God grants life and death. God created the sexes, male and female, from their combined fluids.

47–49. That God promised a resurrection. It's God that gives wealth and contentment. God is the Lord of Sirius [star].

50–54. That God destroyed the tribe of Ad and Thamud. Before them He destroyed the even more unjust and rebellious people of Noah's time. God later destroyed the overthrown cities [Sodom and Gomorrah].

55–62. Which of God's benefits can anyone dispute? This [Muhammad] is a prophet in the tradition of the previous messengers of God. The judgment day is near, and only God knows when. Do you question this message from God? Why do you laugh and not cry? Why do you waste your precious time? Prostrate yourselves and serve God.

Chapter 24 (chronologically)

Sura 80 (42 verses), Abasa (He Frowned)

1–2. [Muhammad] frowned and turned away when a blind man approached him.

3–4. How do you know that the man might purify himself and become more spiritual? Or that he might listen to and benefit from your message?

5–7. As for the person who thinks he is self-sufficient, to him you should preach; even though you will not be blamed if he fails to follow the straight path.

8–10. Meanwhile when a person comes to you earnestly trying to follow the straight path and fearing God, you ignore him.

11–16. This is not how you must act. This message is a reminder to all men, so let whoever wishes to pay heed to it. The message is in honored books, exalted and holy, maintained by honorable and just scribes.

17–22. Cursed is the man who rejects God. God created man from a drop of fluid. God makes a smooth path for man, then causes him to die and be buried. And when God wills it, He resurrects the dead.

23. Yet man has not done what God has commanded him to do.

24–32. Let man consider his food: how God showers the earth with an abundance of water; how God splits the earth and causes the grains, grapes, vegetables, fodder for herds, olives, dates, gardens, and fruits to grow for man and his animals' use.

33–42. On that day of the resurrection, when the deafening cries are heard and man flees from even his own family because he will be so concerned for himself, some faces will be bright with laughter and joy, while other faces will be stained with dust and veiled in darkness. The latter are those who rejected God and were wicked.

Chapter 25 (chronologically)

Sura 97 (5 verses), Al-Qadr (The [night of] Fate/Ordainment)

1–5. God revealed this message [Qur'an] on the night of ordainment. Let me describe the night of ordainment as such: It is better than a thousand months, the Lord sends all the angels and spirits out with commands, and there is peace until the sunrise.

Chapter 26 (chronologically)

Sura 91 (15 verses), Al-Shams (The Sun)

1–10. By the sun, moon, day, and night. By the heavens God built, by the earth God formed, and by the soul [mankind] that God fashioned perfectly and then inspired with an understanding of right and wrong: He who purifies his soul succeeds, and the corrupted fail.

11–15 The Thamud people denied [God] with their rebellious ways. Especially when the most wicked of them went forth and even after the messenger of God told him, "She is God's camel, so allow her to drink," rejected the messenger and hamstrung [crippled] the camel. In retribution God destroyed them and did not fear the consequences.

Chapter 27 (chronologically)

Sura 85 (22 verses), Al-Burooj (The Constellations of Stars)

1–3. By the constellations in the heavens, by the promised resurrection day, by the prophet and the judgment day.

4–9. Cursed are the people who dug the ditch and kept a fire burning in it. Who sat by and watched the believers of God being forced into the flames just because they had faith in an all-powerful and knowing God.

10. Those people who persecute and oppress faithful men and women will burn in hell if they do not repent for their crimes.

11. But those people that are faithful to God and perform good deeds will achieve greatness through salvation and will know heaven's gardens and rivers.

12. God's punishment is strong and severe.

13–16. Remember it is God that can create and restore life. God is forgiving and loving. God is the Lord of the throne and can do whatever He wishes.

17–20. Haven't you heard what happened to the peoples of the Pharaoh and the tribe of Thamud? Yet still the faithless reject the truth of this message, but God unseen surrounds them.

21–22. Indeed, this is a glorious Qur'an, inscribed and preserved.

Chapter 28 (chronologically)

Sura 95 (8 verses), Al-Tin (The Fig)

1–3. I swear by the fig and the olive tree, by Mount Sinai, and by this secure city [Mecca];

4–6. We created man in the best of designs, and then we reduced him to the lowest of the low; except for those men that are faithful and do good works. For those men is an everlasting reward.

7. Then who or what causes man to deny God's judgment at the resurrection?

8. Isn't God the fairest of all judges?

Chapter 29 (chronologically)

Sura 106 (4 verses), Quraish (The Quraish or Quraysh Tribe)

1–4. Because of the covenants with the Quraish tribe, they travel safely during the winter and summer caravans. Let them worship the Lord of this House, who has fed their hunger and protected them from dangers.

Chapter 30 (chronologically)

Sura 101 (11 verses), Al-Qariah (The Catastrophe)

1–3. The Catastrophe! What can explain to you the day of catastrophe?

4–5. It is a day when mankind will be scattered like moths and mountains will weaken and crumble.

6–7. Those who tip the scales of judgment with good deeds shall have a pleasurable life.

8–11. Those who find their good deeds are outweighed by bad shall make their home in a bottomless pit of raging fire.

Chapter 31 (chronologically)

Sura 75 (40 verses), Al-Qiyama (Resurrection Day)

1–2. I swear by the day of resurrection, and I swear by the self-critical soul.

3–4. Do men not think We can reassemble their bones? We are able to perfectly rebuild him to the tips of his fingers.

5–6. Yet man chooses to lead a sinful life and asks, “When is this day of resurrection?"

7–10. When man's sight is confused and the moon is eclipsed as the sun and moon unite, men will cry "Where can we flee?"

11. But there shall be nowhere to hide.

12–15. That day man's place will be with your Lord. That day man will be told about his good deeds and bad. Man shall be a witness against himself through his deeds, yet he may put forward excuses for his actions.

16–17. Do not try to speed up receipt of revelations. It is up to Us to collect the verses and have them recited.

18. But when We have the words recited, follow the recitation.

19–21. For it is up to Us to explain the resurrection to you. For mankind loves the present life and neglects the hereafter.

22–25. On that day, some faces will be resplendent looking towards their Lord, and some faces will be dismal and gloomy knowing that some back-breaking punishment was imminent.

26–30. When man's soul is almost out of the body, there shall be a cry "Who shall save him now?" and then he will know the time of death is near. His thoughts of pending hardship will build the day he is brought to the Lord.

31–35. Men who failed to find faith and pray and instead acted prideful as he lived with his family; woe be unto them.

36–40. Does man think he will be unjudged at death? Wasn't man created from reproductive fluids and shaped perfectly by God into both male and female? Why shouldn't a God so powerful bring the dead back to life?

Chapter 32 (chronologically)

Sura 104 (9 verses), Al-Humaza (The Slanderer)

1–3. A warning to every defamer who gathers his wealth for security, thinking that prosperity makes him immortal.

4–9. Wealth will not stop you from being thrown into the crushing fires of hell kindled by God, where flames will close in upon the hearts of men like great columns.

Chapter 33 (chronologically)

Sura 77 (50 verses), Al-Mursalat (The Emissaries)

1–7. I swear by the successive emissaries, the hurricanes raging, the winds scattering; by those separating one from another, by those spreading revelations, to warn you that what has been promised will surely occur.

8–13. So when the stars become dim and the heavens are split open, mountains are scattered like dust, and when the time comes for the arrival of the messengers, although the date and time is unknown, it will be the day of judgment.

14–15. How can I explain the day of judgment? Misery awaits those who rejected the message that day!

16–19. Didn't we destroy the former generations and then make the latter ones follow? That is how we deal with sinners. Misery awaits those who rejected the message that day!

20–24. Didn't we create you from mere fluid and put you in a safe place until you were born? We designed you perfectly as is our way. Misery awaits those who rejected the message that judgment day!

25–28. Haven't we made the earth a place for the living and the dead complete with lofty mountains and water to drink. Misery awaits those who rejected the message that judgment day!

29–34. On judgment day, it will be said to the disbelievers "Go you to the place you used to deny. Go towards the smoke's shadow; its three columns will not cool you from the flames. Hellfire throws up sparks as large as castles and yellow as camels." Misery awaits those who rejected the message that judgment day!

35–37. On this day, they won't be able to speak or offer excuses for their behavior. Misery awaits those who rejected the message that judgment day!

38–40. This will be the sorting day. We shall gather all living mankind and those who died before. If you have any wits, try to outwit me. Misery awaits those who rejected the message that judgment day!

41–44. But for the righteous that day, they shall be found in the cool shade among watering springs. They shall have all the fruits they desire. They will be told to enjoy their rewards for good deeds. We certainly reward the good.

45–47. But again, misery awaits those who rejected the message that day! So, eat and enjoy yourselves for only a little while on earth, for you are sinners. Misery awaits you.

48. [MD] When it is said to the rejecters "bow down," they do not.

49. Misery awaits those who reject the message!

50. What message after this one will the disbelievers believe in?

Chapter 34 (chronologically)

Sura 50 (45 verses), Al-Qaf (The Arabic letter Qaf/the *Q* sound)

[When a letter is used to start a sura/chapter,
its meaning is considered a mystery of God.]

1. Qaf. I swear by the glorious Qur'an,

2–3. Man wonders about the messenger [Muhammad] that has been chosen from among them. The faithless say, "This is a strange thing; that after we have died and turned to dust, we will be brought back to life again. It seems far-fetched."

4. We [God] know how many will perish on earth and have a

book recording all people.

5–7. But men deny the truth that has been given to them, and they are confused. Can they not see the flawless sky We made; the earth with its plains and mountains and all the living things on it?

8–10. As a reminder to the faithful, We send down rains, and We grow the crops and gardens and the tall and fruiting date palm trees.

11. To provide food for the faithful, We continue to give life to dead lands each cycle. The same will happen at the resurrection.

12–14. Many men before this Qur'an denied the hereafter. The people of Noah and the inhabitants of Rass and Thamud. The Ad tribe, Pharaoh, and the brethren of Lot. The people of the grove and of Tubba. All these people rejected the apostles, and My warning was enforced on them.

15. Were We worn out by the original creation that men should doubt Our ability to resurrect?

16. We created man, and We know what tempts his soul. We know him better than he knows himself.

17–18. There are recorders on the left and right hand, so not a word does man utter that is not written down.

19. When death brings man the truth of his life, it will be said to

man "This is what you have been avoiding."

20–21. The trumpet will sound announcing the day of resurrection. Then every soul will come forward accompanied by two angels, one a guide and another to bear witness.

22–23. The evildoer will be told, "We have removed the veil today so you can see that we have been with you." Then his companion will announce, "Here is my testimony for him."

24–26. God will pronounce sentence on him: "You two angels cast this faithless ingrate into hell." "He who gave to others grudgingly, broke laws, and doubted the truth." "He who worshipped another god besides the Lord; throw him into the dreadful torment."

27. The devil will say, "Lord I did not make him stray; he made the errors himself."

28–29. God will say, "No need to argue in front of me, as the sentence I will give him was warned of in advance and cannot be changed; and I am fair to man."

30. On judgment day We will ask hell, "Are you full?" and hell will reply, "Are there many more to come?"

31–35. That day when paradise will no longer be distant, but be brought near to the righteous. It will be said, "This is what I promised all of you faithful people." "You who were devoted to and fearful of God." "Enter today into immortality and peace." "Here in paradise with Us, you will have all you ever wish for and more."

36. Think of how many generations of man We destroyed before you, who were stronger than the people of today. Did they have a place to hide when God judged them?

37. This is a message for anyone that has a heart and is willing to listen.

38. [MD] We created the heavens and the earth in six days and were not weary.

39–40. Therefore, be patient with what others say and praise the Lord before the sun rises, the sun sets, and also during part of the night after prayers.

41–44. Listen for the day when a cry will signal the day the dead will once again rise. We, who give life and death, will bring you all to your final destination. That day the earth splits and the people all rise is easy for Us to do.

45. We [God] know what men say, and you Muhammad do not need to rule over them as a tyrant. Warn them through the Qur'an of my threats.

Chapter 35 (chronologically)

Sura 90 (20 verses), Al-Balad (The Town/City)

1–4. I swear by this town where you reside a freeman and the ancestors before you, We created man with much effort.

5–6. Does man think that no one has power over him? He shall say, "I have wasted immense wealth."

7–9. Does he think that no one can see him? Did We not give him a pair of eyes, a tongue, and a mouth?

10–11. Did We not show man two paths [good and evil]? But he does not take the uphill path towards goodness.

12–16. How will you be able to see the uphill path in life? It's freeing slaves, feeding the hungry, taking in an orphan, caring for the poor.

17–18. If you take this path, you will be among those who believe, have patience, and encourage others to show compassion. Your place will be on the right hand of God.

19–20. But those who reject the revelations of the good path will be of the left hand, and they will be enveloped with fire.

Chapter 36 (chronologically)

Sura 86 (17 verses), Al-Tariq (The Nightly Visitor/Bright Star)

1–4. By the sky and night visitor [you will know the night visitor by a piercing bright star], know that every soul has a guardian.

5–7. Let man think about how he was created. He was created by fluid gushing from between the backbone and ribs.

8–10. God will be able to bring man back to life on the day that all men's secrets will be examined. At that time, man will be powerless and have no helper.

11–14. By the heavens that give rains and the earth gushing springs, this message is decisive and not a jest.

15–17. As for those who are plotting a plan, know that I am planning against them, so give those faithless a break for now and deal with them gently.

Chapter 37 (chronologically)

Sura 54 (55 verses), Al-Qamar (The Moon)

1–5. The hour is near, and the moon is split, yet if the people see the sign they turn away saying, "This is an illusion." They deny the warnings and follow their own desires. But every era has an end. But there have already been messages and warnings against base behavior. It was useful wisdom, but they have not listened.

6–8. Because of this, you can turn away from them. On the day of the summoning, they will have a terrible affair. They will rise from their graves, with their eyes cast down in humility, scattered like locusts. As they scramble toward the summoner, the unbelievers will say, "This is a difficult day!"

9–15. This disbelief has happened before. The people during Noah's time rejected their messenger, and they said Noah was insane and drove him away. As a result, Noah called on his Lord to help him in his struggle. So We opened the gates of heaven, and water poured forth. We caused the earth to spring water forth to join with the water from the sky. And We carried him on his Ark made of wood, as he sailed above the waters under Our watch as a reward for being rejected by man. We have left this as a sign for all times, but will anyone heed the warning?

16. How terrible was my penalty after my warning?

17. We have made the Qur'an simple and easy to understand, but will anyone heed Our warnings?

18–20. The people of Ad rejected the warnings, and My penalty was great. We sent down a furious wind and caused them a day of violent disaster as men were plucked out like palm trees torn from the ground.

21. How terrible was my penalty after my warning?

22. We have made the Qur'an simple and easy to understand, but will anyone heed Our warnings?

23–31. The Thamud tribe rejected our warnings. They said, "How can we follow a single mortal from among us? What if he strays or goes mad? Has the message been sent to him alone? No, he is a liar."

We told their warner "that tomorrow they will know who the liar is. For We will send them a she-camel as a trial, so be patient and watch. Tell them to share the water among them to drink." The men being tested instead asked a friend to take a knife and slay the camel. What were My punishments? We sent against them a mighty blast and scattered them like dry sticks.

32. We have made the Qur'an simple and easy to understand, but will anyone heed Our warnings?

33–39. Lot's people rejected his warnings. So we sent against them a storm of stones yet spared Lot's family as a favor from God for We reward those who give thanks. Lot warned them of Our punishment, but they doubted him. The people tried to tempt Lot, but we blinded them and they heard, "Taste My warning and My wrath." Early in the morning, Our punishment was served on them. "Taste My warning and My wrath!"

40. We have made the Qur'an simple and easy to understand, but will anyone heed Our warnings?

41–42. The Pharaoh and his people were also warned. They rejected the revelations and signs, so We overtook them with Our power.

43. Are the current unbelievers better than those of the past? Do they have some promised immunity?

44–46. [MD] Do the unbelievers say, "We are able to defend ourselves due to our unity." They will soon be defeated and driven in flight. The hour [judgment] is set, and that hour shall be bitter and severe for them.

47–48. The guilty have made a mistake and are in sorrow. That day they will be dragged into the fire on their faces, and they will hear, "Taste the touch of hell!"

49–55. We have created all things in proper proportion and Our command happens in a twinkling of an eye. We have destroyed disbelievers like you before, but will anyone remember the warning? Everything they did, great and small, is captured in scriptures. For the righteous there is a dwelling among the gardens and rivers in a seat of honor with the Lord.

Chapter 38 (chronologically)

Sura 38 (88 verses), Saad (The Arabic letter Saad) [one of the Arabic *S* sounds]

1–3. *Saad.* I swear by the Qur'an bear this in mind. While unbelievers are prideful and defiant, they should remember how many previous generations We destroyed. Remember those who cried out when they could not escape Our wrath.

4–10. Those earlier disbelievers wondered how a prophet could come from among their people. They said, "He is a sorcerer, a liar." They said, "Has the prophet combined all our gods into one God? How strange." Their leaders told them not to listen and to worship their current multiple gods. They said, "We have not heard of this monotheism from religion before; it's a forgery." They asked, "Has God revealed His message just to him?"

They are in doubt of My message? They have not felt My punishment yet! Maybe the doubters have the treasure of the mercy of the Lord who can grant any judgment. Maybe they have the ownership of the heavens and earth and everything in between. If they do, then let them climb to heaven.

11–13. Have no doubt the disbelievers will be defeated. There were many before these men that rejected the prophets I sent; like the people of Noah, of Ad, of the Pharaoh, of Thamud, and of Lot.

14. For those who rejected my messengers, My just punishment surely came.

15–17. So today when rejecters say, in mockery, they don't want to wait for a call to judgment and ask the Lord to show them a portion of their sentence before their final day of reckoning, I say be patient and like David be strong and faithful.

18–20. Remember that We made the mountains that glorify at sunset and dawn and birds that flock together and sing in chorus. We made David's kingdom strong and gave him wisdom in thought and clear speech.

21–22. Have you heard the story of the two men who climbed over the walls of David's private chamber to bring him their argument? David was alarmed at their entry, but they told him to have no fear as they just needed their dispute solved. They asked that he give them an honest judgment that would provide a fair ending.

23. The man with one sheep explained that his brethren had 99 and yet was bullying him to give up his one lamb.

24–25. David told the man that he had been wronged; that the man should not have demanded his only sheep when he already had 99. He explained that many business partners wrong each other except those men who are righteous in thought and deed, but that those righteous men are few. David then realized he was being tested by God and prayed, asking for the protection of the Lord. In return We forgave him his lapse and he was close to God and enjoys paradise.

26. David, we did make you a king on earth, so judge men with truth and justice. Do not follow the lusts of your heart, for that will mislead you from the path to God. Those who stray from the path to God will have a great penalty on judgment day.

27–28. We created the heaven and earth with a purpose. Those who think it was in vain are disbelievers. The disbelievers will learn of the hellfire on judgment day. Should we treat the faithful and righteous the same as the corrupt and wicked?

29. This scripture We have sent down to you that is full of blessings allows you to think over the revelations so that the intelligent men can understand Our warnings.

30–33. We gave to David a faithful and selfless son in Solomon, who was a penitent soul. Once when the sun was setting he realized he had missed his afternoon prayer while he was looking at horses. Solomon said to the angels, "While I was admiring the horses, I forgot to remember my Lord at the sunset. Bring them back to me," and then he passed his hand over their legs and necks.

34–35. We certainly tested Solomon. Once we placed a dead body on his throne. He turned to repent and said, "My Lord! Forgive me and grant me a kingdom that is suited to me, for you are all-powerful."

36–40. We gave him power over the winds to guide as he wished. He controlled the evil spirits and every kind of builder and diver and those that were bound together in chains. We told him, "Such are Our gifts, and you can give them freely or hold them without accountability." Solomon enjoyed Our favor and was near to Us and will enjoy a happy final return to Us.

41–44. Remember Job, who cried to his Lord, "Satan has afflicted me greatly, and I suffer." And it was said to Job, "Strike the ground with your foot, and wash in the spring that appears." Then We gave him back his household and were merciful, as he was patient and could stand as a reminder to the faithful.

God knew he had taken an oath to give his wife a hundred lashes for questioning his faithfulness, and God ordered him to use a handful of grass to strike her and not a stick.

45–47. Remember Our servants Abraham, Isaac, and Jacob, who all possessed power and insights. We chose them specifically to remember and proclaim the hereafter. They were selected as the best, and so they are with us.

48. Remember Ishmael, Elisha, and Isaiah who were also among the best.

49–55. This is a message for the righteous. The hereafter is a place of beauty for you. The gardens of Eden will have their gates open for you. The righteous will recline and relax with abundant food and drink. Beside the righteous will be virtuous women of equal age. This is the promise to you on the day of reckoning. The gifts of heaven will never be exhausted.

But remember this [is for the righteous.]

For the sinners, there is an evil end.

56–59. They shall burn in hell as a final resting place. They shall taste the evil of scalding water and putrid pus from wounds and a variety of other equal torments. There is a large group rushing to hell with you. There is no welcome for them, and they will surely burn in the fire.

60. They will cry, "No welcome for you, as you have brought this

upon us in life."

61. They will say, "Lord, whoever prepared this hell for us, give him double the penalty of fire."

62–63. They will say, "Why don't we see the men we thought were wicked burning among us?" "Did we wrongly ridicule them in life, or have we just not seen them here yet?"

64. This is what the inmates of the fire will discuss.

65–68. Say to the people Muhammad, "I am only a messenger, and there is only one God with absolute power over all men. The Lord of heaven and earth is mighty and forgiving. This is a message of importance so do not turn away."

69–70. I have no knowledge of the matters discussed by the exalted chiefs; I only know what is revealed to me to say in public.

71–76. Recall when the Lord said to the angels, "I am about to create man from clay, and after I have fashioned him and breathed into him of My spirit, you will fall down in respect for him." And all the angels did bow down, except for Iblis whose pride made him an unfaithful. God said to Iblis, "Why don't you bow to man? Are you prideful or too exalted?" Iblis replied, "I am better than those you create from the dust, as you made me from fire."

77–78. God said to Iblis, "Go away from here, as you are now cursed until the day of judgment."

79–81. Iblis said to God, "My Lord give me a pardon until the day the dead are raised." And God said to him, "I will grant a reprieve until then."

82–83. Iblis replied to God, "By your power I will mislead every man until then, except for your purified servants."

84–85. God said, "The truth is I will certainly fill hell with you and everyone who follows you."

86–88. Say Muhammad unto mankind, "I ask no payment for this message, and I am not a pretender. This is nothing but a reminder for all the world, and you will know its truth in due time."

Chapter 39 (chronologically)

Sura 7 (206 verses), Al-Araf (The Heights)

1. Alif, Lam, Meem, Sad. [A-L-M-S]. [Intent of letters unknown to man.]

2. A book has been revealed to you, so let not your heart be heavy; teach and remind the believers.

3. Say, mankind follow the message given to you by your Lord and not other ideas from man.

4–5. Remember that We have destroyed many towns for their sins. Sudden and swift was the punishment. They only cried out, "Surely we were wrongdoers."

6–9. We will question those men who were sent our message. And We shall question the messengers. And We shall recount their entire life story with them, for We were always present. Our judgment of the scales will be true, and those tipping the scales with good deeds will have been successful; but those whose weight is light will lose their souls, because they did not follow our guidance.

10–18. We put you on earth with power and provisions so you could fulfill your life. But you give Us little thanks. We created you and made all the angels bow to you, except for Iblis. God questioned Iblis, and he felt he was better than mankind, as he was made from fire not clay. So God cast him out for his arrogance. Iblis then asked for respite from his curse until the dead were arisen, and God gave it to him. Iblis told God he would retaliate against mankind by ambushing them along the straight path of life and proving to God that men are not thankful. God vowed to fill hell with Iblis and any man that followed him.

19–21. We said to Adam, live with your wife in the Garden and enjoy all the good things, but avoid that one tree or you will be a wrongdoer. Then Satan whispered suggestions to them trying to convince them that God forbade that one tree so they could not become angels or immortal, swearing he was a trusted advisor.

22-23. Satan tricked them into tasting the fruit of the tree and learning about shame. They began to sew leaves together to cover their bodies. God called to them reminding them of his forbidding the tree. "Satan is an enemy of yours." They said to God, "We have sinned and darkened our souls. Without your forgiveness we will be lost."

24–25. God said to man and Satan, "Go forth from here, and on earth you will be enemies and live for a while. There you shall live, and die, and be raised up from."

26 Children of Adam, We have sent you clothing to cover your shame and to provide beauty. But the garment of righteousness is the best. It is one of the signs of God.

27. Children of Adam, don't let Satan seduce you like he did your parents in the Garden. He and his tribe watch you from the shadows. We have made satans to guard those who don't believe.

28. When you are caught being indecent, do not point to your father's bad behavior as an excuse, thinking God has given you permission to do that act. God never commands us to act shamefully. Are you trying to speak against God?

29. Say, "My Lord commands justice," and give your soul to Him at every prayer and call upon Him. Put your faith only in Him. As He created you, you will return to Him.

30. God guided some of mankind, while others chose to listen to devils instead of God and think they are following the right path.

31. Children of Adam, wear your beautiful clothes at every prayer, and when eating and drinking do not be wasteful. God does not love the extravagant.

32. Who forbade the embellishment of gifts from God that He produced for His servants and the provisions for sustenance? They are for the believers of the world to have on resurrection day. We explain our revelations for those who have knowledge.

33. The things that my Lord has forbidden are shameful deeds, even secret ones; sins, lies, and undue aggression; assigning partners to God without His authority; and saying things about God that you don't have knowledge of.

34. Every nation survives for an appointed time, and when the term is reached you cannot delay the end or cause it to come sooner.

35–36. Children of Adam, when a messenger amongst you reveals My signs, those who are righteous shall need not fear or grieve. But those who reject Our revelations with arrogance are the rightful owners of the flames and shall live in the fire.

37–39. Who is a greater sinner than someone who lies about God or denies His messages? When they are taken from this earth, they will admit to the angels that they made up the lies and rejected God. He will say, "Join the people that have passed before you in the fire." Every time that new people enter, they will curse those who came before them. They will tell the Lord that those who went before them misled them and ask God to give them twice the penalty. God will double it for all people in the fire without their knowledge. Then, the older inhabitants will say to the newer, "You have no advantage over us, so taste the fire."

40–41. Those who reject Our message and turn away in arrogance will not enter the Garden until a camel can pass through the eye of a needle. That is the reward for sin. For they will reside in hell for their unjustness.

42–43. But those who are faithful and do right will not have their soul burdened more than it can handle. They will be companions in the Garden. And We shall remove from their hearts any hatred. Below them rivers will flow and they shall say, "Praise be to God who guided us here. We would not have made it here if not for God and His messengers." They will hear "Behold the Garden you inherited for your good deeds."

44–47. Those in heaven shall call to those in hell exclaiming that the promises of God were true and asking if their Lord kept his promise. The hell dwellers will reply "yes," but someone between them will cry, "The curse of God is on the sinners—those who would hinder [men] from the path of God and lead them astray were those who denied the hereafter." Between them shall be a veil, and on the heights will be certain men who would know everyone by his mark; calling out to their companions of the Garden, "Peace be upon you." They will not have entered yet but will hope to. When they look to the men in the fire, they will say, "Lord please do not send us to the place of the unjust."

48–49. The men on the heights will call to certain men whom they will know from their marks, saying, "How useful to you now were your hoards and your arrogant ways?" "Aren't these the men you swore God would never show His mercy to?" "Enter the Garden and have no fear or grief."

50. Those in hell will call to the people in heaven, "Pour down some water and anything that God has given you." They shall say, "Surely God has forbidden them both to unbelievers."

51. Those who treated religion as a sport for amusement were deceived in life. So on this day We forget them as they forgot Us and rejected Our signs.

52. We sent them a book full of knowledge and in detail explained the guidance to mercy for those who have faith.

53. They wait for fulfillment, and on the day of fulfillment those who ignored Our message earlier will say, "The messengers of God spoke the truth. Is there anyone that can intercede for us? Or can we be returned to earth to follow the righteous path this time?" But they will have already lost their souls, and the false interceders they created will have failed them.

54. Your Lord is God, who created the heavens and earth in six days and then mounted the throne. He makes the night and day continuous and created the sun, moon, and stars to command. He creates and commands all. Blessed be God the Lord of the worlds.

55. Call upon your Lord humbly and privately, for God doesn't love wrongdoers.

56. Do not cause corruption on earth and then call on Him with fear and hope. God has mercy for those who do good.

57. It is He who sends the winds foretelling His mercy, till He brings a rain cloud. We lead the cloud to a dead land and cause rains to descend and bring forth crops of every kind. In this way We shall bring forth the dead so that you should remember.

58. From land that is clean and good, by God's will, grows produce, but from the land that is bad, nothing grows that is useful. We explain the signs by various [ways] to those who are thankful.

59–64. We sent Noah to his people. He said, "O my people! worship God! You have no other god but Him. I fear for you the punishment of a dreadful day! The chieftains of his people said, "We think you are wrong." Noah said, "O my people! I am not wrong; on the contrary I am a messenger from the Lord of the worlds! I convey unto you the messages of my

Lord and give good counsel to you, and am given by God knowledge you don't have. Don't you consider it odd that a message from your Lord, comes through a man from among your own people, to warn you, so that you may fear God and receive His mercy?"

But they rejected him, and We delivered him and those with him in the Ark safely; but We drowned in the flood those who rejected Our signs. They were indeed a blind people!

65–72. To the Ad people We sent Hud, one of their own. He said, "O my people, worship God for you have no other god but Him. Won't you guard against evil?" The unbelieving chieftains of his people said, "We think you are wrong, and We think you are a liar!" Hud said, "My people, I am no fool, but [I am] a messenger from the Lord of the worlds! I convey unto you the messages of my Lord, and I am a faithful advisor. Do you not consider it odd that there should come a messenger from among your people? Do you remember that you were made successors after Noah's people and respected? Remember the benefits you have received from your Lord so you could be successful." The chieftains said, "Are you saying we should worship God alone and forsake the religions of our fathers? If so, then show us your threat if you are telling the truth." Hud said, "Terror and wrath from your Lord have already fallen on you. Would you argue with me over gods you and your fathers named without permission from God?

Then await the consequences and remember I am also waiting."

We saved Hud and his followers by Our mercy, but We cut off the roots of those who rejected our message.

73–79. To the Thamud people We sent Salih, one of their own. He said, "My people! Worship God and have no other god but Him. This is a clear sign from your Lord! This female camel is God's sign unto you, so leave her to graze and let her come to no harm, or you shall be given a grievous punishment. Remember how He made you inheritors after the Ad people and gave you the land where you build your palaces and castles and carve out homes in the mountains. Remember the benefits you have received from God and refrain from evil and mischief on the earth." The arrogant leaders among his people said to those who they despised and those among them who were believers, "Do you believe that Salih is a messenger from his Lord?" They said, "We do indeed believe in the revelation which has been sent through him." Then the arrogant men said, "We reject what you believe in." Then they hamstrung the camel and insolently defied the order of their Lord, saying, "O Salih! Bring forth your threats if are truly a messenger of God!"

The earthquake caught them unawares, and they lay lifeless in their homes in the morning. So Salih left them, saying, "O my people! I conveyed to you the message for which I was sent by my Lord. I gave you good counsel, but you don't love good advisors."

80–84. Lot said unto his people, "Why do you commit indecencies like no one has ever done before? Your wantonness defines you as you lust over men instead of women." His people answered, "Expel them from the town for they are a puritanical family."

So We delivered Lot and his family, except his wife who lagged behind. And We brought a shower of brimstone upon the town, for that is how We finish the guilty.

85–93. We sent Shu'ayb to the Midians, and he told them to, "Serve God and have no other god but Him. Follow the clear path given to you, be fair to men, pay what is owed, and don't cause corruption on earth. It's what's best for you if you are faithful. Don't wait along the righteous path trying to lead others astray. Recall that when you were few, God multiplied you, and recall the punishment for the evil among you. And if some of you believe in my message and some do not, be patient, for in the end God will choose between you, and He judges wisely.

The arrogant chieftains said to Shu'ayb, "Unless you and your followers revert to our old religion, we will drive you from the town.

Shu'ayb questioned, "Even if we are unwilling to revert? We

would be affronting God if we reverted after God delivered us from those ways. Unless God wishes us to revert, it would not be in our interest. We have put our trust in God. Oh Lord, decide between us and our people, for you have the best judgment."

The faithless chiefs said, "If you follow Shu'ayb, you will surely be ruined!" Then the earth shook, and in the morning they were left lifeless on the floors of their homes. The men who rejected the message and called Shu'ayb a liar became strangers in their homes and were ruined. So Shu'ayb left his people, reminding them that he had given them the message of God and good advice and questioning why he should grieve for the unbelievers.

94–100. Whenever We sent a prophet to a town, we also sent suffering and afflictions so that they might learn humility. Then we made them prosperous until they started to think that their ancestors were also touched with distress and then happiness. Then we caught them unaware and called them to account.

If the people had only been faithful and fearful of God, We should have given them all the blessings of heaven and earth. But they rejected the truth, and We punished them for their misdeeds. Why did the people feel secure against Our wrath while they slept or while they acted carefree during the day? Did they feel as if they were immune to God's plan? Those who feel exempt from God's plan will perish. Is it not clear to mankind that the lessons of punishment upon their ancestors proves that We can bring them to account for their sins as well?

101–102. These were the stories of the towns We sent messengers to but were found faithless, so their hearts were sealed by God. In most of them, We primarily found unfaithful men that were disobedient.

103. [The detailed story of Moses] After these events, We sent Moses with Our signs to the Pharaoh and his chiefs, but they too wrongfully rejected them. You should consider the consequences of their disbelief.

104–122. Moses said, "O Pharaoh! I am a messenger from the Lord of the worlds, and I am only able to speak the truth about God. I have come from God with His signs and ask that you let the children of Israel leave with me." Pharaoh replied, "To prove your truthfulness, show me your signs from your God." Moses flung down his staff, and it became a serpent. Then he withdrew his hand from his cloak and it was invisible. The Pharaoh's chiefs said, "He is an expert magician intending to run you out of your lands," and Pharaoh asked the advisors for their ideas.

They advised him to keep him around for a while so they could send for the greatest magicians in the city. The magicians arrived, asking Pharaoh about their possible reward for besting Moses in competitions. Pharaoh promised them important court positions for victory.

The magicians asked Moses whether he or they would begin. Moses told them to start the competition, and they awed the onlookers. God inspired Moses, and he threw his staff again, and it devoured the magician's tricks. The crowd saw that the magicians were clearly defeated, and the wizards then bowed to Moses crying, "We believe in the Lord of the worlds, the Lord of Moses and Aaron."

123–126. Pharaoh spoke: "How dare you believe Moses before I give you permission? Surely, this is a conspiracy you all created to drive his people from the city; but you will soon feel the consequences of your actions. I will cut off your hands and feet and crucify each of you." They said to Pharaoh, "Surely we will be sent back to God, but do you take vengeance on him for simply believing the signs of our Lord? Protect us with patience and take our souls, God, for we die as men who have submitted to you."

127. The Pharaoh's chiefs spoke next to the king: "Do you dare leave Moses and his people untouched and able to cause trouble in the city? We will kill his people's male children and spare their women."

128–129. Moses spoke to his people: "Pray for help from God and wait patiently, for only God can decide who He guards against evil and who will inherit the lands." His people replied, "We have had nothing but trouble even before you came here and still today." Moses reminded them that God may yet destroy their adversary and make them rulers of the earth, but He will surely watch how they behave today."

130–132. God punished the Pharaoh's people with years of drought and famine. But when anything good occurred, they accredited themselves for the goodness. Yet when evil activities returned, they blamed Moses and his people. They didn't understand that evil events were their own fault. They said to Moses, "No matter what signs you bring us, we will not have faith in you."

133–136. So, next We sent a plague of death, locusts, lice, and frogs. They were still so arrogant and continued to sin. And after every plague they would say to Moses, "Pray to your Lord to stop this plague and we will send the children of Israel away with you." But every time the plague ended, they went back on their promise to Moses. So for rejecting Our signs, We drowned them in the sea.

137. We made the people considered to be weak on the east and west of Pharaoh owners of his lands. We blessed the children of Israel and fulfilled our promise for their patience through the suffering. We destroyed the structures the Pharaoh had built.

138–140. We took the Israelis safely across the sea. Then they came across a people devoted to idols and the Israelis said to Moses, "Make us a god like their idols." Moses replied, "You are an ignorant people. These people are a cult vainly worshipping, and their ways will be destroyed. You want me to find you a god other than the God that has just endowed you with favor above all other peoples?"

141. Remember that We rescued you from Pharaoh who had killed your male children.

142–144. We asked of Moses forty days of solitude, and we asked his brother Aaron to lead in his place, to ensure the people were not led astray in his absence. When Moses came to his appointed place, he asked his Lord if he could look upon him. God said, "You cannot see Me directly but to look for Me in the mountain." When God revealed His glory upon the mountain, it came crashing down and Moses fell down. Upon recovering Moses said, "Glory be to you God, I am repentant and am the first of the faithful." God said, "Moses I have chosen you above all mankind for a mission, so take my messages with you and be thankful."

145. So We wrote Our laws upon tablets and commanded that they be followed closely by the people. "Tell the people to do what is right, for soon I will show you the home for the sinners."

146–147. Those who are arrogant on earth and won't do right will not see My signs. Even if they see them, they won't believe. When they see correct behavior, they won't adopt it. They will choose to emulate sins. They will reject Our revelations, and those who reject our revelations will have no good deeds counted in the hereafter.

148–150. While Moses was in seclusion, his people made an ornate idol in the image of a calf, and they unjustly worshiped it. When they realized they had sinned, they said, "If our Lord does not show mercy to us, we will surely perish." Moses returned to them angry and said, "Evil is the course you took in my absence, and you hastily turned away from your Lord." He set aside the tablets and grabbed his brother by the hair and dragged him forward saying, "Brother, the people viewed me as weak and almost killed me. Do not allow our enemies to triumph and do not count me among the sinners."

151. Moses prayed, "Lord forgive me and my brother. Show us your mercy; for you are the most merciful."

152–153. Those who worshiped the calf will feel the wrath of the Lord and they will be shamed for the rest of their life. For We do not forgive those who invent a lie. But, for those who do wrong and truly repent for their sins, in the hereafter the Lord is forgiving and most merciful.

154–156. Once his anger subsided, Moses lifted up the tablets that contained the Lord's guidance. There was mercy in the message for those people who feared the Lord. Moses chose seventy people to attend meeting, and when they arrived, the earth quaked. Moses prayed, "Lord you could have destroyed us anytime you wanted to before. Would you now destroy us for the deeds of some foolish people among us? It is a test from God, and you can surely lead anyone astray and anyone along the righteous path. But you are our protector, so forgive us and give us mercy, for you are most merciful. Tell us what is righteous in this life and the hereafter, for we have turned to you for guidance." He replied, "I give my punishment to whom I please and because my mercy embraces all things, I will ordain it for those who fight against evil, those who are regularly charitable, and those who are believers in Our revelations." [tenets of Islam]

157. Those who follow the messenger, the prophet who can neither read nor write and who is mentioned in the earlier scriptures, will be instructed about what is right and wrong. He will lift the burdens from men. For those who believe in him, honor him, help him, and follow the righteous path will prosper.

158. Mankind, I am the messenger of God who commands the heavens and earth. There is no God but Him. He creates life and causes death. Believe in God and His messenger, the uneducated prophet, and His words. Follow him on the righteous path.

159. Among Moses's people, there are some that establish justice and are guided by the truth.

160. We divided the people into 12 tribes or nations. We inspired Moses so that when his people asked him for water, he could strike a rock with his staff and see 12 springs come forth. Each tribe knew its own place for water. We gave them the

shade of clouds and sent down to them manna and quails, saying, "Eat of the good things We have provided for you." But they rebelled and caused Us no harm as they harmed their own souls.

161. We said to them, "Live in this town and eat here what you wish, but repent with words when you enter the gate and be humble so We can forgive your sins and reward the righteous to help others."

162. But the unjust changed the words we gave them, and so We sent them a plague of pestilence.

163. [MD] Ask the people about the town standing close by the sea. Where they broke the rules of the Sabbath. When they observed their Sabbath, the fish came right to the surface for them. But when they did not observe the Sabbath, there were no fish. We tried them in this way, for they were sinning.

164–167. [MD] When some of the people say, "Why do you preach to a people whom God will later destroy or terribly punish?" say to them, "To fulfill our duty to your Lord, that they might fear Him." When they disregarded Our warnings, We rescued those who stood against evil and punished the wrongdoers for their sins. When they were prideful of their sins, We said to them, "You are to be despised and rejected like monkeys." The Lord announced that We would send cruel torments against them until the day of resurrection. The Lord is swift in retribution and also forgiving and merciful.

168. [MD] We dispersed them into separate communities on the earth. Some were righteous and some were not. And We tested them both with prosperity and adversity to see who will return to Us.

169. [MD] After them came an evil generation that also inherited the Book [religious scriptures of the Abrahamic God], but they chose the vanities of this world and relied on the excuse that we will be forgiven for our excesses on earth. Wasn't the covenant based on an understanding that they would not speak anything about God but the truth? Didn't they study the scriptures and realize that the hereafter is better for those who are righteous? Don't you understand?

170. [MD] For those who follow the rules of the scriptures and regularly pray, it is never a waste to give Our rewards to the righteous when they perish.

171. When We shook the mountains above them and they thought they were going to be crushed, We said, "Follow closely the rules given to you, and use them to ward off evil."

172–173. Remember that when the Lord brought forth descendants from Adam, He made them testify that He was their Lord sustainer. They testified that He was. This was done so that on judgment day, they could not say, "We were not aware of you Lord, so don't destroy us for we simply followed the falsehood of our forefathers when we took false gods and associated them with God.

174. We explain the revelations in detail so that mankind may return to Us.

175–176. Tell them of the stories of men that We sent our signs but who went astray because they ignored Us and Satan overtook them. If it had been Our will, We could have exalted him but he chose to follow the lowly desires of earth. His is the parable of the dog.

If you attack the dog, he pants with his tongue out, and also if you leave him alone, he pants with his tongue out.

Such are the people that deny our revelations. Tell them the stories and perhaps they will reflect upon them.

177. Evil is a parable of the people who reject our revelations and therefore wrong themselves.

178. He whom God leads is on the righteous path, and whomever God sends astray are those who will perish.

179. There are many genies and men that have been sent to hell who had hearts but would not understand and had eyes but would not see. They are like cattle, but worse, for they chose to ignore the signs.

180. The most beautiful names belong to God, so use them to speak of him. Avoid those who use his names as profanity, for they shall pay for their actions.

181–183. There are people that We created that will lead people with truth and establish justice. There are those that reject our revelations and will be punished in ways they cannot imagine, and I grant them respite, for my plan is complete.

184. Do they not think that their companion [prophet] is sane? He is but a simple messenger.

185. Don't they consider the kingdom of heaven and earth and everything that God created? Don't they think that their own end is drawn near? So what will they believe after this?

186. Those who God sends astray are unguided, and He leaves them to wander blindly through life.

187. When they ask about the end of times and when it will occur say, "Only God knows the hour of the end, and it will be momentous when it occurs. All of a sudden it will happen, catching everyone unaware." They will question you to see if you actually know the time, but tell them only God knows.

188. Tell them, "I have no power to control the good or bad except that which God wills to happen. If I had knowledge of the future, I would be rich and would never be harmed, but I am just a messenger and bearer of good news to the faithful."

189–192. It is He who created you from a single soul and gave you a mate. She carries the burden until it is heavy, and then you both call to God, "Please give us a goodly child and we vow to be grateful." But when God gives them a goodly child, they associate others with that gift. God is exalted above all those they associate with Him. Why do they associate partners to God that cannot create anything and are themselves created? And have no power to give help or even to help themselves?

193–194. If you call them to follow the guidance, they will not obey. It's all the same whether you invite them to listen or not. Those who you call upon are like you, mere servants. Call upon them and let them answer if you are truthful.

195–197. Do they have feet to walk with? Hands to grab hold with? Eyes to see with? Or ears to hear with? Tell them, "Call upon your so-called partners of God and with everything you have got, plot against me. For surely my guardian is God, who revealed the scriptures and cares for the righteous. But those who you call upon are not able to help, and they can't even help themselves."

198–199. When you call people to follow the guidance and they refuse to hear you, even if you see them watching you, while they refuse to see, keep forgiving them but demand they do what is right, and turn away from the ignorant.

200–202. If you are wounded by the slander of Satan, then seek refuge with God, for He hears and knows all things. Those fearful of God remember God when Satan troubles them, and they go straight. But the evil ones just increase their errors and never slow down.

203. If you don't bring them a message and they ask why haven't

you created another revelation, say to them, "I only say what is revealed to me from your Lord, who is a guide and provides mercy to those of the faith."

204. When the Qur'an is recited, listen attentively and silently so that you may receive mercy.

205. Always remember your Lord in your soul and be humble and reverent; use a low voice in the morning and evening and always be mindful.

206. Even those closest to your Lord are humble enough to worship Him. They praise Him and humbly bow to Him.

Chapter 40 (chronologically)

Sura 72 (28 verses), Al-Jinn (The Genies)

1–5. It has been revealed to me that a group of jinns listened to the Qur'an and they said, "We have heard a marvelous recitation. That it is a guide for the righteous, and we believe in it. We will not worship any gods in connection with our Lord. We believe in the majesty of our Lord and that He has never taken a wife or created a son. There are fools among us that used to tell lies about God, but we don't think anyone should speak a lie against God."

6–7. Indeed, there were people that used to seek shelter and protection of some specific jinns, and that only increased their wrongdoing against God. They supposed, just as you might suppose, that God wouldn't raise anyone from the dead.

8–9. We jinns who have listened to the Qur'an have attempted to eavesdrop in heaven but found it protected with stern guards and flames. We used to hide there and listen, but anyone trying now would find the flames waiting for them.

10. We do not know if someone on earth is intended harm or if the Lord will give them guidance to correct their path.

11–13. There are righteous and unrighteous among us, as we are sects that follow many paths. But we know that we cannot escape God on earth or in flight. As for us, we have listened to the guidance, and we accept it. Those who believe in the Lord shall have no fear of loss or oppression.

14–15. Among us there are some who have submitted their will to God [Muslims] and some who are unjust and deviate from the righteous path. Those who submit their will to God have chosen the right path. But those who deviate from the right path will be the fuel of hell.

16–17. Those that follow the path of God will have water to drink in abundance, that we may test them, but if anyone turns from God, he will be given increasingly severe penalties.

18. The places of worship are only for God, so don't pray to anyone else alongside God.

19. When the servant of God stood to pray, the crowds nearly crushed him.

20. Say, "I only pray to God, and I don't associate any false god with Him."

21. Say, "I have no power to bring you harm or good."

22. Say, "No one can protect me from God, and I can find refuge only with Him."

23. My sole duty is to transmit messages from God to mankind. Whoever disobeys His message or His messenger will dwell in hell forever.

24. On judgment day they will see what they are promised, and then they will know who has support from the weakest and how small they are in number.

25–28. Say, "I do not know the hour of the judgment day nor whether God has set it soon or far from now. God alone knows the unknown and does not reveal His secrets to anyone, except a chosen messenger who is guarded by sentinels from all sides, so that He knows that they have transmitted His messages, and He knows what's going on around the messenger, and He can record everything."

Chapter 41 (chronologically)

Sura 36 (83 verses), Ya Seen (one of the prophet's names)

1–4. Ya Seen, I swear by the definitive Qur'an, you are one of the apostles and follow the straight path.

5–6. It is a revelation handed down from God the mighty and merciful, in order that you can warn these people whose fathers were not warned. The people are oblivious to this scripture.

7. The word has already proved true against most of them so they will not have faith.

8–11. We have put yokes on their necks, and their heads are craned away from the truth of God's guidance. We have put a bar in front of them and one behind, and they are blindfolded, so they cannot see. So whether you warn them or not, they will not believe you. You can only warn people who follow the revelations and fear God, so to them offer news of forgiveness and reveal the rewards of faith.

12. We alone give life to the dead. We record everything they have done on earth and have kept it in a book of precise evidence.

13–19. Tell them of the example about the people in the city when the messengers visited:

When we first sent two messengers, they were rejected, so we strengthened the group with a third apostle. But the people said you are only men like us, and you are lying, because God has not given you a revelation. The apostles replied, "Our Lord surely sent us as messengers, and we have a duty to proclaim it." The people then said, "We sense you are an evil omen, and if you do not stop we will stone you. A great punishment we will give you." The apostles said, "You are your own evil omens. You would see it, if you heard our warnings, but no, you are an extravagant bunch."

20–21. Just then a man came running up from the city and said, "My people, follow these apostles! Obey the messengers who are not asking for money and are following a righteous path."

22–27. Why shouldn't I worship He who created me and to whom we shall return? Shall I worship other gods instead of Him? If God wants to cause me harm, those other gods can't protect me, nor can they save my soul. That would be a grave error. Lord, I have faith in you, so listen to me. God said to him, "Enter the Garden of paradise." The man said, "If only my people had known what the Lord forgave in me to allow me the honor of entering paradise."

28–30. After that man, We did not send down any hosts from heaven to his people. Nor did we need to. And in one single cry they were extinct. Too bad for them that every messenger that arrived was mocked.

31. Did they never notice how many generations before them were destroyed, never to return?

32. All of them will be brought before Us to stand judgment.

33–35. A sign for man is that We take unfertile earth and return life to it in the form of grain they can eat. We then produce gardens of date palms and grapes, and springs bring water forth so they can eat of the fruit we created. They did not create this life, so why can't they be grateful?

36. Praise be to God for creating all things on the earth, and the humans themselves, and the knowledge they do not yet know.

37–40. A sign for man is the night. We take away the day and plunge the world into darkness. The sun runs its course to a place ordained by the almighty and all-knowing. The moon is appointed to its phases until it becomes thin like an old palm leaf. We do not permit the sun to overtake the moon nor the night to overtake the day; they all move in their own orbit.

41–44. A sign for man is that We carried their ancestors through the flood. We have also created similar vessels for them to ride upon. If it were Our will, We could drown them and leave them helpless with no way to be saved, unless by Our mercy.

45-46. [45 in MD] When it was said to people "Beware of what is in front of you and also what is behind you, so that you may receive mercy." There were no signs from the Lord that they did not disregard.

47. When they are told to spend the wealth that God has provided, the unbelievers ask the faithful, "Should we feed the people that God would have fed if He willed it?" They are in error.

48-52. They say, "When will the promises be fulfilled if you are telling us the truth?" But they will not have to wait long, for a single cry will seize them while they debate. They won't have time to write a will or return to their family. The trumpet shall sound, and the men will rise from their graves to meet the Lord. They will say, "Woe unto us. Who raised us from our graves?" A voice will say, "This is the promise of God the most gracious, as told by His messengers."

53–58. There will be but one single blast, and mankind will be brought before Us. On this day not a soul will be wronged in the least, and retaliation shall only match your past deeds. Those who enter paradise shall be joyful. They and their companions shall recline on couches in the shade. They shall have fruits and whatever else they desire. "Peace" will be the watchword from the Lord most merciful.

59–62. "But you guilty ones, get aside this day." Didn't I tell you children of Adam not to worship Satan, as he was your manifest enemy. And that you should worship me, for that is the right path? Yet he has led a great many of you astray. How did you not understand my guidance?

63–67. This is the hell you were warned of so many times. Embrace the fire for your disbelief. Today We will seal their mouths, but their hands will speak to Us, and their feet will bear witness to all they have done to earn this. If We had wanted to, We could have blinded them so they would have to grope about. If We had wanted to, We could have frozen them in their places so they couldn't go forward or back.

68. If We grant long life to someone, they will once again become weak. Do they not understand this?

69–70. We have not instructed the prophet in poetry, nor does he need it. This is nothing less than a message and a manifest Qur'an, so that he can warn all the living and its word can be fulfilled against the unbelievers.

71–73. Have they not seen how We created the cattle and placed them under their power? And that we made them so some could be ridden and others provide food? And from them they can get milk to drink. Will they not give Us thanks?

74–75. Yet they still take on other gods besides God, hoping for more help. They don't have any power to help, but their worshippers will protect them with arms.

76. So don't let their words bother you Muhammad, for we know what they are doing in secret and openly.

77–83. Doesn't man see that it was We who created him from a drop of sperm? Yet he dares to stand in open opposition? Man makes comparisons to Us but forgets his own origin. Then he says, "Who can revive the old corpses after they have rotted?" Say to them, "He who created you the first time will give them new life. He is well versed in creation. The same [One] who made fire burn from a green tree so you can have a fire. Why couldn't He who created the heavens and earth create them? He is the all-knowing creator. When He intends to do something, He only has to say 'be' and it is done. So, give glory to He that rules over all things, and through Him you shall be brought back."

Chapter 42 (chronologically)

Sura 25 (77 verses), Al-Furqan

(The Criterion for distinguishing right from wrong)

1–2. Blessed is He that sent down the criterion to His prophet so that he can warn mankind; He who is the king of heaven and earth and has no son or partner in the kingdom and created everything precisely.

3. And still, people have taken up other gods instead. Gods that have no power to create, were themselves created, and have no power to cause good or harm nor death, life, or resurrection.

4–6. The unbelievers say that God is but a lie and that others are helping to spread it. In truth, the faithless have created a lie. Unbelievers say this Qur'an is simply the tales of the ancient men and that they are dictated to him every morning and evening. Tell them Muhammad, "The Qur'an was sent down by Him that is all-knowing, all-forgiving, and all-merciful."

7–8. The faithless say, "What sort of messenger would eat food and walk through the markets? Why didn't God send an angel down to help him warn mankind? Why does the messenger lack treasure and a beautiful garden of foods? You are following a bewitched man!"

9. You can see they are talking ill of you and are straying from the straight path that they will never be able to find.

10. Blessed is He who can grant you anything He wishes, like gardens with streams flowing. He will build you palaces.

11–14. For those that deny judgment day we have prepared flames. When they can see it from a distance, they will already hear its crackling roar. And when they are flung into the confined space chained together, they will cry out for death. They will be told not to pray for a single death but for many repeated deaths.

15–16. So say to them, "Is the fire best or the everlasting paradise that is the promised reward for the righteous? They will have everything they desire that is a promise from your Lord."

17-18. On judgment day He will gather those who worship others besides God and ask, "Was it you that led these men astray, or did they choose to be unrighteous?" The faithless will say, "Glory be to you God; it was not appropriate for us to take up other gods but you." But you did warn them and their fathers. They are a lost people.

19–20. They will call you a liar and impugn your character so that you cannot avoid punishment or find help. But those that treat you unjustly will pay a grievous penalty. The messengers before you also ate food and walked in marketplaces. We give you trials to test your patience, and God is all-seeing.

21–23. Those who doubt God's existence ask, "Why hasn't He sent an angel to us, or why can't we see God?" They are arrogant and defiant! When they get to finally see an angel, those sinners will feel no joy. Angels will say, "You are forbidden from paradise!" Then We will assess their deeds and turn them to dust.

24–29. But those resting in paradise will be peaceful and relaxed on that day when heaven will open and angels will descend. The day that God will be most merciful except to the faithless, they shall have a hard day. The day that sinners will bite their own hands crying, "I wish I had followed the path laid by the messenger. I wish I had not taken on my friends that led me astray from the warnings of the messenger." And Satan will fail to help mankind at this hour.

30–31. Then the messenger will say, "My Lord, the people didn't believe the Qur'an." That is how it is for every prophet. We give him an enemy among the faithless, but God is sufficient to help you.

32. The faithless will ask, "Why wasn't the Qur'an revealed to the prophet all at one time?" It is revealed to you in gradual arranged stages so it may strengthen your heart.

33. We have prepared you with a wise explanation for every argument the faithless bring against you.

34. Those who will be gathered in hell on their faces are on a bad path and are straying further from the righteous way.

35–36. We sent Moses the book and gave him his brother Aaron to assist. We commanded them to go to the people who rejected Our messages. Then We destroyed them completely.

37. When Noah's people rejected the messengers, We drowned them as a sign to mankind that the evil will pay a great penalty.

38. And the same for the Ad, Thamud, and Rass people and many generations in between.

39. For each of them We gave warning by parables and then destroyed them for their sins.

40–42. Certainly the faithless saw the towns that were destroyed. How could they miss it? Yet they still didn't expect a resurrection day. And when they see you, the prophet, they mock, asking, "You are the one that God sent as a messenger? He would have led us from our current gods if we hadn't adhered to their worship." Soon they will know their punishment and will see that they were straying from the righteous path.

43–44. Have you seen the men that choose to worship their own desires as a god? Is it your duty to protect them? Do you think that most men listen or even understand? They are like cattle and are moving away from the right path.

45–47. Have you noticed how the Lord casts the twilight and

darkness? If He willed it, He could have made it permanent. But We have made the sun its beacon, and We retract the darkness to Us gently. It was Us that made the night so that man can rest and sleep and made the day so man can rise anew.

48–50. And it is He that sends the winds to warn of the merciful rains coming in the clouds. With the purifying water, We revive unfertile lands and quench the thirsts of the man and beast We created. We have repeatedly brought the rains to man so they would remember Us, but most are ungrateful.

51–52. If We willed it, We could have sent a prophet to every village on earth. Do not listen to the unbelievers, and struggle mightily against them with this message.

53–54. We created the two different bodies of water on earth, one sweet and drinkable and the other bitter and salty; so we created a barrier between them so they would not join. We created man from water and then empowered him to establish relationships by lineage and marriage, for the Lord has power over everything.

55–56. And yet man worships others besides God, things that cannot bring them good or harm. The unbeliever is against God. But We only sent you Muhammad as a messenger of good news and a warning.

57–58. Say, "I ask for no reward for my message except that you choose to follow the righteous path to the Lord and that you put your trust in the living God and celebrate His praise. He is well aware of the sins of His servants.

59. Ensure you ask someone who is aware of God about Him. He who created the heavens and earth in six days, and is well established on the throne, God the most generous.

60. When they are told to bow before the all-beneficent they say, "What is the 'all-beneficent'? Should we bow to whoever you tell us to?" This increases their distance from the right path.

61–62. Blessed is He who made the stars in the sky and the shining moon; He who made the night and day. We have much to show gratitude for.

63–71. The servants of the beneficent are those who are humble, and when the foolish address them, they say, "Peace." They are those who spend the night bowing and standing in prayer to God. They are those who say, "Lord, deliver us from the sure wrath of hell, for it is an everlasting punishment. It is an evil place to stay." They are those that are neither wasteful nor tight-fisted with money, but find the balance of moderation. They are those who do not cry out to any other god but God, who do not kill another without just cause, who do not commit adultery, for anyone that does shall pay a penalty. The penalty on judgment day will be doubled unless he repents and is faithful in life and does good deeds. Because God will change their evil deeds to good, as He is forgiving and merciful. For whosoever repents and follows the righteous path has truly turned towards God.

72–76. Servants of the beneficent are they that do not lie, and when they hear those talking in vain, they just pass on by. They are those that do not pretend to be deaf or blind when they are shown the signs of their Lord. They are those who pray, "Lord, grant us the comfort of a wife and children and help us to guard against evil." They are the ones that will be rewarded with the highest place of honor in Heaven, because they were steadfast and so will be welcomed with greetings of "Peace." They will be happy forever in their place of rest.

77. Say to the unbelievers, "My Lord would care for you if you would learn how to pray to Him, but you have rejected the truth and my advice, so that act will bring you ultimate punishment."

Chapter 43 (chronologically)

Sura 35 (45 verses), Fatir (The Originator or the Angels)

1. Praise be to God, who created the heavens and earth, who made the angels—His messengers with wings. God has power over all things.

2. Whatever mercy God bestows on mankind no one can reverse. And whatever mercy He withholds cannot be granted by anyone else. He is almighty and wise.

3. Mankind, remember God's grace towards you. There is no other creator that can give you a heaven and earth. There is no god but God. So why do you stray from the path?

4. If they impugn you, My messenger, remember that other apostles were impugned before you and that God will have a final decision on those people.

5. Mankind, the promise of God is true. Don't be deceived by your present life, and don't be deceived by Satan about God.

6. Remember, Satan is your enemy, so treat him as such. He only seeks companions on earth to join him in hell.

7. For the unbelievers who reject God, there will be a terrible penalty, but for the faithful who commit righteous deeds, there will be forgiveness and a reward.

8. What if someone is fooled into evil acts, but he thinks he is doing good? God leads astray who He likes and guides on the right path who He wants. Do not worry yourself about those people, for God knows what they are doing.

9. It is God that sends winds out to cause the rain clouds to form and then moves them over unfertile lands so they can be revived by the waters. So too will be your resurrection.

10. If anyone seeks honor, power, or glory, they should know that all glory, honor, and power belong to God. To God give words of praise for your power, as he allows your righteous conduct. And for those who devise evil plots, they will find an

awful penalty, and their plans will come to nothing.

11. God created man from dust and sperm and then made you into pairs. No female conceives or gives birth without His knowledge. No man can have a long or shortened life without Him recording it. All this is easy for God.

12. The two bodies of water are different. One is sweet and drinkable, while the other is salty and bitter. Yet from both bodies can you find meat and jewels to wear. And when you see ships cutting through the waters, you can ask for God's grace and give thanks to God.

13–14. He created night and day and causes them to cycle. The sun and moon are subject to His laws and follows His set course. God has dominion over everything. Those others you invoke have no power. If you call to them, they will not hear you. If they hear you, they cannot answer your prayers. And on the day of judgment they will reject your faith in them. No one can tell you the truth like the one all-knowing God.

15–17. Mankind, you are the ones that need God, because He has everything and is owed all your praise. If He pleased, He could wipe you away and bring about a new creation. This is not difficult for God.

18. No one can carry another's load for them. You can only provide warning to those who truly fear God and pray regularly. And those who purify themselves for their own

sake, to God they will return.

19–23. The blind and sighted man are not alike; nor are darkness and light; nor cool and hot. Those living and those that have died are not alike. Although God can make any deaf person hear, you cannot make those in the graves hear your warning. You are no more than a messenger.

24–26. We have sent you with the truth to bear glad tidings and to warn mankind. Every nation has had a messenger sent to it. If they reject you, those before you were also rejected. Their messengers went to them with clear signs, and scriptures, and psalms, and books of enlightenment. In the end I punished terribly those who rejected the message.

27–28. Have you not seen, mankind, that God sends down rains from the clouds? With it We produce fruits of many colors. In the mountains are streaks of white and red and various hues and an intense black. Also among men and beasts there are diverse hues. The smartest among God's servants fear him, for God is mighty and forgiving.

29–30. Those servants that recite the Qur'an of God, pray regularly, and give to charity in public and private can expect a reward that never ends so that He can pay them for their good deeds from His grace. He is all-forgiving and most appreciative.

31–32. What We have revealed to you of the Book [Qur'an] is the truth and confirms what was revealed earlier in time. God is all-knowing about His servants. We have given the Book as inheritance to our specially chosen servants. Among them are those who do wrong to themselves, who are mediocre, and by God's grace some who excel in doing good works. That is the greatest grace.

33–35. They will enter the Gardens of Eden dressed in silk and wearing bracelets of gold and pearls. They will say, "Praise be to God, who removed our sorrows. God is oft-forgiving and appreciative. It is His grace that gave us this eternal mansion where we shall never feel weariness."

36–38. For the faithless who reject God there will be the fires of hell. They will not die nor be released from the flames early. We punish the ungrateful ones. In hell, they will cry, "Lord let us out, and we will do good deeds and not be evil." Didn't We give you a long life so you could heed Our warnings? And remember We sent you a messenger. Accept your punishment, for you have no help here. God knows all things that occur in heaven and on earth. He knows the secrets in man's heart.

39. He let you inherit the earth. If anyone rejects God, they only hurt themselves. The faithless gain nothing from God by their disbelief.

40. Say, "Tell me about your partner gods you call upon besides God. Show me what they created in heaven or on earth. Have We given them a scripture so that you can prove they exist?" They can't. The wrongdoers only promise each other more

delusions.

41. God sustains the heavens and the earth so they continue to function, and if they should fail, there is no one that can harness them besides God. He is patient and forgiving.

42–44. The people swore by God that if a messenger came to them, they would follow his guidance perfectly. But when a warner came to them, it only increased their loathing. They behaved arrogantly and plotted evil schemes which backfired. So now they wait and look at the traditions their ancestors followed. They will find no change in God's way, nor any revision. Haven't they seen what happened to their ancestors even though they were stronger than today's people? Nothing can stop God's wrath. He is wise and powerful.

45. If God were to give mankind the punishment they deserve, they would all be obliterated. Instead He gives them relief until the appointed time arrives. And at judgment day God will know about all His servants.

Chapter 44 (chronologically)

Sura 19 (98 verses), Maryam (Mary)

1. Kaf, Ha, Ya, Ayn, Saad

2–4. This is the account of your Lord's mercy toward His servant Zachariah, when he called out to his Lord quietly saying, "My

Lord, I have become feeble, and my hair is grey, but I have never failed to worship you in prayer."

5–6. "Now I fear what my relatives will do after I depart, as my wife is without child. Would you grant me an heir? One that would inherit from me and the family of Jacob. Please make him someone that pleases you Lord."

7–10. The prayer was answered saying, "Zachariah, We will give you a son named John, and never before have We given this name." Zachariah replied, "My Lord, how shall I have a son when my wife is barren and I am so old?" The Lord said, "This is easy for Me, as I created man before from nothing." Zachariah asked for a sign. "Your sign will be your inability to speak for three nights even though you are healthy."

11. After prayer, Zachariah went before his people and asked them to pray to God in the morning and evening.

12–15. We commanded his son, "John take hold of the scripture." And We gave him wisdom while only a child. And We gave him compassion and purity, and he was devout. He was kind to his parents and never arrogant or rebellious. Peace be upon him at his birth, at his death, and at his resurrection.

16–19. Mention in the Book of Mary the time when she left her family and traveled eastward. Secluded from family, We sent her Our spirit appearing in the form of a man. Mary said, "I seek refuge from the all-generous, if you are God-fearing."

The spirit replied, "I am only the messenger of the Lord to tell you of the gift of a holy son."

20–21. Mary asked, "How can I give birth to a son when no man has touched me and I have been faithful in marriage?" The spirit said, "It will be so. 'The Lord said it would be easy for Me, and that We will make him a sign to mankind of our mercy.' "

22–26. So she became pregnant with him and she traveled to a remote place. As the birth pains struck her, she paused at a date palm tree and said, "I wish I had died before this pain and been forgotten." From below her a voice cried, "Do not grieve, for the Lord has provided a stream of water below the tree and if you shake the tree, ripened dates will fall at your feet. So eat and drink and find comfort. And if you see anyone, tell them you have made a vow to fast to God and that you may not speak to them today."

27–28. After birth, she brought the babe to her people. They said, "Mary, surely you return with an odd thing. Sister of Aaron, your father was not an evil man and your mother was not unfaithful."

29. But Mary pointed to the babe. They said, "How can we talk to a child still in the cradle?"

30–34. He spoke, "I am a servant of God. He has given me revelations and made me a prophet. He has blessed me wherever I may go and has commanded me to pray and give alms throughout my life. He has made me kind to my mother and commanded me not to be arrogant or unhappy. Peace is upon me from the day I was born, to the day that I die, and on the day I will be resurrected." Such was the true story of Jesus [Isa], the son of Mary, which they vainly dispute.

35–36. It is not appropriate to the majesty of God for Him to father a child. Glory be to God. When He decides a matter, He only needs to say "be" and it is so. God is my Lord and yours, so serve Him on the righteous path.

37–38. But sects disagree on this. Woe be upon the faithless on that awful day. They will see and hear clearly when they come to Us, but today they live in grave error.

39–40. Warn them that on judgment day the matter will be decided. For now they are oblivious, and they don't believe. We will inherit the earth and all who are on it will be brought back to Us.

41–43. Tell them in the book [scripture] about Abraham [Ibrahim], for he was a truthful man and a prophet. Recall when he said to his father, "Father, why do you worship something that you can't hear or see and offers you no benefits? Father, I have been given revelations that you do not know, so follow me, and I will guide you on the straight path."

44–45. "Father, do not worship Satan, for he rebels against God the beneficent. I fear that a great punishment awaits you from the most benevolent and that you will become a servant of Satan."

46. His father replied, "Do you hate my gods Abraham? If you don't stop, I will have you stoned. Go away from me for a long while."

47–48. Abraham said, "Peace be upon you. I will pray to my Lord to forgive you. He is gracious to me. I will leave all of you that pray to gods other than God. I will pray to my Lord. Hopefully I won't fail to be blessed by God."

49–50. When he turned away from the unbelievers, We gave him sons Isaac and Jacob, and We made each a prophet. We gave them Our mercy and great honor and a reputation of honesty.

51–53. Also, explain in the book the story of Moses, for he was especially dedicated to God and was a messenger and a prophet. We called to him from the right slope of the mountain and brought him to Us to talk privately. We also gave him a brother, Aaron, who was a prophet.

54–55. Mention in the book the story of Ishmael [Ismael]. He was true to his word and also a messenger and prophet. He reminded his people to pray and give to charity. The Lord was pleased with him.

56–57. Mention in the book the story of Idris. He was a truthful man and a prophet. We raised Idris to a high status in heaven.

58. [MD] These were prophets blessed by God from among the ancestors of Adam, Noah, Abraham, Israel, and others We

guided and selected. Whenever they heard the signs of God, they would bow down weeping.

59–60. After these men, there were evil generations that failed to pray and were lustful, so soon they will reap the punishment of their activities. Except for those that repent, are faithful, and do good deeds, for they will enter paradise and not be punished.

61-63. The Garden of Eden is God's promise to His faithful servants, and it will exist. In the Garden, there will not be any idle talk but instead "Peace." They will have food every morning and evening. It is the Garden that will be inherited by the devout servants that fight evil.

64–65. The angels say, "We only descend upon the Lord's command, and everything that is in front of, behind, and between us belongs to Him. The Lord never forgets. He is the Lord of the heavens and the earth and everything in between, so worship Him and serve Him faithfully. Do you know anyone that is equal to Him?"

66–67. Man asks, "Will we be resurrected from the dead?" Doesn't he remember that We created him out of nothing?

68–70. Have no doubt, my Lord, We will gather all good and evil men together and place them on their knees around hell. Then We will pluck out the most rebellious to God from among them. And We will also know who are the most worthy among them.

71. [MD] None of them will enter without a decree from your Lord.

72. We will rescue those who shunned evil, and let the unjust remain there on their knees.

73–75. When We show our signs to mankind, the unbelievers say to the faithful, “Which side is in a better station of life and has better company?” How many generations before them did we destroy who had more goods and finer appearances? When men go off the straight path, God will extend their life until such time that God sees what He was promised, in either punishment or the judgment time. Then man will know whose position is worse and whose side is weaker.

76. God gives additional guidance to those who are righteous, as lasting good deeds are the best reward for the Lord.

77–80. Haven't you seen the man that rejects Our signs and says, “I will certainly have wealth and children.” Has he seen the unknown or made a pact with the most beneficent? No, so We shall record what he said and prolong his punishment length. He shall come to us alone, and We shall inherit what he speaks of.

81–87. They have chosen to worship gods besides God so they might have power. They will find no strength, and soon they will be disowned by their so-called gods and become their enemy.

Don't you see that We have sent the devils to the unbelievers to incite them. Don't hurry against them, for We count down their limited days. For on the day We will gather the righteous before God to be honored as guests, and We will drive the sinners into hell like thirsty cattle. No one will have any power to intercede for man except those who have made a covenant with God.

88. They say, "God has taken a son."

89. They utter an abomination.

90–91. The heavens are about to be split apart, the earth torn in two, and the mountains crumbled should they say that God has a son.

92–94. It's unworthy of the beneficent to have a son. Everyone in the heavens and earth comes to the beneficent as a servant. He knows every living thing in His domain by count.

95–96. Each and every one of them will come to God alone on judgment day. God will be gracious to those who were faithful and did righteous deeds.

97. So we have made it [the Qur'an] easy for you to understand. You may bear its good tidings to the righteous and with it warn the contentious.

98. How many generations before this have We destroyed? Can you see a single person from them or hear them at all?

Chapter 45 (chronologically)

Sura 20 (135 verses), Ta Ha
(Arabic letters with *T* and *H* sounds,
possibly a name for the prophet)

1. Ta. Ha.

2–5. We didn't send down this Qur'an to make you miserable but as a warning to the God-fearing. It's a revelation from He who created the earth and heavens and graciously sits on the throne of His dominion.

6–8. He owns everything on earth in the heavens and in between. He knows every word spoken and every thought, even your secrets. God! There is no God except Him. He is known by the most beautiful names.

9–12. Do you know the story of Moses [Musa]? He saw a flame and said to his family, "Wait here, I see a fire and can bring us a hot coal from it or gain some guidance at the campfire." But when he got near the flames, a voice called out, "Moses! I am your Lord, so remove your sandals, for you are in the sacred valley of Tuwa."

13–16. "I have selected you, so listen to my revelations. I am God. There are no gods except Me. Serve Me alone and establish prayers for My remembrance. Surely the hour is coming when every soul will be measured for what it has earned; but My plans are hidden from all, so the time is unknown. Do not be distracted from the coming hour by the faithless unless you want to perish with them."

17–23. "What is that in your right hand Moses?" "It is my staff that I use for support, to move my flock, and for other uses." "Throw it down Moses!" Moses cast his staff on the ground, and it became a snake moving on the sand. God said, "Pick it up, and do not be afraid, for it will become a staff again. Now tuck one hand under your other arm, and when you remove it, it shall become white but will not pain you. This is another sign of other signs We can show you."

24–35. God commanded, "Now go to the Pharaoh, for he has been rebellious." Moses replied, "Lord, make me confident and ease this task for me. Remove my speech impediment, so they can understand me. Allow me a deputy from my family—my brother Aaron. Make me stronger with his backing, and make him share in my task so that we may glorify and remember you even more, for you know us best."

36. God said, "Your prayer is granted Moses."

37–41. We have conferred you a favor already Moses when We inspired your mother to, "place the child in a basket and send him down the river, where he will be taken out by an enemy of Mine and his." "Then I placed love upon you and was able to watch you grow up. Later your sister went to the mother and reunited you two, so she wouldn't be grieved."

"Then you killed a man, and We delivered you from that ordeal and tried you with many tests. Then you stayed for many years among the people of Midian. Then you arrived to Us as planned, and I chose you for My servant."

42–48. "Now go with your brother and My signs and do not falter in remembering Me. Go to the Pharaoh, for he has become rebellious. Try first to speak kindly, and maybe he will accept the warnings." They both replied, "Lord, we are afraid he may quickly punish us or act like a tyrant." He said, "Don't be afraid, for I am with you and will see and hear everything. Go to him and say, 'We are apostles sent by the Lord. Send the children of Israel with us and don't harm them. We bring a sign from the Lord and peace for all who follow His guidance.' Further, 'It has been revealed to us the penalty that awaits for people who reject the guidance and turn their backs on God.'"

49–50. Pharaoh asked, "Who is your Lord, Moses?" Moses answered, "Our Lord is the one that created everything and gave it guidance."

51–52. Pharaoh asked, "What about the previous generations?" Moses replied, "The knowledge of their fates was recorded by the Lord, and He never makes a mistake or forgets."

53–54. He made the earth to hold you, and created paths for you to travel upon, and sent down water from the sky to create vegetation. Eat of it and feed your cattle. Surely these are signs that men can understand.

55. From earth man was created by Him, and back to earth you will return, and from the earth you will be raised a second time.

56–59. We showed Pharaoh all Our signs, but he denied them and refused to believe. Pharaoh said, "Have you come to drive us from our lands by magic, Moses?" "We can produce magic to match yours, Moses, so let us set a meeting at a neutral site." Moses replied, "The meeting shall be on the day of the festival, so let us gather in the afternoon."

60–64. The Pharaoh left, drew up a plan, and returned at the appointed hour. Moses said, "Woe unto you if you create a lie against God, as you will be destroyed. Liars always fail." They spoke among themselves and finally said, "These two are expert magicians, and they aim to drive Pharaoh from these lands and destroy its institutions. So settle your plans and come stand in ranks against Moses, for he who does the best in the competition will prosper."

65–66. So it began; they said, "Moses, who shall go first?" Moses replied, "You may start." Their ropes and staffs began to move as if alive.

67–69. Moses became afraid. Sensing his fear, We said, "Do not be afraid, Moses, for you have the upper hand." We said, "Throw your staff from your right hand, and it will swallow up the magic that the fake magicians have conjured. Wizards will not be successful anywhere they go."

70. After seeing this, the magicians flung themselves down in obedience and cried, "We believe in the Lord of Aaron and Moses."

71–73. Pharaoh spoke, "You believe in Him before I give you permission? He must be your leader that taught you magic. I will cut off your hands and feet and crucify you on palm trees so that you will find out who can give you harsh and permanent punishment." They replied, "We will never choose you over Moses, Lord, after seeing these signs, so do as you wish, for you will only end our lives of this world. For we believe in our Lord, that He may forgive us our sins and the magic you forced us to perform. God is better and forever."

74–76. He who comes to the Lord as a sinner at judgment day will go to hell where he neither lives nor dies. But those that come to Him as believers who have done righteous deeds, they will be exalted in paradise. Beneath them will be rivers flowing where they will live forever in reward for their purity against evil.

77. We then sent a revelation to Moses to travel by night with My servants on a path to the sea and do not be afraid of Pharaoh catching up to you or of the sea.

78. Pharaoh pursued them with his army, but the waters of the sea covered them.

79. Pharaoh led his people off the straight path instead of being righteous.

80–82. Children of Israel, We delivered you from Pharaoh and made a covenant with you on the side of the mountain and then sent you manna and quails. Eat the good things we provided you, but do not overstep your bounds, or My wrath will be upon you. Anyone I unleash my wrath on surely dies. But I am also forgiving towards people who repent, believe, and do good works, and then stay on the righteous path.

83–85. We asked on the mount, "Moses, why do you hurry from your people?" He replied that they are close upon him, but he hurried to God to please Him. We said, "Moses we tested your people while you were away, and the Samiri has led them astray."

86. Moses returned to his people sad and angry, saying to them, "My people, God made you a promise. Was I gone away too long, or do you want God to bring His wrath upon you for breaking your promise to me?"

87–88. They said [to Moses], "We only broke our promise to you because the Samiri told us to take our precious metals and put them in the fire, and then he created a golden-colored calf from the metals, and it seemed to moo. This is your god, the god of Moses, but you have forgotten."

89. Couldn't they see it could not speak and that it had no power

to bring them harm or good?

90–91. Aaron had told them earlier, "People, you are being tested. Your Lord is most gracious, so follow me now and obey my orders." The people replied, "No, we will not abandon our cult worship until Moses returns."

92–94. Moses said, "Aaron why did you stay here when you saw them going in the wrong way? Why didn't you come to me? Did you disobey my commands?" Aaron replied, "Brother, do not grab hold of my beard or head, but I feared you would say that I caused this division among the children of Israel and not hear my explanation."

95–97. Moses asked, "Why did you do this, Samiri?" He replied, "I could see something they could not, so my soul suggested I take some dust from your footprint and toss it in the fire with the metals, making a calf." Moses replied, "Go away from here, and to everyone you meet you must say "Do not touch me," for there is a final meeting you will not break. As for your god, we will melt it down and scatter it in the sea."

98. Your god is God, and there is no god but Him. He is all-knowing.

99–104. We have given you some stories from the past to be used as a reminder to those in the present. Whoever rejects the messages will pay on judgment day. They will carry an evil burden on the day of resurrection, when the trumpet sounds and we gather all the guilty men with terror in their eyes. They will whisper to each other, "You only stayed ten days." We will know everything they will say, even when the best of them whispers, "You have stayed only one day."

105–107. When they ask you about your time on the mount, reply, "My Lord will break you and scatter you like dust and leave only an empty plain, where no one will see a curve or angle."

108–112. On judgment day when the summoner announces the end, who will be straightforward in his call, all sounds will cease in the presence of God the most gracious except a murmur. No one will intercede for any man except those who were given permission by God and whose opinion He trusts. He will know everything in their future and their past, but man will not be able to comprehend it. Everyone will be humbled before Him, the living God who sustains everything. Those who are evil will fail in His judgment. But those who do righteous deeds and are faithful will have nothing to fear in His judgment.

113. We have sent you this Arabic Qur'an and given you some warnings in detail so that you may fear God or feel a need to remember Him. God above is the true king. Do not be in a hurry with the Qur'an before We have finished revealing it to you; instead say, "My Lord, increase my knowledge."

115–124. Remember, We had made a covenant with Adam, but he forgot it, and we found him undependable. We told our angels to bow before Adam, but only Iblis refused Us. We told Adam to watch out for the enemy of him and his wife so he couldn't drive them from the Garden and make them unhappy. In the Garden there was promised food, clothing, drinks, and shade. But Satan whispered to Adam saying, "Let me lead you to the tree of immortality." As a result, they both ate of the tree and realized they were naked and tried to cover themselves. Adam disobeyed his Lord and went off the righteous path. But his Lord was gracious and chose to guide him still. He told them, "Both of you must leave the Garden with enmity towards each other. But if you come to me for guidance, and you follow it, you will not lose your way or be unhappy. But whoever rejects my message will have a wretched life, and on resurrection day I will raise him up blinded."

125–126. The evil will say, "My Lord, why did you raise me up blind when before I could see?" God will reply, "It was because when I sent Our signs, you rejected them, so on this day you will be rejected."

127. We punish those who stray from the right path and reject Our messages. The penalty in the hereafter is harsh and eternal.

128. Is it not clear enough when We remind men of the many generations before them We destroyed, amid His ruins you now walk? These signs are clear for those willing to think and understand them.

129. A message was already sent out from your Lord that their punishment was inevitable, and the end of time date was set.

130. [MD] Be patient with what they say, and constantly glorify the Lord; praise Him before the rising sun and before it sets, praise Him for part of the night, and at the ends of the day so that you may be pleased.

131. [MD] Don't look at the things We have given for enjoyment to certain groups, things by which We test them, because the provision from your Lord is better and enduring.

132. Ask others to pray, and be steady worshipers. We don't ask you to provide sustenance to Us, but rather We provide for you. But the provisions of the hereafter are only for the righteous.

133. They will ask, "Why didn't the Lord show us a miracle?" Say, "What greater sign is there than this book of revelation [Qur'an]?"

134–135. If We had destroyed them with a punishment before revealing the Qur'an, they would have said, "Lord, if you had only sent us a messenger, we would have followed the revelations before we were humbled and disgraced." Say to them, "Each of us is waiting, so continue to wait. One day you will know who followed the straight path and who is righteous."

Chapter 46 (chronologically)

Sura 56 (96 verses), Al-Waqia

(The Imminent Hour—Judgment Day)

1-3. When the inevitable event happens, and there is no denying it will occur—exalting some and demeaning others.

4–11. When the earth shakes violently and mountains crumble to be scattered like dust, people will be divided into three groups. There will be people on the right hand of God, and what of those on the right? There will be people on the left hand of God, and what of those on the left?

12–26. And the most faithful of the three groups will be brought closest to God in the Garden of paradise. People from older generations and people from later times will recline on gem-encrusted couches facing each other. They will be served wine by immortal youths that will not make them drunk or cause headaches. They will have their choice of fruits and meat from birds, and as a reward for past deeds beautiful companions with eyes like pearls. They won't hear any useless talk or sinful speech; they will only hear "Peace, peace."

27–40. And what will happen to the people on the right hand? They will live among the thornless lote trees, with clustered plantains and shade. Nearby also are flowing waters, and abundant fruits of every kind can be eaten without limitations. There also on raised couches they will find virgin companions of Our special creation who are loving and of equal age. These companions on the right hand will contain people from the older generations and also people from the later times.

41–56. And what will happen to the people on the left hand? They will be in the midst of scorching winds and scalding water, surrounded by the shade of black smoke, and it will not be cool or refreshing. They were the wealthy who performed great sins before, and when they say "We will become dust and bones when we die and don't believe we will be resurrected, nor will our ancestors." Tell them, "The early and new generations will all be gathered on judgment day, and you unbelievers will have to eat from the bitter Zaqqum tree until your stomachs are stuffed, and then you will drink boiling water on top of it like thirsty camels." That will be the hospitality for them on the day of judgment.

57–59. Why can't you admit the truth, that We created you? Have you thought about the sperm that you emit? Do you create it, or did We the creators?

60–61. We ordain the deaths among you, and man can't escape Us resurrecting you and changing your form into something you can't imagine.

62. Certainly you are aware of the genesis. Why don't you praise God?

63–67. Have you thought about the seed you plant? Is it you that makes it grow or Us? If We wanted to, We could crumble it to chaff and leave you crying, "We have suffered a great loss and have not seen the fruits of our labor."

68–70. Consider the water you drink. Do you cause it to fall from the sky or do We? If We wanted, We could make it salty. So why do you not give thanks?

71–73. What about the fire you use? Did you cause the tree to grow or were We the growers? We made it a memorial and an item of comfort for travelers in the desert.

74. Therefore, celebrate with praise the name of your Lord the supreme.

75–80. I swear by the stars in the sky, and that is a great oath, that this is indeed a noble Qur'an in a protected book. No one but the purified shall touch the revelation sent down from the Lord of the worlds.

81–82. [MD] Why do you hold this revelation in contempt and make a livelihood declaring it false?

83–87. When a dying man's soul is about to leave his body and you are watching him, not realizing We are closer to him than you are because you can't see Us, why don't you put his soul back into place—if you are truly not subject to Our divine power?

88–91. If someone is among those close to God, then he will have rest, satisfaction, and a garden of delights. If someone is one of those on the right hand of God, then wish him, "Peace be upon you" as a greeting from the people of the right hand.

92–94. If someone is a person who rejects the truth and goes astray, for him is a welcome of boiling water and entry into the flames of hell.

95–96. This is certainly the truth, so celebrate with praise the name of the Lord supreme.

Chapter 47 (chronologically)

Sura 26 (227 verses), Al-Shuara (The Poets)

1. Ta. Seen. Meem.

2. These are the verses of the book that make things clear.

3-5. You may worry yourself to death because people are not converting. If We wanted to, We could send down a sign from above that would bow them in humility forever. Remember that every time the beneficent one sends man a new message, they turn away from it.

6–9. They have surely rejected the message of truth, and soon they will understand the truth they mocked. Have they never looked at the earth and all the wonderful things of every kind that We produce on it? This is a sign, but most still don't believe. Your Lord is mighty and merciful.

10–14. When your Lord called Moses, He said, "Go to the unjust people. The people of the Pharaoh. Will they not fight evil?" Moses replied, "My Lord, I fear they will reject me as a liar, and I will become scared, and I won't be able to speak; so you should send Aaron as your messenger. And also, they have charged me with a crime, so I fear they will kill me."

15–17. God said, "Certainly not. I will send you both instead with Our signs. We will be with you listening in. So, you both will go before Pharaoh saying, 'We have been sent by the Lord of the worlds. You should send away the children of Israel with us.'"

18–22. Pharaoh said, "Didn't we let you grow up here as a child among us, and didn't you stay here for many years of your life? Until you committed that deed and were ungrateful." Moses replied, "I did commit that deed when I was not on the righteous path. So, I fled from you in fear, and my Lord granted me wisdom and made me an apostle. And is it because you have enslaved the children of Israel that you remind me of my past treatment?"

23–28. Pharaoh said, "Tell me what is the Lord of the worlds?" Moses replied, "He is the Lord of the heavens and earth and everything in between— if you are faithful." Pharaoh spoke to those gathered: "Do you hear him?" Moses stated, "The Lord of your forefathers." Pharaoh scoffed, "The messenger that has been sent to us is clearly crazy." Moses stated, "He is the

Lord of the East and West and everything in between, if only you could understand."

29–31. Pharaoh spoke: "If you choose any other god besides me, then I will imprison you." Moses asked, "Even if I showed you convincing signs?" Pharaoh said, "Show them if you are truthful."

32–33. Moses threw his staff down, and it became a snake. Then he drew his hand from his cloak, and it was white.

34–37. Pharaoh spoke to his chiefs saying, "This is a skillful wizard who plans to drive us from our land by sorcery, so what should we do?" They replied, "Keep him here while we send our people into the city to find the best wizards."

38-40. The sorcerers met at the appointed time, and the people gathered to watch so they might begin following the wizards if they won the contest.

41–42. When the Egyptian sorcerers arrived, they asked Pharaoh, "We will be rewarded if we defeat him, correct?" Pharaoh promised them high positons if they succeeded.

43–48. Moses asked them to begin the contest. So they threw down their ropes and rods and said, "By the might of Pharaoh we will certainly win." Moses then threw his staff down, and it swallowed up the false magic. The sorcerers then bowed down deeply in adoration saying, "We believe in the Lord of the worlds, the Lord of Moses and Aaron!"

49–51. Pharaoh then spoke, "How dare you put your faith in Him before I give you permission. He must be the chief that you taught you magic. Soon you will know [my power], as I will cut off your hands and feet and crucify you all." They replied, "It doesn't matter, because we will return to our Lord. We hope that He will forgive our sins for being His first believers."

52. We revealed to Moses to "Travel by night with My servants, for Pharaoh will be following you."

53–56. Pharaoh sent out his messengers announcing that the Israelis are a small band, and they have offended us, but we are many and prepared.

57–59. We expelled the Pharaoh's people from the gardens and springs and made the children of Israel the inheritors of their treasures and estates.

60-62. At sunrise Pharaoh pursued the Israelis. When the two groups saw each other, the people warned Moses that they will surely be overtaken. Moses replied, "No, the Lord is with me and He will guide us."

63–68. We revealed to Moses to strike the sea with his rod, and the sea divided into two mountains of water and let the other party get close to Moses. We delivered Moses and his people through but drowned the others. This is indeed a sign, but most of them don't believe it. Your Lord is indeed the mighty and merciful.

69–76. Tell them about Abraham and the time he asked his father and his people what they worship. They told Abraham, "We worship idols, and we will continue to worship them." Abraham asked, "Do they listen when you call to them? Do they benefit you or cause you harm?" They said, "No, but we learned this worship from our fathers." Abraham asked, "Have you ever considered what you and your forefathers have been worshipping?"

77–82. Abraham said, "I have made them all angry at me now, but I have the Lord of the worlds, who created me. He guides me and provides me with food and drink. When I get sick, He cures me, and He will make me die and resurrect me again. I hope He will forgive my sins on the day of judgment."

83–93. "My Lord, grant me wise judgment and unite me with the righteous. Pass on a worthy reputation of me to my ancestors. Let me pass into the garden of bliss. Forgive my father, for he is among those who have left the straight path. Don't let me be a disgrace when I am resurrected. On that day wealth and the number of children won't matter, as only those who come to God with a faithful heart will pass into paradise with the others who fended off evil and feared God. When hell will be shown to the perverse, they will be asked, "Where are the gods you have been worshipping? Can they help you or even help themselves?"

94–102. "Then they will be thrown into the fire with those who seduced them along with Satan [Iblis]." They will say as they argue, "By God, we were led astray by you when we thought you equal to the Lord of the worlds. You seducers are the guilty ones here for misleading us. Now we have no one to intercede on our behalf with God. Not even a single friend. If we only had another chance, we would be faithful."

103. There is a sign indeed, but most men do not believe.

104. Your Lord is the almighty and all-merciful.

105–110. The people of Noah rejected the messengers sent to them when Noah said to them, "Will you all fear God?" "I am a faithful prophet sent to you, so fear God and obey me. I ask nothing in return from you, as my reward lies in the hands of the Lord of the worlds. Fear God and obey me."

111-115. They responded, "Why should we believe in you when your followers are the lowest of society?" Noah replied, "How would I know what they had done? Their past deeds are for God to assess; if you only knew my message you could understand. I am not here to drive away anyone who is faithful. I am only a simple messenger."

116. They stated, "If you don't stop, Noah, we will stone you."

117–118. Noah called out, "My Lord, they have rejected my message. Judge us all appropriately and deliver me and the faithful."

119–122. So, We delivered him and those that were with him in his heavily loaded ship. Then We drowned the others. This is a sign, but most do not believe it. The Lord is mighty and merciful.

123–127. The Ad people rejected God's messengers. Hud asked them to fear God and said that he was a faithful messenger. He told them to fear God and obey Him and that God would take care of Hud's reward.

128–135. He pointed out to them that they build landmarks to themselves and fine buildings as if they will live forever. That they act as tyrants when they seize land. He told them to fear God and obey him and to keep their duty to the God that gave them cattle and sons and gardens and springs. "I fear for your retribution on judgment day."

136–140. They replied, "We don't care what you say; you speak of the old traditions, and we know we won't face punishment." They rejected Hud, so We destroyed them. This is also a sign, but most will not believe. Your Lord is mighty and merciful.

141–152. The Thamud people rejected the messengers. Salih asked them would they fear God: "I am your faithful messenger. Fear God and obey me." He didn't ask for reward, as it was in God's hands. He asked them if their earthly things made them safe: gardens, springs, farms, date palms, and carved cliff homes. "Fear God and obey me. Don't follow the extravagant people who are corrupt and harm society."

153–159. They replied, "You are bewitched and only a human." Then they asked for a sign. He said the sign was a she-camel that they must share a well with, at alternate times. They could not touch her or face a harsh penalty. But they hamstrung her and then were regretful. They received their penalty. This is a sign, too, but most do not believe. The Lord is mighty and merciful.

160–166. The people of Lot rejected the messengers. Lot asked them if they would fear God. He told them he was a trustworthy messenger and to fear God and obey Him. He relied on God for his reward not the people. He asked, "Why do you leave the wives that God created for you to be with men? You are breaking all the rules."

167-175. They told Lot, "If you don't stop talking, we will throw you out of the city." Lot said, "I detest your behavior. Oh Lord, deliver me and my family from such conduct." So We delivered him and his family, except for a an old woman lagging behind. We utterly destroyed the others in a rain of brimstone that they were warned about. This is a sign, but most do not believe. The Lord is mighty and merciful.

176–184. Those who lived in the wood near Midian rejected the messengers. Shu'ayb asked them if they would fear God and told them he was a trusted messenger. "Fear God and obey me." He asked for no reward from men and left it to God. "Be fair in trade and don't give people too little; and balance the scales so no one is cheated. Do not act wickedly or be corrupt. Fear the creator who made you and those before you."

185–191. They said, "You are bewitched! You are just a human like us, and we think you are a liar." They asked for him to make fragments fall from the sky to prove he was truthful. Shu'ayb said, "My Lord is aware of all that you do." They rejected him, and the punishment came in a gloomy and grievous day. This is a sign, but most do not believe. The Lord is mighty and merciful.

192–195. This is a revelation from the Lord of the worlds brought to your heart by a trustworthy spirit so that you may warn others, in a plain Arabic language.

196. The revelation was predicted in the ancient scriptures.

197. [MD] How can it not be a sign if the educated children of Israel know it's true?

198–199. If We revealed it to one of the non-Arabs and had him recite it to them, they would not have believed.

200–203. In this way, We have caused it to enter the hearts of the guilty. They won't believe in it until they see a painful punishment. But the penalty will come swiftly, and they will not see it coming. They will then ask, "Can we have some relief?"

204–207. Do they want Us to speed up their punishment? Do you understand? If We let them enjoy a longer life and then We give them the punishment We promised them, what joy will they get from that time?

208–213. We never destroyed a population without sending a messenger. We always remind them that We are fair. The revelations are not brought down by devils; it's not their purpose, nor do they have that power. They aren't even able to hear the revelations from where they stay. So do not call on any gods besides God, or you will be punished.

214–220. Warn your family, and show kindness to the faithful that follow you. But if followers disobey you, tell them you aren't responsible for their actions. Put your trust in the almighty and all-merciful. He sees you when you stand for prayer and as you move among those who prostrate. He hears and knows all things.

221–223. Do you know who the devils descend to find? They go to every sinful liar and eavesdrop. Most of them are liars.

224. [MD] As for the poets, only the sinners follow them.

225–227. Haven't you noticed that they wander around in every valley and that they don't do as they say, except those who believe, do good deeds, give remembrance to God, and defend themselves from unjust attacks. The unjust will soon know their punishment.

Chapter 48 (chronologically)

Sura 27 (93 verses), Al-Naml (The Ants)

1–3. Ta. Seen. These are the verses of the Qur'an, an evident book, and a guide and good news for the believers—those who pray, and give to charity regularly, and are certain of the hereafter.

4–5. For those who do not believe in the hereafter, We have caused them to think their works on earth are good, so they are bewildered. These are the people who will receive a grave penalty, and in the hereafter, will lose the most.

6. You have received the Qur'an from One who is wise and all-knowing.

7–8. Remember Moses when he said to his family, "I see a distant fire, so I will go get information from them or a coal to light our fire so we can warm up." But as he neared the fire a voice told him, "Blessed are those in the fire and around it. Glory be to God the Lord of the worlds."

9–11. "Moses, I am God the mighty and wise. Throw down your staff!" It started to move like a snake so Moses retreated. "Moses, messengers should not be afraid in my presence, but if they have done wrong and then did good deeds to compensate, they find I am often forgiving and most merciful."

12–14. "Now put your hand into your robe near your torso, and when you pull it out it will be white but won't hurt. Take these, of the nine signs, to Pharaoh and his people for they are an evil lot." But when Our signs were shown to them, they said it was only magic. They rejected the signs aloud in an unjust and arrogant manner, while their souls were actually convinced. See the fate of the wrongdoers.

15–19. We gave knowledge to David and Solomon, and they both said, "Praise be to God who has granted us favor above what He gave many of His followers." Solomon was David's heir, and he said, "People, we have been taught the language of the birds and been given all things in abundance, and this is a sign of God's grace. Before Solomon his people were assembled: genies, humans, and birds. When they came to a valley of ants, one of the ants said, "Fellow ants get in your burrows so that Solomon and his armies don't crush you without knowing it." Solomon smiled, amused at the queen's speech [Queen Sheba], and said, "My Lord, I am grateful for the favors you have given me and my parents so that I may do righteous acts that are pleasing to you. I pray one day to be among your righteous servants."

20–25. He reviewed the birds assembled and asked where the hoopoe bird was. "I will punish him severely or kill him if he doesn't have a good reason for his absence." Soon the hoopoe bird came to him saying, "I was gathering information you were not aware of in Sheba. I found a woman ruling over the people there; and she has provided them with abundance, and she sits on a magnificent throne. I found the people of Sheba worshipping the sun instead of God. Satan has made their activities seem right and has led them off the straight path. They are not righteous. They do not worship God, who reveals what is in heaven and earth and knows everyone's secrets."

26. God is the Lord of the great throne and there is no god but Him.

27–32. I will find out if you are telling the truth, hoopoe; take this letter to them and then move away and watch their reaction. The queen said, "My chieftains, I have been sent a noble letter from Solomon and his people. It says, 'In the name of God most gracious and merciful, do not defy me and submit.'" Then she asked for advice from her chiefs so she could hear their opinions before responding.

33–35. They advised her that Sheba was powerful and mighty and that they awaited her decision. She stated, "When the kings enter a country, they devastate it and bring even the mightiest people low. That is what I expect now. So, I am going to send him a present and hear from my ambassadors when they return."

36–37. When the envoys arrived, Solomon said, "Are you trying to give me more wealth, when everything that God has given me is better than what He has given you. You are more impressed by your gift than I am. Go back to Sheba, for we will be coming with a power that you cannot resist. We will expel you from the land in disgrace and you will be humbled."

38–40. Solomon spoke to his chiefs: "Which of you can bring me Sheba's throne before they come to us to submit?" A cunning genie said, "I can bring it back before we end this council session, for I am very strong, and you can trust me." Another who had knowledge of the scripture said, "I will bring it here in the twinkling of an eye." And the throne appeared in front of Solomon and he said, "This was done by the grace of God to test me to see if I am grateful or not. Those who are grateful receive gratitude for their own soul. Those who are ungrateful must realize that my Lord is bountiful and generous."

41–42. Solomon ordered the throne to be transformed so that the Queen of Sheba would not recognize it, so he could test her to see if she is rightly guided. Solomon asked her when she arrived if the throne in front of her was like hers. She replied, "It appears to be my throne. We were told of your power before we arrived, and we submit to you."

43. She had been hindered from worshipping God by the gods she was worshipping instead, and she came from a faithless people.

44. Solomon asked her to enter the palace hall, and when she did she thought it was a lake, so she lifted her skirts, uncovering her legs. Solomon said, "Your eyes deceive you; this is a floor of crystal slabs. She cried, "My Lord, I have been unjust, and I submit alongside Solomon to God the Lord of the worlds."

45–47. We sent the messenger Salih [their brother] to the Thamud people telling them to serve God; but they split into two quarrelling factions. Salih said, "My people, why would you rather do evil instead of good? If you would just ask God for forgiveness, you may receive His mercy." They replied, "We believe that you and your followers are a bad omen bringing us bad luck." Salih replied, "Your bad omens are from God, and He is testing you."

48–50. In the city, there were nine corrupt men that would not change. They said, "We swear an oath by God that we will secretly attack Salih and his people, and when they seek vengeance we will all say it wasn't us, and they are liars." The evil men planned, but We plotted too, and they were not aware of Us.

51–53. In the end, they failed, and We destroyed them and their followers. Their houses were left in ruin, because they were unjust. This is a sign for people who can understand it. We saved those from Thamud who were faithful and righteous.

54–55. We sent Lot as a messenger to his people, and he asked them why they commit such indecent acts when they know it's wrong. Lot said, "Why would you lust after men instead of women? Are you that senseless?"

56–58. His people simply said, "Drive out Lot and his followers from our city, for we want to be pure and clean." We spared Lot and his family, except for a wife We destined to be one of those remaining behind. Then we rained down a shower of brimstone, an evil rain for those who have been warned.

59–60. Say, "Praise be to God and peace be upon His servants chosen to be His messengers. Who is better, God or the false gods they associate with Him? Is He not the best that created the heavens and earth, who sends rains from the sky? With rain We cause orchards and trees to grow beautifully, as it is not in your power to cause them to grow. Can there be another god besides God? No, those who believe that are unrighteous."

61. "Is He who made the earth firm, and poured the rivers, and set the mountains, and created a barrier between the seas not the best? Can there be another god besides God? Most people don't know."

62. "Isn't He best that listens to souls crying to be cleansed of evil and that made mankind the inheritors of earth? Can there be another god besides God? Few pay any attention."

63. "Isn't He best who guides you on land and sea in the darkness and who sends winds as messengers of His mercy? Can there be another god besides God? God is exalted high above those they associate with Him."

64. "Isn't He best who caused the creation and then can repeat it and gives you nourishment from heaven and the earth? Can there be another god besides God? Show us your proof if you are truthful."

65–66. Say, "No one in heaven or on earth, except God, knows the future or when the judgment day will come." No one knows about the hereafter. They doubt it, because they cannot see it.

67–70. When the unbelievers say, "We doubt that when we become dust like our fathers we shall be raised from the dead. We and our forefathers were promised this before, but it's just an ancient fable." Say unto them, "Travel around and look at the end that came to the sinners." But don't grieve for them nor let their plots against you bring you grief.

71–72. They will also say, "Tell us when this promise will occur if you are not a liar!" Tell them, "If you want to see judgment day sooner, it may not be far off."

73. Your Lord is gracious to mankind, even though most of them are ungrateful.

74–75. Your Lord knows everything they say and the secrets they keep. Everything that occurs in heaven and on earth is recorded clearly.

76–77. The Qur'an explains to the children of Israel most of the ideas that they disagree upon, and it is a guide and mercy for the believers.

78. Your Lord will judge who is just and unjust by His wisdom. He is mighty and all-knowing.

79. Put your trust in God, for you are on the right path.

80–81. You cannot make the dead listen nor cause the deaf to hear your message when they turn from you, and you guide the blind from going astray. Only those who believe in Our signs and will submit can hear you.

82–85. On judgment day, when Our promise is fulfilled against the unjust, We will have a beast of the earth speak to them, because mankind would not believe Our signs. We will gather all the people from every nation that rejected Our message and form them in groups. When each passes before God to be judged, He will ask, "Did you reject My revelations because you could not understand them or for some other reason? [or What did you do in life?]" And then the promises of judgment will be kept because of what they did wrong. They will not be able to speak.

86. Can they not see that We created the night for them to rest, and in the day We gave them light? These are surely signs for anyone that is faithful.

87. On the day the trumpet is sounded everything will be terrified in heaven and on earth, and except for those God exempts, everyone will come to God in humility.

88. You see the mountains that you think are firmly affixed to the earth; they are actually drifting like passing clouds. That is the work of God, who has made everything faultless. He is aware of everything you do.

89–90. Those who do good will receive more in reward for those deeds and be safe from terror that day. But those who do evil will be flung face-first into the flames. "Are you to be rewarded for something you didn't do?"

91–93. I have been commanded to serve the Lord of this city [Mecca], who has made it a sacred place and is Lord of all things. I am commanded to be among the people that submit to God and commanded to recite the Qur'an. If anyone accepts guidance, they do it for their own souls. And if they go astray say, "I am only one of the messengers [warners]. All praise belongs to God, as soon He will reveal His signs, and you will recognize them." Your Lord is aware of all you do.

Chapter 49 (chronologically)

Sura 28 (88 verses), Al-Qasas (The Story)

1–3. Ta. Seen. Meem. These are the verses of the scripture that makes things clear. We recite for you some of the story of Moses and the Pharaoh for people who believe.

4. Pharaoh the tyrant cast his people into factions; oppressing one tribe by killing its sons and not its women. He was an agent of corruption.

5–6. We wished to be gracious to the tribe being oppressed and make them leaders [imams] and let them inherit the lands and to grant them power in the region, while making Pharaoh, Haman, and their followers see what they have been fearing.

7–9. We sent a revelation to Moses's mother to suckle her infant, but when she felt fear for him, to cast him in the river and don't be afraid or grieve. For We would bring him back to her and make him one of the messengers. The people of the Pharaoh plucked him from the river, fearing he might be an enemy and cause regret, for Pharaoh and Haman were sinners. The Pharaoh's wife said, "He is a joy to me and Pharaoh, so do not kill him. Maybe he will be a benefit to us, or we may adopt him as a son." They were not aware.

10–13. Moses's mother missed him, so We strengthened her heart right before she was about to reveal him to Pharaoh, so she would remain faithful. Moses's mother asked his sister to follow him, so she secretly kept an eye on him without Pharaoh noticing. Then we made Moses refuse to suckle, so his sister could tell the Pharaoh's nurses that she knew a good family that could nourish him and care for him. In this way We restored Moses to his mother, so she wouldn't weep or grieve and so that she would see that God's promises are true. But most of mankind doesn't understand.

14. When Moses reached adulthood, We gave him wisdom and knowledge. We reward those who do good.

15–16. One day Moses entered the city when people were distracted and came upon two men fighting. One was a follower of Moses and the other an enemy. His coreligionist asked for help, so Moses struck the enemy with his fist and killed him. He said, "This was Satan's doing, for the man was an enemy and he misled people." Moses prayed, "My Lord I have sinned; do you forgive me?" So He forgave him, for He is forgiving and merciful.

17. He said, "My Lord, because you have bestowed grace on me, I will never help any sinners."

18–19. Moses was in the city at dawn being watchful, and again he saw the man who had asked for his help, and he was asking yet again. Moses told him he must be very quarrelsome. As he prepared to strike the man who was an enemy to them both, he spoke, "Moses, do you intend to kill me like you killed the man yesterday? Do you plan on becoming a tyrant in this place and not a reformer?"

20–21. Just then a man came running from the edge of the city and yelled to Moses that the chiefs were talking about killing Moses. "Run away from here; I am trying to help you." Moses ran from there and in a state of fear he prayed, "Lord please save me from the unjust people."

22–24. When Moses stood facing Midian he prayed, "Lord maybe you can show me the right path." When he arrived at the watering hole in Midian, he found a group of men watering their flocks and two women standing back with their flock. Moses asked what they were doing, and the women said, "We cannot water our flock until the shepherds move away from the water." They also mentioned that their father was very old. Moses watered the flock for the women. Upon returning to the shade he prayed, "Lord I am in need of whatever goodness you might send me."

25. Later one of the women came walking bashfully towards him and said, "My father wants to reward you for watering our flock for us." When Moses went to the man and recounted his story, the man said, "Don't be afraid; you have escaped the unjust people."

26–28. One of the daughters suggested he hire Moses, because he was strong and faithful. The father said he intended for Moses to marry one of his daughters in exchange for him working there eight years, ten if possible. The father said he would not be too hard on Moses and that if God wills it, he would be found righteous. Moses considered the agreement to be sound and asked that he be treated well regardless of which option he chose, and with God as his witness he would agree.

29–32. After fulfilling his promise, Moses was traveling with his family when he saw a distant fire by a mountain. He told his family to wait while he went to the fire to get information or a coal to start a warming fire. Nearing the fire Moses heard a voice from the valley coming from a tree, "Moses I am God, the Lord of the worlds. Throw down your staff!" Moses watched it start to move like a snake, and he retreated. "Moses, come closer and don't be afraid; you are one of the people that is safe. Then the voice told him to put his hand in his cloak and pull it out, and it would turn white but not hurt. "These will be two signs from the Lord to show Pharaoh and his chiefs who are rebellious and evil."

33–35. Moses told the Lord that he had killed a man in that city and that he feared being killed in return. He suggested the Lord send his brother Aaron along with him to strengthen him, for he could speak well. He feared they would accuse him of lying. He said, "We will make you stronger by sending your brother too and giving you both authority so they can't touch you. With Our two signs you and anyone that follows you will be victorious."

36–37. Pharaoh was not impressed by Moses and the signs and claimed it was fake magic that no ancestors knew of either. Moses told them, "My Lord knows best who speaks His guidance and who will enter heaven. The unjust will not be successful."

38. Pharaoh said sarcastically to his chiefs that he had heard of no god to be worshipped besides himself and asked them to build a brick tower so he could go look at Moses's God. "I think they are liars."

39–42. Pharaoh was arrogant and insolent. We thought he and his people would not have to return to Us. So We seized him and his hosts and cast them in the sea. That is the ending for the unjust. We made them leaders in hell that invite people to the fire. On judgment day, they will find no help. And on earth We cursed them. On the day of judgment, they will be hated.

43. Of course We revealed the Book to Moses, only after We destroyed previous generations, to serve as a reminder to mankind, to provide guidance, and to be a mercy so they might reflect.

44–46. You weren't there on the mount when We revealed the commandments to Moses. After a passage of time you were also not there in Midian revealing Our signs to them, but We continued to send messengers to men. You were not there on the side of the mountain when We called to Moses. But We have sent you as mercy from your Lord to warn people that have not heard the message before so that they may be warned.

47. If We didn't send you to these people and a disaster had struck them for their deeds, they might say, "Lord, why didn't you send us a messenger? We would have listened and been among the faithful."

48–50. But now when the truth has come from Us, they say, "Why hasn't the messenger been given what Moses was given?" But people didn't believe Moses either. They said he was a magician and liar. So say to them, "Bring me a book from God better than the Torah and Qur'an, and I will follow that guidance, if you are telling the truth." If they don't respond to your request, then know that they only follow their desires. Who is more unjust than someone that follows his own desires without any guidance from God? God does not guide the evil men.

51. Now We have revealed the Word to them so they may choose to take warning.

52. [MD] Those people We previously sent the Book before this Qur'an believe in the Qur'an.

53. [MD] When the Qur'an is recited to them, they say, "We believe in it because it is the truth from our Lord. We were Muslims before the Qur'an was revealed."

54–55. [MD] Those who have the patience to repel evil with goodness and give to charity will be given twice their reward. When they hear useless talk, they avoid it saying, "Our deeds belong to us and yours to you. Peace be upon you, but we do not associate with the ignorant."

56. You will not be able to guide everyone you want to, but remember that God guides those He will and knows very well those who do receive guidance.

57. When they ask, "If we follow this guidance with you then will we have to leave our lands?" We have established a secure life for them, where produce of all kinds is traded. This is provided by Us, but most do not understand.

58–59. How many populations have We destroyed because the people took excessive pride in their life of ease and were thankless? Now in those empty lands live a miserable few, and We are the inheritors. But never did your Lord destroy a population until He had sent them a messenger to recite our revelations. Never did We destroy a place unless the people were unjust.

60. The material items of this world have been given to you as a comfort and an ornament. What you will find with God is better and eternal. Have you no sense?

61–62. Are these two the same? Is the person We made a promise of paradise to in the afterlife and the person whom We gave nice things to in this life but found out on judgment day that he would be punished equal? On that day, God will call out, "Where are my so-called partners that you imagined I have?"

63–64. To those that will be proved guilty of the charge of polytheism We will hear, "Lord, these are the people we led astray just as we were led astray ourselves. We declare we are innocent, because they weren't worshipping us." It will be said to them, "Call upon your partner gods of God for help." No one will answer them, and they will see the penalty of doom, and they will wish they had listened to the guidance and followed the right path.

65. On that day He will call out, "What did you say to My messengers?"

66–67. None of the doomed will hear any good tidings that day, and they won't ask each other for them. But anyone that had repented, been faithful, and done righteous work will have hope of achieving salvation.

68–70. The Lord can create and choose as He wishes. No other has a choice. Glory to God! He is more noble than the partners they associate with Him. He knows everything that is secret and public. He is God and there is no god besides Him. Give Him praise in this life and the next. He sits in judgment ,and everything is brought back to Him.

71. Ask, "If God were to make the night last until the judgment day, what other god is there that can bring out the light? Why won't you understand?"

72. Ask, "If God were to make the day last until the judgment day, what other god is there that can give you darkness so you can rest? Why won't you understand?"

73. Out of His mercy He made you night and day, so you may rest and also see His grace and then give thanks.

74–75. On the day He will call to them and say, "Where are My partners that you pretended existed?" And We will draw a witness from each group of people and say, "Bring us your witness!" Then they will all know the truth is God's alone, and the lies they told will have failed them.

76. Korah was one of Moses's people, but Korah rebelled against them. We gave him so much treasure that even a company of strong men couldn't carry it. His people said to him, "Do not rejoice over treasure, for God does not love those who rejoice. Use the means that God has given you to seek a home in the hereafter; don't be corrupt because God hates the corrupt."

78. Korah said, "God gave me this because of the knowledge I possess." Didn't he know about all the generations God had destroyed before him who were even stronger and richer? The guilty will not even be asked about their sins.

79. So Korah went among his people dressed in his fine clothes. Those who worried about life on earth said, “If we only could have what Korah has; he has been very fortunate.” Those who were truly knowledgeable said, “Woe unto you, Korah, for the best rewards in the hereafter are for the people that are faithful and do good acts, and only the patient will receive it.

81. Then We made the earth swallow him and his home. He had no one to help him against God and could not defend himself.

82. Those who had envied him before then said, “Clearly it is God that controls who gets rich or loses wealth. If God had not been gracious to us, He would have made the earth swallow us, too.” Those who reject God will never prosper.

83. We will give the home in the hereafter to those who were not arrogant or corrupt. The good eternity is for the righteous.

84. Those who did good works will be rewarded better than they gave. But those who did evil will only be punished in equal measure for their actions.

85. He who gave you the Qur’an will bring you back to home. Say, “My Lord knows best who gives true guidance and who is lying.”

86. You did not expect the Book would be sent to you, but it is mercy from your Lord, so never help anyone that rejects God.

87. Never let anything stop you from sharing the revelations that God has sent you. Continue to call men to faith in God, and do not associate with those who associate other gods with God.

88. Never call upon any god besides God. There is no god but He. Everything will disappear but His face. He reserves judgment on all and to Him you will be resurrected.

Chapter 50 (chronologically)

Sura 17 (111 verses), Al-Isra/Bani Israel
(The Night Journey or the Tribe of Israel [Israelis])

1. Adored is He that carried His servant on an overnight journey from the sacred mosque to the farthest mosque, whose ground We did bless. A journey where We could show him some of Our signs. Surely, He sees and hears all. [believed to specify Al-Aqsa (the farthest) Mosque in Jerusalem]

2–3. We gave Moses the Book so there would be guidance for the children of Israel. [We told] the offspring of those We carried in the Ark with Noah, "Do not choose any guardian besides Me." He was a grateful worshipper.

4–8. We revealed in the Book that twice the children of Israel would cause corruption on the earth and for that arrogance would be punished. When the first promise came true, We sent Our followers to ravage their lands, and they did. After that We gave them a second chance and aided them with resources and children to build a great army, warning, "If you perform good acts, it benefits your souls, and likewise evil acts will harm your soul. When the second promise occurs, We will raise another group to ravage your leaders, enter your temple as before and lay waste to your lands. The Lord may yet show mercy to you, but if you revert to sin, We will revert to punishment. We have made a hell as a prison for those who reject the faith."

9–10. This Qur'an is a guide to what is righteous, and gives good news to the faithful who perform good acts, that they will receive a great reward. For those that don't believe in the hereafter, We have created a great punishment.

11. Man is quick to pray for evil when he should be praying for good.

12. The night and day are two of Our signs. The sign of the night is unseen, but the sign of the day gives you sight so you may seek grace from your Lord and compute the days and the years [time]. We have explained this in detail.

13–14. We have affixed every man's deeds to his neck, and on judgment day We will open a book in front of him. "Read your own recorded acts; your own soul is a sufficient witness against you."

15–16. Whoever is guided rightly benefits their own soul, and whoever goes astray only hurts their own soul. No man can bear the burden of another man. We do not punish any population unless we have sent them a messenger. And when We want to destroy a town, We first reveal a warning to the wealthy. And after they act unjustly, the warning is proved true, and We utterly destroy them.

17. How many generations have We destroyed since Noah's? God knows and sees every sin of His servants.

18–20. For those people who desire materials of this current life, We give the desired things to whomever We want as We please. But in the end We also make a hell for them where they will be rejected and condemned in the hereafter. For those who wish for things in the hereafter, attempt to do right, and have faith; We will give them favor. To both groups of people We freely offer the bounty of the Lord.

21. On earth you have seen We have given more to some than others. In the hereafter there is strict ranking based on people's merit.

22. Do not take any other gods besides God, or you will be despised and rejected.

23–24. The Lord decrees that you worship no one but Him and are kind to your parents. When they reach old age, don't disrespect them or desert them, but treat them with honor.

Care for them with compassion and humility and say, "My Lord have mercy on them for their care for me when I was a child."

25. The Lord knows everything man does. If you are righteous in actions, He is forgiving to all those who repeatedly repent.

26. [MD] Fairly give relatives their inheritance and also to the needy and travelers; but don't spend wastefully.

27–30. Wasteful people are the brothers of devils, and Satan is ungrateful to his Lord. If you must ignore wasteful people as you pursue the Lord's mercy, simply speak kindly to them. Don't be stingy, but don't spend wildly, or you will be responsible for becoming poor. The Lord increases and decreases His provision of sustenance fairly when He pleases, for He knows and sees everything about His servants.

31. Do not kill your children because you fear poverty. We shall provide for them and you. Killing children is a great sin.

32. [MD] Do not commit adultery [fornication/sex without marriage], for it is shameful and an evil way.

33. [MD] Do not kill that which God has forbidden, unless it's for a just cause. The family of anyone killed wrongfully has been given the right to forgive the murderer or ask for equal punishment but cannot exceed the law and seek vengeance against others.

34. Do not take any property of an orphan, but instead protect it until they reach adulthood. Fulfill every promise, for every promise will be evaluated on judgment day.

35. It will help you in the end to give people the correct amount of goods and to weigh goods on a balanced scale [do not cheat].

36. Don't believe in ideas [or follow ideas] you don't understand. All you see, hear, and feel will be judged in the end.

37. Don't walk the earth with disrespect like you own it. You can't split the earth in two or extend the height of the mountains.

38. All these things are evil, and the Lord hates them.

39. This is part of the wisdom the Lord revealed to you. Do not associate God with any other object of worship, or you will be thrown into hell, guilty and rejected.

40. Do you think that your Lord wanted you to have sons while He took for Himself daughters from among the angels? You have spoken an appalling thought.

41. In various ways We have explained messages in this Qur'an, so that people may take warning, but it seems to increase their dislike of the truth.

42–43. Say to them, "If there truly are other gods as you claim, wouldn't they have tried to move against the Lord of the throne? Glory to Him, for He is nobler than the gods you claim."

44. Everything in the seven heavens and on the earth declares the glory of Him in praise. But you don't understand how they declare His glory. He is lenient and merciful.

45–47. Sometimes when you recite the Qur'an, We place a hidden barrier between you and the unfaithful; We cover their hearts so they don't understand it and plug their ears so they can't hear you honor the only Lord, causing them to turn from you. We do this because We know best why men come to listen, when they come to listen, and when they talk secretly about you, saying My servants follow an insane person.

48. Look at the descriptions they create for you. They have gone astray and will never be righteous.

49–52. They ask, "How can we be resurrected in a new creation from dust and bones?" Answer them, "Even if you are stones or iron or some unimaginable creature, you will be resurrected." They will ask, "Who will cause us to return?" Answer them, "He who first created you." They will then nod at you and ask, "When will it happen?" Say, "Maybe quite soon." On the day He calls you up, you will answer His call with praise and think to yourself it has only been a little while.

53–54. Tell My servants that they should only speak kind words, for Satan tries to create discord among men. Satan is the enemy of mankind. Your Lord knows a man's soul best. If He wants to, He can grant you mercy or give you punishment. We have not sent you [Muhammad] as a warden over all men.

55. Your Lord knows the most about every being in heaven and on earth. We did give some prophets more advantages than others; We gave the Psalms to David.

56. Say to them, "Try to call on those beings or idols besides God, and they will not have any power to remove your misfortunes or to bring about change."

57. [MD] Those beings you call upon besides God are actually all trying to find a way to access their Lord, even those you pray to that are closest to Him. They hope for His mercy and fear His punishment. The punishment of your Lord is something to fear.

58. We will destroy every population and town before the day of judgment or severely punish it. That is written in the Book.

59. Nothing today stops Us from sending more signs, but the earlier generations always thought they were false signs. Like when we sent the she-camel to the Thamud to warn them, but they mistreated her. We only send signs to warn men of possible destruction.

60. We said to you that your Lord encompasses all of mankind; We only showed you the vision that you saw as a trial for

mankind and the cursed tree in the Qur'an. We warn them, but it only causes them to commit more wrongdoing.

61–62. Remember when We told all the angels to bow down to Adam; they all did except for Iblis. He asked why he should bow down to someone made from clay. Iblis said that if Adam was the one that We would honor above him, then he wanted to have grace from God until resurrection day. He vowed in that time period to bring all but a few of Adam's descendants under his sway.

63–64. God said, "Go your way, Iblis, and anyone that follows you will receive hell as an ample payment. Attract anyone you can with your voice, collect your force of infantry and cavalry against them, share with each other wealth and children, and make promises to them." But Satan only promises them to deceive them.

65. "But you will have no authority over My followers." Your Lord is a sufficient guardian.

66–67. Your Lord makes the ships travel smoothly through the seas so you can collect its bounty. He is most merciful to you. When you are in distress on the sea, there is no help from those you pray to instead of God. And when He brings you back to dry land, you turn away from God. Man is ever ungrateful.

68. Do you not worry that He will cause the earth to swallow you from beneath on land or that He will send a violent tornado of stones, and then you will not have anyone to protect you?

69. Or do you not worry that He will send you back out to sea and then bring a heavy storm to drown you for your ingratitude, and you will not have anyone to protect you from Us?

70. We have honored the children of Adam, provided them safety across land and sea, given them good provisions, and given them more advantages than most of Our creations.

71–72. On that day, We will call forth every man and his leader and give each their record book in their right hand, and they will read it, and they will be dealt with fairly. But those who were blind [willfully] on earth will be blind in the hereafter and continue to stray from the path.

73–75. [MD] Their purpose was to tempt you away from Our revelations and to substitute Our revelations with something you created, but pretending it's in Our name. They would have accepted you as a friend in return. Had We not strengthened you, they may have started to persuade you a little. If you had done this act, We would have given you double the punishment in this life and after death, and you would have found no one to help you against Us.

76–77. [MD] Their goal was to scare you from your lands. If you had left, they would have only dwelled there a short time after you. This is Our custom with messengers like those We sent before you. You will find We don't change Our customs.

78–79. [MD] Perform prayer at the sun's decline until the dark of night and then the dawn recital. The dawn recital is always witnessed. Pray for a part of the night as an extra prayer for you, and maybe your Lord will give you a higher class.

80. [MD] Say, "My Lord, let me enter through the gate of truth and honor, and also let me exit through the gate of truth and honor. Grant me Your power to sustain me."

81. Say, "Truth has arrived and lies have vanished, for lies always vanish."

82. We send down in the Qur'an healing and mercy to the faithful, but to the unjust it increases their ruin.

83. When We give man Our favor he turns from Us and disregards it. And when evil afflicts him, he is in misery.

84. Say, "Everyone acts according to his own character, but your Lord knows those who are guided on the right path."

85. When they ask you about the spirit say, "The spirit is commanded by the Lord, and my knowledge of it is only what little I have given you."

86–87. If We wished it, We could take back what We revealed to you, and then you would have no guardian against Us, except for mercy from your Lord, for His kindness to you is abundant.

88. Say, "Even if every man and genie worked together to try to produce a Qur'an like this, they would not be able to."

89. We have used every type of parable in this Qur'an to explain it to man, and yet the majority of them refuse to believe.

90–93. When they say, "We refuse to believe you until you make a spring gush out water from the earth; or until you create a garden of date palms and grapes with a river flowing through it; or until you cause the sky to fall down in pieces, as you predicted; or you bring us face to face with God and the angels; or you have a house covered in gold; or you climb a ladder up into the sky—No, we shall not even believe you climbing the ladder until you bring back down to us a book that we can read." Reply to them, "Glory be to God. Am I anything more than a mortal messenger?"

94–96. What caused men to reject belief when guidance came to them was just the question, "Why has God only sent us a mortal to be His messenger?" Reply to them, "If angels walked on earth living among man, then We certainly would have sent an angel as a messenger. It is enough that God acts as a witness between me and you; He knows and sees everything about His servants.

97–98. Whoever God guides is rightly guided, but whoever He leads astray will never find a guardian for himself. On the day of judgment, We shall gather the unjust together, lying on their faces, blind, dumb, and deaf. Their destination will be hell, and whenever the heat decreases, We will increase the fire. That is their retribution, because they didn't believe Our revelations saying, "When we are but dust and bones, will we really be resurrected?"

99. Can they not see that God, who created the heavens and the earth, has the power to recreate them? He has created an end date for them, of that there is no doubt. Yet the unjust refuse to believe.

100. Say, "Even if you possessed all the treasures of the Lord's mercy, you would not distribute them for fear of spending it; man is wretched."

101–102. We gave Moses nine signs, as the children of Israel can attest. When he stood before Pharaoh he said, "I think you have been bewitched." Moses replied, "You know that these signs have been sent down by the Lord of heavens and earth as clear evidence. I deem that you, Pharaoh, are doomed."

103. Pharaoh resolved to remove Moses from the face of the earth, but We drowned Pharaoh and every one of his followers.

104. Then We told the children of Israel, "Live safely in this land, and when the promise of the hereafter comes, We will gather you all together."

105. With truth We sent it down, and We sent you as only a messenger of good news and warnings.

106. We divided the Qur'an into parts, and We send it down to you in pieces so that you can recite it to men as it's revealed.

107–109. Say, "Whether you believe it or not, when people who were given knowledge beforehand hear the Qur'an recited, they bow down on their faces in humility and they say, 'Glory to our Lord; our Lord's promise must be fulfilled.' They fall down on their faces in tears, and it increases their humility."

110. Say, "Call upon God or call upon the beneficent, you can call him either for it is the same. The most beautiful names belong to Him. But do not speak loud or silent when you worship but something in between."

111. Say, "All praise belongs to God, as He has no son and no partner in sovereignty, and He needs no partner to protect Him. Proclaim His greatness."

Chapter 51 (chronologically)

Sura 10 (109 verses), Yunus (Jonah)

1. Alif. Lam. Raa. These are the verses of the definitive book.

2. Why is it a wonder to the people that We have sent Our message by revealing it to a man that lives among them and telling him to, "Warn mankind and give good tidings to those who believe so that they can be in good standing with the Lord?" The faithless say, "He is a sorcerer."

3. Your Lord is God. He created the heavens and the earth in six days and then established himself upon the throne. No one can plead for you with Him unless He allows it. God is you, Lord. Worship Him. Will you accept this warning?

4. To Him you will all return; that is a promise of God. It was He who caused the original creation, then He will bring it back, and He can reward justly those who were faithful and did righteous deeds. But for those who reject Him, He will deliver boiling water to quench their thirst and a painful punishment.

5–6. He made the sun radiant and lit the moon and ordained its phases so that man can calculate time. Everything God created was for a purpose. He explains His signs in detail for those who understand. For in the repetition of night and day and in everything that God created in the heavens and on earth there are signs for the righteous to understand.

7–8. Those people that do not expect to meet Us and are perfectly pleased with life on earth and do not see Our signs will have a home in the fires because of their deeds.

9–10. Yet those people who are faithful and do good acts will be guided by their Lord through their faith. Streams will flow for them in the garden of paradise. They will call out, "Glory to you, God." And they will be greeted with, "Peace." And their concluding statement will be, "All glory belongs to God, the Lord of all the worlds.

11. If God were to quicken the end of the lives of sinful men as fast as He brings an end to the just, then He would end their lives immediately. But We leave those people on earth that don't plan on meeting Us in the hereafter to wander confused in their rebellion.

12. When man is in pain, he cries to Us from all positions. But when We have solved his problems, he will go about his life as if he had never cried to Us for help. This is how man can make his wrongdoing seem allowed in his mind.

13–14. We destroyed generations before you when they sinned. Their messengers warned them, but they wouldn't believe. That is how We punish the guilty. Then We let you inherit the lands after them so We can see how you behave.

15–16. When Our clear signs are revealed to the people that don't look forward to meeting Us, they say, "Bring us a revelation other than this one or change this one." Reply, "It is not in my power to change it. I simply follow what is revealed to me. If I were to disobey my Lord, I would fear my punishment on that great day. If God had willed it, I would not recite it to you, nor would He have made you aware of it. I lived with you my whole life before it was revealed to me. Why don't you understand?"

17. Who commits the greater sin, those who create a lie against God or those who deny His revelations? Sinners are never successful.

18. When they worship things other than God, that can neither help them nor harm them, and they say, "These will be our negotiators with God." Reply, "Do you intend to tell God something He has never heard of before in the heavens or on earth? Praise be to Him, for He is more noble than all you associate with Him."

19. Mankind was once a single nation, but later it separated. If God had not previously commanded that they stay separate, they would have settled their differences by now.

20. When they say, "Why didn't the Lord send us a sign?" Reply, "Only God knows the unknown, so let's wait together to find out."

21. When We allow mankind to feel Our mercy after they have suffered, they immediately start to plot against Our signs. Say

to them, "God can plot faster than all." Our messengers are recording all the plots mankind makes.

22–23. He enables you to move across land and sea. You can board a ship and sail with fair winds and rejoice. Then when a storm strikes them with waves, and they think they will drown, they call out to God in sincere prayer, "If You save us from this, we will truly be grateful!" But when He saves them, immediately they brazenly disobey again. Mankind, you rebel and stain your own soul. Enjoy of this earth now, and in the end return to Us; We will inform you of your actions.

24. A parable of life in this world: It's like water which We rain down from the sky; it causes vegetation to grow, which provides food for men and beasts. When the earth wears this radiant ornament and is beautiful, men think they have power over it. We send down Our command, by night or day, and the earth is mown flat as if it had never flourished. We explain the signs for those who reflect.

25. God calls you to the place of peace. He guides whomever He chooses on the right path.

26. People who are virtuous will be rewarded and then some. No shame or blackness will cover their faces. They are companions of the garden and will live there for eternity.

27. Those who have committed evil acts will be rewarded with evil. Shame will cover their faces. No one will protect them

from God. Their faces will be covered with a cloak as dark as night. They are companions of the fire and will endure it.

28–29. On judgment day when We gather everyone together, We shall tell the people who associated gods with Us, "Stand back, both you and your supposed partner of God." Then We will separate them, and their supposed partner of God will say to them, "It was not us you worshipped, and because God is a sufficient witness between you and us, we were unaware that you were worshipping us."

30. On judgment day every soul shall learn of their deeds. They will be returned to God, their rightful Lord, and their false gods will fail them.

31. Say, "Who gives you provision from the sky and earth? Who controls your hearing and vision? Who brings the dead back to life and death from the living? Who provides guidance?" They will reply, "God." Then say, "Will you be faithful to Him?"

32–33. God is your true Lord. When you take away truth, you are left with error. So where are you being led? The word of your Lord is the truth against those who do wrong. They will not believe.

34. Say, "Can any of those you associate with God cause creation and then repeat it? It is God who caused the genesis and can reproduce it. How can you be misled?"

35. Say, "Can you ask those you associated with God for guidance towards truth? It is God who provides guidance towards truth. So, isn't God more deserving of your faith than those you associate with God? What is the matter with the way you make decisions?"

36. Most of them follow assumptions, but assumptions won't protect them from the truth. God is aware of all they do.

37. Only God could create this Qur'an. It is a confirmation of previous revelations and a more complete explanation of the Book. It is, without a doubt, from the Lord of the worlds.

38. When they say, "He forged it." Reply, "Bring me a chapter that is equal to this, and you can ask anyone besides God for help. If you are truthful."

39. They will call you a liar if they can't comprehend the knowledge even before you have given them the explanation. Those generations before you also called messengers liars, and you can see what happened to those wrongdoers.

40. [MD] Among the people there are some who believe and some who do not. The Lord knows who the corrupt ones are.

41. If they call you a liar say, "My deeds are mine, and yours are yours. I am responsible for my actions, and you are for yours."

42. There are some people who will pretend to listen to you. But can you make the deaf hear, even though they won't understand?

43. There are some people that will look toward you. But can you guide the blind, even though they won't see?

44. God will not be unjust to mankind, but mankind will corrupt his own soul.

45. On judgment day He will gather all beings together, and it will seem to them like they had only been apart for a day, and they'll recognize each other. Surely those who denied they would ever meet Him and rejected His guidance will perish.

46. It doesn't matter if We show you something that We promise to them or if We call you home [before we show you]; mankind will return to Us, and God is a witness to all their acts.

47. Every nation is sent a messenger so that on the day of judgment they can be tried justly.

48–49. When they ask, "If you speak the truth, on what day will this threat happen?" Reply, "I have no power to harm or benefit myself [like God does], so I can only do as God wishes. Every people [nation] has a limited term and they can neither defer the date nor reach it faster."

50–51. Further, say to them, "You cannot avoid His punishment when it comes, and it can happen anytime, night or day; so what is it about judgment day that you sinners would actually want to reach it faster? Right now you wouldn't believe in the day unless it actually came to pass, right? You have already wished to speed its arrival by not believing in it."

52–53. That day it will be said, "To those who were unjust, taste the eternal torment! You will be paid for what you earned." They will ask you if it's true, so reply, "Yes, by my Lord it's the truth, and you cannot escape it."

54. If every sinning soul were able to possess all the treasure on earth, they would try to buy their way out of judgment; and they will declare repentance, when they see hell. But all will be judged fairly and given only justice.

55–57. God owns everything in the heavens and on earth, so His promise must be true. But most of them do not understand. It is He that causes life and death, and you shall return to Him. Mankind, God has sent you a warning and a cure for your souls and for those who are faithful, guidance and mercy.

58. Say to them, "Let us rejoice in the grace and mercy of God." It is better than everything they hoard.

59–60. Ask them, "Why have you made some of the sustenance God sent to you lawful and some unlawful? Did God command you to do this, or have you created a false rule and attributed it to God?" What do you think the penalty is on the day of judgment for people that invent a lie against God? Surely God is full of grace, but most men do not give thanks for it.

61. God is witness to all conduct of business, every reading of the Qur'an, and every deed being carried out. Not even something as tiny as an atom in the heavens or earth is invisible to God. Everything great and small is recorded.

62–64. Friends of God do not fear, nor do they grieve; they are faithful and righteous in the face of evil. For those friends it's good news in this life and the hereafter. There can be no changing the words of God—it [the words] is a mighty triumph.

65. Don't let their statements cause you grief. All the power and honor belongs to God, and He hears and knows everything they say.

66. All the creatures in heaven and earth belong to God. So who are the "partners" of God that people worship? They are just a concoction, and they always lie.

67. He gave you a night to rest in and a day so you could see. These are signs for people who would listen.

68–70. They say, "God has created a son!" All glory be to Him. He is self-sufficient. He owns the heavens and the earth. You have no authority to say He made a son. Do you dare to tell God about something you don't really know? Reply, "Those who invent a lie concerning God will not succeed." They will only enjoy this world a little while, and to Us they will return.

Then We will give them a severe punishment for how they chose to defy God.

71. Tell them the story of Noah. He told his people, "If me being here and sharing the signs of God with you is offensive, then I put my trust in God. So hatch your plan and gather your men. If you have no doubts, then attack me and give me no relief."

72–73. "But please remember, I haven't asked for any money, for God gives my reward, and I have been commanded to submit to God." They rejected him, but We saved him and those in the Ark, and they inherited the earth. We drowned those who denied Our revelations. See what happened to those who reject Our signs?

74. After Noah We sent many messengers bringing signs to later generations, but they also rejected the revelations like the people before. That is why We mark the souls of sinners.

75–78. After more messengers, We sent Moses and Aaron to the Pharaoh and his leaders with Our signs. They too were arrogant and guilty. When they saw the truth in Our signs, they said, "This is only magic." Moses asked them how they could deny the truth once it was shown to them. And then, "Is this magic? For magicians don't find salvation." Pharaoh questioned, "Have you two come to us to lead us from the faith of our ancestors, so that you two can become powerful in Egypt? We will not believe in you!"

79–82. Pharaoh called for his most skilled wizards to battle Moses. Upon arrival Moses challenged them to cast their spells. Upon seeing their best, Moses said, "You have merely brought deceptions, and God will make your actions futile. God does not help the corrupt to prosper. And God will prove His truth by His words, even though the sinners will oppose Him."

83–86. At this point, only some of the children of Moses's people believed his message, as the others were afraid of the tyrant Pharaoh and his likely persecution of them for being faithful. Moses told them, "My people, if you truly believe in God, then submit and put your trust in Him." His people replied, "We do put our trust in God, but please Lord don't make us a target for oppression. Please deliver us from the unfaithful by your mercy."

87–89. We inspired Moses and Aaron by telling them, "Provide homes for your people in Egypt and turn them into a place of worship. Establish regular prayers and share the good word to the faithful." Then Moses prayed, "Our Lord, you have given Pharaoh and his chiefs wealth and glory in this life, and with it they lead men from your righteous path. Please destroy their wealth and harden their hearts so that they won't be faithful until they finally see their mortal doom." God replied, "Your prayer has been accepted, so stand tall and follow the righteous path of the believer."

90. We allowed the children of Israel to cross the sea, and when the Pharaoh followed them, we drowned him and his men. As he was drowning Pharaoh said, "I believe there is no god besides the God of the children of Israel, and I am now one of those who submit to him!"

91–92. We said to him, "Of course now you submit, while before you were rebellious and corrupting!" But, We will deliver your dead body from the sea to be a sign to all those who come after you. Unfortunately, most men don't heed Our warnings.

93. We brought the children of Israel to a bountiful place. They were united until We gave them knowledge, and they created schisms. Your Lord will judge them at the resurrection for the things they disagreed upon.

94–95. [MD] If you doubt what We are revealing to you, then ask someone who has read the Book. This is the truth from your Lord, so do not doubt it nor reject the signs of God, or you will join those who will perish.

96. Some will not be faithful, especially those who were justifiably marked by God's word . . .

97. . . . even if every sign is personally shown to them, until the end when they see their final grievous penalty.

98. Why was it that only Jonah's community listened to Our warnings? When they became faithful, We removed the

disgrace they were living under and let them enjoy their lives for a while.

99. If your Lord wished it, so all mankind would believe. Would you [Muhammad] force men to believe?

100. No soul can be faithful except by the will of God. He places impurity on those men who cannot understand.

101–103. "Behold all that is in the heavens and on earth." But no signs, revelations, or warnings can benefit the unbelievers. Do they expect any different outcome than their ancestors before them at death? Tell them, "Then wait, and I will wait with you." We will surely save Our prophets and the faithful in the end. We are bound to save the believers.

104. Tell mankind, "If you doubt my religion, then know that I don't worship your other gods, I only worship God. The God that will bring about your death. I have been commanded to be one of the believers."

105. "Always worship religion righteously and do not be one of those that ascribe partners to God."

106. "It is surely a sin to call upon any other being besides God, like any of those that cannot harm or help you."

107. If God gives you pain, only He can stop it, and if He intends you to receive benefits, then no one can stop His gift. He can grant His will to any follower He chooses, for He is forgiving and merciful.

108. Tell them, "Mankind, the truth has been revealed to you by your Lord. Whoever lives righteously helps their soul, and those who stray from the straight path harm their souls. I am not here to keep you on the straight path."

109. Follow the revelations sent to you and be patient until God passes judgment. He is the greatest judge.

Chapter 52 (chronologically)

Sura 11 (123 verses), Hud (Hud)

1–2. Alif. Lam. Ra. [ALR] This is a book from the all-knowing, with perfectly simple verses explaining all matters in detail. It says "worship no one besides God, and I am just a messenger of His revelations and good tidings."

3. Seek forgiveness from your Lord and be remorseful, so that He may grant you an enjoyable life and bestow His grace on all those worthy. But if you turn from God, I fear you will face a great penalty on judgment day.

4-5. To God you all will return, and He has power over all things. God is all-knowing, and what men try to hide in their hearts and cover with their clothes is known to Him. He knows the secrets of men.

6. Every creature on earth owes its nourishment to God's provision. He knows where everything resides and where it is or will be buried. All knowledge is recorded clearly for Him.

7–11. It is He that created the heavens and the earth in six days. His throne was over the waters so that He might test the best behaved of you. But if you were to tell them, "You shall be raised up after you die," the unfaithful would reply, "That is obviously nothing but magic." And if We delay their punishment until a specified time, they will say, "What delays it?" On the day that they receive their punishment, there is nothing that will hold back what they have mocked. And if We give man a short gift of mercy from punishment, when it is removed he will be thankless for Our mercy. And if We show him favor after he has suffered adversity, he will simply say, "The evils have left me." Man is boastful and will just rejoice, [giving no credit to God]. But, the exception to this is the man that shows patience and does good deeds; for that man there is forgiveness and a great reward.

12. [MD] Do not abandon what We have revealed to you [Muhammad] because mankind makes you upset. Surely, they will say to you, "Why didn't God send us a treasure or an angel?" You are only the messenger; God has the power over all things.

13–14. When people say, "You fabricated the Qur'an," say to them, "If you are right, then try to fabricate ten chapters like these.

You can call upon anyone besides God to help you. If your gods don't respond to your requests, then you must know that this is a revelation from God and that there is no God except Him. Then will you submit to God?"

15–16. If people desire the present life and all that glitters, We shall give it to them in full payment for their deeds, and they will not suffer any loss. But they will receive nothing in the afterlife except the fire. For what they achieved in this present world will come to nothing.

17. [MD] Can people who accept a clear sign from their Lord as recited by a messenger—like those who were guided by the book of Moses before them—be equal to people that don't? For those who reject the signs will meet in the fire in the afterlife. Never doubt that outcome, for it's the truth from your Lord. Unfortunately, most men to do not believe the signs.

18–22. Is there any man more unjust than those who create lies concerning God? When they are brought before God, witnesses will say, "These are the people that lied against their Lord, and now the curse of God will be upon them." Anyone that hinders another man from the path to God by twisting the path will be denied in the hereafter. They will not escape God's plans for earth and will have no protectors, thus their punishment will be doubled. They lost their power to hear and they did not see. They are the ones who have lost their own souls, and the lies they invented will fail them in the end. They will be the greatest losers in the hereafter.

23. But those who are faithful, do righteous works, and humble themselves before their Lord will be the rightful companions in heaven and abide in the Garden.

24. There is a parable comparing two kinds of men: those who are blind and deaf and those who can see and hear. Are the two equal? Will man not take heed of the warnings?

25–26. We sent Noah to his people and he said, "I am a messenger. Serve no one but God. If you don't, I fear a harsh penalty."

27. But the chiefs of the unfaithful said to him, "We think you are but a man like us, and we only see the most wretched among us following you with poor judgment. You have no power to speak to us, and we think you are liars."

28–31. Noah replied, "My people, if I have been given a clear sign from my Lord and received His mercy but you cannot see the signs, shall we be able to force you to accept a sign you are averse to? My people, I don't ask for any payment in return, for my reward comes from God. I will not drive away the faithful, for they have to meet their Lord. But I see you are the ignorant ones." He continued, "My people, who will help me against God if I drove them away? I have not told you that I have the treasures of God or that I know the future, and I don't claim to be an angel. And I haven't told these men you despise that God will grant them their every wish, for God knows what is in their souls, and it would be wrong of me to say those things."

32. The men replied, "Noah, you have argued with us long enough now, so why don't you just bring these threats you have been promising to us, if you are actually telling the truth?"

33–34. Noah replied, "Only God can bring His promises to you, and when He does there is no escape. My advice will not help you, if God wills you to be led astray. He is your Lord, and to Him you shall return."

35. If they say to you, "He has invented the Qur'an," say to them, "If I did, then I am only responsible for my sins. I am innocent of all the sins that you will commit."

36–37. Noah was told, "The only people that will believe you are those that have already been faithful. Do not grieve for the evil the others commit. Build an Ark as We have inspired you to, and do not call upon Us anymore about those who have sinned. The sinners are going to be drowned."

38–39. Noah began to build the Ark. And every time the chiefs would pass by and mock him Noah would reply, "Although you ridicule us now, we will soon mock you. Soon you will know who is going to receive punishment and a lasting doom."

40–41. Then the commandment happened, and the earth gushed fountains of water. We said to Noah, "Load a pair of every kind of beast and then your family and Our followers." But there were few faithful men to load. Noah cried, "Get on the Ark in the name of God, whether it is docked or sailing. The Lord is forgiving and merciful."

42–43. The Ark was lifted on the waves, which were as tall as mountains. Noah called to a son that had become separated, "Come aboard so you won't be stuck with the unfaithful!" His son replied, "I will just climb up a mountain and be safe from the flood." Noah told him that on this day nothing could save him from the wrath except the mercy of God. The waves continued and Noah's son was destroyed among the unbelievers.

44. So it was, the command was given, "Earth, swallow the waters, and sky clear up your clouds." The waters drained, and the event was over, leaving the Ark to rest on Mount Judi. The word went forth declaring, "Gone are the unjust people."

45–47. Noah called to his Lord, "Surely my son is part of my family. Your promise is true, and you are the most fair of judges." God replied, "Noah, he is not part of your family because of his evil ways. Do not ask me about things you don't understand. I give this advice so you don't act like the ignorant." Noah responded, "My Lord, I seek refuge with you, so that I won't ask things I have no knowledge of. Unless you forgive me, I shall be among the lost."

48. The word came to Noah, "Leave the Ark with peace from Us. We lay blessings upon you so that some of your offspring will become nations. But other offspring will be granted the pleasures of the earth for a while before We overtake them with great penalty."

49. These are some of the unknown stories We reveal to you. You didn't know them before, and neither did your people. Have patience knowing that the end is for the righteous.

50–52. We sent Hud to the Ad people; he was one of them. Hud said, "My people, worship God. There is no other but God. Your other gods are invented. My people, I don't ask for rewards from you for sharing this message. My reward is from the creator. Do you understand me? My people, ask your Lord for forgiveness and turn to Him in remorse. He will bring down the rains and make you stronger, so do not turn from Him in sin.

53–56. The Ad people said, "Hud, you haven't brought us any proof, and we will not abandon our gods based on your word. We do not believe you. Perhaps some of our gods have made you evil?" Hud responded, "As God is my witness, I am not possessed, as you have suggested, by any partners of God. So do your worst in opposing me, and give me no relief. I trust in God my Lord . . . and your Lord. There is nothing on this earth that He doesn't control. My Lord is on the righteous path."

57. "If you turn from God, I know that I have given you His message. My Lord will replace you with another generation of men, and you will do no harm to Him. My Lord is the guardian over all things."

58. When Our commandment came, We saved Hud and all the believers from the severe penalty the Ad received.

59–60. That is the story of the Ad people, who rejected the signs of their Lord and disobeyed Our messenger, while following the commands of every brazen ruler. They were cursed in this life and also on the day of judgment. They rejected their Lord, and We removed them from the followers of Hud.

61. We sent Salih, one of their people, to the Thamuds. Salih said, "My people, worship God and have no other god but Him. He created you from the earth and made you caretaker of it. Ask Him for forgiveness, turn to Him repentantly, for the Lord is near and ready to respond."

62. The Thamud replied, "While you are surely one of us, do you really ask us to stop worshipping as our fathers worshipped? We are suspicious of your request to worship one God."

63. Salih continued, "My people, can't you see? I am acting on a sign from God, who has given me mercy. Who could save me from God if I disobeyed Him? You could not save me."

64–65. He continued, "This female camel is a gift from God to you. Let her feed freely on the earth, and do not harm her, or a swift penalty shall befall you." But the Thamud people hamstrung her. Salih then told them, "You only have three days now to enjoy life, and this is a promise that will come true."

66–68. When Our promise was fulfilled, We saved Salih and those who believed his message. Through Our grace they survived the penalty of that day, for your Lord is mighty. A mighty and awful cry blasted upon the evil Thamud people, and they were found dead in their homes in the morning. It was as if they had never existed there at all. The Thamud rejected their Lord, and they were removed from the world.

69–70. When Our messengers went to Abraham, they offered news of peace. Abraham responded with the words of peace and quickly brought them a roasted calf. When the messengers didn't reach for the food, Abraham was distrustful of them and fearful. The messengers assured him he need not fear, for they were sent to deal with Lot's people.

71–73. Abraham's wife laughed when the messengers told her of a son for her named Isaac and of his son Jacob. She said, "How could an old woman and an old man bear a child? That would surely be wondrous." They responded, "Do you question the decree of God? The grace of God and His blessings are upon your house. He is the glorious one worthy of praise."

74–76. Once the awe of the visit left Abraham and he absorbed the good news, he began to plead with Us for the lives of Lot's people. Abraham was forgiving and compassionate and always respectful of God. We told him, "Abraham, do not ask for this. The Lord's commandment has been given and cannot be stopped."

77. When Our messengers reached Lot, he was saddened and felt powerless to protect his people. Lot said, "This is a difficult day."

78–80. Lot's people gathered around them. [They had been committing sexual abominations for a long time.] Lot spoke to them: "My people, take my daughters, for they are pure for marriage. Fear God and don't act disgracefully in front of my guests. Is there not one upright man among you?" The people replied, "Lot, you know we have no interest in or need for your daughters; you know what we desire." Lot responded, "If only I had the power to suppress you or had strong supporters among you."

81. The messengers said, "Lot, we are the messengers from your Lord. They will not harm you. Travel now with your family while it is still dark, and don't let anyone look back at this place. Your wife will remain behind though, and she shall be struck with the rest. They aim to get you in the morning, and it's very near."

82–83. Our decree came to pass, and We turned the city upside down and rained fire and brimstone upon them, as they were marked by the Lord for their unjust behavior.

84–86. We sent Shu'ayb, a brother, to the Midian people. He said, "My people, worship God and have no other gods but Him. Never cheat in your measures and weights. I see your prosperity and fear a coming day of doom. Be fair when you measure and weigh goods, and never withhold what is due to your customers. Do not commit evil on this earth nor corrupt it. Your fair earnings left to you by God will be better for you if you are faithful. But I am not here to watch over you.

87. The Midians questioned, "Shu'ayb, does your religion require that we stop worshipping as our fathers did? Or that we no longer do as we please with your own property? You are surely a kind and practical person."

88–90. Shu'ayb spoke: "My people, have you not considered that I am acting based on a sign from my Lord and that He has given me sustenance to sustain my work? I do not ask you to be fair so that I may cheat and profit behind your backs. My only desire is to reform us. My success in this endeavor is determined solely by God. On Him I rely and pray." He continued, "People, do not let your disagreement with me cause you to sin, or you will suffer the same fate as the people of Noah, Hud, Salih, and Lot in the near future. Instead ask your Lord for forgiveness and turn to Him in repentance. My Lord is merciful and kind.

91. The Midians responded, "Shu'ayb, we don't understand most of what you are saying. You are weak compared to us, and if not for your family, we would have stoned you by now.

92–93. He said to them, "My family is somehow more important to you than God? God is merely something you can cast aside and neglect? Don't you know that my Lord is involved with everything that you do? My people, do as you wish based on your beliefs and know that I am acting upon mine. Soon you will know who will receive a great penalty and who is a liar. We shall both be watching for it."

94–95. When Our commandment was enacted, We saved Shu'ayb and the faithful among them with Our mercy. The mighty blast overtook the sinners, and they lay motionless in their homes in the morning. It was as if they never existed at all. The Midian were cleansed of the earth just like the Thamud!

96–99. We sent Moses with our revelations and authority to Pharaoh and his chieftains, but they listened to the Pharaoh, and his commands were not righteous. Pharaoh will lead his people on judgment day straight into the fire. He will lead them to an evil place. They are cursed on earth, and they will receive a miserable gift on the day of resurrection.

100. These are the accounts of some of the communities of the world; some of them stand today, while others have been destroyed.

101-108. We did not bring injustice to them, for they have wronged their own souls. The gods they called upon besides God did nothing to save them when God's decrees came to pass. This shows the power of the Lord's punishment. When He penalizes communities for their sins, it is painful and severe. This is a clear sign for those who fear doom in the hereafter, that day when mankind will gather and have their day of testimony. That day will not be delayed past its appointed time. On that day no soul shall speak unless He wills it. Some of the souls will be wretched, and some will be eager. The wretched will enter the fire, where there will be nothing but groaning and crying. The wretched shall remain there for eternity, unless the Lord removes them. The Lord can do whatever He likes. The blessed shall be in the Garden. They shall remain there forever, unless the Lord removes them. It is an eternal gift.

109. Let there be no doubt about the consequences for which god men choose to worship. If they worship the gods like their fathers before them, then We shall repay them in full.

110. We gave Moses the scripture, but it was not followed by all. Had it not been for an earlier message from your Lord, they

would have solved their differences among them. They are in doubt about it.

111–113. The Lord will surely repay everyone for their deeds, for He knows everything man does. So stand strong and do as commanded. You and everyone you turn towards God must not stray from the straight path, for He watches every step. Don't slant towards those who sin, or the fire will also seize you. You will have no protectors to help you against God.

114. [MD] Establish regular prayers at either end of the day and at some times at night. Surely good acts can make up for sins, so be mindful.

115. Be steadfast, for God rewards only the righteous.

116. There were only a few men, who We saved, before you that possessed the understanding that men should be warned not to corrupt the earth. Why weren't there more? The sinners pursued only the pleasures of life, and they were a guilty lot.

117. Your Lord never destroyed entire communities wantonly if they were trying to reform themselves.

118–119. If your Lord had willed it, He could have created mankind as a single nation, but they still would have argued over differences. The only ones that would coexist were those He bestowed with His mercy, and that is why He created them. The word of your Lord has been fulfilled: "I will fill hell with genies and men all together."

120. We have related the stories of the other messengers to strengthen your heart. In this chapter, you have learned the truth and a warning and reminder for the faithful.

121–122. Say to the unfaithful, "Act according to your beliefs, as we too are acting on ours. Wait! For we are waiting, too."

123. To God belongs all that is unknown in the heavens and the earth. To God all things will return. So worship Him, and put your trust in Him. Your Lord is aware of every deed of man.

Chapter 53 (chronologically)

Sura 12 (111 verses), Yusuf (Joseph)

1–3. [MD] Alif Lam Ra. These are the signs of this clear Book. We have sent it down as a lecture in Arabic so that you may learn. We reveal to you the stories in the best narration in this inspired Qur'an. Before this Book, you were among those who were ignorant.

4–6. And Joseph told his father, "In my dream I saw 11 planets and the sun and moon all bowing towards me." His father replied, "My son, do not tell your brothers, or they will plot against you. Satan is the enemy of mankind. Your Lord will surely choose you and teach you how to interpret visions. He will place His grace on you and families of Jacob, just as He placed it on your forefathers Abraham and Isaac. Your Lord is all-knowing and wise."

7. [MD] In Joseph and his brothers are signs for those who seek the truth.

8–10. The brothers said, "Joseph and his brother [Benjamin] are loved more by our father than we are. But we are a stronger group, and our father is clearly wrong." One said, "Kill Joseph or force him out into some unknown land, so that father may give his favor to you, for there will be time enough for you to become righteous afterwards." Another said, "Don't kill Joseph, but instead throw him in a well, for he will surely be picked up by some travelers eventually."

11–14. They spoke to their father later: "Why don't you trust us with Joseph? We are surely his good friends. Send him with us tomorrow to play, and we shall take care of him." Jacob replied, "It saddens me, because if you take him with you, I fear a wolf may eat him while you are not watching him." They replied, "If a wolf should reach him while he is in a large group like ours, it's only because we have all been eaten."

15. The brothers did take him with them and agreed that they would throw him in a well. We put a message in Joseph's heart that one day he would tell them the truth of their plans to their faces, but they would not know who he was.

16–18. The brothers came crying to their father at nightfall saying, "You will never believe us even though we speak the truth, father, but we all ran away and left Joseph with the gear, and a wolf devoured him." They showed him a blood-stained shirt they created, and the father said, "Your souls have allowed you to fabricate this tale, but for me I choose patience. Only God alone could help in a situation such as you describe."

19–20. A caravan of travelers sent their water carrier to the well, and when he retrieved his bucket he said, "Good news. We have found a fine young boy." They hid the boy as treasure, but God knew what they had done. Later they sold him for a very low price of a few silver coins, for they underestimated his worth.

21. The Egyptian man who bought him told his wife to "give him an honorable home, so that maybe he will prove useful to us or maybe we will adopt him as our son."

22. When Joseph became an adult, We gave him wisdom and knowledge, for We reward those who do good.

23–24. One day the woman in whose house he lived tried to seduce him into an evil act. She bolted the door and said to him, "Come to me." Joseph said, "It is forbidden! I seek refuge in God. Your husband is my master, and he has given me a good home. Wrongdoers are never rewarded." She desired him, and he would have also desired her but knew the will of his Lord, and he could turn away from evil and shameful acts. He was one of Our most sincere servants.

25–28. They both raced towards the locked door, and she tore his shirt from behind, and as they opened the door her husband arrived. She asked, "What shall be the punishment for someone that tries to do this act to your wife, prison or a painful penalty?" Joseph responded, "It was she that tried to seduce me into sin." One of the house servants saw the event spoke: "If she is truthful and he is a liar, then his shirt should be ripped in the front, but if the shirt is ripped from the back, then she is a liar, and he is truthful." When he looked at the shirt torn from behind, the husband said, "Woman, you are guilty in this case, and your scheme is a strong one."

29. He declared, "Joseph, leave this matter alone now, and woman, ask forgiveness for your sins, for you are guilty."

30. The ladies of the city were gossiping about the wife of the ruler Aziz trying to seduce her slave boy. They said he must have affected her deeply and that she was clearly in the wrong.

31–32. She heard of the gossip and invited them to a banquet. She placed a knife before each of them and said to Joseph, "Walk in the room in front of them all." When the women saw him, they worshipped his beauty and cut their hands absentmindedly saying, "God is great. This is no mortal man but instead a graceful angel!" The wife spoke to them: "Here is the man you blamed me for lusting after. I did try to seduce him, but he resisted nobly. But now if he doesn't do my bidding, he will be cast into prison among the disgraced."

33–34. Joseph cried, "Oh Lord, prison is better for me than to do the acts they ask of me. If you don't fend off these women, my youthful foolishness will drive me to become a sinner." So his Lord heard his prayer and fended off the women. For He hears and knows everything.

35. The men decided after seeing the signs of his innocence that it would still be best to imprison him for a while.

36. In the prison he met two young men. One said, "I dreamed I was a wine presser." The other said, "I dreamed I was carrying bread on my head, and the birds were eating it." "Please tell us what these meant, for we know you are a person that can interpret dreams well and are virtuous."

37–38. He explained, "Before your next meal arrives, I will reveal the meaning of the dreams. This is a duty placed on me by my Lord. I have abandoned the ways of people who don't believe in God and deny the existence of the hereafter. I follow the ways of my forefathers, Abraham, Isaac, and Jacob. Never would we attribute any partners to God. This is due to the grace God has placed upon us and mankind. Most men do not give thanks."

39–40. "My fellow prisoners, I ask, 'Are many gods better than one supreme God?' Those other gods you worship besides God are just names created by you and your fathers, and they have no authority from God. Command belongs solely to God, and He commands that you worship no one but Him. This is the correct faith, but most men are ignorant."

41. "My fellow prisoners, one of you will pour the wine for your Lord to drink, while the other will be crucified, and the birds will eat from your head. This is the meaning of the dreams you asked for."

42. Joseph asked the prisoner that was about to be released to mention his name outside in the presence of his King. But Satan made the prisoner forget to mention Joseph, and he remained in prison for a few more years.

43–44. The king of Egypt said to his dream interpreters, "I have a vision of seven fat cows being eaten by seven thin ones and seven green ears of corn and seven more dry ears, so what does it mean?" They answered, "It's a jumbled dream, and we do not know its meaning."

45. The released prisoner recalled Joseph in prison and said, "I can tell you its meaning if you allow me to go."

46. At prison he said, "Joseph the truthful, explain the vision of seven fat cows being eaten by seven thin ones and seven green ears of corn and seven more dry ears, so that I can return to the court, and they may understand it."

47–49. Joseph said, "For seven years you should sow as usual, but only reap what you need to eat and leave the rest in the storage. For the next seven years will be dreadful, and you will eat up almost everything that you have stored. Then there will be a year when people will have abundant rains and be able to press wine and oil."

50–51. Upon hearing the interpretation, the king called for the messenger [prisoner Joseph]. Joseph asked the king, "Go to my master and ask him about the ideas in the minds of the women who cut their hands? My Lord knows well what their schemes were." The king asked, "What was your plan when you sought to seduce Joseph into an evil act?" The ladies replied, "God save us, but we knew of no evil in him." Aziz's wife uttered, "Now the truth is out for all, I admit it was I who tried to seduce him into sin, but he is one of the virtuous ones."

52–53. Joseph said, "I asked for this so that my master would know that I have never betrayed him and to show that God never guides the acts of the unfaithful. I do not absolve myself of blame, for the human soul is prone to evil unless God shows us mercy. My Lord is most merciful."

54–55. The king said, "I will take Joseph on to my personal staff." Once he had spoken to Joseph, he said, "On this day I publicly deem you honorable and faithful." Joseph asked, "Place me in charge of the storage houses, and I will guard them, as I know their importance."

56–57. This is how We gave power to Joseph in the lands. To take possession as he pleased. We place Our mercy on whom We please, and we never lose track of the rewards for the good men. But the reward in the hereafter is the best for those who are faithful and righteous.

58–60. Then Joseph's brothers arrived and stood in front of him, and while he knew them, the brothers didn't recognize Joseph. After Joseph furnished them with provisions he said, "If you bring me a half brother who you share a father with, you will see that I pay out equally and am a good host. But if you don't bring him to me, then I will not do business with you, and you needn't come back."

61. The brothers replied, "We will try to get our father to let us bring him to you."

62. Joseph told his young attendants to place the money that the brothers used to buy grain into the brothers' saddlebags, so they wouldn't find it until they got home, so that they might come back.

63–64. When the brothers returned to their father, they told him what happened and added, "The man threatened to withhold our future measure of grain and said we must bring our brother to him. So send our brother with us so that we may obtain our measure. We will take care of him." Jacob replied, "Why should I trust you to protect this brother any better than the last?" God is the best keeper, and He is the most merciful one.

65. Later the bothers opened their saddlebags and found their money returned to them. They said, "Father, what more can we desire? Our money has been returned to us, so now we can get more food for the family. We can take care of our brother and also retrieve another full camel load of grain for this is a small amount."

66–67. Jacob replied, "I will only send him with you if you swear an oath to me in God's name: That you will bring him back to me unless you are rendered powerless." After they swore the oath he added, "God is the witness to our pledge." Then he said, "When you enter the city, each must go in by different gates. I cannot help you against God, as the decision rests with God alone. In Him I put my trust, and in Him we all must trust."

68. The brothers entered as their father had instructed them, which did not protect them against God's wishes but only fulfilled a desire of Jacob's soul. Jacob possessed a knowledge that We had given only to him and most of mankind does not know.

69. Once again with Joseph, the brother was given to him. Joseph pulled him nearby and told him, "I am your brother, so do not grieve for what the others did."

70. Once Joseph finished giving the brothers their fair provision, a drinking cup was placed inside his brother Benjamin's saddlebags. Then a man shouted, "This caravan has a thief!"

71. The brothers turned, asking, "What is it that has been lost?"

72. "We are missing the king's drinking cup. Whoever brings it forward will have a camel load," said Joseph.

73. The brothers responded, "By God we did not come to this place to cause trouble, and we are not thieves!"

74. The Egyptians asked what the penalty should be if the brothers were found to have lied.

75. The brothers said the person who has it should be held for punishment, because they believe in punishing evil.

76. When Joseph searched the bags, he found the cup in his brother's baggage. We planned this for Joseph. He could not arrest his brother by law of the king unless God willed it. We increase the wisdom of whom We please, but no matter how wise one gets, there is always one who is all-knowing.

77. The men said, "If he has stolen, then it's because he had a brother who stole before him." Joseph kept his thoughts to himself thinking, "You all are in a bad situation, because God knows the truth about what you are saying."

78. The brothers pleaded, "Ruler of the land, he has an old father, so take one of us in his place, as surely you are a gracious man."

79. He responded, "God forbids us to take another in his place, for it would be wrong to charge another with theft."

80–81. When they saw that the Egyptian wouldn't yield, they conferred in private. The eldest said, "Father made us take an oath in God's name, and previously we failed to return with Joseph, so I am not leaving this land until father allows it or God commands me, as He is the best of judges. You all return to father and tell him his son committed theft. We can only testify to what we know and cannot stop unseen acts."

82. They told Jacob, "You can ask at the town we stopped at and of the caravan we traveled with that we are telling you the truth."

83–84. Jacob spoke: "You have created a story that you believe, but my course is patience. God willing, all my sons will be brought together for me. God is all-knowing and wise." Then he turned from them and said, "How great is my sorrow for Joseph." His eyes became white with grief, and he fell silent.

85–86. The brothers said, "By God, you will not stop remembering Joseph until you ruin your health or die!" He responded, "I only tell my grief and sorrow to God, for I know things from God that you don't."

87. "Now go, sons, and look for Joseph and his brother, and never give up on gaining God's mercy. No one gives up on seeking God's mercy except the most unfaithful people."

88. Back in Joseph's place they said, "Dear ruler, our family has faced misfortune, and although we haven't enough money,

please pay us our full measure. Treat us as a charity case, for God rewards the charitable."

89. Joseph asked, "Didn't you all know what you did to Joseph and his brother in your moment of ignorance?"

90. The brothers questioned, "Are you Joseph?" He replied, "I am Joseph, and this is my brother. God has been gracious to us. God will never forget to reward those who are patient and righteous."

91–93. They admitted, "By God, it's clear God preferred you over us, and we have been sinful." He said, "On this day have no fear. God will forgive you, for He is the most merciful. Take my shirt and place it over my father's face. When he can see again, bring all your family here to me."

94–95. As the caravan was leaving Egypt, their father spoke saying, "Unless I am crazy, I sense the presence of Joseph." Those around him said, "By God, it's your old mind."

96–98. The brothers arrived and placed the shirt on his face. The father regained his sight again and said, "Do you recall that I once told you I know things from God that you do not?" The brothers begged, "Father ask for our sins to be forgiven, for we were at fault." He said, "I will ask for God's forgiveness of your sins, for He is most merciful."

99. Upon returning to Egypt, Joseph took his parents into his home and said, "Enter into Egypt safely if God wills it."

100. Joseph placed his parents on high, and they bowed down to him. He said, "Father, this is my vision fulfilled. God made it so. He was good to me when He took me from prison and then brought my family out of the desert, even though Satan had placed hatred between my brothers and me. The Lord knows all the mysteries of life's plan and is knowledgeable and wise."

101. "My Lord, you have given me power and the ability to interpret visions. You are the creator of heaven and earth. You are my protector in this life and the hereafter. Take my soul at death in submission to you, and unite me with the righteous."

102. This is one of the stories about unseen events which We reveal to you. You were not present with the brothers when they created their plans.

103–105. Yet no matter how much you try, most men will not believe you. You will not ask them for any reward for this message as it's simply a reminder for all mankind. How many signs in the heavens and earth do men pass by and still they ignore them?

106. Most men can only believe in God by associating others with Him.

107. Do men feel safe from God's coming wrath? Do they feel secure from the sudden and unknown hour of judgment?

108. Say to them, "This is My way: I invite you unto God based on clear evidence for me and whoever follows me. Glory be to God. I am not an idol worshipper or polytheist."

109. Before you We only sent messengers or apostles that were simply men that we inspired from among the humans living in the communities. Does man not travel and see the remains of the people who were punished before them? The home in the hereafter is best for those who are righteous. Have men no sense?

110. When the apostles became hopeless about converting anyone and began to think they were being fed lies from Us, that is when We began to help them, and We delivered who We chose into safety. But We never withheld Our punishment from the sinners.

111. In this history there are lessons for men that want to understand. It's not an invented story but rather a confirmation of earlier times; a detailed explanation of all things. It's a guide and a mercy to the faithful.

Chapter 54 (chronologically)

Sura 15 (99 verses), Al-Hijr

(Rock City, where the people of Thamud were said to reside)

1–3. Alif Lam Ra. These are the signs of the Book and a clear revelation [Qur'an]. The unfaithful will wish they had been

Muslims. Let the unfaithful eat, be joyful, and get distracted by desires of this life, for they will soon learn the truth.

4–5. We never destroyed a community without warning. No nation can delay or speed up their time limit.

6–9. People will say, "You, who are receiving these messages, are clearly insane. If you are being truthful, then why didn't you send an angel down to us?" We only send angels down to mankind in rare cases, and when We do, they are relentless to the unfaithful. Have no doubt We have sent down the message, and We are its protectors.

10–15. We sent many messengers to mankind throughout history, and every single apostle was mocked. We let faith pass through the souls of the guilty, for they never believe the messages and cling to their ancient and outdated ways of worship. If We opened a gate straight into heaven so they could climb right in, they would say, "Our eyes are not seeing correctly; we must be bewitched."

16–18. We have set the stars in the sky and made them beautiful to those who gaze up. We have guarded them from every cursed devil, and any that eavesdrop are pursued by a flame.

19–21. We spread the earth out like a carpet, setting the mountains firmly, and caused all suitable things to grow upon it. We made on earth many ways of subsistence for you and for other things outside your care. Everything that exists We have in our unlimited supply, and We only send it down to man in allotted amounts.

22. We control the fertilizing winds and then bring abundant rains from the sky. You are not in control of the waters.

23–25. We cause life and death and are the eternal heirs of the universe. We know who came before you and the generations to come. Your Lord will resurrect them all, for He is wise and all-knowing.

26. We create mankind by molding potter's clay drawn from mud.

27. Earlier We created the genie from an intense fire.

28–29. Your Lord said to the angels, "I am creating man from a potter's clay drawn from the mud. Once I have molded him and breathed My spirit into him, you shall bow down in respect to him."

30-35. All the angels bowed in reverence to mankind except for Iblis. God said, "Iblis, why don't you bow in respect to mankind?" Iblis replied, "I will not bow to a man that you created from clay and mud." God then cast out and cursed Iblis, a curse that would last until judgment day.

36–38. Iblis pleaded that he be pardoned of his penalty until the resurrection begins. God granted his reprieve until the appointed time.

39–40. Iblis declared to God that because He had cast Iblis into a life of evil, he would lead mankind astray in return. That he would tempt all men to evil except those that were righteous servants of God.

41–43. God replied, "The path of my righteous followers leads straight to me. You will surely not have any authority over men unless they are deviants. For hell is the promised place for them."

44. Hell has seven gates, and the seven classes of sinners will enter there.

45–48. Meanwhile, the righteous will reside among the gardens and fountains. They will enter there in peace and security. We will remove all bitterness from their souls, so they can be as brothers resting closely on raised couches. They shall not tire and never be asked to leave.

49–50. Tell My servants that I am forgiving and merciful. And that My penalty is a painful punishment.

51–57. Tell them about Abraham's guests: When the guests appeared to Abraham and said, "Peace," Abraham replied, "We are afraid of you." The guests told him not to fear, for they brought him good news of a wise son. Abraham questioned their good message, as he was an old man. They assured Abraham they spoke the truth. Abraham said, "Only those who have gone astray would despair a mercy from their Lord. Why do you messengers from God come to earth?"

58–60. They replied that they had been sent for the guilty people on earth, except for the followers of Lot, who would be saved—excluding his wife who will lag behind.

61–66. Eventually the messengers appeared to the followers of Lot. Lot declared that they were strangers to him. They replied that they arrived to end the debate about the fate of these people. "We speak the truth, so leave while there is still night left and do not lag behind or look back on this place." We revealed by decree that the guilty would all be punished by morning.

67–69. The people of the town came to see the new arrivals. Lot asked that they not disgrace him in front of the guests: "Fear God, and do not shame me."

70–72. The people said, "Didn't we forbid you from entertaining guests?" Lot replied, "Here are my daughters. Please take them if you must act out." But, the people were just wandering blindly in their intoxication.

73. An awful cry left them dead by sunrise.

74. We turned that city upside down and rained fire and brimstone on them as decreed.

75. These are signs for those willing to understand them.

76–77. The city's remnants are along the main road as a sign for the faithful to see.

78–79. Those who dwelled in the woods [Aykah] were also sinners. So We brought retribution on them. Both places are on a main road for all to see.

80–84. Those who dwelled in al-Hijr [the rocky place] also rejected the apostles. We sent them our messages, but they would not listen. They hewed out their homes in the rocky mountains and felt secure. But a mighty blast seized them by morning, and their life's works could not save them.

85–86. There was a reason We created the heavens and earth and everything in between. The hour is close at hand, so be gracious and forgiving of man. Your Lord is the all-knowing creator.

87. [MD] We have given you the seven frequently used verses [the opening chapter] and the noble Qur'an.

88–89. Do not be envious of the things We give to certain people nor grieve for them, but instead be kind to the faithful. Say to mankind, "I am but a simple messenger."

90. Just as We sent down [wrath] on those who made divisions of the Qur'an into parts, your Lord will judge them for all their deeds.

94-99. Proclaim to all what you are commanded, and separate from people that are polytheists. We will defend you from those who ridicule you. Those who worship another god besides God will soon learn the truth. We know you are distressed by their comments. So celebrate loudly the praise of your Lord, and be among those who bow to Him. Serve your Lord until death arrives.

Chapter 55 (chronologically)

Sura 6 (165 verses), Al-Anam (The Cattle or Livestock)

1. Praise be to God the creator of heaven and earth, who made the darkness and the light. Yet the unfaithful still hold up others as equal to God.

2. He created you from clay and gave you a limited life, its length known only to Him. Yet you still have doubts.

3. He is God of the heavens and earth. He knows everything you utter in secret and in public and knows the worth of your deeds in life.

4–5. Every single sign the Lord revealed to them was ignored. Those that rejected the truth when it was revealed to them will soon learn the truth about what they mocked.

6. Don't they see the generations before them We destroyed? We built them stronger than your current community with a plentiful earth and abundant rains that made flowing streams.

Yet because of their sins, We destroyed them and created another generation.

7. If We sent them the messages written on parchment that they could hold in their hands, the unfaithful would say, "This is just magic."

8–9. They ask, "Why didn't you send an angel to us?" But if We sent them an angel, he would resolve the matter at once without more time for mankind to reflect on the issue. If we had sent Our messenger as an angel, We would have him appear as a man, so he could talk to men. This would have surely made the matter even more confused than it is.

10. Many messengers were mocked before you, but those who ridiculed were eventually overpowered by the things they mocked.

11. Tell them to travel around the land to see what happens to those who reject Our message.

12. Ask them, "Who do the heavens and earth belong to?" Tell them, "It is God, and He has the power to give mercy. He will gather you all together on the day of judgment. Those who will not be faithful have lost their own souls."

13. Everything that exists in the day and night belongs to Him. He hears all and knows all.

14–16. Ask them, "Shall I ask another besides God to be my protector? When He is the creator of heaven and the earth and feeds everyone but needs no nourishment? No. I was commanded to be the first to submit to God and to never be one of the polytheists. If I disobeyed my Lord, I would fear a great penalty on an important day. On that day, only God's mercy can save a soul. Salvation would be a signal triumph."

17–18. If God gives you an illness, only He can remove it. He can give you happiness, for He has power over all things. He reigns supreme over all His servants and is all-knowing and wise.

19. Ask them, "What gives the most weight as a witness in testimony? God! God is the witness between us, and this Qur'an has been revealed to me so that I may warn you and everyone it reaches. Do you testify that there are other gods other than God? I cannot say that. There is one God, and I am not to blame for any others you associate with Him."

20. [MD] Everyone that has received this Book must recognize its truth as they recognize their own sons. Those who choose not to believe it damn their own souls.

21. Is there anyone more sinful than someone who lies against God or rejects His revelations? The evildoers will never prosper.

22. When We gather them all together, We will ask them who attributed any partners to God and then make them present those associates.

23. [MD] They will have no excuses and will say, "God, we were never polytheists."

24. See how they harm their own souls with their lies. A lie that will fail them in the end.

25–26. Some of the people that pretend to listen to you We gave hardened hearts and deaf ears, for even if they saw all the signs, they would not find faith. When they come to you to argue, they will say, "These are just stories of ancient times." Some forbid themselves and others from the message, but they don't know they only destroy their own souls.

27–28. When they are confronted with the fire, they will beg to be sent back to earth, so they could accept the signs of their Lord, so they could be among the faithful. But they would only say it to save themselves when faced with the truth that they had been denying. They would only return to sin if they had it to do over again. They are liars.

29–31. Some say that there is nothing after their lives on earth and that there won't be a resurrection. But when they stand before God, He will ask them, "Is this real?" and they will admit it is. Then they will receive their punishment for rejecting the faith. Those who reject the existence of judgment day will be lost when they stand in front of God. They will grieve for not accepting it and will bear all of their burdensome misdeeds on their shoulders alone.

32. The hereafter is the true life, while this current one is but a pastime. Don't you understand?

33–34. We know that their words cause you grief. It is not you they reject. These sinners reject the message of God. Apostles before you felt rejection, but they were patient under persecution until We aided them. No one can alter the words of God. You have already received some accounts of the previous messengers.

35. If their rejection becomes too much for you, then you can try to find a tunnel into the earth or a ladder into the sky to retrieve a sign for them. Look, if it was God's will, He would have already made all men faithful. Be patient and do not be swayed by the ignorant.

36. Only those who truly listen will accept the message. Don't worry about the dead, for when God raises them up they will become faithful.

37. They will ask, "Why didn't God send us a sign from above?" Tell them, "God has the power to send down a sign, but most of them won't understand it."

38. Every living creature on earth is living in a community like you. We have left nothing out of the Book. They will all be gathered back to God.

39. Those who reject Our signs are deaf and dumb, wandering in the dark. God can will who He likes to wander aimlessly or to move on the straight path.

40–41. Ask them, "Answer me truthfully. If you found yourself facing the wrath of God on judgment day, would you call out for another god besides Him? Of course not; you will call upon God to remove your sins if He chooses to. You will forget your false gods."

42–45. We sent messengers before you to many communities. We afflicted the people with suffering and trials so that they might learn to be humble. But did they become humble during our affliction? No. Instead their hearts hardened, and Satan made their sins appealing to them. Later when they forgot the warnings we sent them, We showered them with good things. And while they were rejoicing in their fortune, We suddenly brought them to judgment, and they fell into despair. In this way We found the last of the sinners. Praise be to God, Lord of the worlds.

46. Ask them, "If God took away your sight and hearing and hardened your hearts, is there any other god besides God that could restore you?" See how We can give the revelations in many ways, but they still reject the message?

47. Ask them, "If God's punishment arrived on a schedule or all of a sudden, would anyone die besides the unjust people?"

48–49. We send apostles simply to bear Our good tidings and to send a warning. Those who are faithful and follow a righteous path shall have nothing to fear and will not grieve. Those who reject Our revelations will find torment, for they did not change their ways.

50. Say to them, “I do not claim to have the treasures of God, or know the future, or to be an angel; but I follow what is revealed to me. Can the blind man be equal to a man with sight? Won’t you reflect on this?”

51. With this Qur’an, warn the people that fear being brought before their Lord on judgment day, so that they will live righteously. There is no one that can intercede for them except for God.

52. Do not send away those who pray to their Lord, seeking his favor at morning and evening. You won’t be accountable for their actions, nor they for yours. So don’t become one of the unjust by turning them away.

53. When We have judged some people in comparison to others, they dare to say, “How is it that God finds those people to be better than us?” Doesn’t God know who His most grateful followers are?”

54. When faithful people who believe in Our signs speak to you, say, “Peace be upon you.” Your Lord has the power of mercy, so when people commit sin out of ignorance and then get

back on the straight path, He can forgive. He is most merciful.

55. We explain Our messages in detail, so that the unrighteous ways are clear.

56. Say to them, "I am forbidden to worship any gods other than God that you worship. I will not follow your ways, for if I do, then I will stray from the righteous path."

57. Say to them, "I stand on the revelations from my Lord, while you reject Him. What you seek to speed up is not in my power to do. He declares what is true and is the wisest of judges."

58. Tell them, "If I had power to hasten what you seek, then the matter would have been settled already. But God knows best who is unjust."

59. He holds the keys to unknown treasures. He knows everything about the earth and sea. No leaf may fall without His awareness. Every grain in the darkness and everything, whether fresh or withered, is written clearly in the Book.

60. He examines your soul every night and knows what you did in the day. He raises you up daily until you reach the end of your life, and then you return to Him. Then He will reveal your record to you.

61–62. He is supreme over all His servants, and He provides guardians to you. When death nears any of you, His angels never fail to take their soul. Then they are taken to God, their just master. He alone gives a judgment, and He is swift in His reckoning.

63-64. Ask them, "Who will deliver you from the darkness of the lands or sea, when you call out humbled and frightened? When you are secretly saying that you will be truly grateful to Him if He rescues you?" Tell them, "It is God that delivers you from these and other horrible situations, and yet you still associate partners to Him!"

65. Say to them, "He has the power to punish you from above and below or to confuse your people with dissension, making you violent towards each other." Notice how We explain our messages in various ways, so that they are understood.

66. Your people reject this revelation, although it is the truth. Say to them, "I am not in charge of you."

67. Every prophesy has a set date to occur, and soon you will know of it.

68–69. When you hear men mocking Our revelations, stay away from them until they change the topic. If Satan causes you to forget this, then once you remember it, do not congregate with the sinners. The righteous are not accountable for the deeds of those who mock, but it is their duty to remind them that they too can be righteous.

70. Abandon those who treat their religion as mere amusement or a joke and have been seduced by the present life. Instead proclaim to mankind this message: That every man must pay for his misdeeds. That they will find that no one can intercede on their behalf except God and that no amount of money will be accepted. Those who have acted in ways that lead to punishment will only be able to drink boiling water in a painful hell for rejecting God.

71. Say to them, "Shall we invoke other gods besides God, who have no power to help or hurt us, and turn our backs after we have received guidance from God? Shall we be like the fools that devils have taken off the straight path to wander the earth bewildered, even as his friends try to show him the righteous way?" Tell them, "God's guidance is the only way, and we have been commanded to submit ourselves to the Lord of the worlds."

72. Tell them to establish regular prayers and to fear God. We shall all be returned back to God.

73. He created the heavens and earth. On that day when He says "Be!" it will be so. His word is the truth. He will be the king on the day the trumpet calls. He knows the visible and invisible. He is wise and aware of all things.

74–75. Recall when Abraham said to his father Azar, "Do you worship idols as gods? Then I can see your people are obviously wrong." We had shown Abraham the kingdom of heaven and earth so that he would be sure of his faith.

76–79. When he saw a star appear at night, he said, "That is my Lord." But after it set, he said, "I don't love the setting stars." Then he saw the moon rise, and he said, "This is my Lord." But when the moon set, he said, "If my Lord had not given me guidance, I would surely be among those gone astray." Then he saw the sun rising and cried, "This is my Lord, for it's the greatest of all." But when the sun set, he said, "My people, I am not responsible for your sins in associating partners with God. I have dedicated myself entirely to He who created the heavens and the earth. I shall never be a polytheist."

80. Abraham's people argued with him, and he asked, "How can you dispute me about God, when He is guiding me? I do not fear anything that you associate with God. Nothing happens without God's will. He is all-knowing. Listen to my warning."

81–82. Why should I fear any beings you associate with God, when you have associated them with God without His permission? Of the two of us, who should be frightened? Those who are faithful and do not contaminate their faith with sins are truly safe on the righteous path.

83. That was the logic We gave to Abraham to correct his people. We can improve one's wisdom in stages as We see fit, for your Lord is wise and knowledgeable.

84–87. We bestowed Abraham with Isaac and Jacob, and we guided all three of them. Before that we guided Noah and his offspring, David, Solomon, Job, Joseph, Moses, and Aaron. We reward the righteous. Also righteous were Zachariah, John, and Jesus. We gave favor to Ishmael, Elisha, Jonas, and Lot. We chose them from among their fathers, brother, and offspring to be guided on the righteous path.

88–89. God gives guidance to whomever He pleases from His servants. But if any of them sets up others in association with God, then all their good works will be useless. These were the men We gave the Book, authority, and prophethood. If any of their descendants reject the faith, We will entrust those powers to another faithful generation.

90. Follow the ways of the prophets that received God's guidance. Say to men, "I ask no money from you, as this is a message to all nations."

91. [MD] They disrespect God when they say that God never passed anything to man by revelation. Ask them, "Who revealed the Book to Moses? The Book was a guiding light for mankind, but you have placed the Book on separate sheets, and you show what you like and conceal most parts from people. Yet through the Book, you and your people were taught things you never knew. God sent down the Book!" Then leave the people to their futile discussion.

92. Blessed is the Book We have revealed to you. It confirms the earlier revelations and warns the people of Mecca and outlying areas. Those who believe in the hereafter believe in this Book and worship carefully.

93. [MD] The most wicked people lie about God, or say they have received inspiration when they have not, or say they can create the words like those that God reveals. If only they could see how these wicked men will suffer in the hereafter. The angels will reach to them saying, "Give us your souls, for this day you will receive your shameful penalty for lying about God and rejecting His signs."

94. Men will return to Us alone just as We created them, leaving behind their worldly goods. No false gods will be there to help them, as the bonds between them will be broken, and the promises will go unkept.

95. God causes the split in the seed grain and the date stone so they may sprout. He brings the dead to life and the living to death. This is your God. Why do you go astray?

96. He created night and day. He made the night for rest and solitude. He gave us the moon and sun to measure time. These are examples of the judgment and precision of the all-knowing and powerful.

97. He made the stars so you may navigate the dark on land or at sea. We have made Our revelations clear for people to recognize.

98. He made you from a single person. He gave you a place for temporary and permanent lodging. We make Our revelations detailed for those who understand.

99. He sends down rains, and with it We produce vegetation like crops that produce grain, dates, grapes, olives, and pomegranates. Each is similar yet differs in variety. As the vegetation bears fruits, look at it as it ripens. In these things are signs for the faithful.

100. Some think genies equal to God; although God did create them, they are not. Some falsely attribute sons and daughters to God with no knowledge of the truth. Praise God, for He is supreme above everyone people ascribe to him.

101. He is the original creator of heaven and earth. How can He have a son when He has no spouse? He created all things and is all-knowing.

102. God is your Lord! There is no god but God. He created all things, so worship Him as He takes care of all matters.

103. He cannot be seen, but He sees all things. He is aware of the most subtle things.

104. Signs have been shown to you from your Lord so you may see the truth and better your soul. If you choose not to see, then you only harm yourself. I am not your guardian.

105. We explain revelations to you in various ways so that no one can say you have simply read this in the books. This also helps make the revelations clear to intelligent people.

106. Follow the revelations inspired by your Lord, for there is no god but God. Stay clear of polytheists.

107. If God willed it, they would not take up false gods. We did not appoint you as man's keeper, and you are not responsible for them.

108. Do not condemn people who call upon others besides God, so that they don't spitefully insult God in their ignorance. We have made all people feel their deeds are fair. When they return to God, He will tell them the truth of their deeds.

109–110. They swear to God that if they see an actual sign from God they will believe it. So, say to them, "All signs are only from God. What is it that makes you not believe when you see the signs?" We shall confuse their hearts and eyes for refusing to believe in the first signs, and they will wander blindly.

111. Even if We sent them angels, made the dead speak, and brought all the signs together for them, they would not believe, unless God willed it. Most of them ignore the truths.

112–113. Every prophet is provided an enemy, someone evil, to lead men astray with flowery lies and treachery. If God willed it, they could not lead them astray, so ignore them and their lies. Let those who don't believe in the hereafter be deceived and delight in the lies, for they will pay for their deeds.

114. [MD] Say to men, "Why should I ask for another to judge me besides God? It was He that sent us this detailed Book." They know that this Book was truly sent from their Lord. Do not be among the doubtful.

115. The words of your Lord have been realized in truth and justice. No one can change His words. He hears all and knows all.

116. If you followed the majority of people in life, they would lead you from the righteous path. They base life on opinions and make guesses.

117. Your Lord knows who goes astray and who follows His guidance.

118–119. Eat only meats slaughtered while God's name was invoked if you are faithful. Why would you eat meats that were slaughtered without God being invoked [Halal] after He explained to you what is forbidden, except for emergency situations? Many people give in to their desires and their ignorance. Your Lord knows who sins.

120. Stop sinning, openly or in secret, for you shall receive what you earn on judgment day.

121. Eating meats that weren't slaughtered while invoking God is a sin. Evil ones have caused people to dispute this. If you listen to them and eat wrongly, you will be among the polytheists.

122. Can these two people be equal? We gave life to one and a guiding light as he walks among men. And the other lives in eternal darkness that he can't escape. The unfaithful think their actions are correct or fair.

123–124. We have created powerful evil men in every community to conspire. Yet they don't know that they only plot against their own souls. When signs come to them from God they say, "We will only believe messages if delivered to us like God's apostles receive them." God knows best who He gives His messages to and how to carry out His mission. Soon the evil ones will be humiliated and punished severely by God for their scheming.

125. God wills the faithful to the righteous path and wills whom He likes to go astray. God will heap punishment on the unfaithful.

126–127. This is the righteous path of your Lord. We have explained the revelations clearly for those who are faithful. They will have a peaceful home with their Lord. He will protect them for their righteousness.

128. On the day when He gathers everyone together, God will describe to the genies how many humans they seduced. The human followers of the genies will say, "Lord we benefited from each other, but now our time is up." God will tell them, "You will stay forever in the fire unless I remove you." Your Lord is wise and knowledgeable.

129. We let some sinners influence others because of what they earn.

130. Men and genies, didn't messengers come to you delivering Our signs and warning you of this day? They will reply, "We are testifying against ourselves." The earthly life seduced them, so they shall testify against themselves that they did not believe.

131. Your Lord does not destroy communities that are ignorant of their sins without first sending a messenger.

132. God knows everything that man does, and there will be degrees of judgment for their deeds.

133. Your Lord is supreme and merciful. If He wills it, He could destroy you and replace you with others, just as He raised you from the seed of other people.

134. All these promises will occur, and you cannot avoid them.

135. Say to them, "People, strive with all your might, just as I am striving. Soon we will know who will have a better hereafter. Know that the sinner will not prosper.

136. Polytheists claim to assign shares of their crops and cattle to God and other shares to the partners they ascribe to God. But the portions assigned for the ascribed partners don't go to God, and the portions assigned to God go to the "partners." This is an evil assignment of portions.

137. The so-called partners of God have made killing their children seem correct, in order to ruin their community and make their religion confusing. If God willed it, they would not have done so. Leave these people alone to their folly.

138. Some have said that certain cattle and crops are forbidden and that no one should eat them, unless they are told to. Some say that certain cattle are not allowed to be yoked or carry a load, and that you can't invoke God's name over some cattle during slaughter. These are lies against God and they will be punished for them.

139. Some say that what is in the womb of a cow is reserved for the men and not the women, but if it is stillborn then both can eat it. These lies against God will be punished, for He is wise and knowledgeable.

140. The people who foolishly kill their children out of ignorance and forbid foods that God has provided are lost, and they lie against God. They have gone astray and are not following His guidance.

141. Men who produce gardens with vines, and dates, olives and pomegranates should eat fruit in its season; but pay your dues on the harvest date and don't be wasteful. God despises the wasteful.

142. Some cows were created for burden and others for meat. Eat what God has provided you, and don't follow the path of Satan, for he is your enemy.

143. Ask of men, "Given eight head of livestock in pairs: two of sheep and two of goats. Has God forbidden two males or two females or what is in the wombs of the females? If you are honest, explain this to me with your knowledge."

144. Ask of men, "Given a pair of camels and a pair of oxen, has God forbidden the two males, two females, or the animals in the wombs of the females? Were you there when God ordered this? Who can be more wrong than to lie against God and lead men astray when they have no knowledge of such things? God does not guide the unjust.

145. Say to mankind, "The only revelations about forbidden foods sent to me are as follows: meat from animals found dead, bloody meat, the flesh of swine, or animals slaughtered while invoking someone other than God. In an emergency if man must eat of these animals for survival, God is most merciful."

146. For the Jewish people, every animal with an undivided hoof is forbidden and also the fat of the ox and sheep unless it's

attached to their backs, in the entrails, or attached to the bone. This is a punishment for their disobedience. We speak the truth.

147. If they lie to you, say to them, "Your Lord is merciful, but He never withholds punishment from the guilty.

148. When the polytheists say, "If God willed it, we would not have given partners to God, nor would our fathers have done so, nor would we have made anything forbidden." Remember their ancestors argued against the revelations until We brought Our wrath. Ask of them, "Do you have any revelations to share with us? If so produce it now. You follow nothing but opinions and continue to guess."

149. Say to them, "God has the final word, and if He had willed it, He could have been a guide to you all."

150. Say to them, "If you have witnesses that can prove God forbade certain things, bring them to us." If they bring out any such witnesses, then do not testify with them. Don't follow the requests of people who deny Our revelation, do not believe in the hereafter, or worship others as an equal to God.

151. [MD] Say to them, "Listen and I will list what God has forbidden. Do not equate anything as equal to God; treat your parents well; do not kill your children because you fear poverty, for We will provide your sustenance; do not act vulgar in private or public; do not kill a soul that God made

sacred, unless it's in the name of justice within the law." These are God's commands, so now you are informed.

152. [MD] Do not touch an orphan's wealth unless you increase it, before he becomes mature. Fairly give full measure and weight. We place no burden on any soul unless they can bear it. Whenever you speak, speak the truth, even if it's about a close relative. Fulfill your promises with God. He commands this so be careful.

153. [MD] This is My [God's] straight path, so follow it and do not stray. Other paths will lead you away from His way. He commands this so that you may be righteous.

154. We gave Moses the Book in reward for being righteous, and it explained all things in detail. It was a guide and mercy for those that might believe in the hereafter.

155. We now reveal this Book as a blessing. Follow its path and be righteous so you may receive mercy.

156–157. Some may say, "This Book was revealed to two communities before us, and we somehow did not know what it said." Or some may say, "If the Book had been revealed to us, we would have followed it more closely than they did." Remember that clear signs from your Lord, a guide and a mercy, have already been sent. So who is more wrong than someone that rejects God's signs and ignores them? Soon those who turn away from the revelations will meet a dreadful punishment.

158. It's as if they are waiting for an angel to come to them, or for the Lord himself to appear or send them a certain sign. On the day that certain signs appear from God it will be too late for those who did not have faith before or earn reward from good deeds. Tell them, "You must wait, and We are waiting too."

159. Do not bother with those people that break up their religion into sects. Their issues are with God, and God will tell them the truth about what they have done.

160. Those who do good deeds shall be rewarded ten for one. Those who commit sins will be rewarded in equal amount. Everyone will be dealt with justly.

161. Say to them, "My Lord guides me on the straight path, the same righteous path that Abraham walked. He was righteous and was not a polytheist."

162. Say to them, "My worship and sacrifice, my living and my dying are all done for God, the Lord of the worlds.

163. God has no partner. Of this I was commanded, and I am the first person to submit to His will.

164. Say to them, "Why should I seek any lord besides God, for He is the Lord of all things? Everyone's soul earns its own reward or punishment. No one may bear another's burden.

When you return to God, He will explain where you went wrong.

165. He made you the successors of earth. He made some of you rank above others so that He may test you about the gifts He gave you. Your Lord is swift in punishment, but He is forgiving and merciful.

Chapter 56 (chronologically)

Sura 37 (182 verses), Al-Saffat (Those Arranged in Ranks)

1–3. I swear by those who are drawn up in ranks, who are strong in repelling or driving, and those who recite the message of God.

4–5. Your Lord is certainly one. The Lord of the heavens and the earth and everything in between; and the Lord of the sun's rising points.

6–7. We decorated the heaven nearest to earth with stars to protect you from rebellious devils.

8–10. They cannot overhear the exalted ones talk, for they are attacked from every side. They are outcasts in perpetual torment, except ones that steal a fragment, but they are pursued by shining flames.

11. Ask of them, "Are they a stronger creation than those We have created?" We created them of malleable clay.

12–18. You marvel, while they ridicule. And when they are warned, they pay no attention. And when they see a sign, they mock it saying, "This is nothing but magic." They ask, "When we die, our dust and bones will somehow be resurrected? And our ancestors too?" Answer them, "Yes. And you will be humiliated."

19–23. There will be just a single cry, and they will see. They will say, "What misery; this is the day of judgment." This is the day of judgment that you denied. The unjust and their wives and things they worshipped instead of God will be gathered and led to hell.

24–32. On the way to hell, they will be questioned: "Why aren't you helping each other today?" On that day they will be submissive. They will begin to question one another: "It was you that came to us swearing you knew the truth." "No you were unfaithful." "We had no power over you, but you were rebellious." "The promise of our Lord has come true, and we are about to face doom." "We misled you, and we were on the wrong path."

33–34. On that day, they all shall share in the penalty. That is how We deal with the sinners.

35–37. When those people were told that there was no god but God, they were disrespectful. They said, "You expect us to give up our gods for the ramblings of a mad poet?" Actually, he brought them the truth and confirmed the messages of the apostles before him.

38–40. Everyone, except the sincere servants of God, will endure a painful punishment. But you will only be punished for what you did.

41–47. For the faithful there is a special sustenance. They will eat fruits and be honored in the gardens of pleasure, facing each other on couches. They will pass around a cup from a clear fountain; the fluid is crystal white and tastes delicious. Those who drink it will not get intoxicated or feel headaches.

48–49. Beside them, will be virtuous women with big eyes that look like delicate and guarded eggs.

50–53. Some will speak to each other and say, "I had a close friend on earth that used to question why I was a faithful person who believed in the messages. He questioned how we could rise up from dust and bones after death to face judgment."

54–57. A voice would say, "Look down!" And when they look down, they would see his close friend in the depths of hell. He would yell down, "You almost lured me into hell with you. If not for the grace of my Lord, I would have been there with you."

58–61. They will ask, "Is it true we shall not die again and that we shall not be punished? This is a supreme accomplishment. Everyone should strive for this result."

62–68. That is a better welcoming than the tree of Zaqqum. We have made it as a torment for the sinners. It is a tree that is rooted in the bottom of hell. Its fruits are like the heads of devils. They must eat from the tree until they are full, and then they have to drink boiling water. Finally, they get to return to the blazing fires of hell.

69–72. They saw that their fathers were going astray, but still they rushed down the same path. Their ancestors went astray, even though We had sent them messengers.

73–74. Remember what We did to everyone that was warned; We spared only Our most devoted worshippers.

75–82. When Noah prayed to Us, We were gracious and saved him and his people from agony. We made his descendants the successors on earth, and We made his name honorable in history: "Peace to Noah, among all the people!" We reward the righteous, and Noah was one of Our most faithful. The others, We drowned.

83–87. Abraham was one of Noah's followers and came to his Lord with a pure heart. When Abraham went to his father and his people he asked, "What do you worship? Do you desire gods other than God? A falsehood? What is your understanding of the Lord of the worlds?"

88–90. Then he looked up at the stars and said, "I feel sickened!" They turned from Abraham and walked away.

91–96. Abraham then went to find their "gods." He asked, "Why don't you eat the offerings they place before you? Why don't you answer me? Can't you speak?" Then he swung at them with his right hand, and the worshippers came running in the sanctuary. He asked, "Why do you worship things you carved yourselves when God has created you and all that you create?"

97–98. They planned to build a furnace and throw him into its fires, but We caused their plot to fail.

99. Abraham said, "I will follow the sure guidance of my Lord."

100–101. He prayed, "My Lord, grant me a righteous son." And so, We told him to expect a patient son. [Although not specified by name here, this section of the chapter refers to Ishmael.]

102. When his son reached working age, Abraham told him that in a vision he saw himself having to sacrifice his son. Abraham asked his son for his thoughts. The son replied, "Father you must do as you are commanded, and God willing you will see that I am unwavering."

103. Having both submitted to the will of God, Abraham placed his son face down for sacrifice.

104–109. Then We called out to him [before he killed his son], "Abraham, you have already fulfilled your vision!" We always reward the righteous. This was an obvious trial. We rewarded him for this tremendous sacrifice and have given him an honorable place in history: "Peace be upon Abraham!"

110–113. We reward the virtuous, and he was one of Our faithful servants. We next gave him the news of the pending birth of Isaac, a righteous prophet. We blessed him and Isaac, although some of their offspring were righteous, and others were clearly unjust even to their own souls.

114–122. We also bestowed Our grace on Moses and Aaron. We saved them and their people from catastrophe and helped them to be victorious. We gave them an illuminating scripture and guided them on the straight path. We praised them for future generations to remember: "Peace unto Moses and Aaron!" We reward the righteous, and they were two of Our faithful servants.

123–132. Elias was also one of Our messengers. He asked his people, "Will you not be righteous? Why do you call on Baal instead of God, the creator, your Lord and the Lord of your ancestors?" But they rejected him, and so every one of them that is not a worshipper of God will be punished with doom. We gave blessings to his name so later generations can praise: "Peace be upon Elias!" We reward the righteous, and he was one of Our faithful servants.

133–138. Lot was one of Our messengers, so We saved him and his followers, except an old woman who We destroyed with the others. You pass by their ruins daily, but still you do not understand?

139–148. We sent Jonah as a messenger. He had joined a ship's crew and was forced to cast lots to see who would be tossed overboard. He drew short. In the sea a large fish swallowed him for his sin. Luckily, he was respectful to God, or else he would have remained in the fish. We brought him sickly from the fish and onto a deserted shore. We caused a gourd tree to grow above him. Then We sent him to a large community of at least a hundred thousand, and they became faithful, so We let them enjoy their lives.

149–150. Ask them, "What is your opinion? Did God create only daughters, and are men only born of women? Did you actually witness God making female angels?"

151–157. They surely lie when they say God has children! Did He prefer daughters over sons? What is your problem? How can you decide these things? Will you not heed warning? Do you have some authority? If you speak the truth, show me your written authority!

158. They have invented a familial relationship between Him and the genies. The genies know that they too have to face His judgment.

159–163. Glory be to God! Except for what His faithful servants reveal about Him, He is innocent of what people say about him. Neither you nor those that you worship will have your lies about God believed, unless the listener is bound for hell.

164–166. None of us has an assigned place; even though we are the ones arranged in ranks; even though we celebrate the glory of God.

167–170. Some said, "If only we could see a sign from the old messengers, we would become faithful servants only to God." Yet, now that the revelations have come, they reject them. Soon they will learn.

171–173. We have already sent Our word to benefit our faithful, and our messengers and make them triumphant. Our people will be victors.

174–175. So turn away from the unfaithful for a while, and watch them learn.

176–177. Do they ask Us to give Our punishment to them sooner? When it descends on them, it will be an evil morning for the unfaithful who rejected the message.

178–179. So turn away from the unfaithful for a while, and watch them learn.

180–182. Glorious is your Lord, the Lord of honor, which does not resemble what they say about him. Peace be on the messengers and praise be to God, the Lord of the worlds.

Chapter 57 (chronologically)

Sura 31 (34 verses), Al-Luqman

(Luqman's account is given in this chapter)

1–5. Alif. Lam. Meem. These are the revelations of the definitive book. A guide and mercy for the righteous men who pray regularly, give to charity, and are faithful and confident about the hereafter. Those who follow their Lord's guidance will be successful.

6. The men that buy amusing dialogue so they can mislead ignorant men from the straight path of God and ridicule it the righteous way, will earn a humiliating punishment.

7. Inform the men of their painful penalty if they turn from you in contempt, as if they were deaf, when you recite Our signs.

8–9. For those who are faithful and righteous, there is an eternal Garden of happiness. That is the promise of God the almighty and wise.

10. He created the heavens that seem to float in the sky; He placed the mountains firmly on the earth; He scattered beasts of all kinds on the earth. We sent down the rains and caused a variety of plants to grow.

11. These are the creations of God. Show me what anyone other than God has created? The sinners are clearly wrong.

12. We gave wisdom to Luqman: "Give thanks to God. Tell whoever gives thanks that it benefits their soul. Tell the unthankful that God is self-sufficient and worthy of their praise."

13. Luqman taught his son, "Never associate any partners with God, for false worship [polytheism] is a grave sin."

14. We have asked man to respect his parents, for his mother carried him and weaned him. Give thanks to your parents and to Me, for you will return to Me.

15. But if your parents ask you to worship things other than Me or give me partners, for which you have no authority, do not obey them. Continue to be kind to them, but follow those who are on the righteous path to Me. You will return to me, and I will recount your deeds.

16. My son, He taught, whether it is just the weight of a mustard seed hidden in a rock, in the heavens, or on the earth, God can see it. God knows all the subtleties and is always aware.

17. My son, pray regularly; take part in good things and forbid evil. Remain patient in all situations; this will require courage.

18. Don't act proud towards others or walk rudely through life, for God does not love conceited braggers.

19. Exhibit modest behavior and speak respectfully. The harshest voice is a braying ass.

20. Can't you see that God has made everything in the heavens and the earth obedient to you? He has showered you with blessings inside and out. Still there are people that argue about God when they are ignorant, have no guide, and have no scripture.

21. When they are told to follow God's revelations they reply, "No, we will just worship the way our fathers did." Satan is calling them to the flames of hell.

22. Whoever submits completely to God and does good deeds has the best grasp on paradise. God decides everyone's ending.

23–24. If anyone rejects the faith, do not let it bother you. They will return to Us, and We will tell them about their deeds. God is aware of everything in a man's heart. We will let them enjoy a little comfort and then cast them into unrelenting punishment.

25. If you ask them who created the heavens and earth, they will surely say it was God. Tell them, "Praise be to God!" But most of them do not understand.

26. Everything on heaven and earth belongs to God. God wants for nothing and is worthy of praise.

27. [MD] Even if all the trees on earth were pens and all the oceans, filled with seven more oceans, were ink, God would not run out of words to be written. God is almighty and wise.

28. [MD] Your creation and resurrection are only of a single soul. God hears and knows all.

29. [MD] Can't you see that God turns night into day and day into night? That He controls the sun and the moon, setting their course and movements? That God is aware of all you do?

30. This is because God is the truth, and anyone people invoke besides Him is false. God is magnificent, the greatest.

31. Can't you see how ships sail on the waters by the grace of God, showing you His signs? The signs are there for those who are patient and thankful.

32. If a wave covers them like a canopy, they cry for God, offering Him their faith. But once He delivers them to dry land, there are some who don't fully believe. Those who reject Our signs are ungrateful traitors.

33. Mankind, do your duty for your Lord, and fear the day when no father can vouch for his son, nor any son vouch for his father. The promise of God is true. Don't let this life distract you or let Satan deceive you about God.

34. Only God is aware of the hour. He sends down the rains. He knows what's in the womb. No soul knows what they will merit tomorrow, and no one knows where they will die. God is all-knowing and fully aware.

Chapter 58 (chronologically)

Sura 34 (54 verses), Saba (Sheba)

1–2. Praise be to God, the ruler of the heavens and the earth. Praise be to Him in the hereafter, for He is wise and aware of all things. He knows of everything going into or out of the earth; everything that leaves or enters the sky. He is merciful and compassionate.

3–4. When the unfaithful say that the hour will never come, say, "By God, it will come from He who knows even the unseen. From Him not even an atom can be hidden in the heavens or on the earth. Everything, great and small, is recorded in the Book, so He can reward the faithful and righteous with forgiveness and bountiful meals.

5. For those who try to oppose Our revelations, there will be a painful and humiliating punishment.

6. People who see the revelations as truth and are guided on the righteous path are worthy of praise.

7–8. When the unfaithful will say, "If we show you a man that believes our bones and dust will be recreated again, is he a liar or crazy?" Say to them, "It is those who don't believe in the hereafter that are wrong and will be tormented."

9. Can they not see what is before them and behind them? The sky and the earth? If We willed it, We could have the earth

swallow them, or make the sky fall on them. There is a sign for every worshipper that submits to God repentantly.

10–11. We gave David grace: "Mountains and birds echo the psalms of praise." We made iron supple in his hands: "Make coats of chain mail with measured chain links; make them right, for I see all you do."

12–13. We made the wind obedient to Solomon, making a month's journey in the morning and another in the evening. We made him a fountain of molten copper, and We gave him genies to work under his command. Any genies that deviated from Our command felt the penalty of fire. They made whatever he asked: temples, statues, reservoir-sized basins, and caldrons affixed to the ground. Give thanks, sons of David! But few of my servants are grateful.

14. When We decreed his death, only a worm gnawing on his staff foretold of it. So when he fell dead, the genies realized that if they knew the future they would not have stayed toiling for him.

15–16. For Sheba there was a sign in their homeland. Two gardens stood to its right and left. "Eat of the provisions of your Lord, and give thanks! A good land and forgiving Lord." But they rejected God, and so We sent a flood from the dams, and the gardens then bore bitter fruit, tamarisks, and some lote trees.

17. That was the retaliation We gave them because of their ingratitude. Do we punish anyone besides the ungrateful?

18–19. In between them and the other cities We had blessed, We made them easy to find and made journeys between them easy and safe by night and day. But they complained, saying, "Lord make the journey stages longer between us." They had wronged themselves, so We made them but a tale in history and scattered them completely. There are signs for every patient and grateful soul.

20–21. Iblis [Satan] proved his beliefs about them, as all but a few believers followed his path. He had no authority over them, but We may test any man to see if he believes in the hereafter, as your Lord takes note of all things.

22–23. Say to them, "Call upon those you worship besides God, for they have no power to move even an atom in heaven and earth. They have no partnership with God, and none of them are His helpers. No one can intercede for you unless He lets them. But when fear is removed from their hearts, a voice will ask, 'What did your Lord say?' and they will reply, 'The truth. He is the highest, the greatest?'"

24. Ask them, "Who gives you sustenance from the heavens and earth? God does! So one of us is righteous, and one of us is gravely mistaken."

25–26. Say to them, “You will not be asked about our sins, and we will not be asked about yours. Our Lord will gather us, and He will judge us fairly, for He is the best judge and knows everything.”

27. Say to them, “Show me those you have associated as partners to God! You can’t of course, because He is God, the mighty and wise.”

28. We sent you solely as a messenger to all men to share the good news and warn them. Most men don’t understand.

29-30. They will ask, “If you are truthful, then tell us when His promise will come true?” Respond to them, “You have an appointment for a day that cannot be postponed or moved up.”

31–33. The unfaithful will say, “We do not believe in these revelations or any that came before.” If only you could see them argue with each other when they are standing in front of God for judgment. The despised will say to the arrogant, “If it wasn’t for you, we would have been faithful.” Then the arrogant will yell at the despised, “You blame us? You rejected the signs that were shown to you. You are the guilty ones.” The despised will reply, “No, you plotted night and day and ordered us to reject God and to worship others in His place as equals.” They will all declare their repentance once they witness the punishment. We shall shackle the necks of the unfaithful, but they will only be punished for their exact deeds.

34–38. Whenever We sent a messenger to a community, the wealthiest would say, "We don't believe what you are saying. We have more money and sons than you and shall not be punished." Say to them, "My Lord can make whoever He wants wealthy or poor, but most people don't know this." It is not your wealth or the number of sons you have that will bring people closer to Us. Only those who believe and are righteous in deed will get an expanded reward and rest safely in the best parts of heaven. And those who fight to stop our messages will be rewarded with doom.

39. Say to them, "My Lord can enlarge or decrease the sustenance for His servants as He wishes. Whatever you spend for good causes He will replace, for He is the best of providers."

40–42. On that day He will gather everyone together and ask the angels, "Did these men used to worship you?" The angels will reply, "You are our Lord, not mankind. Most of them worshipped the genies." On that day no one will have the power to help each other. We will say to the sinners, "Now taste the punishment of the fires that you denied existed!"

43–45. When Our revelations are spoken [by you] to them, the rejecters of the truth will say, "This man is trying to make you stop worshipping as your fathers did. He is making the whole story up. This is clearly just magic." Remember, We did not give them scriptures to read or any messengers before you. Their predecessors denied the revelations before, and We gave them only a tenth of what you are revealing. My punishment on those disbelievers was memorable.

46. Say to them, “Let me advise you about one point; rise up for God in pairs or individually and reflect upon the message. Your companion is not possessed; he is simply a messenger warning of you of a great punishment.”

47. Say to them, “I ask you for nothing in return for this message. My reward comes from God, and He is the witness to all things.”

48. Say to them, “My Lord casts the truth. He knows all the unknown things.”

49. Say to them, “The truth has come. Lies will not dare show their face and will not return.”

50. Say to them, “If I go astray, I do so at risk of my own soul. If I follow a righteous path, it’s because of the inspirations of my Lord, who hears everything.”

51–54. If only you could see them when they are shaking with fear and have no escape. They will cry, “Now we believe in the truth.” How can they now quickly believe in the revelations when before they were so far from believing? They rejected faith entirely and fired shots at what they could not see. So We will place a barrier between them and their desires, as was done to their kind in the past. They used to be such grave doubters.

Chapter 59 (chronologically)

Sura 39 (75 verses), Al-Zumar (The Throngs [masses])

1–2. The revelations in this Book are from God, the mighty and wise. We have sent this true Book to you, so be sincerely devoted to serving God.

3. Only God is worthy of complete devotion. Those who choose protection from anyone other than God like to say, "We worship others so that they can bring us closer to God." God will judge them for their beliefs. God does not guide the liars and ungrateful.

4. If God had wished for a son, He could have taken anyone He chose, from amongst all those He created. Glory be to God, the absolute and irresistible.

5. He created the heavens and earth perfectly. He makes the night turn to day and the day give way to night. He controls the sun and moon, setting their specific course. He is the almighty and most merciful.

6. He created you from a single soul, created a mate, and sent down eight pairs of cattle. He creates you in the wombs of mothers, one after another in triple darkness. This is God,

your Lord! All sovereignty is to Him. There is no god but Him. Where are you being led astray?

7. God does need your thanks if you are ungrateful, but He doesn't like ingratitude from His worshippers. If you are grateful, He will be pleased with you. No one must bear the burdens of another person. When you return to your Lord, He will list your all your deeds, for He knows even the secrets of man.

8. Some men pray frequently to their Lord in times of trouble, but after He grants them favor they are ungrateful. Then he creates other gods to rival God and lures other men from God's straight path. Say to them, "Enjoy your ungratefulness while you can, for the fires wait for you."

9. Is a man that prays properly and devoutly, who believes in the hereafter, and hopes for the mercy of his Lord equal to one that does not? Say to them, "Are those who know equal to those who do not know? Only the wise men will take this warning."

10. Say to them, "My faithful servants fear your Lord. Those who are righteous on God's vast earth will be rewarded. Those who are patient will receive a full reward."

11–13. Say to them, "I was commanded to worship God sincerely and to be the first to submit to Him completely. I fear a great penalty one day if I disobey my Lord."

14–15. Say to them, “I worship only God and put all my faith in Him. Serve who you want instead of God. The true losers on judgment day are those who lose their souls and the souls of their people.”

16. They shall be covered with flames above and below them. With this God deters His servants: “Servants, fear Me!”

17-18. For people who ward off evil and don’t worship idols and turn repentantly to God, there is good news. Give the good news to the men who listen to the messages and follow the best meanings of it. They are the men guided by God and endowed with understanding.

19. Can someone found deserving of punishment be saved? What can you do to rescue them from the flames?

20. Those who are dutiful to their Lord will live in lofty mansions with streams flowing below. That’s a promise from God, and He doesn’t break His promise.

21. Didn’t you see how God sends down the rains from the sky or brings up through springs? How He causes crops to grow and then wither to crumble and blow away. There are signs to remind men who want to see them.

22. If God opens a man’s heart to Islam so he can be guided by the light, isn’t it better than a man’s [heart] that is not open? Those who have hardened hearts and can’t praise God are clearly wrong.

23. God's revelations contain beautiful messages. While often repeating a similar lesson, the verses are consistent throughout the scripture. For the fearful it makes the skin crawl and the hearts open to receiving God's guidance. God guides who He wishes, but for those He sends astray there is no guide.

24. What if someone tries to dispute the punishment handed out to them on judgment day? The sinners will be told to take what they have earned.

25–26. People before them also rejected the revelations, and to them, their punishment came out of nowhere. Just as God made them taste disgrace on earth, He will give them a greater punishment in the hereafter. If they had only known.

27. We have given men, in this Qur'an, every kind of parable so that they may be warned.

28. An Arabic Qur'an [given] with no deviousness, so that man can ward off evil.

29. God gave a parable comparing one slave belonging to masters and one slave owned by only one. Can the two slaves be equal? Praise God! But most men don't understand. [Can one slave serve two masters' wishes correctly? Can a polytheist serve more than one god well?]

30–31. You will die, and they will die one day. In the end, all will face judgment day, and you will settle your disputes in front of your Lord.

32. Is there any worse sinner than someone that lies about God and rejects the truth when it's revealed? Isn't hell the destination for the disbelievers?

33–35. But those who bring the truth and those who believe it are righteous. They will share in the Lord's bounty as a reward. God will deduct their bad deeds and pay them for the good they did.

36–37. Isn't God alone strong enough for His worshippers? Yet people try to frighten you with other gods besides Him. For those that God sends astray, there is no guide. Whoever is guided by God cannot be led astray by anyone. Isn't God the Lord of retribution?

38. If you ask them who created the heavens and the earth, they will say God. So say to them, "If God places a penalty on me, can those things you worship besides God remove it? If God grants me a mercy, can they block me from receiving it? God is sufficient for me. Let the faithful put their trust in Him."

39–40. Say to them, "People, you act in your way, and I will act in mine. Soon we will know who will receive a disgraceful punishment and who will receive an everlasting punishment."

41. We have revealed this Book to you to share with mankind. Those who receive guidance help their soul, but those who stray damage their soul. You are not a custodian over them.

42. God takes the souls of men at death and the souls of those that have not died in their sleep. Then He keeps those He has decreed to death and sends the others back for a set time. There are *clearly* signs here for those who are thoughtful.

43-44. If you find they have taken intercessors besides God ask them, "[Can they intercede] even if they have no power or intelligence?" Tell them, "God alone can grant intercession. He rules the heavens and the earth. In the end everyone is brought back to Him."

45. When God is mentioned alone, the faithless are filled with disgust. When things they worship instead of Him are mentioned, they are joyful.

46. Say to them, "God, the creator of the heavens and the earth, knows everything public and secret. You will judge between Your servants about the matters we disagree upon."

47–48. If the sinners possessed everything on earth and then some, they would offer it all to save their souls on judgment day. God will give them a punishment that they never could have imagined. All of their evil deeds will confront them, and everything they used to mock will surround them.

49. When man needs Our help, he prays to Us. But when We grant him Our favor, he says he earned it because of something he was knowledgeable about. He is wrong, but this is a trial, and most men don't understand it.

50–51. The previous generation used to say that what they did would not be counted towards them. But the results of their deeds earned them punishment. The sinners of this generation will soon be accounted for their deeds too. They cannot escape what they earn.

52. Don't they know that God can increase or decrease supplies for anyone He pleases? The signs are there for those who believe.

53–55. Say to them, "My servants, who have sinned at the cost of their own souls, don't worry about God's mercy. God forgives all sins. He is forgiving and merciful. Be remorseful towards our Lord and submit to His will before the punishment arrives. After that time, you cannot be saved. Follow the best of the guidance revealed to you from your Lord, because the penalty can arrive when you least expect it."

56. And some may make excuses: "Unfortunately, I fell short of my duty to God, and I mocked Him."

57. Or "If God had guided me, I surely would have been righteous."

58. Or when they see their punishment, "If only You had given me a second chance, I would be more righteous."

59–61. The answer will be, "I sent you My revelations but you rejected them, were proud, and were unfaithful." On judgment day, you will know those who lied about God because of their blackened faces. Isn't hell the home for the proud? Meanwhile, God will save the righteous; no harm will touch them, and they won't grieve.

62–63. God is the creator of all things and caretaker of all affairs. He holds the keys to the heavens and the earth. Those who reject the signs of God will be lost.

64. Ask of them, "Are you asking me to worship something besides God? You are ignorant men!"

65–66. It has been revealed to you and to your ancestors, "If you join others to God, you will fail in life, and you will be among the lost. So worship God and be grateful."

67. They do not hold God in the esteem that He deserves. On judgment day He will have the whole earth in His grasp and the heavens in His right hand. Glory be to God, He is more noble than any partners associated with Him.

68. The trumpet will blast, and everyone in heaven and earth, except those selected by God, will collapse. Then a second blast, and all will be standing and waiting.

69. The earth will shine in the glory of her Lord. The record of deeds will be opened. The prophets and witnesses will be brought in for a fair judgment, and they won't be treated unjustly.

70. Every soul will receive what their deeds have earned them. God knows all that they did.

71. The unfaithful will be led into hell in throngs [masses]. When they arrive, the gates will open, and the wardens will say, "Didn't messengers come from among you and reveal the signs of your Lord and warning you of this day?" The throngs will answer, "Yes." Still the decreed punishment for unfaithfulness will be carried out.

72. They will be told, "Enter the gates of hell to dwell, for evil is the home of the proud."

73–74. The righteous and faithful to their Lord will move to the Gardens in throngs. The gates will be opened and the wardens will say, "Peace be upon you. You have done well, so dwell here." They will say, "Praise be to God, who truly kept His promise. He made us inherit this land where we can live anywhere in the Garden. What a grand reward for the righteous."

75. You will see the angels thronging around the throne singing praises to their Lord. The decisions made between them in judgment will be perfect. Praise be to God, the Lord of the worlds.

Chapter 60 (chronologically)

Sura 40 (85 verses), Al-Ghafir (The Forgiver [God])

1. Ha. Meem.

2–3. The revelations in this Book are from God, the mighty and knowledgeable, the forgiver of sins, the acceptor of repentance, the severe punisher, and the merciful. There is no god but Him, and to Him all finally return.

4. No one disputes the signs of God except the unbelievers. Do not let their apparent fortunes and frequent travels mislead you.

5. Before them were others that rejected the signs. Noah's people and factions after them and every nation schemed to harm their apostles and argued against Our message, refuting the truth. But We destroyed those factions with an awful punishment.

6. The decree of your Lord about the punishment of the unbelievers was fulfilled. They are the inmates of the fire.

7–9. For those that bear the throne and those around it singing glory and praises to the Lord, they believe in Him and they ask for forgiveness for the other believers: "Lord, you rule over all things with mercy and knowledge. Forgive those who are repentant and follow your path. Save them from the punishment of hell. Lord, grant them entry into the Garden of Eden as you promised to them, the righteous among their fathers, their wives, and their descendants. You are the mighty and wise. Preserve them from evil deeds with your mercy. It will be for them the highest achievement."

10. The unfaithful will be told, "For rejecting the faith, God feels more outrage towards you than you can for each other."

11. They will reply, "Lord, twice you made us die, and twice you gave us life. We now recognize our mistakes. Is there a way out of this punishment?"

12. The answer will be, "This is because when you were told to worship only God, you rejected the faith. Instead you worshipped things you made partners to him. Your judgment belongs to God alone, the magnificent and greatest.

13. He showed you signs and sent down sustenance from heaven, but only the repentant became faithful.

14. Pray to God in sincere devotion, although the unbelievers will detest it.

15–17. The Lord of the throne and the supreme master sends inspiration to any servant He pleases, so that they may warn man of the judgment day. That day, all will gather for God when not a thing can be hidden from God, the king of all dominion, the almighty, the one God. That day, every soul must account for what it earned. There will be no injustice that day; God is swift in judgment.

18. Warn them of the day that is coming soon, when their hearts will rise in their throats to choke them. No friend or intercessor of the sinners will be heard from that day.

19. He knows the sins committed by the eyes and the secrets in a man's heart.

20. God will judge with the truth. He sees and hears all. Anyone else worshipped by man will not be a judge that day.

21–22. Have they not travelled the lands and seen the consequences that struck communities that rejected Me before them? Those people were mightier in strength, but God destroyed them for their sins and they were defenseless. God had sent them messengers with clear signs, but they rejected them. So God destroyed them, so He is mighty and severe in punishment.

23-24. We sent Moses with our signs and clear authority to Pharaoh, Haman, and Korah. They called him a lying sorcerer.

25. When he came to them in truth on Our behalf, the Egyptians said, "Slay the sons of those who believe him and spare the females." But the schemes of unbelievers fail.

26. Pharaoh said, "I should kill Moses and make him cry to his Lord. I fear he might change your religion and cause confusion in the lands.

27. Moses said, "I seek refuge in my Lord, and your Lord, from all the arrogant people that do not believe in the day of judgment."

28–29. One of the men among Pharaoh's people who had hidden his faith asked, "Should you kill a man because he declares 'My Lord is God?' after he has shown you clear signs from your

Lord? If he is a liar, then that sin belongs to him. If he is truthful, then the punishments he warned you of fall on you. God surely does not guide sinners and liars. My people, while you are the kings of the lands today, who will save us from the wrath of God if it comes?" Pharaoh spoke, "I only tell what I think is correct. I only point you towards wise policies."

30–31. The faithful man spoke again: "My people, I fear for you a disastrous day like past communities received. A punishment like the one from Noah's time, or the Ad, or the Thamud, or those who came later. God does not want injustice for His servants."

32–33. "My people, I fear for you a day when all will be summoned. When you will all turn and run, because you have no defender against God. Whoever God sends astray will have no guide."

34. We sent Joseph to you with clear signs, but you doubted his message. After he died, you said that God would never send another messenger. That is how God allows doubters to deceive themselves.

35. God and His followers detest men that argue about God's signs when they have no authority to do so. As a punishment, God seals their sinful arrogant hearts to His message.

36–37. Pharaoh said, "Haman, build me a tall tower so that I may reach the heavens and see this god of Moses, although I think him a liar." This deed seemed alluring to Pharaoh, and he was lured from the straight path. The activities of Pharaoh ended in destruction.

38–40. The faithful man spoke again: "My people, follow me and I will guide you on the righteous path. This present life is only temporary; you will make your true home in the hereafter. If you commit evil deeds, you will receive equal punishment for them. If you live through righteous deeds, whether you are a man or woman, and are a believer, you will enter the Garden of paradise with endless reward."

41–43. He continued, "Why is it that I call you to salvation in the hereafter, and you call me to the fire? You ask me to stop believing in God and to ascribe partners I have never heard of to Him, and I ask you to put faith in the almighty forgiver. You are asking me to put faith in one that has no claim on this world or the hereafter. We will return to God, and the sinners will reside in the fire."

44–46. "Soon you will recall what I am telling you now. I commit myself to God, for He knows who His servants are." Soon Pharaoh's people were punished from all sides, but the faithful man was spared. In the fire they will endure day and night. On the day of judgment, Pharaoh's people will be sentenced with the harshest penalty.

47–48. In the flames they will argue with each other. The weak will say to the arrogant, "We were only following your lead, so why don't you absorb some of our fire?" The arrogant will reply, "We were all cast here together; surely God judges every servant accurately."

49–50. The dwellers in hell will say to the wardens of the flames, "Please pray to your Lord to lessen our punishment by just one day." The wardens will reply, "Did messengers come to you with clear signs?" Dwellers will reply, "Yes." The wardens will dismiss them: "Then pray to God yourself, but the requests of the unfaithful are in vain."

51–52. We will always help Our messengers and the faithful, both in this world and on resurrection day. On that day excuses from the sinners will not help them avoid their curse and their evil dwelling place.

53–54. We gave Moses the guidance and made the children of Israel inheritors of the Book as a guide and reminder for those who were wise.

55. Have patience. God's promises are true. Ask forgiveness for your sins, and sing praise to God in the evening and morning.

56. [MD] Those who argue about the signs of God without authority have nothing in their hearts but a lust for greatness that they won't achieve. Seek refuge in God, for He sees and knows all.

57. [MD] Surely the creation of heaven and earth is more extraordinary than the creation of men, but most people don't understand that.

58. The blind and those with sight are not equal, and neither are the faithful and righteous when compared to evildoers. You are learning little from your reflection.

59. There is no doubt that the hour is coming. Yet few men believe it.

60. Your Lord says, "Pray to Me, and I will answer. Those who are too arrogant to worship Me will enter hell humiliated."

61. It was God that made the night for you so you may rest and the day time so you can see. God is gracious and generous to mankind, but most men are not grateful.

62. God is your Lord, the creator of all things, and there is no god but God. How is it you are lured away from the truth?

63. Those who reject the revelations of God are led astray.

64. It is God that made the earth for you to dwell upon and the sky as a canopy; He created you in a perfect shape and provided you with pure and useful sustenance. God is your Lord. Blessed is God, the Lord of the worlds.

65. He is the living God. There is no god besides Him. Pray to Him in exclusive devotion. Praise God, the Lord of the worlds.

66. Say to them, "I am forbidden to worship those gods to worship besides God. Because of the clear messages I received

from God, I am commanded to submit to the Lord of the worlds."

67. He is the One that created you from the dust, then from sperm and seed, then from a clot, then brings you out as an infant, so that you may reach maturity and become older [although some may die young] until you reach your final age, so that you may become wise.

68. He gives life and death. When He decrees an activity, He simply says "be" and it occurs.

69–72. You have seen people that dispute the signs of God. How they are being led from the righteous path? Those who reject the Book and the revelations of Our messengers, will soon learn the truth, when iron collars are chained to their neck, so they can be dragged through boiling waters to burn in the fire.

73–76. There they will be asked, "Where are the gods you set up as partners to God?" In reply they admit, "They have left us. We were not praying to anything real before." That is how God sends the unfaithful astray. "Because you celebrated things on earth that were false and you were disrespectful, enter now through the gates to reside in hell." Evil is the destination of the arrogant.

77. Be patient; the promise of God is true. Whether We show you a piece of what We have promised them, or We take your soul beforehand, they will all return to Us.

78. Before you We sent messengers; some of their stories you know, and some you don't. All messengers delivered only revelations that were authorized by God. When God issues His command, all will be judged by the truth, and the followers of lies will be lost.

79–80. God made the cattle for you, some to be ridden and others for food. There are numerous other uses for them that you can choose, like using them to carry a load like a ship.

81. He shows you His signs. Which of God's signs will you reject?

82–85. Do people not travel the land and see what happened to earlier generations? They were more numerous and stronger than current generations, yet it did not protect them. For when the messengers showed them clear signs, they instead gloated about their own previous knowledge. Then what they had mocked consumed them. As they saw Our punishment close in, they cried, "We believe in God and reject all others we partnered with Him!" But their new profession of faith, after they saw their doom, came too late to save them. This has been God's way of treating His servants since ancient times. The unfaithful will perish.

Chapter 61 (chronologically)

Sura 41 (54 verses), Fussilat (Elaboration)

1–4. Ha. Meem. A revelation from the most benevolent and most merciful. A book that explains the signs in an Arabic Qur'an [reading/recitation] for enlightened people. A herald of good news and warnings; yet most people turn from Him and do not hear.

5. They will say, "Our hearts will not allow you to invite us, and our ears cannot hear you. There is a curtain between us, so do what you will, and we shall follow our ways."

6–8. Say to them, "I am a man like you. It was revealed to me that your God is one God. So follow the path to Him, and ask His forgiveness. Anguish awaits the polytheists, those who don't give regularly to charity, and those who don't believe in the hereafter. But for those who are faithful and do righteous deeds, the reward is everlasting."

9. Ask of them, "Do you really not believe in He who created the world in two days? Do you create equal partners to him? He is the Lord of the worlds."

10–11. He placed mountains standing high and firm and blessed its contents and created food for all who needed it in four days. Then He looked at the sky made of smoke and said to the sky and earth, "Come together whether you want to or not!" They replied, "We come together obediently."

12. He completed the seven heavens in two days and assigned each layer its duty. We decorated the lower heaven with lamps and commanded it to protect. That was ordained by the almighty and knowledgeable.

13–14. If they don't listen to you, say to them, "I warn you now of a torment that like a thunderbolt struck the Ad and the Thamud people." The apostles came to them saying, "Serve no one but God!" They replied, "If our Lord had willed it, He would have sent down angels to us, so we reject your message and do not believe."

15–16. The Ad people were arrogant for no reason and asked, "Who is mightier than us?" Did they not see that God, their creator, was stronger? Still, they rejected our messages. Therefore, We unleashed a furious wind of destruction, so that they could taste humiliation on earth. The punishment in the hereafter will be more shameful, and they will have no help.

17–18. The Thamud people chose to ignore the guidance We sent them, so We sent a stunning punishment to humiliate them. We saved those among them who were faithful and lived righteously.

19–21. On the day that the enemies of God are gathered, they will be marched in ranks towards the fire. At its edge their ears, eyes, and skin will testify against them about their past deeds. They will ask their own skin, "Why did you testify against us?" The skin will reply, "God has given us speech. It is He who gives speech to all things, and created you for the first time, and to whom you will all return."

22–23. You didn't hide yourselves thinking that your eyes, ears, and skin would not testify against you. You didn't think that God knew everything that you did. But your belief about the power of God has brought you destruction. Now you are utterly lost.

24–25. If they are resigned, the fire will remain their home. If they beg to receive mercy, they will find they are not allowed any. We will give them companions that will make them think their past and present deeds were fair. The punishment came true for them, just as it did for people before them. They are utterly lost.

26. The disbelievers will say, "Don't listen to this Qur'an [recitation] and yell during its reading to disrupt it so we may overcome him."

27. We will give the unfaithful a taste of their severe penalty and will repay them for their evil deeds.

28. The payment for God's enemies is the fire. It will be their eternal home as punishment for rejecting Our revelations.

29. The unfaithful will say, "Lord, show us those genies and men that misled us, and we will crush them under our feet so they become the lowest of all."

30–32. For those who said, "Our Lord is God," and then stand upright and are patient, the angels will descend saying, "Have no fear and do not grieve; instead hear the good news of the paradise you were promised. We are your guardians in this life and in the hereafter. There you will have everything that your souls desire and anything you ask. It's the hospitality from the forgiving and most merciful."

33. Who can speak better than a man who prays to God, lives righteously, and says, "I am one of the Muslims." [Muslims in Qur'anic Arabic is spelled "moo-sel-meen," which is why you see that anglicized spelling in some books.]

34–35. Good and evil are not equal. Repel evil acts with something better. You will find that that action can make friends of enemies. No one will be granted it [power of goodness] unless they are patient and are among the best.

36. If Satan tries to interfere and disturbs you, then seek refuge in God. He hears and knows all.

37. Among His signs are the night and day and the sun and moon. Do not bow to the floor towards the sun and moon but instead pray towards God who created them, if you truly serve Him.

38. If they are too proud, then there are always those close to the Lord that will praise Him day and night and never tire.

39. You see His signs when you watch a deserted land stir to life and yield crops after We send down the rains. He who can

revive the earth can revive men who are dead. He has the power over everything.

40. Those who distort Our revelations cannot hide from Us. Would you rather be cast in the fire or pass safely through on the day of judgment? Do what you like, but He sees everything you do.

41–42. Those who reject Our message when it's shown to them cannot hide from Us. It is an unassailable Book: No lies can be added to it from anyone, as it was sent down by One that is wise and worthy of all praise.

43. Everything being said to you was told to the messengers before you. Your Lord can be forgiving and a severe punisher.

44. If We had sent this Qur'an [lecture] in a language other than Arabic, the nonbelieving Arabs would have said, "Why haven't the messages been translated or clearly communicated? What is this, a non-Arabic scripture and an Arab-speaking prophet?" Say to them, "This is guidance and healing for those who believe. For those who do not believe, there must be deafness and blindness, as if they are being spoken to from a distant place."

45. We gave the Book to Moses, and soon arguments about it arose. If not for a word that was told to them earlier by your Lord, their arguments would have been settled. They remain suspicious doubters.

46. If you do righteous deeds, it benefits your soul. If you commit evil works, it harms your soul. Your Lord will never be unjust to His servants.

47–48. He knows everything necessary about everyone at the hour [judgment day]. No fruit leaves its peeling, and no woman conceives or births without His awareness. On that day God will ask men, "Where are the partners you associated to me?" They will reply, "They are not here with us." Those besides God that they used to worship will fail them, and they will realize there is no escape.

49. Man never tires of asking for good things, but when evil touches him he loses hope and becomes desperate.

50. When We bestow a taste of Our mercy on man when he is faced with adversity, he will say, "I helped myself, and I don't think there will be a judgment day. But if I am ever returned to my Lord, my good deeds will be enough." We will show the disbelievers everything they did and give them a taste of Our severe punishment.

51. When We bestow our favors, man ignores Us and keeps to himself. But when he is in trouble, he sends up prolonged prayers for help.

52. Ask them, "If these revelations are from God and you reject them, who is making a bigger mistake than someone that is openly fighting with God?"

53. We will soon show our signs on the horizons and in their souls until it becomes clear that they are true. How is it not enough proof that your Lord is witness to all things?

54. How are they still doubtful about their meeting with the Lord? He is involved with all things!

Chapter 62 (chronologically)

Sura 42 (53 verses), Al-Shura (The Consultation)

1. Ha. Meem.

2. Ain. Seen. Qaf.

3–5. God the almighty and knowledgeable inspired you like those messengers before. Everything in the heavens and on earth belongs to Him the exalted and great One. His majesty nearly rips open the heavens, and the angels sing their praises for their Lord and pray for forgiveness for all beings on earth. He is God the forgiving and merciful.

6. If anyone chooses guardians besides God, do not worry, God is watching them, and you are not serving as a warden over them.

7. We have inspired a message in you as an Arabic Qur'an [lecture in Arabic] so that you may warn the mother of cities [Mecca] and those around it of the certain day of gathering.

Warn about that day when one group will be in the Garden and another group in the flames.

8. If God had willed it man could have been made one community, but He brings who He wants to His mercy, and the sinners will have no friend or guardian.

9-10. If they have chosen to worship guardians besides Him, say, "God is the protector. He gives life to the dead and is able to do all things. Whatever you are arguing about, the verdict lies with God. God is my Lord, and in Him I place my trust, and to Him do I turn."

11–12. Say, "He created the heavens and the earth. He made you in pairs and cattle in pairs. By this pairing He can multiply you. There is nothing like Him. He is the one that hears and sees everything. He holds the keys to heaven and earth. He increases and decreases the sustenance of whomever He chooses. He knows all things."

13. He proposes for you the same religion that We instructed Noah on, which He sent by inspiration to you. That We proposed to Abraham, Moses, and Jesus. The tenets are that you should be obedient in worship and establishment and make no divisions [sects] within it. You will be making a difficult request of the unbelievers. God chooses for Himself who He likes and guides to Himself those who look to Him frequently.

14. After the knowledge [revelations] reached them, they became divided for selfish reasons. If it wasn't for an agreement that occurred between them and your Lord, specifying an appointed term, the matter would have been settled between them. Those who have inherited the scriptures after the division are in grave doubt about it.

15. Summon them to this faith and be steadfast, as you were commanded. Do not follow their desires, but say to them, "I believe in what God has revealed of the Book, and I was commanded to do justice between you. God is our Lord and your Lord. We are responsible for our deeds and you for yours. There is no argument between us and you. God will return us all to Himself.

16. Those who argue about God after He has been accepted should know their argument carries no weight with the Lord, and they will feel His severe penalty.

17. God sent down the truthful Book and the balance [the method of judgment for conduct]. What will make you realize that the hour is happening soon?

18. Only those who don't believe in it want to speed up the arrival of the hour, while those who are faithful are apprehensive of it and know its the truth. Those who argue about the coming hour are very unrighteous.

19. God is gracious to His servants. He provides for whomever He chooses. He is strong and mighty.

20. If you seek the harvest in the hereafter, We will increase your harvest on earth. If you seek the harvest on earth, We will give it to you, but you will get none in the hereafter.

21. Do some people have gods that have made things legal in their religion without the permission of God? If not for a judgment given to them before, the matter in question would have been resolved already. The sinners will have a painful punishment.

22. You will see the unjust fearing their judgment for all they did, and the burden will fall on them. Meanwhile the faithful and righteous will be found in the meadows of the gardens with every desire met. That is the greatest mercy.

23. [MD] God gives this good news to His faithful and righteous servants, "The only reward I ask of you is to love your family." Every good deed you conduct is being counted. God is merciful and appreciative.

24. [MD] If they say, "He has created a lie against God." [Tell them] if God willed it, He could seal your heart. God will wipe out lies and prove the truth with His words. He knows what secrets men hide.

25. [MD] He accepts repentance from His servants and forgives sins. He knows everything you do.

26. He answers [the prayers of] those who are faithful and do good works and increases their reward. For the unbelievers there is a severe penalty.

27. [MD] If I were to increase the provision of my servants all at once, it would cause chaos. We send it down in careful measure. He is aware and watches His servants.

28. He sends down the rains after men have lost hope, and He spreads His mercy. He is the guardian and praiseworthy.

29. Some of His signs are the creation of the heavens and earth and the beasts He scattered through the lands. He is able to gather them all at His will.

30. Your own hands are responsible for whatever misfortune you encounter, and still He forgives most of your faults.

31. You cannot escape on the earth, and you also have no guardian or helper besides God.

32–34. Another sign of God are the ships sailing like mountains through the sea. If He wills it, He can calm the winds, leaving the ships motionless on the surface. There are signs for everyone steadfast and grateful. Or, He can wreck them because of the evil that the men have committed. But He forgives much.

35. Let people know that whoever disputes Our revelations will have no way to escape.

36. Whatever you have on earth is just to get you through this life. What God has for the faithful and trusting is much better and longer lasting.

37. It's for those who avoid the worst sins and shameful deeds and who choose to forgive when they are angry;

38. For those who respond to their Lord's call, who maintain regular prayer, who take counsel among others in decisions, and who spend what We have given to them;

39. And for those who react when faced with aggression by coming to each other's aid.

40. The repayment for a bad deed is an equal bad deed, but those who will forgive and reconcile receive a reward from God. God does not love the unjust.

41. But those who defend themselves after being wronged cannot be blamed.

42. The blame falls upon those who commit the wrong actions and revolt unjustly. They shall receive a grave penalty.

43. The most courageous and steadfast way to act is to show patience and forgive.

44. If God leads someone astray in life, they will not have a guardian in the hereafter. You will see the unjust when they first see their punishment, asking, "Is there any way we can go back?"

45. You will see them facing their doom, standing humbly with their eyes lowered in disgrace. The faithful will say, "The biggest failures are those who lose themselves and their followers on resurrection day. The unjust will be in eternal punishment."

46. There will be no one to protect them besides God. Whoever God leads astray, will find no path.

47. Listen to your Lord before the day arrives from God that you cannot avoid. You will have no refuge that day, and you won't be able to deny His charges.

48. If men reject you, remember We didn't send you to be their warden. Your duty is only to deliver the message. When man is enjoying the mercy We gave him, he revels in it. If he causes a horrible situation by his own actions, he is ungrateful.

49–50. God is the king of the heavens and the earth. He creates what He wants. He gives sons to whom He wants, daughters to whom He wants, or both boys and girls to whom He wants. He can also make women sterile. He is all-knowing and all-powerful.

51. No man should speak to God directly. God speaks to man via inspired revelation, from behind an object, or through a messenger authorized to spread His words. He is triumphant and wise.

52–53. We inspired you, when you didn't know what the Book was or what faith was. But We created it as a light so that We may guide Our servants to righteousness, to the path to God. God, who owns the heavens and the earth. All matters return to God.

Chapter 63 (chronologically)

Sura 43 (89 verses), Al-Zukhruf (Gold Ornaments)

1–3. *Ha. Meem.* [H. M.] This Book makes things clear. We made an Arabic language Qur'an [recitation] so that you may understand it.

4. It [the recitation] is in the religious Book [mother Book] that We possess, and it is wise and dignified.

5. Should We callously withhold this message from you because you are sinful people?

6–8. How many prophets did We send to the generations before you? And every time a prophet arrived, he was mocked. Remember from the stories of old that We have destroyed communities much stronger than these.

9. If you ask them, "Who created the heavens and the earth?" they will surely reply, "The mighty and all-knowing One did."

10–14. It was He that created the earth for you to live on and made paths for you to follow so you can find your way. That sends down rains, as needed, so We can bring new life to dead soil, just like We will bring man back to life. Who created all things in pairs and made ships and cattle that you can use for transport. And as you rest on their backs, you can remember the gift from your Lord that has made things happen that you couldn't do for yourselves. "We will surely be returning to our Lord."

15. They associate some of His servants with Him. This is blasphemous and ungrateful.

16. Would He have chosen a daughter from among those He created and then chose to give you sons?

17. When news is given to one of mankind that his wife delivered what [a daughter] they dare partner with the gracious God, they become gloomy and angry.

18. Do they liken to God a girl that is raised among trinkets and unable to speak clearly in an argument?

19. Mankind assumes angels, the servants to God, are female. Did they witness the creation? This belief will be recorded and called into account!

20. They will say, "If the gracious One had willed it so, we would not have worshipped these things." They have no idea what they are talking about. They lie.

21–22. They act like We had given them a Book before now and are following it. But they have said before, "We are just following the footsteps of our father's religious worship."

23. This is how it has been every time We sent a messenger before you. The wealthy people would say, "We are just worshipping the way our fathers did."

24. Messengers would say, "But what if I brought you better guidance than what your fathers follow?" The people replied, "We do not believe that you have been sent by God."

25. That is why We brought them great punishment. That is the consequence of rejecting the message.

26–28. Recall Abraham said to his people and his father, "I reject what you do in worship. I will only worship He who made me, and He will be my guide." This statement endured in the people who came after him so they could turn back.

29–31. I have allowed good things in the lives of these men and their fathers, but only until a time when they would receive a messenger revealing the truth. But when they hear the truth they said, "This is just magic, and we do not believe in it." Then they ask, "Why wasn't this Qur'an sent to any of the great men of the two towns?" [Mecca and Yathrib; Yathrib became Medina.]

32. Are these people in charge of where your Lord gives His mercy? We decide who does what on the earth and who rises

above other men to become leaders. The mercy of your Lord is finer than the wealth those men stockpile.

33–35. If not for the danger that all men would become disbelievers, We would have provided all the unfaithful with silver roofs, stairs, doors, and thrones, plus ornaments of gold. But those gifts would only please men in the present life. The hereafter, near your Lord, is a place only for the righteous.

36–39. For those who fail to glorify the all-merciful one, We assign him a devil to be his friend. The devil keeps them off the path of God and makes them think they are acting righteously. When they stand before Us, the man will say to his devil friend, "I wish there were a world between us." He is an evil friend. But when you are unjust, no good will come that day. You will share doom with him.

40. Can you make the deaf hear again or guide the blind or guide the unjust? Maybe We remove you and exact retribution on them. Or Maybe We show you what We are promising them, because We have the power to do as We like to them.

43. Be patient and follow closely what We have revealed to you. You are on the right path. It is a reminder for you and your people, and soon you will be questioned.

45. Ask the prophets We sent before you if We ever authorized any gods to be worshipped other than the most gracious.

[Related to a journey Muhammad would make, where he would see earlier prophets.]

46–48. We sent Moses with Our signs to the Pharaoh and his chief, where he said, "I am a messenger of the Lord of the worlds." But when he showed them Our signs, they mocked him. We had him show them sign after sign, each clearer than the last, and We punished them with torment so that they might listen.

49. They cried, "Wizard, call on your Lord for us, as you have a covenant with him. We will accept His guidance."

50. And when We lifted our torments, they broke their pledge.

51–53. Pharaoh then said, "My people, doesn't Egypt belong to me? Don't you see the rivers flowing under my palace? Aren't I better than this despicable wretch that can hardly speak? How come he doesn't have gifted gold bracelets on his arms? Why didn't angels accompany him to us?

54. [MD] Pharaoh misled his people against Moses, and they obeyed him. They were a sinful people.

55–56. When they provoked Us again, We punished them harshly, drowning them all. We condemned them to history, as an example to later generations.

57–58. When the son of Mary [Jesus] is used as an example, the people mock him saying, "Aren't our gods better than him?" They ask that question just to be disagreeable.

59. The son of Mary was simply a servant that We bestowed Our favor upon. We made him a role model for the children of Israel.

60. If We had willed it, instead of you, We could have sent generations of angels to run the earth.

61–62. He will be a sign of the coming of the resurrection day. Don't have any doubts concerning it, and follow Me; this is the righteous path. Don't let Satan block the path, because he is your sworn enemy.

63. When Jesus brought signs, he said, "I bring you wisdom so that I can settle your disputes. Hear your God, and obey me."

64. "God is my Lord and our Lord, so worship Him. This is the straight path."

65. Factions soon appeared among the people. The unjust must beware of the painful penalty day.

66. Why should people try to learn the hour of the resurrection day, just so it won't surprise them?

67–73. On that day friends will become enemies to each other unless they are among the righteous. My worshippers will not have any fear that day or any grief. Those who believed Our signs and submitted to Islam will enter the garden with their wives in happiness. You will be served everything your souls desire on trays and dishes of gold and your eyes will find delight.

This is the Garden you will inherit by your good deeds. In the Garden are many fruits for you to eat.

74–78. The guilty will endure the punishment of hell. They shall find only despair, and their punishment will not be lessened. It's not that We were unjust to them, but rather they were unjust to themselves. They will cry out, "Master, ask the Lord to kill us now." The reply will be, "No, you shall remain here." We have brought the truth to you, but most of you were opposed to hearing it.

79. We hear they have created a plan. But We are the ones that resolve things.

80. They do not think that We can hear their secret thoughts and their private conversations. But our messengers are among them, writing it all down.

81. Say to them, "If the most gracious had a son, I would be the first to worship him."

82–83. Glory to the Lord of the heavens and the earth; the all-powerful is free from what people allege about Him. Leave them to babble and gossip until they arrive at the promised day.

84–85. God is in the heavens and on the earth and is wise and all-knowing. Blessed is the ruler of the heavens and the earth and all in between. He knows the hour, and you will all return to Him.

86. Anyone they invoke instead of God is powerless to intercede, except for those who bear witness to the truth and know Him.

87. If you ask them who their creator is, they will certainly tell you it was God. So why are they turning away from the truth?

88. God will hear His prophet's cry, "My Lord, these people truly refuse to believe!"

89. "Turn from them and say 'Peace!' They will soon know the truth."

Chapter 64 (chronologically)

Sura 44 (59 verses), Al-Dukhan (Smoke)

1. Ha. Meem.

2. I swear by this clarifying Book. We revealed it during a blessed night. We have always warned mankind.

4. Every matter is resolved in it.

5–7. It is an edict from Us. We are the ones sending revelations as a mercy from your Lord. He knows and hears all things. He is the Lord of the heavens and the earth and everything in between. You simply need to have conviction.

8. There is no God but Him. He gives life and causes death. He's your Lord and the Lord of your ancestors.

9. Yet they are doubtful.

10-11. Be sure to watch on that day the sky brings forth a visible smoke. It will envelop the people and be a painful punishment.

12. They will cry, “Our Lord, relieve us of this punishment, for now we are believers!”

13–14. What good will their cries be then? After We had already sent them a messenger sharing the truth, which they rejected and mocked, saying, “He is an educated madman.”

15–16. We will remove a little of the penalty for a moment, but they will simply revert to their wicked ways. Then one day We will strike them a mighty blow, and We will exact Our retribution.

17–19. We tried the people of the Pharaoh when We sent them a noble messenger, saying, “Give me the servants of God, for I am a messenger you can trust. Do not defy God, as I have His full authority.”

20–22. “I have the security of my Lord and your Lord in case you try to stone me. If you don’t believe me, then leave me alone.” He cried to his Lord, “These are a guilty people!”

23–24. The reply: “Take My servants away by night, knowing you will be pursued. Leave the sea behind, for surely the pursuers will be drowned.”

25–28. Think of how many gardens and springs were left behind, plus cornfields and great buildings, and the conveniences of life that brought them so much joy. That was their end. We gave those things to another people.

29. Neither heaven nor earth cried for them. They got no pardon.

30–31. We delivered the children of Israel from a humiliating punishment at the hands of Pharaoh, who was an arrogant tyrant.

32–33. We chose the Israelis above all other nations and gave them signs which contained a clear trial.

34–36. When they say, "Nothing will happen after we die. We will not rise again. If you are telling the truth, then bring our fathers back from the dead."

37. Do they think they are better than the Tubba [Yemeni King] people or their ancestors? We destroyed them because they were guilty.

38–39. We didn't create the heavens and the earth just for the fun of it. We created them for a specific purpose, but most do not understand it.

40–42. On the day of judgment, all will determine the end of their term. That day when no friend will be able to aid another, and only those with God's mercy will be aided. He is mighty and merciful.

43–46. The sinful will eat the tree of Zaqqum. It will be like molten metal in their stomachs, scalding like boiling water.

47–50. A cry will sound: "Seize him and drag him into the fires of hell! Pour boiling water over his head! Taste this; you thought you were strong and noble! This is what you used to doubt!"

51–53. The righteous will be safe among the gardens and springs, reclining near each other, dressed in fine embroidered silks.

54. They will be wed to fair women with beautiful wide black eyes. [Houries, fair creatures not descendants of Adam.]

55–57. They can safely call for any type of fruit they desire and not feel death after their initial death. They will be saved from the punishment of hell by the mercy of their Lord. It will be a great triumph.

58–59. We have revealed this in your language so it will be easy to understand and you may be warned. "Wait, for surely they are waiting."

Chapter 65 (chronologically)

Sura 45 (37 verses), Al-Jathiya (Kneeling)

1. Ha. Meem.

2. The revelations of this Book are from God the all-powerful and wise.

3. In the heavens and the earth are the signs for those who believe.

4. Your creation and the fact that beasts roam the earth are signs for those who are faithful.

5. The exchange of night for day, the revival of the earth after God sends down the rains, and the movements of the winds are all signs for the wise.

6. We reveal these truths to you. What path will they choose after hearing of God and His signs?

7. There is misery for the sinful liars.

8. They that hear the signs of God recited and yet are arrogant and obstinate, as if they never heard them, tell them of their painful punishment.

9–11. When they learn about Our signs, they make light of them. Theirs will be a humiliating penalty. In front of them is only hell. Their good deeds won't count, and the guardians they worshipped instead of God won't save them from a grievous penalty. This guidance is the truth. Those who reject the revelations of their Lord face painful punishment.

12. God tamed the seas so that your ships may sail on them under His command; so that you may share in His bounty and give thanks to Him.

13. He commands everything in heaven and earth to your service. There are signs for those who reflect.

14. [MD] Say to the faithful, "Forgive those who do not look forward to their days with God. When He can examine each person and repay them according to what they earned.

15. Righteous deeds will benefit a man's soul, while evil deeds damage it. In the end all will return to your Lord.

16–17. We gave the children of Israel the Book, the mantle of prophethood, and sustenance, and we chose them above all other nations. We gave them clear commandments, and it was after all this knowledge was received that they divided into sects due to rivalry. Your Lord will judge them on the day of judgment concerning the issues they argued about.

18–19. We have now set you on the right legal path [sharia], so follow it; and don't follow the low desires of people you don't know. They will not be of use to you when you face God. Sinners will have only other sinners to protect them, while the righteous will have God to guard them against evil.

20. This is a clear warning for mankind and provides guidance and mercy for the truly faithful.

21. Do sinners think We will count them as equal to those who were righteous in life and death? They have bad judgment.

22. God created the heavens and the earth for just intentions so that every soul can be repaid for what they have earned and be judged fairly.

23–26. You have seen the men that worship their desires instead of God; God has sent them astray, sealed their hearts and ears, and covered their eyes. Who will guide them after God has withdrawn His guidance? Will you not accept this warning? They will say, "There is nothing but this life in this world. We live, then we die, and nothing can destroy us besides time." They don't know what they are saying; it's all guesses. When Our signs are recited to them, they have a flimsy rebuttal, "If you are being honest, then bring back our dead fathers!" Say to them, "It is God that gave you life, He will give you death, and He will gather you all on resurrection day. There is no doubt about this." Yet most men don't understand this.

27. God reigns in heaven and on earth. On judgment day, the liars will perish.

28–29. You will see men of every nation bowing down on their knees. They will be called before their Book: "Today you will be repaid for your deeds. This is our record, and it will bring justice, for We wrote down everything you did."

30. Those that believed and did righteous deeds will be admitted by their Lord to His mercy. It will be a triumph.

31. Those who rejected God will hear, "Weren't Our signs recited to you? You were an arrogant and guilty people."

32. When it was said to you, "The promises of God are true, and there is no doubt of the coming hour," you used to say, "We do not know the hour. We think it's made up. We cannot be sure of it."

33. The evils of what they did will then appear to them, and what they used to mock will be all around them.

34–35. It will be said, "Today We will forget you just as you used to forget this day was coming. Your home is in the fire, and there is no help for you, because you used to joke about the signs of God, and the life on earth misled you." They will not be taken out after this, nor can they make amends.

36–37. Praise to God, Lord of the heavens, earth, and all the worlds. His majesty reigns in the heavens and earth, as He is mighty and wise.

Chapter 66 (chronologically)

Sura 46 (35 verses), Al-Ahqaf (The Dunes)

1. Ha. Meem.

2. This Book was revealed by God, the mighty and wise.

3. We created the heavens and earth and all that is in between with honest intentions but only for a limited time. Unbelievers, consider yourselves warned.

4. Say to them, "If you are truthful, then tell me more about what you worship instead of God. Tell me what they created on earth. Do they control a part of heaven? Show me a revealed scripture from them or tell me some evidence of their knowledge."

5–6. Who can be more lost in life than someone that prays to something besides God? Something that doesn't answer your prayers and won't be there for you on judgment day. On judgment day, when mankind gathers, these things you worshipped will become your enemies and deny your worship.

7. When Our signs are recited to the unfaithful, they will say, "The truth you reveal is just magic."

8. Or they will say of you, "He invented all this." Say to them, "Even if I made it all up, you still would have no power to turn me against God. He knows what you say about this. He is all the witness I need of our interactions. He is forgiving and merciful."

9. Say to them, "I am not the first apostle, and I don't know what yours or my future will be. I follow what is revealed to me. I am simply a messenger bringing warnings."

10. [MD] Say to them, "Consider this. If what I recite is from God, and you are rejecting it, after the children of Israel accepted a similar scripture from an earlier prophet, how arrogant are you?" God does not guide the unfaithful.

11. The unfaithful say to the faithful worshippers, "If this revelation were a noble truth, then surely we would have been converted before you!" Because they will not follow the righteous path, they cry, "This is an ancient lie."

12. Before this revelation, the Book of Moses was a guide and a mercy. This Book confirms that scripture in the Arabic language. It's a warning to the unjust and good news for the righteous.

13–14. Those who say that our Lord is God and walk the righteous path shall never fear nor grieve. They will be content in the Gardens eternally as reward for their good deeds.

15. [MD] We command mankind to be kind to his parents. Their mothers bear them and birth them in pain. After reaching full maturity at forty years old, man should say, "My Lord, inspire me to be grateful for the favors you gave to my parents and me, so that I may live righteously with your approval. I ask your grace in bestowing on me children of my own. I am repentant to you, and I surrender completely."

16. They [the faithful and righteous] are the ones We will reward fully for their good deeds and overlook their sins. They will live in the Garden, in keeping with the promise We made them.

17. Some men will tell their parents, "You disgust me. You tell me a tale about rising from the dead even hundreds of years

after I die." The parents will pray to God for help, telling their son, "Have faith or you will be sorry. The promise of God is true." The son will reply, "These are old tales told by men."

18. They are just like the many nations of men and genies that have previously felt the promise of God come true. They will be utterly lost.

19. All will be divided into categories of sin according to the deeds they committed, so God can repay them for their acts in a just manner.

20. On the day of judgment, the unfaithful will stand before the flames and will be told, "You have already received good things in your life on earth, and you took great pleasure in them. Today you will be penalized with humiliation for your arrogance and constant sinning."

21. Tell them about the messenger We chose from among the Ad people. He warned his people that lived among the dunes, like the apostles before and after him, "Worship no one besides God, or I fear that you will face doom on a grievous day."

22. They replied, "You are trying to turn us away from our current gods! If you are not a liar, then bring down the disaster you are threatening us with."

23. He replied, "Only God knows when it will come. I am simply telling you what I have been sent to say. You are an ignorant people."

24–25. When the Ad people saw a cloud traveling towards their valley, they cried, "Here comes a cloud full of rain!" But it was the penalty they had asked for. It was a wind capable of painful punishment, destroying everything by the command of the Lord. The morning left only the ruins of their homes. We repay those who sin.

26. They [Ad] had received from Us power, hearing, sight, hearts, and intellect that We haven't given to you. None of those things could save them when they rejected the signs of God. They were lost when they were faced with the things they used to mock.

27. We have destroyed many communities all around you in the past. We repeatedly showed them signs, so that the people may turn to Us.

28. Do you wonder why none of the things [false gods] they worshipped instead of God failed to save them from penalty? They were left to answer for the lies they created.

29–30. Once We sent a group of genies to listen to you recite. In your presence they told people to listen in silence. Afterward they went to their people to warn them, saying, "People, we have heard from a book revealed after Moses that confirms what was revealed previously. It instructs us to follow the righteous path to the truth."

31. "People, listen to God's messenger and believe in Him [God]. He will forgive your sins and protect you from a great punishment."

32. "Those who reject the message of God's apostle cannot hide from God's plan on earth and will have no guardian in his place. You wander in great error."

33. Don't they see that God, who created heaven and earth and never grew tired, can give life to the dead? He has power over all things.

34. On the day the unfaithful are standing in front of the flames, they will be asked, "Is this real?" They'll respond, "Yes, my Lord." Then they will hear, "Taste your doom for denying the truth."

35. [MD] Be patient just like the previous messengers were, and don't wish to hurry the punishment onto them. On judgment day when they see what We promised them, it will seem like only yesterday you warned them. This is a clear message. Will anyone be destroyed besides the sinners?

Chapter 67 (chronologically)

Sura 51 (60 verses), Al-Dhariyat (The Scattering Winds)

1–6. Know by the winds that scatter, that bear the rain clouds, that guide the ships and the seas, that carry the angels to dispense blessings with God's command; that what is promised is the truth. Judgment day will surely come to pass.

7–8. I swear by the heavens full of constellations, you all have differing opinions.

9–11. Those that would reject the revelations do reject them. A curse on the liars that wander carelessly in confusion.

12–14. When they constantly ask, "When will the day of judgment arrive?" Tell them it will be a day when they are tormented by the flames and will hear a voice saying, "Taste your persecution! This is the event you kept asking [the prophet] to cause to occur at your command [to prove his truthfulness]."

15–16. The righteous though, will find themselves amidst the gardens and springs, finding joy in things their Lord gives them. A reward for a good life.

17–19. They slept little at night and in the early dawn rose to pray for forgiveness. They shared their wealth with the beggars and the needy.

20–21. There are signs on earth for those confident in their faith; and there are also signs in yourselves, if you will look.

22. In heaven is your reward and all that has been promised.

23. I swear by the Lord of heaven and earth that this is the truth, just as it's true you can all speak.

24. Have you all heard about the honored guests of Abraham?

25. They came to Abraham and said, "Peace." He replied to them, "Peace. I do not know you all."

26–28. He left them to retrieve a roasted calf and, placing it before them, asked them if they would eat. The guest did not eat, and Abraham became worried. They said to him, "Do not be afraid," and then told him that he would receive a wise son.

29-30. His wife then stepped forward laughing and slapped her forehead, saying, "I am a barren old woman." They replied to her, "It doesn't matter, because your Lord has decided, and He is wise and knowledgeable."

31. Abraham asked, "Messengers, what is your next assignment?"

32–34. They told him they were being sent to a community that was full of sinful people. "We are sending down on them a shower of brimstone aimed at everyone marked by the Lord as guilty."

35–36. We looked in the community for those that were faithful, so We could evacuate them. We only found one home that had Muslims in it.

37. We will leave this sign as a reminder of the painful punishment.

38–40. We sent Moses with clear signs when he traveled to see Pharaoh on Our authority. Pharaoh just turned his back and told his chiefs, "He is a wizard or a lunatic." For his punishment, We flung him and his army into the sea.

41–42. The Ad people were another sign. We delivered a punishing wind on them. It left nothing behind but ruin and dust.

43–45. The tribe of Thamud also received a sign, and We told them to enjoy themselves for a little while. They revolted against the command of their Lord, and while they watched, a thunderbolt overcame them. They were unable to even rise and help each other.

46. The people of Noah's time were also a wicked bunch.

47–49. We built a sky with Our might, and We can expand the vastness of space. We laid out the spacious earth and created things in pairs, so that you may take notice [of Us].

50. Say to them, "Run towards God. I am merely a messenger from Him."

51. "Do not create other objects to worship along with God. I am merely a messenger from Him."

52. Every time a messenger was sent to any people in history they all responded the same: "He must be a wizard or else he is possessed."

53. Do they somehow pass this response on to one another? They are all rebellious people.

54. Just turn away from them, for you won't be held to blame for them.

55. Remind mankind, for surely the message will aid the faithful.

56. I only created genies and men so that they might worship Me.

57. I do not require any nourishment from them or ask them to feed Me.

58. God is the provider of sustenance, the Lord of power and an unbreakable might.

59. The sinners will receive the same punishment as the guilty people before them. Don't let them ask Me to hurry its arrival.

60. There is misery for the unfaithful on that day that is promised to them.

Chapter 68 (chronologically)

Sura 88 (26 verses), Al-Ghashiya (The Overwhelming)

1. Have you heard about a future overwhelming event?

2–7. That day when some faces will be wearing humiliation, as they wearily enter the flames and must drink boiling water?

They will have only cactus to eat, which will not provide nourishment or stop the hunger.

8–16. Others on that day will be joyous, pleased with their past life, and reside in gardens on high, where they won't hear any more lies or idle talk. The fountains will gush near the raised thrones, and goblets will be set out. There the cushions will be placed on the carpets.

17–20. Does mankind not look at the camels? Wonder about their creation? Look at the heavens held aloft? See how the mountains have been affixed? And how the earth is a spreading expanse?

21–22. Warn them! For you are Our reminder and have not been sent to manage men's affairs.

23. For those who reject the message and do not believe,

24. God will punish them with a great penalty.

25–26. All will return to Us, and they will be called to account [for their life].

Chapter 69 (chronologically)

Sura 18 (110 verses), Al-Kahf (The Cave)

1–3. Give praise to God who sent this Book to His servants and only filled it with truth. This Book offers a path for the righteous and also a warning of punishment. It offers good news to the faithful that do good works that they will receive a fair reward where they will reside eternally.

4–5. It also warns those who say that God has taken a son, that they have no knowledge about what they are saying and neither did their fathers. They are speaking a monstrous lie.

6. You would worry yourself to death if you constantly have concerns about those who don't believe this message.

7–8. Everything on earth We created as a glittering distraction, so that We can test mankind and see who lives a righteous life. In the end, We will make the earth a barren wasteland.

9. Do you think that the experience of the "companions of the cave" and the inscription were part of Our wondrous signs?

10. One day some young men took refuge in a cave and prayed, "Lord, send us your mercy and help us through this crisis."

11–12. We made them deaf and left them in the cave for a number of years and then woke them to see which of the two was able to determine how long they had been in the cave.

13. We share this true story with you because they were two youths that were faithful, and therefore We increased their guidance.

14–16. We strengthened their hearts and they stood, preaching, "Our Lord is the Lord of the heavens and the earth, and we will never call upon another god except Him. If we called upon another god, it would be an atrocious lie. Our people are worshipping gods besides Him, and they do not have clear authority to do so. Who is more evil than someone that lies against God? When you reject all the gods other than God, then seek refuge in the cave. Your Lord will extend His mercy and guide you comfortably through any crisis."

17. You have surely seen the sun moving from right to left as it passed their cave while they were inside. This is a sign of God. Whoever God guides is righteous, but whoever God lets go astray will not have any guardian to show him the right path in life.

18. If you saw them in the cave, you would have thought they were awake while they slept. We turned them from their left to right sides. Their dog lay stretching his paws across the cave threshold. If you had come upon them, you would have run from them in terror.

19–20. When We woke them from their long sleep, they questioned each other. One asked, "How long have we been here?" One of them said, "Maybe a day or a part of a day?" Later one said, "God alone knows how long we have stayed here. Let's send someone with money into the nearest town to find some pure foods for your hunger. Have him act courteously and take care not to tell anyone about you all. If they should figure out who you are, they might stone you to death or force you back into their religion."

21. We did let the people of the city know about the young men in the cave, so they could learn that the promise of God is true and that the hour of judgment would surely come. After much discussion in the city, the occupants said, "Construct a building over them. Their Lord knows what's best for them." Those who won the argument said, "We shall raise a mosque [place of worship, *masjeed*] above them."

22. Of this story, some say there were three young men with the dog being a fourth. Others say it was five and with the dog six—they were guessing at random. Yet another said seven with a dog eight. You say to them, "My Lord knows the true number, and only a few men truly know the full story." Do not enter any arguments about them with men that are seeking confrontation, and do not ask anyone about the young men in the cave.

23–24. Do not say, "I will do that tomorrow," without adding the phrase "if God wills it so!" [*Insha'Allah*], and pray to your Lord if you forget the phrase and ask, "Maybe my Lord will guide me to a more righteous path than this."

25. In truth they stayed in their cave for 309 years.

26. But say to them, "God knows truly how long they stayed. He knows the secrets of the heavens and the earth. He is clear in sight and keen of hearing. Man has no guardian besides Him, and He does not share His authority with anything or anyone else."

27. Recite what has been revealed to you of your Lord's book. Nothing can change His words, and you can't find any other sanctuary except for Him.

28. [MD] Congregate with those who pray to their Lord morning and evening, and don't look beyond them in desire for the splendor and beauty of this life. Do not obey anyone who We have allowed to become unfaithful to Us, who follows their own desires, and who has gone beyond redemption.

29. Say to them, "I speak the truth from your Lord, anyone that chooses to can believe, and anyone that chooses to can fail to believe it." We have created a fire for the unfaithful. It will enclose them like a tent. When they cry for relief, they will be given water like molten metal. The dreadful act of drinking will scald their faces. They will not rest in comfort.

30–31. For the righteous and faithful, We will count every good deed. They will be in the eternal Gardens with rivers flowing beneath them, as they wear bracelets of gold and green clothes made of fine embroidered silk. They will recline on couches, an excellent reward and a fine resting place.

32. Tell them the parable of the two men. For one man, We had provided two gardens of grapes and surrounded it with date palms. Between the two men We placed a cornfield.

33–36. These two gardens were very successful. They always bloomed, and We placed a spring inside them. One day when the men were arguing, the man with the bountiful gardens said to his neighbor, "I am richer than you and more men follow me." He then stood in his gardens full of pride and said, "These gardens will never fail. I don't think the judgment hour will ever come. And even if I am brought in front of my Lord for judgment, surely he will reward me with something even better."

37–41. His neighbor said to him during their talk, "Do you mean to deny Him? He who created you from dust and a drop of seed and molded you into a man?" He continued, "I say that God is my Lord, and I do not create any partners equal with God." Then he asked the prideful farmer, "Why didn't you walk in your garden and say, 'God has made this as He wishes. There is no power besides God's.'" He continued, "While you think I am inferior to you in wealth and children, have you considered that my Lord might give me something better than your garden and that He might send down thunderbolts on your land and leave it scorched? Or that the water level may sink so low that you can't reach it?"

42–43. Then his fruits came to ruin and he sat wringing the dirt and vines dead on the trellises in his hands. All he could say was, "Poor me, if only I had not attributed a partner to my Lord."

He now had no one to help him except for God, and he couldn't help himself.

44. The only protection comes from God, the true Lord. He is the best judge of rewards and payback.

45. Explain to them the parable of their life in this world. It is like the rains that We send down, so the vegetation can grow into a tangled mess that eventually breaks into pieces and is scattered by the winds. God has power over all things.

46. Wealth and children are but ornaments of this life. The things that endure are good deeds. They are the thing most rewarded by your Lord and provide you the best foundation for hope.

47–48. One day We will flatten the mountains, and the earth will be level. We shall gather them all and will not leave any behind. They will stand before their Lord in ranks and hear, "You have now returned to Us just like We first created you, even though you thought this promised hour wouldn't arrive."

49. The book of deeds will be opened in front of them and the sinners will have a look of terror on their face because of what is written. They will say, "Pity us, look at this book. Everything is recorded in it no matter how big or small the detail." They will be presented with everything they have ever done, and the Lord will give fair justice to all.

50–51. We told the angels to bow down to mankind, and all but Iblis heeded Our command. He was one of the genies, and he disobeyed his Lord. Why would you seek him or one of his offspring to be your guardian instead of Me? They are mankind's enemy and an evil choice for the sinners. I did allow them to witness the creation of the heavens or the earth and certainly not their own creation. Those who mislead mankind are not my assistants.

52–53. When He asks one day for you to, "Call upon those who you thought were my partners," they won't respond to your cry, as they will be separated by an abyss. Then the sinners will see the flames and realize that they are about to enter them. There will be no way to escape it.

54. We made this Qur'an [scripture] for the benefit of mankind, and it contains various examples [to explain Our guidance]. Unfortunately man is the most argumentative being.

55. Nothing prevents mankind from having faith when the guidance comes to them and from praying for forgiveness from their Lord. Why do they seek the painful penalties We cast on their ancestors or wish to face personal doom?

56. We simply send Our messengers to spread the good news and to give warning, but the unbelievers always argue with them in vain. They argue to try to weaken the truth. They take Our revelations as a hoax and mock Our warnings.

57. Is there any greater sinner than the man who hears out revelations and then rejects them and tries to ignore the deeds he has done with his own hands? We have hardened their hearts and plugged their ears, so when you try to share Our guidance, they will never accept it.

58. Your Lord is forgiving and merciful. If He called the unfaithful to account immediately, it would be speeding up their punishment. They have a certain lifespan ahead of them, but after that they cannot escape justice.

59. It was the same for the communities We destroyed in the past. They were sinning, and We set a specific time for their destruction.

60–63. Moses spoke to his servant during their travels: "We will journey until we reach the junction of the two seas or until I've traveled for years." When they reached the junction, they forgot about the fish they carried, and it made its way into the sea. Farther along on the journey, Moses said to the servant, "Let's eat a meal, as we have grown tired." The servant replied, "Satan made me forget to tell you, but when we were on the rock by the sea, the fish somehow made it into the water."

64–66. Moses spoke: "That was what we were looking for!" Then they retraced their path to the rock. There they found one of Our servants that We had bestowed Our mercy on and gave Our knowledge to. Moses asked, "May I follow you on the condition that you share with me the knowledge you have been taught?"

67–68. The servant of God replied, "You will not be able to bear me. How can you have the patience to learn something of which you have so little understanding?"

69–70. Moses replied, "You will find that I am patient and I will not disobey you." The man replied, "OK, but you may not ask me any questions about my knowledge until I explain it to you."

71–73. They traveled on together, and then one day the man made a hole in their boat. Moses screamed, "Have you scuttled this boat in order to drown the passengers? You have done a strange thing." The man replied, "I told you that you would not be able to bear with me." Moses responded, "Please forgive me for forgetting my promise and don't be angry with me for this slip."

74–76. They journeyed some more until the man met a youth and killed him. Moses exclaimed, "You have killed an innocent man who was not guilty of murder. This is horrible!" The man responded, "I told you that you couldn't be patient with me." Moses replied, "If I ever ask another question of you, then you may send me away, for it would be my fault."

77–78. On they went until they arrived at a town where the citizens refused them as guests. The man found a crumbling wall in the town and started to repair it. Moses stated, "If you wanted to, you could ask for a payment for this work." The man looked at Moses and said, "This is where we will part. Let me tell you the significance of the things you were too impatient to understand."

79. "First the boat. It belonged to poor men that worked the river. But I needed to make it unserviceable, for there was a king nearby seizing every boat they could find seaworthy."

80–81. "The young man was killed because his parents were faithful, and we feared that he would be disobedient to them and bring them grief. We intended for their Lord to give them a better son that was pure and merciful."

82. Finally the wall. It was the wall of two young orphans in the town. Beneath the wall was a treasure that their father left to them. He was a righteous father, and the Lord desired that the boys would retrieve their treasure when they reached maturity. I did none of this by my own accord. That is the justification of the actions you were too impatient for me to explain to you.

83. [MD] When they ask you about Dhul Qarnayn, say to them, "Let me recite his story."

84–86. [MD] We established him as a power on the earth and gave him ways to achieve anything. He followed a certain road until the sun set, and he found a muddy spring. Nearby were a people, so We spoke to him, "Dhul Qarnayn, you have the authority to be kind or to punish them."

87-88. [MD] Dhul said, "If you do wrong, we will punish you, and then you will be sent to your Lord, and He will deliver a most awful penalty. But if you are faithful and act righteously, you will be rewarded and we will make your lives easier."

89–91. [MD] Then he followed another road until he came to a sunrise shining on another people that We had not given any shelter from the sun. He left them as he found them, and We knew what he was thinking.

92–97. [MD] He again followed another road until he reached a valley between two mountains. Here he found a people that were nearly illiterate. They begged, "Dhul Qarnayn, the Gog and Magog are corrupting the lands. We wish to pay you to erect a barrier between them and us." He replied, "What my Lord has given me is better than your reward, so just help me with your labor, and I will build a barrier." He commanded, "Bring me pieces of iron." Soon they had filled the space between the mountainsides, and he said, "Now blow your bellows, and then bring me the molten metal to pour over this wall." The neighbors were unable to scale the barrier or dig through it.

98. [MD] He explained to them, "This was a mercy from my Lord. One day when His promise comes true, He will level this barrier. The promise of my Lord is the truth."

99–101. [MD] On that day We shall let men surge against each other like waves. Then the trumpet will sound, and We will gather them all together. Then We shall give the unbelievers a clear view of hell. Those unbelievers that were blinded to My revelations and couldn't bear to hear them.

102. Do the unfaithful think that they can choose My servants to be a guardian instead of Me? We have prepared hell as a welcome for the unbelievers.

103–104. Say to them, "Shall We tell you who will lose the most by their deeds in life? It's the people who waste their whole lives' effort while thinking that they were doing good deeds."

105. Anyone who denies the signs of their Lord and mocks the idea that they will meet Him in the hereafter will find that their work was in vain. On resurrection day, We will give no weight to their deeds.

106. Hell is their reward, because they rejected faith and mocked My revelations and messengers.

107–108. But for the faithful and righteous, We will welcome them in the Gardens of paradise. They will stay there eternally and never wish to leave.

109. Say to them, "If we used the oceans like ink to try to write all of my Lord's words, we would run out of ocean; even if you doubled the size of the ocean, you would still not have enough ink."

110. Say to them, "I am mortal like you. The inspirations have come to me that God is your only one god. Whoever wants to meet his Lord must do righteous deeds and never try to join anyone as a partner to God."

Chapter 70 (chronologically)

Sura 16 (128 verses), Al-Nahl (The Honeybee)

1. God's commandments will happen. Do not try to hurry them along. God is glorious and dignified above any of the partners men associate with Him.

2. He sends His angels down inspired by His commandments to any servant He wishes, and they say, "Warn mankind that there is no god besides Me, so worship Me."

3. He created the heavens and the earth with truth. He reigns above any partners they associate with Him.

4. He created man from a drop of seed, and yet man is openly defying Him.

5–7. He created cattle for mankind to give them warmth and meat and for other uses. There is beauty in them, as man drives them home at sunset and out to pasture in the morning. They can carry your loads to far-off places you cannot carry it. Your Lord is most kind and merciful.

8. He also created horses, mules, and asses for you to ride and to show them off. He has created other things too that you aren't aware of.

9. God provides the straight path and also deviant ways. If God willed it so, all men would be guided correctly.

10–11. He sends down the rains you drink and that grows vegetation for your herds to eat. He also uses it to produce crops, olives, date palms, grapes and other kinds of fruits. These are all signs for those who reflect upon them.

12. He controls the night and day and the sun and the moon to make them useful to mankind. These are signs for those who are wise.

13. All the color variations on the earth are His creation and are also a sign for those who are grateful.

14. He controls the seas, so that you can catch fish from them and extract the jewels for decorations to wear. You can see the ships move on their waves, so that you can enjoy their abundance and be grateful.

15–16. He made the mountains firm, so they wouldn't quake, and gave you rivers and roads to travel upon. He made landmarks and stars, so you can guide yourselves.

17. Has He created all this like an amateur that doesn't know how? Why won't you take warning?

18. If you tried you couldn't add up all the favors God has given man. God is forgiving and merciful.

19. God knows what you do in public and all your secrets.

20–21. Those you worship instead of God were created by God and do not have the power to create. They are dead things and are not aware of the resurrection date.

22–23. Your God is the one and only God, and those who don't believe in the hereafter have ignorant hearts. They are arrogant. God knows what their hearts conceal and what they proclaim. He does not love the arrogant.

24–25. When you ask man, "What has your Lord revealed?" They will say, "Merely the ancient stories." On judgment day they will bear all of their own burdens and also part of the burdens of those that misled them. They will bear a great and evil burden.

26. The people before this also schemed, but God tore their foundations out of their buildings, and the roofs fell on them. Doom came at them while they were unaware.

27–29. On judgment day, He will disgrace them and ask, "Where are My partners that you used to argue existed?" Those who are wise will note, "On this day the unfaithful are covered with shame and misery." And those that the angels grabbed while they were committing sin will cry, "We submit fully, and we were not sinning!" The angels will remind them that, "God knows everything you did. Now enter the gates of hell and stay forever. Evil is the home of the arrogant."

30–31. When the righteous are asked, "What has your Lord revealed?" They will reply, "Everything that is good." For the righteous there is good in this life and a reward in the hereafter. The faithful and righteous will have a fine home. They will enter the eternal Gardens where streams flow, and they will have whatever they wish. That is how God rewards the righteous.

32. Those who are taken by the angels while in a state of purity will be welcomed with, "Peace be onto you; enter the garden in reward for your deeds."

33–34. Do they just wait for angels to come to them or for the Lord's decree to occur? That is what people did before these. God did not act unjust towards them; they brought it upon themselves. The consequences for the evil they had done arrived, and the warnings they used to mock encircled them.

35. The polytheists will say, "If God had willed it, neither we nor our ancestors would have worshipped anything besides God, and we would not have forbidden anything that He didn't advise." The people before them said the same thing. Do we ask our messengers to do anything besides reveal a clear message?

36. We sent a messenger to every people proclaiming, "Serve God and shun false gods!" Afterwards there were some people that became righteous and also some that went astray. If you travel the lands, you can see the consequences of the unfaithful.

37–39. Even if you want them to be rightly guided, remember that God won't guide those who mislead others. They will have no guardian. They will swear by their strongest oaths that God doesn't have the power to resurrect the dead, but it is surely God's true promise. Most men don't know this. They'll be raised so that He can settle the arguments between men, and so the unfaithful will realize they were liars.

40. To make something happen all We have to say is "Be!" and it occurs.

41–42. For anyone that has to leave their homes to serve God because of oppression, We will provide them a good home in this world. But the true reward in the hereafter will be the greatest. If only they could realize this! It's for those who are patient and persevere, putting trust in their Lord.

43–44. In the past, We sent other men as messengers; they carried Our inspired words. If you have not heard of their messages, ask people about it. We sent them with clear signs and scriptures. We have also revealed this message to you so that you can reveal it to mankind to reflect upon it.

45–47. Of those men who make evil plans, do they feel safe from God? That He won't make the earth swallow them or that a punishment of doom won't strike them by surprise? Safe that He won't suddenly grab them on a journey? There will be no escape. Safe that He won't make them suffer by a slow attrition? Indeed, your Lord is kind and merciful!

48. Haven't they seen how everything that God created casts a shadow from right to left as they bow to God humbly?

49–50. Everything in the heavens and on earth bows respectfully to God, because they are not arrogant. They fear their Lord and follow His commands.

51. God said, "Do not worship two gods; there is only one God. Only be afraid of me."

52. Everything in the heavens and on the earth belongs to Him. Religion is His. Would you fear anyone besides God?

53–55. Everything that brings you joy is from God. When you are troubled by distress, you call to Him for help. And yet when He removes the distress from your life, some of you associate other partners to God, unthankful for the favor God granted you. For you ungrateful, enjoy your life for a little while, because soon you will learn your mistake.

56. Even after We bestow upon them their sustenance, they set aside a portion of their tithe for the make-believe things. By God, you will be asked about these things you falsely created.

57–59. Glory be to God! They even associate a daughter with God! While to themselves they seek what they desire [sons], yet when news arrives of a newborn girl, they get angry and grieve inside. Fathers hide themselves in shame because of the bad news, asking themselves whether they should keep the girl disapprovingly or bury her in the sand. They will surely make an evil choice.

60. For anyone that doesn't believe in the hereafter, an unimaginable evil awaits them, and God has the most powerful and vivid imagination. He is the mightiest and wisest.

61. If God immediately punished all sinners in mankind, there wouldn't be a soul left on earth. So He gives them their appointed lifetime to live. But once they leave the earth, they cannot postpone their justice for a single hour. Man also can't bring that specific end time forward.

62. Some associate something to God that they wouldn't even want for themselves. While doing so, they lie to themselves, thinking they will be rewarded in the future. There is no doubt that the fires of hell are their unavoidable destination and will be the first to enter it.

63. By God, We sent messengers to the people before you, but Satan made them think they were living righteously. Today Satan is their patron, and they will bear a painful penalty.

64. We sent down this Book to you, so you can clarify the arguments that men have between each other. It is a guide and mercy for the faithful.

65. God sends down rains to the earth to revive the soils that are dry, so they can give life. This is a sign to all who want to see it.

66. If you study the cattle, you will see Our sign. From inside their body where intestines and blood flow, We allow a pure and tasty milk to flow for you to drink.

67. Look at the date palm and grapes. They provide you nourishing food and strong drink. This is a sign for the wise to see.

68–69. The Lord taught the bee to build hives on the hills and in trees and homes. He taught them to eat from all the vegetation of the earth. From the bees comes a drink in varying color that can be a healing aid to mankind. This is a sign for those who believe.

70. It is God that creates man and recalls their souls at death. There are some among you that will reach an age in life where you will no longer remember what you once knew. God is all-powerful and all-knowing.

71. God gives His gifts to some men in greater number than others. Those He favors more in wealth and property should not give their rightful gifts from God to their servants in a

quest to make them equal. Are they trying to deny gifts from God?

72–73. God makes mates for you from your own kind. From this relationship come sons and daughters and grandchildren and provisions for you. Why then do they believe in lies? Are unbelievers ungrateful for God's grace? The unfaithful worship things besides God that are powerless to provide them sustenance on earth or in heaven.

74. Don't create anything and liken it to God. God knows what you don't know.

75. God gave us a parable of two men. One is a slave to the other. The slave is powerless, while the other man has been granted God's favors, and he spends his riches publicly and privately as he wishes. How can you think these two are equal? Praise God, most men don't understand.

76. God gives us another parable of two men. One man is dumb and powerless. He is a burden to his owner, and no matter what the owner asks of him he causes no good. Can the dumb be equal to a just man on the righteous path?

77. God knows the secrets of the heavens and the earth. The judgment day's occurrence could come in a blink or even sooner. God has power over all things.

78. He brought you from your mother's womb with a blank mind. He gave you hearing and sight and also a heart; you could give thanks.

79. Don't people see the birds floating in the sky? They are held up by the power of God. There are signs for the faithful.

80. God gave you a place to rest safely in your homes. He gave you animal skins to make tents when you travel. From animal wool, fur, and hairs, He gives you household items.

81. God made places to give you shade, shelters in the hills, and garments that can protect you from the heat and from weapons in battle. This is how He keeps his promise to you, so that you can submit to Him.

82. Remember it's only your duty to deliver a message; they may reject it.

83. They can recognize the favors of God and still deny them. Most of them don't believe.

84. But on that day when We raise a witness amongst every nation, there will be no excuses allowed from the unbelievers, and they won't be able to ask for favors.

85. When the unjust finally see the great penalty they face, there is no way its intensity will be lessened, and they won't get any relief from it.

86–87. When the sinners who created partners and associated them with God see them in the hereafter, they will say, "Our Lord, these are the other gods we worshipped instead of you." They will reply, "You are all liars." So on that day the sinners will openly submit to God and all of their invented gods will have failed them.

88–89. For anyone that rejected God and then led men away from the righteous path, We will double their grievous penalty. On the day We raise a witness amongst all nations, We will bring you forth as a witness against those sinners. For We have sent the Book to you, so it can answer all questions, be a guide, be a mercy, and offer good news to all who submit to God. [Muslims]

90. God commands justice and kindness and generosity to your relatives. He forbids indecencies, evil acts, and aggression. He warns you, so you may take heed.

91. If you fulfill your promises to God and keep all your oaths once you have made them, you have ensured God's guardianship. God knows everything you do.

92. Don't be like the woman who would unravel her yarn into strings and weaken it after making it strong, by lying among yourselves so that one group of people can become more wealthy than another. This is a test from God. He will explain to you, on the day of judgment, everything you used to argue about.

93. If God chose to, He could have made all mankind into one nation. But He chooses to guide who He wants and lead astray who He wants. He will call you to account for your deeds.

94. Don't make promises among yourselves with the intent of making a solid man's foot slip. Or you will have to bear the evil consequences of pulling men away from the righteous path to God.

95–96. Do not trade your promises to God for a small gain. If you only knew that the reward from God is so much greater for you. What you have on earth will be gone, but God's reward is everlasting. We will reward the faithful and steadfast, relative to their good deeds.

97. Whether they are a man or a woman, We will give a good life to the righteous and faithful and will reward them in the hereafter in accordance with their good works.

98–100. When you recite the Qur'an [scripture], seek God's protection from Satan. He does not have any power over people that are faithful and put their trust in God. He does have power over people that make him their guardian and associate partners with him.

101. God knows best what He wants to reveal and when to reveal it. So when We send down a revelation that replaces another

they say, "You are making this up!" Most of them do not understand.

102. Say to them, "The holy spirit delivered this revelation from your Lord truthfully, so that it can strengthen the faithful and be a guide and good news for Muslims." [those who submit to God]

103. We know that disbelievers say, "He is being taught these verses by a man." But the language of the man they are referring to is foreign, while these recitations are pure and clear Arabic.

104. God will not guide the people that don't believe in the signs of God, and they will receive a great penalty.

105. The real liars are the people that don't believe in God's signs and try to say that they are made up.

106. Anyone that stops believing in God after accepting the faith of their own free will feel the wrath of God and bear an awful penalty. There is an exception for people that are forced to denounce their faith publicly but keep the faith in their hearts.

107. The penalty is because these people have chosen the life in this world over their life in the hereafter. God will no longer guide people who stop being faithful to Him.

108–109. They will have their hearts, ears, and eyes sealed by God and will not receive the messages. There is no doubt they will be the scum in the hereafter.

110. Your Lord will be merciful and forgiving to anyone that must leave their home to escape persecution and then struggles [*jihad*] and is patiently steadfast.

111. On the day when all souls are judged independently and rewarded for what they did in their life, they will be judged fairly.

112–113. God gave us a story about a city that was safe and quiet. They had all they needed in abundance, yet they were ungrateful for God's gifts. So God made them hungry and terrified for their misdeeds. Then a messenger appeared from among them, but they rejected him. Then a great torment overtook them for their injustice.

114. Therefore eat the lawful and pure things God gives you and be grateful for God's gifts, if it is God that you worship.

115. He has forbidden you from eating any animal that was found dead before it was slaughtered, blood, pig meat, and any foods that were blessed using any other name instead Gods. But if you are forced to eat these due to emergency and not because you are being disobedient or gluttonous, then God is forgiving and merciful.

116. Do not lie and pretend that you know what is lawful and what is forbidden, because it is a lie against God. Those who lie against God will not succeed.

117. You may get brief enjoyment from this but will face a painful punishment.

118. We forbid the Jews from these things. We did not mistreat them, but they were wrong to themselves.

119. Of course, for those who sin out of ignorance and later repent for their misdeed, your Lord is merciful and forgiving.

120. Abraham was a model to mankind. He was obedient to God, righteous [upright; *hanif*] and not a polytheist [heathen].

121. He [Abraham] was grateful for God's favors. So in return He [God] selected him and put him on a straight path.

122. We gave him good things in this world, and in the hereafter he will be among the righteous.

123. We have taught you this inspired message so say, "Follow the faith of Abraham, who was righteous and not a polytheist."

124. The Sabbath was ordained because of the people who were arguing about its correct date. Your Lord will settle their arguments on the day of judgment.

125. Invite man to follow the path of your Lord using wisdom and sound counsel. Argue with them with dignity. Your Lord knows who strays from the path and who follows the guidance.

126. If you retaliate towards them, then only respond equally to their treatment of you. But if you are patient instead, then you are following the best course.

127. [MD] So be a patient man. Your patience is possible only through God. Don't grieve for those who argue, and don't feel anguish from their scheming.

128. [MD] God sides with those who are God-fearing and live virtuously.

Chapter 71 (chronologically)

Sura 71 (28 verses), Nuh (Noah)

1. We commanded Noah to tell his people about an impending doom.

2–4. Noah said, "My people, I am a messenger sent to tell you that you should worship and serve God and obey me. If you do, He may forgive your sins and let you live for a while longer. The given term of life cannot be postponed when it approaches an end. If you only knew this."

5–6. He prayed, "My Lord, I have spoken to my people both night and day. It seems the more I talk the more they go astray."

7. "Whenever I tell them that you might forgive them, they just place their fingers in their ears, cloak their heads, and become more arrogant."

8–12. "I call to them loudly in public and also talk to them in private. I tell them to ask their Lord for forgiveness for He is merciful. That He will send abundant rains. That He will increase their wealth and the number of sons and give them gardens and rivers."

13. I asked them, "What is the matter with you all? Why don't you revere God and pray for His favor?"

14–16. "You know He created you in stages. Can't you see that God created the seven heavens in layers? That He made the moon to light them? That he made the sun like a lamp?"

17–18. "God caused you to grow gradually from the earth. After life He will return you into the earth and then resurrect you."

19–20. "God has laid out the earth in vast expanses, so you can travel its spacious paths."

21–22. Noah cried, "My Lord, they disobey me and instead follow men who earn nothing from their wealth and children. They have schemed to create a great plan."

23–24. "They say to each other, 'Do not abandon your gods, not Wadd, Suwa, Yaghuth, Ya'uq, nor Nasr.' They have misled many people, while you don't empower them with anything but failure."

25. For their sins they were drowned. They entered the fire and found that all the gods they worshipped instead of God could not help them.

26–28. Noah prayed, "Lord, don't leave a single unbeliever on the earth. If you leave any of them behind, they will mislead your servants, and their descendants will be wicked and ungrateful. My Lord, forgive me, my parents, all who enter my home faithfully, and all the men and women who believe. Only give the sinners more punishment."

Chapter 72 (chronologically)

Sura 14 (52 verses), Ibrahim (Abraham)

1–3. Alif. Lam. Ra. We have revealed this Book to you so that you can bring mankind into the light from the darkness. With the permission of their Lord, they may enter the straight path towards the almighty and praiseworthy God. He owns everything that is in heaven and earth. For the unfaithful there will be a mighty penalty. Those that like the life of this world more than the hereafter and who block other men from following God's path and seek corruption have gone the furthest from righteousness.

4. We always send Our apostles with a message in their own people's language, so they could clearly relay it. Then God allows to stray who He likes and guides who He likes. He is all-powerful and wise.

5. We sent Moses with Our signs and authority, saying, "Bring your people from the darkness and into the light. Teach them

to remember the days of God." There are signs here for the steadfast and grateful hearts to see.

6–8. Moses said to his people, "Never forget the mercy of God for His deliverance of you from the Pharaoh. Those people tormented you and killed your sons, while sparing your women. It was an incredible trial by your Lord." Remember your Lord's proclamation, "If you are grateful, then I will reward you, but if you are ungrateful, there will be a severe punishment." Moses then said, "God is self-sufficient and always worthy of praise even if every last man on earth proves to be ungrateful to Him."

9. Haven't you heard the story of Noah? Noah, the Ad or the Thamad people, and those of earlier generations? Only God knows about them. They received messengers with clear revelations, but they stuck their hands in their mouths while saying, "We reject your mission and are suspicious about what you are asking us to do."

10. Their apostles replied, "Do you doubt God, the creator of the heavens and the earth? He, not I, calls to you. He can forgive your sins and pardon you until the end of time. The people replied, "You are just a human like us! You are trying to turn us away from our ancestor's gods. Bring us a clear sign!"

11-12. The messengers responded, "Yes, we are just humans, but God bestows His grace on whichever servants He wants. I can only bring you the signs that God allows. Let all faithful men put their trust in God. Why shouldn't we put our trust in God? He has guided our way. We will endure any pain you may cause us. The faithful should put their trust in God."

13–14. The unbelievers replied, "We will drive you from our lands and return to our old religion." But the Lord gave the message to the apostles that, "We will destroy these unrighteous men. We will allow you to live in their lands after they are gone. It's the promise to men who fear facing Me on judgment day and fear My threats."

15–17. The messengers sought help from their Lord, and all the disrespectful sinners fell. In front of the unjust is hell, where he will drink only boiling water. They will sip it slowly but never be able to swallow. Death will surround him yet he won't die. An unrelenting misery.

18. A parable of the unfaithful. Their works will be like ashes being blown daily by a storm. They will have no power to control their earnings. Their's is a great mistake.

19–20. Can't you see that God justly created the heavens and the earth? If He wanted to, He could remove you and bring forth a new creation. It is not a difficult thing for God.

21. Everyone will be present before God, and the weak will ask the arrogant men, "Can you save us from God's wrath, because we were simply following you?" The arrogant will reply, "If God had given us any guidance we surely would

have shared it with you. It doesn't matter how we react to the punishment now, because there is no escaping it."

22. Next Satan will say to the people, "God promised you the truth, and I gave you false promises. I had no authority over you, but still you listened to my call. Don't ask me to take any blame; blame your own souls. I can't help you, and you can't help me. I reject the actions you took to associate me with God. Sinners will face a great punishment."

23. But for those who were faithful and righteous, you will enter the Gardens, with rivers flowing, and live there by God's grace. You shall greet each other saying, "Peace."

24–25. God tells us that a good phrase is like a good tree. Its roots are firmly planted, and its branches reach up to the heavens. Every season God allows it to bear fruit. God uses parable to provide a warning to mankind.

26. God tells us that an evil phrase is like an evil tree; poorly rooted in the ground, it has no stability.

27. God will strengthen those who are faithful with words that stand firm, in this life and the hereafter. God will let those who do wrong go astray. God does as He wishes.

28–29. [MD] Haven't you seen the people that lost God's grace by becoming unfaithful and led their people into hell? They will enter the evil place and remain.

30. To those that set up others as equals to God in order to mislead men from the righteous path say, "Enjoy your brief life for you are headed straight to hell."

31. Tell My faithful servants to establish regular prayer and give to charity in public and private before the day comes when there will no bargaining or helpful friends.

32–34. It is God that created the heavens and the earth and sends down rains from the sky to produce fruits. He made the ships take your guidance, so they can sail the sea by His authority, and made the rivers serve you. He set the sun and moon on their constant courses and gave you night and day to serve you. He gives you everything you ask of Him. If you try to count God's favors to man, you cannot do it. Man is unjust and ungrateful.

35. Abraham once prayed, "My Lord, make this city safe, and save my sons and me from idol worship.

36. My Lord, they have led many men astray. But, whoever follows my ways is with me; and for those who disobey me, You are surely forgiving and merciful.

37. Our Lord, I have placed some of my family in a barren valley near Your sacred house, my Lord, so that they can establish proper worship. Fill some of their hearts so that they will move towards You, and feed them fruits so they can be thankful.

38. Our Lord, You know what we say and what we hide, because nothing on earth or in heaven is hidden from God.

39. Praise God, who gave an old man two sons, Ishmael and Isaac. He is my true Lord and hears prayers.

40. My Lord, make me worship properly and raise children that do, too. Lord, please accept my prayer.

41. Lord, forgive me, my parents, and all the faithful on the day of judgment."

42–43. Don't think that God doesn't know what the wicked are doing! He simply gives them some relief until the day they will look in horror, running in fear, with their heads looking upwards and their hearts empty.

44-45. Warn mankind of the day of doom, and the sinners will say, "Lord, give us more time, so we can begin to obey Your messages and follow Your apostles." They will hear, "Didn't you already swear that there would be no penalty for you? Didn't you live in the lands of the sinners before you that We dealt with harshly? We gave you many examples to learn from."

46. Those men devised powerful plans, but they were known to God. Their plans couldn't move the mountains.

47. Never think that God will fail to keep His oaths to His messengers. God is mighty and the Lord of retribution.

48. One day the earth and heavens will be changed, and mankind will be brought before God, the One, the almighty.

49–51. You will see the sinners linked by chains, with clothes made of pitch, and fire covering their faces. God may pay each soul what it earned, and God is swift in judgment.

52. This is a message for mankind. Take heed of it and know that He is the one God. Let the wise understand this.

Chapter 73 (chronologically)

Sura 21 (112 verses), Al-Anbiya (The Prophets)

1. The judgment day for mankind is approaching, but they reject the warnings.

2–3. When new revelations from their Lord arrive, men don't listen seriously. Their hearts are preoccupied with unimportant things. Sinners secretly question others: "Is Muhammad more than a mortal man? Can't you see his magic? Why would you believe him?"

4. Say to them, "My Lord knows every word and thought in heaven and on earth. He hears all and knows all."

5. Man will say, "These revelations are just his mixed-up dreams, and he is a forger and a poet. He must bring us a sign like the prophets of old used to present."

6. Would they believe if they recalled that We destroyed every disbelieving community before them—and We sent them signs?

7–8. Before you We sent other messengers, and they were all men We inspired. If you didn't know this, ask their followers about the earlier signs. They were not immortals, and they needed to eat like other men.

9. We always fulfilled Our promises. We saved those We wanted, and We destroyed the unbelievers.

10. We have revealed a Book to mankind with a message. Why can't you understand this?

11–13. There were countless communities that We destroyed for their sins and then raised up another generation to replace them. Yet, when each saw Our punishment coming, they tried to run from it. They were told to stop and to return to their lives and their homes, so they can be examined.

14–15. They cried, "We are in misery, for we have done wrong." They kept up this behavior until We mowed them down like vegetation.

16–17. We didn't create the heavens and the earth just for amusement. If We were seeking a hobby, We would have found one amongst Ourselves.

18. We fling the Truth against lies and knock out its brains until the lies are gone. Misery will visit you for what you say about Him.

19–20. He owns everything in the heavens and on earth. Even those who serve in His direct presence are humble enough to worship Him, and they never grow tired. They glorify Him day and night and never get weary.

21–23. Have you worshipped any gods from earth that can resurrect the dead? If there were any other gods besides God, everything would be in a state of disorder in the heavens and earth. Glory to God, the Lord of the throne that towers above everything they associate with Him. He cannot be questioned for His actions, but they surely will be.

24. If they have taken up other gods besides Him, then say, "Bring me evidence of them. That is the requirement for me and those messengers before me." Most of them don't know the truth and will reject it.

25. Every apostle We sent before you was inspired to give Our message: "There is no god but Me, so worship Me."

26. They say, "The most gracious One has a son. Glory to Him." No, they [sons] are just honorable servants.

27. They do not speak before He does, and they obey His commands.

28. He knows the future and the past. They can only intercede for those already deemed acceptable. They stand in awe of Him.

29. Anyone who claims to be a god besides God will be punished with hell. That is how We repay sin.

30. Don't the unfaithful see that We created the heavens and earth from one mass? We made everything out of water. Why don't they believe?

31–33. We set the mountains firm on the earth and made broad paths between them, so man can pass through to their destinations. We made the heavens a secure roof, and yet they reject these signs. We created the night and day, and the sun and the moon in their orbits.

34–35. We have not granted any man immortality here. If you die, how can you be immortal? Every soul must taste death. We will test you through good and evil trials. You will return to Us.

36. When the unfaithful see you they ridicule you, saying, "Is this the one that speaks of your gods?" They deny you when you mention the most gracious One.

37–40. Man is always in a hurry, but soon enough I will show you My signs, and you will not want to speed their arrival. They ask, "If you are honest, then tell us will this threat occur?" If only the unfaithful could foresee the moment when they won't be able to keep the flames away from their faces and backs and they won't have any assistance. The fire will be upon them suddenly as it confuses them. They won't have any power to stop it, nor will they get any relief.

41. Many messengers before you were mocked, and those who ridiculed them were soon surrounded by the thing they taunted.

42. Say to them, "Who can protect you both night and day from the wrath of God?" But they will turn away at the mention of their Lord.

43. Ask them if they have any gods than can protect them from Us? They can't defend themselves, let alone protect men from Us.

44. We have provided the good things in life to these men and their fathers until they became aged. Can't they see that We gradually reduce their lands at its borders? How do they expect to be victorious?

45. Say to them, "I am revealing what is inspired to me." But the deaf will not hear your message when you speak.

46. If only a breath of the wrath of your Lord touched them, men would say, "We are doomed! We have been unjust!"

47. We shall erect scales of justice on the judgment day so that every soul will receive fairness. Even deeds that are the weight of a mustard seed will tip the scales, and We are completely adequate to judge.

48–49. We gave Moses and Aaron the standards for judging right and wrong, a torch, and a warning for the righteous. They who secretly fear their Lord and who dread the final hour.

50. We have sent down a blessed reminder, so how can you reject it?

51–53. We bestowed dignity upon Abraham and knew him well. He said to his father and people, "What are these images you worship?" They replied, "They are the ones our fathers worshipped."

54–55. He told them, "You and your fathers are making a grave mistake." They replied, "Have you brought us some truth, or are you joking?"

56–57. He said to them, "Your Lord is the Lord of the heavens and earth, and He created you. I can testify to this. By God, I will deal with your idols when you are gone."

58–59. Then he broke all but the largest of them to pieces, in hopes that they would return. They saw it and said, "Who did this to our gods? He must be an evil man."

60. Someone said they had heard of a young man named Abraham.

61. "Bring him to us, so he can testify in front of the people."

62-63. He was questioned: "Abraham, are you the person that did this to our gods?" He replied, "No, this was done by the largest of your gods, so if he can speak, why don't you question him?"

64. They talked among themselves, concluding, "We are the ones that have been wrong."

65. Perplexed, they said, "You know that these idols can't speak!"

66–67. Abraham asked, "Why do you worship things, instead of God, that cannot do anything good or bad to you? You and the things you worship besides God disgust me. Can't you understand?"

68. Hearing enough, they said, "If we are to do anything, then burn him and protect your gods."

69–70. We told the flames, "Be cool and safe for Abraham." They had sought to harm him, but We made them lose the most.

71–73. We saved Abraham and sent him and his nephew Lot to the land we had blessed for all people. We gave him Isaac and then also Jacob. We made them all righteous men. We made them leaders who could guide men by Our authority. We inspired them to do good deeds, properly worship, and give to charity. They worshipped Us alone.

74–75. Lot was given judgment and knowledge. We later saved him from a town that was full of disgraceful people. They were an evil and rebellious group. But We gave Lot Our mercy, as he was a righteous one.

76–77. Recall when Noah cried to Us, that We listened to his prayers and delivered him and his family from a great disaster. We aided him as he challenged people who had rejected Our signs. They were an evil people, and We drowned them.

78–82. There was David and Solomon giving judgment in a field where neighbors argued about sheep that strayed in the night. We saw their judgment. We inspired Solomon to truly understand matters. To each of them We gave judgment and wisdom. We willed the mountains and birds to celebrate Our praise of David. We did all these things. We taught him how to make coats of mail to protect you in battle. Aren't you grateful? We placed the howling winds under the command of Solomon, as it headed towards his lands that We had blessed. We know all things. Among Solomon's divers and workers were devils that We kept an eye on.

83–84. Job cried to his Lord, "I am facing severe hardship, and you are the most merciful One." We heard Job and removed his hardship and restored to him the people he had lost, while doubling them in size. This was a mercy from Us and is a remembrance to those who worship Us.

85-86. We must remind you of Ishmael [Isma'il], Enoch [Idris], and Isaiah [or Ezekiel (Dhul-kifl)]. They were all steadfast men, so We took them into Our mercy. They are among the righteous.

87–88. There was Jonah [Dhun-Nun], who didn't believe that We could punish man with hardships. In the depth of his despair, he cried out, "There is no god but you! Glory unto you! I have been a sinner." We heard his cries and saved him from his hardships. That is how We save the faithful.

89–90. Zachariah called out to his Lord, "My Lord, please don't let me remain childless. You are the best of the inheritors." We heard him and made his wife fertile, so she could bear him a son named John. The three of them were in competition to do good deeds, prayed to Us with love and reverence, and were humble towards Us.

91. Recall the woman who remained a virgin. We breathed Our spirit into her, making her and her son a sign for all people to see. [Likely Mary and Jesus]

92. This is your only community, and I am your Lord. Worship Me.

93. Others have divided their communities, but they will all come back to Us.

94. Whoever acts righteously and is faithful will have their efforts recorded.

95–96. Every population that We had to destroy is prohibited from returning to Us, until the Gog and Magog are loosed from their positions and swarming over every hill.

97. Then the promise will be fulfilled. The unfaithful will gaze in horror, crying, "We are doomed! We were oblivious to this and were sinners.

98–100. You, along with those things you worshipped instead of God, will become fuel for the flames of hell. If they had truly been gods, they would not go there. But that's where they will end up. Those in hell will hear nothing but wailing.

101–103. The people that have already heard Our good warnings will be kept from hell. They won't hear the slightest sound from there and will rest where their souls desire to. They won't be bothered by the great terror. In fact the angels will welcome them, saying, "This is the day that was promised to you."

104. Just as We orchestrated the original creation, We promise that We shall reproduce it on the day that We roll up the heavens like a scroll.

105. After the Torah, We wrote in the Psalms, "My righteous servants shall inherit the earth."

106. In here is a clear message for those who are faithful.

107. We have sent you simply as a mercy for all nations.

108. Say to them, "I have been inspired to reveal that your God is the one God. Won't you submit to Him?"

109–111. If they reject you, say to them, "I have given this message to you all, but I don't know if the promises will occur soon or at a distant time. He knows everything that you say out loud and what is in your heart. I don't know whether this is a trial for you and a chance to enjoy life for a while."

112. "My Lord, judge with certainty. Our Lord is the most gracious and should be sought to guard against the things you claim."

Chapter 74 (chronologically)

Sura 23 (118 verses), Al-Mu'meenoon (The Believers/The Faithful)

1. The faithful will be successful.

2. Those who were humble in prayer;

3. avoided vain conversations;

4. who give to charity;

5–7. who guard their chastity; exceptions of course for people who are married and people who have sex with their slaves, for they are not committing a sin. But anyone desiring [any relations] outside of that are sinning;

8. who keep their pledges and covenants;

9. and who strictly conduct their prayers.

10–11. They will be the heirs of paradise, and there they shall live.

12–14. We created man from a bit of clay and then placed him as a drop of sperm in a safe place. Then We turned the sperm into congealed blood and made a lump of bones that we covered with flesh. Then We developed another creature from this. Blessed is God, the best of creators.

15–16. Eventually you will die. Then on the day of resurrection you will be raised again.

17. Above you We have created seven heavens. We are ever mindful of all our creations.

18–20. We send down the rains in the right amounts, and then cause it to enter the soil, and We can carry it away with ease. We use it to grow your gardens of date palm and grapes, and here you find abundant fruits to enjoy. It brings you a tree in the Mount Sinai area that can produce oil and be used as a condiment.

21–22. The cattle provide a message to man. Not only do they provide a drink from their stomachs and meat to eat, there are also many other uses for their bodies. Much like a ship, they can carry you.

23-25. We sent Noah to his people to say, "My people, you must worship God. He is the only God. Why won't you fear him?" The chiefs replied, "He is just a man like us. He wants to become superior to you. God could have sent angels to us if He willed it. We have never heard of what he is saying from our ancestors." Others said, "He is simply possessed, so let's keep an eye on him."

26. Noah prayed, "My Lord, please help me, for they are calling me a liar."

27. So We revealed to him to, "Build an Ark under Our supervision and inspiration. Then when We command the waters to gush forth from the earth, place two of every species, both male and female, and your family on the Ark—except those that rejected the message. Don't plead with Us about any of the sinners being saved, for they will be drowned."

28–29. Once you and your companions are safe on the Ark, pray, "Praise God who saved us from the sinners. My Lord, guide me to a safe harbor for landing the Ark, for you are the best navigator."

30. There are surely signs here for wise men to see. We are always testing mankind.

31–32. After We raised another generation of men, We raised a messenger among them, saying, "Worship God. There is no other god but Him. Won't you fear Him?"

33–38. The chiefs were unbelievers and denied the hereafter even after We bestowed a comfortable life on them. They said, "He is just a man like us. He eats and drinks like us. If you listen to a mere man like yourselves, you will be lost. He promises that after death your dust and bones will be resurrected. What he promises is far from the truth. There is nothing for you but the life in this world. We live and we die. We will not be brought back to life. He is just a man inventing lies about God, and we are not putting our faith in him."

39. The messenger said, "My Lord, help me, because they are calling me a liar."

40. In reply, "Wait a little while, and they will be sorry."

41. Soon an awful punishment overtook them, and We turned them to rubbish to be blown in the wind. The evil people were gone.

42. Then We raised more generations of men.

43. No community can lengthen or shorten their duration.

44. We continued to send messengers one after another, and every time they spoke they were rejected. They were accused of lying. So We caused each community to follow the others to doom. We made them examples to later generations. Those who reject the faith are removed.

45–48. Later We sent Moses and Aaron, his brother. They had Our signs and authority when they met the Pharaoh and his chiefs, who the brothers found disrespectful and arrogant. They said, "Why should we believe two men like you? Your people are our slaves." After they accused them [Moses and Aaron] of lying, they [Pharaoh and his chiefs] joined the communities that had been destroyed.

49. We gave Moses the Book, so they [his people] could be righteous.

50. We made Mary and her son as a sign. We gave them shelter on a high meadow with a flowing stream.

51. Apostles, eat purely and do good works, for I know everything you do.

52. This community is one, and it is yours, and I am your Lord. Be faithful to Me.

53–54. People have broken their united community into sects, where each group enjoys its own creeds. For now, leave them in this confused state.

55–56. Do they think that We have granted them wealth and male children because We are eager to give them the best things? They don't understand.

57–61. Know this: Those who are fearful of their Lord, who believe in the signs of their Lord. Who never associate partners to their Lord, and those who give to charity with fear in their hearts, because they know they will one day return to their Lord—it is those people that race to do good works and are examples on that path.

62. We never ask any soul to bear any burden it cannot handle. We keep a record that shows the truth of their deeds, and they will be judged fairly.

63. But many hearts are confused about this, and they are performing other deeds instead.

64–67. When We punish those leading luxurious lives in this world, they will cry for relief. They will be told, "Do not cry for relief today, because We will not help you. My signs were recited to you, but you rejected them. You were arrogant towards the messages and told fables in your nightly meetings."

68–69. Haven't they thought about these revelations? Haven't they learned anything new that their fathers had not passed on to them? Do they reject the messenger because they don't recognize him?

70–71. They say, "He is possessed," but he has brought them the truth. Most of them hate the truth. If the truth in the messages would have matched their desires, then the heavens and the earth would have fallen apart. We have sent them a warning, but they have rejected it.

72. Are you asking them for payment for your messages? The reward of your Lord is better, because He is the best provider.

73–74. You are calling them to the straight path. Those who don't believe in the hereafter are deviating from the path.

75–76. If We took mercy on them and relieved them of their distress, they would simply revert to their lost ways and stray from the path. We inflict them with pain, but they will not humble themselves in prayer to their Lord and submit to Him.

77. When We open the gates to their severe punishment, they will plunge into despair.

78. He gave you the ability to hear, see, and feel with your heart. Yet you give little thanks.

79. He multiplied you on this earth, and you will return to Him.

80. He gives life and causes death. He created the night and the day. Don't you understand?

81–83. They still speak like the ancient men, saying, "How could we be resurrected when we are but dust and bones? This was promised to us and our fathers before us. It's just an old story."

84–85. Ask them, "Who owns the earth and all its beings?" They will reply, "God." Then ask them, "Why won't you listen to this warning?"

86-87. Ask them, "Who is the Lord of the seven heavens that sits on the supreme throne?" They will reply, "It all belongs to God." Ask them again, "Why won't you worship Him?"

88–89. Ask them, "Who has dominion over all things and who protects all, yet who you cannot protect yourself from?" They will reply, "God." Ask them how they are being deluded.

90. We send them the truth, but they still lie.

91. God has not taken a son. There have never been any partners to Him, because each god would have taken away what He

created, and there would be fighting amongst them for power. God sits above all that they say about Him.

92. He knows the seen and the unseen. He is exalted above any partners they associate with Him.

93–95. Say, "My Lord, if you will show me the things you promise to them, then please don't put me among the sinners." Know that We are capable of showing you the things We are warning about.

96. Repel evil with things that are better. We are aware of the things they are saying.

97–98. Say, "My Lord, I seek refuge in You from the temptations of the devils. I seek refuge from their mere presence."

99–100. When they die, they will say, "My Lord send me back, so that I may live righteously this time." They will hear, "By no means." In front of them will be a barrier until the resurrection.

101–104. When the trumpet sounds, there will be no kinship between men, and they won't ask about each other. Those whose good deeds weigh heavy will be saved. But those whose good deeds weigh light will lose their souls and reside in hell. The fire will burn their faces, and they will be gloomy.

105–107. They will hear, "When My signs were recited to you, didn't you reject them as lies?" They will reply, "My Lord, we let evil overcome us, and we were sinners. Lord, remove us from this, and if we return to evil ways, then we are truly sinners."

108–111. They will be told, "Go deeper into hell, and don't speak to Me. Some of My servants used to pray to Me, saying 'Lord, we are faithful. Please show us mercy, for you are the most gracious.' But you people ridiculed them. You mocked them so much that you forgot My warnings while you were laughing at them. So you know, I rewarded those people for their steadfastness, and they are triumphant now."

112–114. He will continue, "How long did you exist on earth?" They will reply, "A day, maybe a half of a day; it's best to ask those who kept count." He will respond, "You stayed for only a little while, if only you had known it.

115. "Did you think that We created you all just for the fun of it and that you wouldn't be called to account to Us?"

116. Glorified is God the king. There is no god except He who sits on the throne of honor.

117. Anyone that calls upon any gods besides God for which he has no proof of existence will be called to judgment to his Lord. The unfaithful will not succeed.

118. Say, "My Lord, be forgiving and grant your mercy, for You are the most generous and gracious."

Chapter 75 (chronologically)

Sura 32 (30 verses), Al-Sajda (The Worship)

1–2. Alif. Lam. Meem. The revelation of this Book is surely from the Lord of the entire world.

3. They will say, "He fabricated it." This truth is from your Lord so you can be an apostle to men that haven't received the warnings yet, so they can be guided correctly.

4. God created the heavens and earth and all that's in between in six days and then rested on the throne. There is no one besides God that can protect you or intercede on your behalf. Won't you receive these warnings?

5. He rules over the heavens and earth. In one day all will return up to Him. That is around one thousand years as you measure it.

6–9. He knows everything that is public and private. He is the mighty and merciful One that perfectly created everything and made man from just a lump of clay. He made man's offspring from a drop of fluid. He completed man and breathed life into him through His spirit. He gave them eyes and hearts. Yet you are most ungrateful.

10–11. When they say, "How is that when we lie hidden in the earth, somehow we will be resurrected?" They are denying that they will meet their Lord. Say to them, "The angel of death will be charged with taking your souls back to your Lord."

12. If you could only see the guilty as they hang their heads in shame facing their Lord, saying, "Lord, we have seen and heard it now, so please send us back so that we can act righteously. Now we truly are faithful."

13. Had We willed it, We could have guided every being's soul, but the message from Me will come true. "I will fill hell with genies and mankind together."

14. Now taste evil, for just as you overlooked the day you would meet Us, We, too, will overlook you. Feel eternal punishment for your sins.

15. There are those who believe in Our signs and fall down in prostrate worship when they hear Our revelations. They celebrate their Lord and are not arrogant.

16. [MD] They leave the comfort of their beds to worship their Lord at night in fear and hope. They spend from what We gave them.

17. [MD] No soul knows what hidden delights await them in reward for their good deeds.

18. [MD] Is a faithful man no better than a sinner? They are not equals.

19. [MD] For those who believe and commit righteous deeds, there are garden homes as a reward for their behavior.

20. [MD] But for those who are wicked, there will be a place in hell. Whenever they want to leave it, they will be forced deeper into it, hearing, "Taste your penalty of fire, the punishment you denied existed."

21. We shall let them taste the nearer punishments in life before the final penalty in the hereafter, in an effort to bring them closer to God.

22. Who can be more wrong than the person that hears the revelations from his Lord and then rejects them? We shall seek vengeance on the guilty.

23. Do not doubt that We gave the scripture to Moses and made it a guide to the children of Israel.

24. Then We chose leaders among them to give Our guidance under Our authority, for they were patient and believed in Our revelations.

25. On judgment day, your Lord will solve all the matters that men used to argue about.

26. Does man not notice how many generations We destroyed that lived in the lands they now travel? These are surely signs, so why don't they listen?

27. Can't they see how the dry soils are renewed with rains that create crops for both men and cattle? Why can't they see this?

28. They will ask, "If you are telling the truth, then when will judgment day occur?"

29. Tell them, "On judgment day, the unfaithful will not prosper by becoming believers, and they won't get any relief."

30. So turn from them and wait, for they are waiting, too.

Chapter 76 (chronologically)

Sura 52 (49 verses), Al-Tur (The Mount)

1–8. I swear by the mount, the scripture written on parchment, the house frequently visited, the roof high above, and the swollen sea that surely the punishment from your Lord will happen. There is no averting it.

9–12. On the day that the heavens are in an uproar and the mountains fall away, it will be a grievous event for those who reject the truth and toy with lies.

13–16. They will be thrown violently into the fires of hell. The fires they used to deny existed. Will they think it's magic or see that it's real? "You will burn in the heat, and whether you can bear the pain patiently or impatiently, you are just being rewarded for your own deeds."

17–20. The righteous ones will be delighting in the Gardens. They will enjoy the place their Lord gave them after saving them from the fire. They will hear, "Eat and drink as a reward for your deeds." They will recline on couches, and We will wed them to fair women with wide beautiful eyes."

21. We will ensure those who were faithful and had families that were faithful are joined with them again. We shall not deprive them of the rewards of their deeds, as every man is owed what he earns.

22–28. We will give them all the fruit and meat they desire. They will pass among themselves a cup that is not vain and will cause no sin. They will be served by young males treating them like precious pearls. They will talk to each other, saying, "We used to be so fearful, but God has been good to us and saved us from torment of the flames. We used to pray to Him often, and behold He is gentle and merciful."

29. So tell mankind that, by the grace of your Lord, you are not a fortune-teller or madman.

30–31. When they say, "He is a poet! We will wait for an accident to befall him." Tell them, "I am waiting here with you."

32. Is it their minds that tell them to say these things? Maybe they are a rebellious people.

33–34. If they say, “He invented this scripture,” then they are faithless. If they are not liars, then have them create a recitation like it.

35–37. Were they created out of nothing? Maybe they are the creators themselves. Did they create the heavens and the earth? They believe in nothing! Do they own the treasures of your Lord? Have they been given ultimate authority?

38. Do they own a ladder that can reach to the heavens, so they can listen to the discussion? If they do, then ask the eavesdropper to provide clear proof.

39. Does He only have daughters while they have sons?

40. Do you ask them for a fee for your message that overburdens them with debt?

41. Do they somehow possess the unseen so they can write it down?

42. Do they seek to plot against you? Those who don’t believe in God will themselves be plotted against.

43. Do they have a god other than God? God is above all the things they associate with Him.

44. If these people were to witness a piece of the heaven falling down, they would just say is was a pile of clouds.

45–47. Leave them alone, and they will be terrified when the day arrives. That day when their plots will not help them at all and no assistance will come. For the evil, there is a punishment beyond what they can understand.

48–49. Wait patiently for the command of your Lord, knowing you are in Our sight. Praise your Lord when you rise and at night and when the stars set.

Chapter 77 (chronologically)

Sura 67 (30 verses), Al-Mulk (The Sovereign One)

1-2. Blessed is the Sovereign One that controls all things. He created life and death in order to try men and find the best of you. He is the mighty and forgiving One.

3–4. He created the seven heavens. You won't find any fault in His creation. Look again at it, and try to find a flaw. If you look at it again, your vision will be weakened and dim.

5. We have placed lamps on the lowest level of heaven like missiles to drive away evil beings. For them we have prepared a blazing fire.

6–11. Those who reject their Lord will face the evil penalty of hell. When they are thrown in it, they will hear the roaring of the blaze as it nearly bursts with fury. Every group will be asked on their way in, "Didn't a messenger come to warn you of this?" They will reply, "Yes, a warning came to us, but we rejected it. We told our messenger, 'God never revealed a message to you; you are seriously mistaken.'" Then they will say, "If we had only listened or had any sense, we would not be dwelling in hell." They will confess their sins, but those in hell are far from forgiveness.

12–14. For the ones that fear their Lord in secret, there is forgiveness and great reward. For whether you announce your beliefs or hide them, He knows what is in all men's hearts. Shouldn't the creator know everything? He is aware of and understands all of man's subtleties.

15. He is the One that made the earth bend to your will, so walk on the land and eat of what it provides, for unto Him you will be resurrected.

16–17. Do you feel confident that He who sits in heaven won't cause you to be swallowed by the earth when it quakes? Do you feel confident that He will not unleash a tornado upon you? Then you will understand My warning.

18. There were men before you that rejected warnings, and My wrath was severe.

19. Can't they see the birds on the wind as they flap their wings? No one can hold them aloft besides the most gracious. He watches over everything.

20–21. Who will be there to assist you as a host except for the most generous? The unbelievers are simply delusional. Who else can provide for you if He withholds His sustenance? Yet they continue to be prideful and reject the truth.

22. Who is more rightly guided? He who gropes on his face or the one that walks upright on the straight path?

23–24. Tell them, "It is He that created you and gave you sight, hearing, and hearts, and you give Him little thanks. It is He that multiplied your numbers on the earth, and you will all be gathered back to Him."

25–26. When they demand, "If you are truthful, then tell us when He will fulfill this promise." Say to them, "Only God alone has knowledge of the time, as I am but a simple messenger."

27. Later when they see it up close, the unbelievers' faces will show grief, and they will be told, "This is the promise that you asked to be fulfilled."

28–29. Say to them, "Consider this. If God destroys me and those with me, or if He has mercy on us—who will save the unbelievers from a severe penalty? He is the most gracious. We have faith in Him and trust Him. Soon you will know which of us is clearly wrong."

30. Ask them, "Have you wondered who can supply you with flowing water if your source were to dry up?"

Chapter 78 (chronologically)

Sura 69 (52 verses), Al-Haqqah (The Reckoning)

1–3. The reckoning. What is the inevitable reckoning? What can make you understand the inevitability of the reckoning?

4–8. The Thamud and the Ad people didn't believe in the inevitable reckoning. The Thamud were then destroyed by a terrible cry. The Ad were later destroyed by a furious wind that He sent upon them for seven continuous nights and eight days. You could see them all lying in its path like fallen palm tree trunks. Do you see any trace of them?

9–12. There was Pharaoh and the people that came before him and the communities destroyed for committing sins. They disobeyed the messengers of their Lord, so He punished them intensely. When the flood waters rose, We carried you on the Ark, so that We could make a reminder of you so that those who heard the stories would remember.

13–17. When the trumpet sounds a single blast and the earth is moved, with its mountains crushed effortlessly, on that day the reckoning will come to pass. The heavens will split, for they will be fragile on that day. The angels will stand on the sides that day, while eight of them hold the Lord's throne above them.

18. On that day you shall be judged. None of your prior deeds will remain secret.

19–24. Those who are handed their book in their right hand will say, "Here is my record to read. I knew that one day I would stand to face judgment. He will live a life of pleasure in a high garden where bunches of fruits hang low. They will hear, "Relax and eat and drink, in reward for how you lived your life."

25–37. Those who are handed their book in their left hand will say, "I wish I was not handed my record and I didn't have to know my reckoning. If only death were the end of things. My wealth has not saved me. My power has left me." They will hear commanded, "Seize and shackle him. Burn him in the hell fire! Bind him to a seventy-cubit length of chain. He did not believe in God most great. He didn't urge people to feed the poor. Therefore he shall have no friend here today. He will eat filth, as only sinners do."

38–42. I swear by what you see and what you cannot see that this is the word of an honorable messenger. It is not the word of a poet; oh, you of little faith. It is not the speech of a fortune-teller; you are not receiving much of this warning.

43. This is a revelation being sent down by the Lord of all the worlds.

44–47. If the messenger invented any verses and claimed they were Ours, We would have seized him by the right hand and then cut his aorta, and none of you could stop Us from doing it.

48–52. It is a reminder for the righteous. We know that there are some among you that reject the message. It will be a matter greatly regretted by the unfaithful. It is the absolute truth. So give glory to the name of your great Lord.

Chapter 79 (chronologically)

Sura 70 (44 verses), Al-Marrij (The Ascending)

1–3. Someone asked God, Lord of the ascending paths, about the unavoidable penalty that will happen to the unfaithful.

4–7. On a day that will span fifty thousand years, the angels and spirit will ascend unto Him. Be gracefully patient, for they see it as a far-off event, while We see it as near.

8–9. On that day the sky will turn to molten copper, and the mountains will be like tufts of wool.

10–14. Though they will stand in each other's sight, no friends will speak to each other. The sinners will be willing to sacrifice their children, wife, and even brother to escape the punishment of that day. He would trade all the kin that sheltered him and everything that is on earth to escape.

15–18. For it is a flaming fire that which burns off his scalp. The flames invite those who rejected the messages and hoarded their wealth.

19–21. Man was created as impatient. He grieves when evil affects him and is grudging in thanks when he receives goodness.

22–28. But this is not so for those who are devoted worshippers: those who constantly pray, who know it's right to give a portion of wealth to the poor and beggars, who believe in the day of judgment, and who fear their Lord's punishment. For their Lord's punishment cannot be averted.

29–31. Also not so for those who guard their chastity around everyone except their wives and their slaves; there is only blame for those who seek intimacy beyond this.

32–35. Also not so for those who keep their promises and who give honest testimony. Those who are attentive in their prayers and all the other things above will be honored people in the Gardens of heaven.

36–37. What can be the matter with the unfaithful that they rush about you? They are on your left and right in groups.

38–39. Do all of them hope to enter into the Gardens of bliss? No, for We created them, as they well know.

40–41. I swear by the Lord of all the earth that We are able to replace them with better men, and We will not have our plans undone.

42–44. So leave those men to gossip and waste their lives until they face the judgment day We have promised. That day, when they will come from their graves, racing toward a goal with a humbled look of shame covering them. That is the day We promise.

Chapter 80 (chronologically)

Sura 78 (40 verses), Al-Naba (The Great Announcement)

1–3. What is that they are arguing about? Is it the announcement of the great event that they cannot agree upon?

4–5. Soon enough they will learn the truth. They will surely know the truth.

6–7. Didn't We make the earth flat with mountains protruding,

8–9. and create you in pairs and gave you sleep so you can rest,

10–11. and make night like a cloak and daytime so you can make a living,

12–13. and build you seven strong heavens and place a shining lamp among them,

14–16. and send down rain from the clouds in abundance so that We can create grains and plants and lavish gardens?

17–20. The day of reckoning has been set. That day when the trumpet sounds and the multitudes come forth, when the heavens open their gates, and the mountains move, vanishing like a mirage.

21–26. Hell lies in wait as a home for the wicked, where they will dwell for ages. They shall not drink or taste anything cool there. For them is only boiling water and pus-like fluid. It is a fitting repayment.

27–29. They didn't fear the reckoning, and they called Our revelations lies. But We have everything recorded in a book.

30. Taste what you have earned, for We will only increase your punishment.

31–38. The righteous will have all they desire as reward: gardens and vineyards, full-breasted women equal to their age, and full cups of drink. They won't have to hear gossip or lies as a reward from your Lord—a well-deserved gift from the Lord of the heavens and the earth and all that is in between. [A gift] from the most gracious one, who no one can talk to on the day the angels and the spirit stand in ranks. No one shall speak except those permitted by the most gracious. He will decide who speaks truthfully.

39–40. That day will surely come. So let those who want it take refuge in their Lord. We have warned you of a pending doom. Of the day that man will look upon the deeds of his life and the unbeliever will say, "I wish that I was dust."

Chapter 81 (chronologically)

Sura 79 (46 verses), Al-Naziat (Those Who Tear Out [souls])

1–7. By the angels who tear the souls from the wicked, by those who gently draw them out, by those who glide smoothly and those who race ahead, by those who arrange the affairs on the day when the quaking begins and the resurrection begins.

8–12. On that day hearts will tremble, and men will look humble. They will ask, "Are we really being restored to our former selves, when we are but rotten bones? This would be a vain activity."

13–14. There will be just a single cry, and all will be awakened to judgment.

15–26. Did you hear the story of Moses? His Lord called to him in the sacred valley of Tuwa, saying, "Go to Pharaoh, for he is rebellious. Say to him, 'Would you like to purify yourself? For I can guide you to your Lord so you can fear him.'" Next Moses showed him a great sign, but Pharaoh rejected it and was disobedient. He turned his back and gathered his men, making a proclamation: "I am your highest Lord." But God punished him and made him an example for those in the hereafter and in this life. There is a lesson here for those who fear God.

27–33. What was harder for Him to create, you or heaven? He raised its vaulted ceiling and created order in it. He created a night and a day in it. After spreading the earth, He created waters and pastures. He affixed mountains firmly, for you and your cattle to use.

34–39. On the day when the great event occurs, when man remembers what he did in life, and the fires of hell are in sight, then those who sinned and preferred the life of the world to the hereafter will find their place in hell.

40–41. But for those who stand in fear of their Lord's judgment and who restrained their souls from base desires, there will a home in the Garden.

42–45. When they ask you, "When will the reckoning occur, because you keep talking about it?" Tell them it is known only to the Lord, and you are just a messenger to those who fear the day.

46. On the day that they see the reckoning, it will seem as if they only waited an evening or at most a full night.

Chapter 82 (chronologically)

Sura 82 (19 verses), Al-Infitar (The Severing)

1–5. When the sky is split apart, the stars are scattered, the oceans merge, and the graves are turned upside down, then a soul will learn what good and bad deeds he has done.

6-8. Mankind, what has seduced you away from your most gracious Lord? Away from He who created you so perfectly, just as He wished it?

9–12. Yet you reject the day of judgment! There are honorable guardians watching you and recording your life. They know everything you do.

13–16. On the day of judgment, the righteous will live in bliss, and the wicked will be sent to burn in hell. They cannot escape hell.

17–18. I ask you twice what will convey to you what will occur on the day of judgment?

19. It will be a day when no soul will be able to help another and God's command will be final.

Chapter 83 (chronologically)

Sura 84 (25 verses), Al-Inshiqaq (The Splitting Open)

1-5. When the heaven is split open, as it dutifully follows its Lord's commands, when the earth is flattened, and casts out its inhabitants becoming empty, following the commands of its Lord.

6–12. Mankind, you must toil towards your Lord until you meet Him. If you are given a record of your deeds in your right hand, you will receive an easy reckoning. You will return to your people joyfully. But if you are given your book recording your deeds behind your back, you will pray to be killed as you enter the burning flames.

13-14. He lived joyously among his people in life, never believing he would be returned to Us.

15. Indeed, his Lord saw everything.

16–19. I swear by the glow of the sunset, by the night and all that gathers in darkness, and by the full moon, you shall journey from stage to stage.

20. What is the matter with mankind that they won't believe?

21. When the Qur'an is recited to them, why don't they prostrate in worship?

22–23. But the unfaithful reject the revelations, and God knows full well all the secrets they keep.

24-25. Warn them of the painful penalty that awaits unless they are faithful and perform good deeds, for those people will receive an unfailing reward.

Chapter 84 (chronologically)

Sura 30 (60 verses), Al-Room (The Romans/Byzantium)

1. Alif. Lam. Meem.

2-5. The Byzantium Empire has been defeated in a nearby land, but after this defeat and within a few years, they will become victorious. All decisions in the past and in the future are in God's hand. On that day, the faithful will rejoice at God's assistance. He helps whoever He chooses. He is the almighty and merciful.

6–7. This is a promise from God, and God never breaks His promise. Most men don't understand this. They only know a few things about this world, and they are ignorant of the hereafter.

8. Haven't they thought to themselves? God must have created the heavens and the earth with a clear purpose and for a set time frame. Still, there are many men who deny that they will meet their Lord in the hereafter.

9. Haven't they walked the earth and seen the fates of those who came before them? Those people were stronger than these, and they were agriculturalists and had larger populations and towns. Their messengers showed them clear signs. God punished them, but they brought it on themselves.

10. The evil found punishment in the end for their deeds. They rejected God's revelations and ridiculed them.

11–12. God started creation, He will repeat it, and then you shall be brought back to Him. The guilty shall despair on the day that hour comes.

13. None of the partners that man ascribed to God will be able to assist him then, and they will actually reject the partners they created.

14–16. On the day that the hour comes to pass, all men will be sorted. Those who believed and committed righteous acts will be happy in a garden. Those who rejected faith and denied Our revelations and denied that We would meet in the hereafter, they will be brought to punishment.

17. [MD] Give glory to God when you begin the evening and when you rise in the morning.

18. All praise from the heavens and the earth belong to Him. Praise late afternoon and at midday.

19. He brings the living from death, brings the dead from the living, and gives life back to earth after it dies. Therefore you shall be brought back from the dead.

20. One of His signs is that He created you from dust, and now humans range the earth.

21. One of His signs is that He created mates among you so you could live in peace with them. He created love and forgiveness between you. These are the signs for those that would see them.

22. One of His signs is the creation of the heavens and the earth and the variations in your languages and skin pigments. These are signs for the wise among you.

23. One of His signs is that at night you sleep and during the day you earn your living by His grace. These are signs for those who would listen.

24. One of His signs is that He sends down lightning, causing fear and hope. He sends water from the sky and revives the earth after it dies. Here are signs for those who are wise.

25. Among His signs is that the heavens and earth respond to His commands, and when He gives a single call, you will all come from the earth at once.

26. Every being in the heavens and on the earth that is obedient to Him belongs to Him.

27. He began the process of creation, and He repeats it. For Him it's very easy. The best descriptive words in the heavens and the earth are reserved to describe Him. He is the almighty and wise.

28. He gives examples to you that you can understand. Do you have slaves in your possession that share the wealth We gave you equally? Do you fear them as you fear each other? We explain Our signs in detail to people who are wise.

29. The sinners simply follow their own lust without any wisdom. Who can guide the people that God has sent astray? For them there are no guides.

30. Set your heart to be truly faithful to the religion in accordance with God's plan as He used to create mankind. There is no

altering God's "laws of creation." That is the correct religion, but most men do not know it.

31. Turn to Him in repentance, fear Him, keep regular prayers, and don't be among the polytheists,

32. . . . those who split up their religion and become sects. Each party rejoices in their own beliefs.

33–35. When man experiences trouble, he cries to his Lord, turning to Him repentantly. But when man receives His mercy he acts like it was his own doing. Some of them even attribute the mercy to a partner they ascribe to their Lord. For those who We have bestowed favors on that have been ungrateful, enjoy your brief lives, for soon you will learn your mistakes. Have We sent down any decree that explains what they associate with Him?

36–37. When We give men a bit of Our mercy, they rejoice in it. But when some evil visits them, that they brought upon themselves, they are hopeless. Don't they see that God increases and restricts His provisions for whoever He wants? The signs are there for those who believe.

38. Give your family what is their right, and give to the needy and travelers. For those who want God's preference, that is the best way to live and be prosperous.

39. What you pay others in taxes benefiting others does not help you earn God's respect, but the money you give to charity to seek God's preference will earn reward.

40. It is God that created you, provides for you, causes you to die, and brings you back to life. Can any of the so-called partners you associate with God do any of these things? Praise Him, for He is above any partners attributed to Him.

41. Corruption has appeared in the lands and on the sea due to some evil men's actions. May He give them a taste of their evil so they might repent.

42. Say to them, "Travel the lands and see the consequences that befell those before you. Most of them were polytheists."

43–45. Set your purpose towards the righteous religion before the inevitable day comes. On that day man will be separated. Those who were unfaithful will suffer for that rejection. While those who were righteous will prepare for only their own souls, so that He can reward those who were faithful and righteous from His bounty. He does not love the unbelievers.

46. One of His signs is that He sends the winds to carry good news to give you a sample of His mercy. Also to allow the ships to sail by His command so that you can seek His bounty and be grateful.

47. We sent apostles before you, each to their respective communities. They went to them with clear signs. We took

vengeance on those who sinned, and We assisted the faithful, as is Our promise.

48–49. God sends the winds to raise clouds that He can spread in the sky and eventually issue rain. When He makes the rain fall on His servants of His choice, they celebrate. Although just before the rains, they were hopeless.

50. Mankind, look at the signs of God's mercy. He gives life again to the earth after it dies, just as He will revive the dead beings, for He is able to do all things.

51. But if We send the wind and they see their crops turn yellow, they will become ungrateful.

52–53. You cannot make the dead hear nor make the deaf hear the message once they have turned their backs and rejected it. You cannot lead the blind back to the path they strayed from. You can only make those that believe in Our signs and submit hear you.

54. God created you in a state of weakness, then made you strong, and then made you weak again and gave you grey hair. He creates what He wants. He is knowledgeable and mighty.

55. On the day the hour of reckoning arrives, the sinners will swear they have only waited an hour. They are used to deceit in life.

56. Those who are wise and faithful will say, "You waited in accordance with God's command, and now you are at the day of resurrection, but you didn't know it."

57. On that day no excuse will save the sinners, and they won't be allowed to earn God's mercy.

58. We have given to man in this Qur'an all kinds of parables. But when you bring them a sign, the unbelievers will say, "You are making up lies."

59. Therefore God seals the hearts of those who don't understand.

60. Wait patiently, for the promise of God is true. Don't let those who lack conviction shake your faith.

Chapter 85 (chronologically)

Sura 29 (69 verses), Al-Ankaboot (The Spider)

1–3. [MD] Alif. Lam. Meem. Do men think they will be left alone and never tested just because they say "We are faithful"? We tested the generations that came before them. God will find out who is sincere and who lies.

4. [MD] Do the sinners think they can escape Us? Their conclusion is evil!

5. [MD] Those who want to meet God should know the appointed reckoning is coming and that He hears and knows all.

6. [MD] Those men that strive only do so for their own souls. God is self-sufficient and doesn't need any creatures [assistance].

7. [MD] Those who are faithful and work righteously won't have their sins counted. Instead We will reward them for the best of what they did.

8. [MD] We command mankind to be good to their parents. But if they try to force you to associate anything with Me in worship that you are not familiar with, then disobey them. You will return to Me, and I will reveal all the deeds you did.

9. [MD] We shall allow those who are faithful and live righteously in life to be among the other righteous in the hereafter.

10. [MD] Even though they say "We believe in God," when some men are faced with suffering at the hands of mankind, they will act like the oppression is coming from their Lord. Then when help arrives to them from their Lord, they will say, "We have always been with you!" But God knows everything that creatures think in private.

11. [MD] God knows who is faithful, and He will find out who are hypocrites.

12–13. The unbelievers will say to the faithful, "Follow our path, and we will bear your sins." They cannot even bear their sins, and they are liars. They will bear theirs and others' sins on the day of judgment, and they will pay for their lies.

14–15. We sent Noah to his people, where he remained for 950 years until the flood overtook them for their sins. We saved Noah and his companions in the Ark and made it a sign for all to see.

16–23. We saved Abraham, too. He said to his people, "If only you knew that it would be better for you to serve God and be wary of Him. Instead you worship idols and invent lies. Those things you worship have no power to provide for you. Seek provision from God. Serve Him and be grateful, for it is to Him you will return." If you choose to reject the messages, as generations before you did, then know that it's the messenger's job only to deliver them clearly. Haven't they thought about how easy it is for God to cause creation and then to reproduce it? Say to them, "Travel the lands and see how He created it. God can recreate things. God is able to do all things." He punishes and shows mercy to whoever He chooses. To Him you will return. You cannot escape Him in heaven or earth and there is no one besides God that can protect you. People who reject the revelations of God and deny they will meet Him again will not receive My mercy. They will suffer a great punishment.

24–25. But all that Abraham's people could say was, "Kill him or burn him!" But God saved him from the fire. These are signs for those who believe. He told them, "You are worshipping idols instead of God. You have love between yourselves in this life, but on the day of judgment, you will disown and curse each other. You will dwell in the fire, and no one will help you."

26–27. Lot then believed his words and said, "I am migrating towards my Lord, the almighty and wise." So We gave Abraham Isaac and Jacob and destined his offspring to prophethood and revelation of scripture. We gave him a reward in this world, and in the hereafter he is among the righteous.

28–29. Lot told his people, "You are committing lewd sins unlike anyone has ever done before. Don't you approach men, rob travelers, and commit evil deeds in your councils?" But his people didn't answer these questions, instead saying, "Bring upon us the wrath of God if you are truthful."

30. Lot prayed, "My Lord, help me with these corrupt people."

31–32. When Our messengers told Abraham about Lot's people, they said, "We are going to destroy the people of that town, for they are an evil group." Abraham said, "But Lot is there!" They replied, "We know exactly who is there, and we will save him and his followers, except for his wife, who will lag behind."

33–35. When Our messengers told Lot of the plan, he was troubled and felt powerless to intervene. They told him, "Fear not and don't grieve. We are here to save you and your followers, except for your wife, who lags behind. We are going to bring a punishment upon these people for their sinful life." Clearly We have left signs for anyone that cares to understand them.

36–37. We sent Shu'ayb to his Midian people, saying, "Serve God and fear the last day. Don't commit evil on the earth causing corruption." They rejected him, and a mighty quake struck them, leaving them lying in their homes by dawn.

38. You can see the destruction of the Ad and Thamud dwellings. Although they used to be intelligent, Satan made their evil ways seem appealing and blocked the straight path.

39–40. Remember the Korah, Pharaoh, and Haman. Moses brought them clear sings, but they were disrespectful and could not escape Us. We punished each for their crimes. We sent a storm of stones, used a mighty blast, made the earth to swallow them, and drowned some, too. God was not unfair to them; they were unjust to their own souls.

41–42. There is a parable about the people who choose others to be their guardians besides God. They are like a spider who builds itself a house. If they only knew that the spider builds the frailest of houses. God knows who you invoke instead of Him; He is mighty and wise.

43. We give parables such as this to mankind, but only the wise will understand them.

44. God created the heavens and the earth with reason, and that is a sign for the faithful.

45. Recite the scriptures that you have been inspired with and pray regularly. Prayer restrains you from indecent and unjust acts, and celebration of God is without a doubt the greatest act. God knows all that you do.

46. Don't argue with those who follow the scripture unless it's in a kind manner or if you are arguing with people who cause injury. Say to them, "We believe in the same revelations as you, and your God and our God are the same. We submit to Him."

47. We have revealed the scripture to you. Those before you that received the scripture believe it, and some of you believe in it. Only the nonbelievers reject Our signs.

48. You [Muhammad] didn't recite any other scripture before this. You did not write one with your right hand. If that were the case, then the liars would have doubted.

49. These are clear revelations for those who are wise, as only the unjust reject Our signs.

50–52. When they ask, "Why didn't your Lord send down signs?" tell them, "The signs are only with God, and I am just a messenger." We have sent down a scripture that you have recited to them. Isn't that enough? There is mercy in this and a warning for the faithful. Tell them, "God is a witness of actions between you and me. He knows everything that is in the heavens and on earth. Those who are arrogant and reject God will perish."

53. Every time they ask you to speed up the promised punishment, they are saved from instant doom, because the day of reckoning has already been set. It will occur suddenly, when they least expect it.

54–55. They ask you to speed up the punishment, but surely hell awaits the unbelievers. On that day that they are overwhelmed by doom from all sides, a voice will say, "Taste the evil you earned."

56–59. My faithful servants, My earth is vast, so serve only Me. Every soul will die and then be returned to Us. Those who were faithful and righteous in deed will be given a lofty home in heaven with rivers below. You will live there safely. What a reward for the good works of those who were steadfast and trusted in their Lord.

60. How many animals don't carry their own nourishment? God feeds both them and you. He hears and knows all.

61. If you ask people who created the heavens and the earth and designed the path of the sun and moon, they will reply, "God." So why do they reject the truth?

62. God increases the provisions that He gives to who He wants, and likewise decreases it. God is aware of everything.

63. If you ask people who sends down the rains and revives the earth after it dies, they will say, “God.” So reply, “All praise is for God.” But most people don’t understand this.

64. This life is but a pastime. If they only knew that their home in the hereafter is the true life.

65. When men sail on ships, they pray exclusively to God. But when they are delivered safely to shore, they associate partners with Him, as they are ungrateful for Our gifts. Let them enjoy this life, for soon they will learn.

67. Can’t they see that this is a safe place, while all around them men are being carried away? Why do they believe in lies and reject the grace of God?

68. Who is a greater sinner, those who create lies against God or those who reject the truth when they hear it? Don’t the faithless end up in hell?

69. Those who strive for Us will receive Our good guidance, for God helps those who are righteous.

Chapter 86 (chronologically)
(The last chapter given before the move to Medina)

Sura 83 (36 verses), Al-Mutaffifeen (The Cheaters)

1–6. Shame on people who cheat others during trade by manipulating the scales and measurements. Do they doubt that they will be resurrected on a great day when all men will stand before the Lord of the worlds?

7–9. The recordings of evil deeds are in the register [*sijjeen*]. How do I explain the register? It is a written record of wicked men's deeds.

10–12. That day will be misery for those that deny the judgment day. Only the worst sinners deny that day exists.

13–14. When Our messages are recited to them, they say, "These are just ancient stories." But their hearts are just stained because of their evil deeds.

15–17. They will be shunned by their Lord on that day. They will enter the flames of hell. Someone will explain to them, "This is the reality that you denied existed."

18–21. On that day, the record of the righteous will be in the register [*Illiyin*]. How do I explain the register? It is a written record of righteous men's deeds, witnessed by those closest [to God].

22–28. The righteous will be delighted as they recline on couches gazing out. You will see their faces beaming with happiness.

They will drink a pure musky wine, and for those who want this, you must strive. It will be mixed with *Tasnim,* a spring water source only for those closest [to God].

29–33. The sinners used to laugh at the faithful. When they passed by them, sinners would mock them by winking at each other. When they were among their friends, they would be joking. And when they saw the faithful, they would say, "Those people have lost their way." But they [sinners] were not sent as guardians over them [faithful].

34–35. On that day the faithful will laugh at the unbelievers from the couches where they relax.

36. Surely the unfaithful will pay for what they did.

Author's Note

This ends the time in the Prophet Muhammad's life when he is simply a messenger sent by God to deliver sermon-like revelations [recitations/the Qur'an] to the people in Mecca. As he leaves Mecca and travels north to the Yathrib Valley [later Medina/Madina], he takes on a new role. He becomes the religious and political leader of the early converts to Islam. The sermons/revelations he delivers in Medina and after his return to Mecca have some messages from God that vary greatly from his earlier ones.

This change in the life of Muhammad and also those of his early Muslim converts is marked forever as the beginning of the Islamic calendar. The Hijrah, or migration, to the North marks the clear beginning of Islam as a major religious movement but also as the beginning of the first Islamic nation-state.

The year of this migration was 622 AD/CE, which marks the beginning of the Muslim calendar that is notated as AH [After Hijrah]. The Islamic date of my book publication is 1438 AH or 2017 AD/CE.

I would urge you to keep this change in Muhammad's role in mind as you read the passages that follow. This time period includes community building, betrayals by neighbors, battles with old friends and new enemies, and peace negotiations with a powerful ruling class.

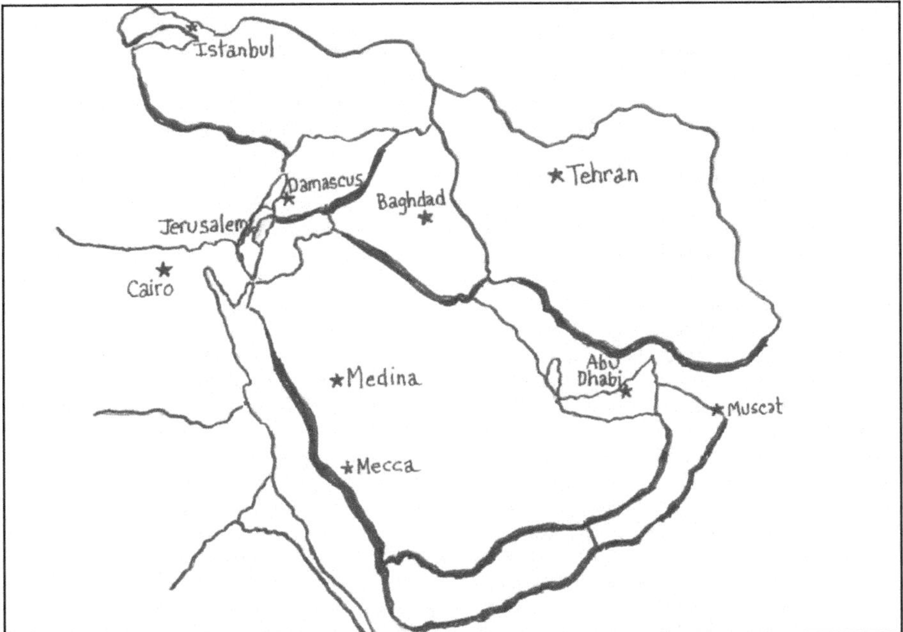

Map © 2017 by Pat Dowden

Medina Period [MD] and Later, 622–632 AD

(10 Years/28 Chapters or Sections)

Chapter 87 (chronologically)

Sura 2 (286 verses), Al-Baqara (The Cow)

1–4. Alif. Lam. Meem. This is the indisputable Book. It contains guidance to the righteous, who believe in the unseen, maintain prayers, spend from what We provide them, believe in the revelations sent to you [Muhammad], and the revelations given before, and are sure about the hereafter.

5. People who follow this righteous course from their Lord will prosper.

6–7. Those who reject faith will still not believe, whether you recite to them or not. God has sealed their heart and ears and covered their eyes. They face an awful punishment.

8–10. Some men will say, "We believe in God and the last day," but they are not faithful. They are trying to deceive God and other faithful people, but they only lie to themselves, and they don't even know it. There is a disease in their hearts, and when God enlarges the disease, they will receive an awful punishment for their lies.

11. When they are told, "Do not cause harm on the earth," they reply, "We are only the peacemakers."

12. But they are the agents of harm, and they don't realize it.

13. When they are told, "Believe as the faithful do," they reply, "You want us to be faithful like the fools do?" They are the fools and don't even realize it.

14. When they meet faithful people, they say, "We believe." But when they are around only their devils, they say, "We are actually with you, and we just mock the faithful."

15. God will mock them in return by letting them wander aimlessly, like a blind man, on their sinful path.

16. These are the people that paid for mistaken guidance, and they won't profit from it, as they are lost.

17–18. They are like a man who had a lit torch shedding light all around him, and then God took the light away, leaving them blind in the darkness. Deaf, dumb, and blind; they will not find the path.

19–20. They are also like a man that sees a rainstorm with thunder and lightning contained in the dark cloud. They just put their fingers in their ears to keep out the thunder, because they fear death. God is all around those who reject faith. The lightning nearly blinds them with its light. They move when it flashes and stop when it's dark. If God wished, He could destroy their vision and hearing. God can do anything.

21–22. Worship your Lord. He created you and those before you, so that you can become righteous. He made the earth for you to rest upon and the heavens as your roof. He sends down the rains and produces fruits for you to eat. Do not create rivals to God because you know [the truth].

23–24. If you doubt the recitations that We have revealed to Our apostle, then create a chapter equal to it. If you are right about their validity, you can call upon any being you created besides God to help. If you are unable to do it—and you won't be able to—then beware of the fire that is waiting for the unfaithful, where men and stones fuel the flames.

25. Give the good news to the faithful and righteous about their part of the Gardens, where rivers flow below them. They will eat fruits and notice that they all look similar. They will abide forever with pure and clean women.

26. God is willing to use a parable about things as small as a gnat. The faithful will know that it's the truth from their Lord, but the unbelievers will say, "What is God trying to tell us in this parable?" By His parables, He leads some on the straight path and some astray, but only the sinners are led astray.

27. People who break their promise to God after they agreed to it, and who break the bonds that God ordered, and do harm in the lands are really causing themselves to fail.

28–29. How can you not believe in God? He gave you life, will cause you to die, and will resurrect you, so you can return to Him. He created all things on the earth and then created the seven heavens. He is all-knowing.

30. God said to the angels, "I am creating a viceregent or deputy king [caliph] on earth." The angels responded, "Will you choose someone that causes corruption and sheds blood, while we sing Your praises and proclaim Your holiness?" He replied, "I know things that you don't."

31–33. Then He taught Adam the names of all things. Then He placed those things before the angels, saying, "If you are correct, then name all these things." The angels replied, "You are glorious! We only know what you taught us. You are the all-knowing and wise." He turned to Adam, saying, "Tell them their names." After he did, God asked them, "Didn't I tell you that I know all the secrets in the heavens and earth, and I know what you say and what you hide?"

34. When We told the angels, "Bow to Adam," they all bowed except Iblis. He refused and was arrogant. He became unfaithful.

35–36. We told Adam, “Live with your partner in the Garden and eat of whatever bounty you desire, but don’t approach this tree, or you will become sinners.” Satan soon caused them to fall from the Garden. And We told them, “Leave here. Some of you will become enemies of others. On earth, for a certain time, you will find shelter and provisions.”

37. His Lord gave Adam revelations, and He forgave Adam. He is often forgiving and merciful.

38–39. We said, “All of you leave here, and when guidance comes to you from Me, the people who follow it will not need to fear or have grief. But those who reject faith or deny Our signs will dwell in the fire.”

40. Children of Israel, always remember My special regard for you and fulfill your covenant to Me as I keep my promises to you. Fear only Me.

41. Believe in the [new] revelations that confirm the earlier one. Do not be the first to deny them. Don’t sell My revelations for a small amount of money. Fear only Me.

42. Do not confuse these truths with lies, and don’t hide the truths that you know.

43. Regularly pray and give to charity. Bow your head alongside fellow worshippers.

44. You encourage righteous behavior among other men and then forget to do it yourself, and you claim to study the scriptures? Can you not understand [them]?

45–46. Seek assistance. Be patient and pray. It is difficult for those who aren't humble. The humble are certain they will return to meet their lord.

47. Israelis, remember that I hold you in special regard, and I preferred you over all creatures.

48. Be wary of the day when no person can help another. When no one will be allowed to speak on your behalf. No ransom can be paid. There will be no help at all [for your souls].

49–52. Remember that We saved you from the Pharaoh's people. They were tormenting you and killed your sons while sparing your girls. It was a great trial for you from your Lord. We parted the sea to save you and then drowned the Pharaoh and his people while you watched. We placed Moses in forty nights of solitude, and while he was away, you began to worship a calf; it was a great sin. But We forgave you for your sin, so that you might become grateful [to Us].

53–54. We then gave Moses the Book and knowledge about what is right and wrong. Here was a chance for you to be guided correctly. You recall that Moses told his people, "You have sinned against yourselves by taking a calf for worship. All of you must turn remorsefully to your maker and kill your people [universally translated as "guilty people"]. This will make things better for you in the eyes of your creator." After this He was forgiving towards you. He is sympathetic and forgiving.

55–56. Later you demanded, "Moses, we will not believe in you unless we can see God with our own eyes." So We sent thunder and lightning to severely stun you as you looked. Then We revived you from death, so that you might become grateful and give thanks.

57–59. We next provided clouds for shade and sent down manna [sustenance] and quails with instructions to, "Eat the good things We have provided you." In the end, they only wronged themselves, as [your/mankind's] sins cannot harm Us. Recall We told them, "Enter the town and eat as much as you like. But you must enter the gates with total humility, uttering 'repentances,' and We will forgive your sins and reward the most righteous." But the sinners changed the words that We asked them to say. So We sent down a plague on them for their wickedness.

60. Recall that when Moses was praying for water to give his people, We said, "Strike that rock with your staff!" Water then poured out from 12 springs. So each tribe was given a fountain. Eat and drink from what God has provided you. Do not make corruption or cause harm on the earth.

61. His people then said to Moses, "We cannot eat just one kind of food every day. Please ask your Lord, on our behalf, to give us other things that grow on the earth, like herbs, cucumbers, garlic, lentils, and onions." Moses replied, "You seek to replace superior food with inferior ones? Then go to the town and you can find what you want!" The people were humbled and impoverished, and this drew the wrath of God. [The wrath was] for rejecting the signs of God, unjustly killing prophets, disobedience, and past wicked behavior.

62. But from among the faithful, the Jews, Christians, and Sabians—the ones that believe in God and the last day and live righteously will be rewarded by their Lord. They shall not fear, nor grieve.

63–64. We took a covenant with you [the Jewish people] and raised a mountain over you as We said, "Hold on tightly to what We gave you. Always remember what is in it, so that you can be dutiful to God." But you turned away [from God]. You all would have been truly lost if not for the grace and mercy of God.

65–66. You surely know what We told those who broke the rules of the Sabbath. "May you be hated like apes!" We made this an example to their generation and future ones. A lesson for those who are God-fearing.

67–68. Moses told his people, "God commands you to sacrifice a cow." They replied, "Are you making fun of us?" Moses prayed, "God save me from this ignorance." They then said, "Ask your God, on our behalf, to clearly describe the cow He seeks." Moses replied, "He says the cow shouldn't be too old or too young, but instead middle-aged. Do as you are commanded!"

69. [Again they pestered him,] "Ask your Lord, on our behalf, to tell us what color He seeks." Moses replied, "He says find a yellow cow. Intensely yellow that is pleasing to the eye."

70–71. Again, they asked, "Ask your Lord, on our behalf, to tell us what cow He seeks. They all look alike to us. We seek God's guidance, if He wills it." Moses replied, "He says find a cow that hasn't been trained to plow or irrigate the fields and that is healthy and unblemished." [His people] replied, "Now you have given us the truth." Then they offered the cow in sacrifice, but they almost didn't.

72. Remember when you killed a man and then argued with each other about the crime? God exposed what you were hiding.

73. And We said, "Hit the body with a piece of it [possibly the cow]." God can bring the dead back to life, as He shows you His signs so that you may begin to understand.

74. Afterwards your hearts were hardened. They were harder than rocks. But there are rocks that rivers flow from, rocks that split open and spew water, and there are rocks that fall in fear of God. God knows everything that you do.

75–77. Are you [faithful] hoping they will believe you? Some of them heard God's words and purposely altered it, even after they understood its meaning. When they meet the faithful they will say, "We believe!" But when they are talking among themselves, they ask, "Do you tell them about what God has revealed to you, so that they can argue with you about it in front of your Lord?" Can't you understand their goals? Don't they know that God is aware of all their secret and public statements?

78. Some of them are illiterate and only know the contents of the Book by what they have been told. And yet they still speculate about it.

79. There will be anguish for the ones that write the Book with their hands [not inspired] and then tell people, "This is from God!" while they sell it for a small price. They will suffer for what their hands have written and the earnings they make.

80. When they say, "The flames will only burn us for a set number of days," reply to them, "Didn't you take a covenant with God? He never breaks His promise. Or are you saying things about God that you can't back with truth?"

81–82. It's clear that those who commit evil acts and are surrounded by sins will dwell in the fire eternally. But those who are faithful and commit righteous deeds will dwell in the Garden forever.

83. Recall that We made a covenant with the Israelis to: Worship only God; be kind to your parents, family, orphans, and the needy; speak kindly to others; and pray and give to charity regularly. Then all but a few of you turned your backs [on the covenant].

84. We then made a covenant with you that said you would not kill your people or force any of them from their homes. You ratified this covenant as witnesses.

85. But after this event, you killed each other and drove part of your people from their homes. You backed some as they fought others, which was a sin and unlawful. Then when people came to you as captives, you ransomed them, even though it was unlawful for them to be banished. Why do you believe in part of the Book and reject the other? You wonder what the reward is for those who live so disgracefully? On the judgment day, you will be given a painful punishment. God is aware of all that you do.

86. These people pay this life by spending from the hereafter. The penalty they receive won't be lessened, and they won't be helped.

87. We gave Moses the Book, and then We sent other messengers after him. We gave clear signs to Jesus, the son of Mary, and reinforced him with the holy spirit. Why does it seem that whenever a messenger arrives that you don't want, you become arrogant? Some you call liars, and some you kill.

88. They reply, "Our hearts are covered." In truth, God has cursed them for their disbelief. They believe so little.

89. In earlier times, they prayed for victory over the unbelievers. Yet now when a book from God is shown to them, and it contains information they know to be true, they are the ones in disbelief. God curses the unbelievers.

90. They have sold their souls for an evil price, for denying what God has revealed because they disrespect God for sharing His grace with other worshippers. They have asked for more wrath on top of His anger. A humiliating penalty awaits the unbelievers.

91. When they are told, "Believe in what God has sent down." They respond, "We believe in what God has sent to us." But then they reject everything that came later, even if it confirms the truth that was sent to them. So say to them, "Then why did you kill the previous prophets of God if you are actually believers?"

92. Moses brought you clear signs, and still you started worshipping a calf while he was away. You sinned.

93. Recall that We made a covenant with you and raised a mountain above you as We said, "Follow strictly what We have given you and be steadfast in retaining it." They replied to Us, "We hear you, yet we will not." Their rejection of the covenant caused their love for a calf to enter their hearts. Say

to them, "If you are faithful to your beliefs, then they will push you towards evil acts."

94–95. Say to them, "If you are telling the truth, then you should seek death. Because if the hereafter and the grace of God are set aside just for you and no other people, [you should seek death.]" But they won't seek death. They know the nature of the sins that they have committed and that God is aware of all the sinners.

96. You will learn that they are the greediest of all people for life [in this world], even more [greedy] than the polytheists. But they could be given a thousand years of lies, and it would not save them from their final punishment. God sees all that they do.

97–98. Tell them, "God sent Gabriel to deliver His revelations to your heart, to confirm earlier revelations, to provide guidance and good news to the faithful. If you are an enemy of Gabriel—or an enemy to God, His angels, His messengers, or Gabriel and Michael—then know that God is an enemy to those who reject faith."

99. We have sent down clear signs to you. Only the wicked sinners reject them.

100. Isn't it true that every time they make a covenant, some part of the group breaks it? Most of them are faithless.

101. Then when a messenger from God arrives and confirms to them previous revelations, some of those that have received the Book pretend that they don't know if he [the messenger] is confirming their Book.

102. They are following Satan's false message that was used against the kingdom of Solomon. But Solomon didn't become faithless. The faithless were the devils that taught magic to men and other things that the angels Harut and Marut had brought to Babylon. These angels always said to their audience, "We are a temptation for you, so don't become faithless." From these two angels, mankind learned how to cause issues between a man and his wife. But they couldn't harm anyone without God's permission. They learned what could harm them and what wouldn't be profitable. They also knew that those who bought [magic] would not be destined for a happiness in the hereafter. If they only knew what evil price they had sold their souls for.

103. If they had been faithful and avoided evil, they would have gotten a better reward from God. If only they knew.

104. Oh faithful, do not say, "Listen to us" [*raina*]. Instead say, "Make us understand and hear" [*unzurna*]. There is a painful punishment for the unbelievers.

105. The unbelievers among the people of the Book and the polytheists never want anything good to come to you from

your Lord. But God has infinite grace, and He can share His mercy with whoever He chooses.

106. For every revelation that we revoke [abrogate] or cause you to forget, We replace it with a similar or better revelation. Don't you know that God has unlimited power?

107–108. Don't you know that everything in the heavens and the earth belongs to God's kingdom and that there is no guardian except for God? Why would you question your messenger in the same way they questioned Moses before? Whoever chooses disbelief instead of faith is going down the wrong path.

109. Many people of the Book [describes those who practice Judaism and Christianity], because they are envious, are trying to turn believers back towards disbelief. They do this after the truth was made clear to them. Forgive and pardon them until God issues His proclamation. God has power over everything.

110. Pray and give to charity regularly. Whatever good you do is sent ahead of you [to heaven] to improve your souls, and God will acknowledge it. God knows all that you do.

111–112. When they say, "Only Jews and Christians will enter paradise," it's only their false desire. Say to them, "If you are honest, show us your proof." Whoever submits [Islam] completely to God and does good deeds will earn their reward with their Lord. They shall not fear or grieve.

113. The Jews say the Christians are not following the truth, while the Christians say the Jews are not following the truth. Yet, they are both reading the same Book. This is how ignorant people speak. God will judge between them, and they will know the truth about their differences on resurrection day.

114. Is there a worse sinner than someone that blocks entry into God's mosques to stop His name from being celebrated? They hope to ruin them. It's not right for these people to enter the building unless they are fearful. There is only disgrace for them in this life and great punishment in the hereafter.

115. The East and the West belong to God. Wherever you turn, you are in God's presence. God is abundant and all-knowing.

116–117. They say, "God has taken a son." No! But everything in the heavens and earth belongs to Him, and everything is obedient to Him. Glory unto Him. He is the creator of the heavens and the earth. When He declares something, He only needs to say, "Be!" and it exists.

118. The ignorant ask, "Why doesn't God speak to us?" or "Why haven't we been sent a sign?" This is what people before them asked too, for their hearts are the same. We have made Our revelations clear to the people that are certain [in their faith].

119. We sent you with the truth to bring good news and to warn mankind. You will not have to answer for the people that will end up in the fire of hell.

120. The Jews and the Christians will never be satisfied with you unless you follow their religion. Say to them, “God’s guidance is the true guidance.” If you followed their beliefs after you received the knowledge, then you would be without a guardian or assistant when facing God.

121. The people who We sent the book to that read it correctly will believe. Those who reject it are lost.

122–123. Israelis, remember the special courtesy I gave to you and that I gave preference to you over all others. Beware of the day when no one shall be able to help another. No payment can help you, no mediation will be allowed, and no one will assist you.

124. Once, the Lord tested Abraham by giving him certain commands. He fulfilled them and was told, “I am making you a leader of men.” He [Abraham] asked, “And what of my offspring?” He [God] replied, “My covenant will not include any unrighteous people.”

125. Recall that We made the sanctuary house for men to gather in, saying, “Take this as your spot for prayer, where Abraham once stood.” We tasked Abraham and Ishmael to, “Purify My house for all those that will circle it, use it as a retreat, or bow and prostrate in prayer.”

126. Recall that Abraham prayed, “Lord, make this a safe place, and provide fruit for the people that believe in God and the

last day." He replied, "But for the unbelievers I will allow only a short time of pleasure before I drive them into the fiery doom. It's an evil destination."

127. While Abraham and Ishmael were building the foundations of the house, they prayed, "Our Lord, accept our actions, for you hear and know all things."

128–129. "Our Lord, make us submissive to you [*muslemeen*] and build from our offspring a people submissive to you. Show us how to worship and be merciful to us. You are sympathetic and merciful. Our Lord, send a messenger to us that they know, who will recite Your revelations and teach them about the Book and Your wisdom to purify them. You are mighty and wise."

130–131. Anyone that ever turns away from the creed of Abraham is foolish. We chose him from all the world, and he will stand among the righteous in the hereafter. When his Lord told him, "Submit! [Islam]," he replied, "I submit to the Lord of all the worlds."

132. Abraham left this legacy to his sons. So did Jacob, saying, "My sons, God has chosen this religion for you. Do not die unless you have become submissive [to God]."

133. Were you witnesses as Jacob was dying and he asked his sons, "What will you worship after me?" They replied, "We will worship your God [not using the word "Allah" in this verse],

and the God of your forefathers, Abraham, Ishmael, and Isaac. The one true God. We submit to Him.

134. The people that died before you will receive what they earned. You will receive what you have earned. You will not be called upon to answer for their actions.

135. When they say to you, "Become Jews and Christians, and then you will be guided correctly," tell them, "We will follow the beliefs of Abraham—the righteous one, that was not a polytheist."

136. Say to them, "We believe in God and what [revelations] was sent to us and sent to Abraham, Ishmael, Isaac, Jacob, the tribes, Moses, and Jesus, and what was given to all the prophets from their Lord. We make no distinctions between any of them. We are submissive to Him."

137. If people believe as you do, then they are on the right path. If they turn away [from belief], then only they are defiant. God will assist you against them. He knows and hears all.

138. [Our roots/beliefs are] colored by God, for who can color us better than God? We worship Him.

139. Ask them, "How can you argue with us about God, knowing that He is our Lord and your Lord; that we are responsible for our actions and you are for yours? And while we sincerely worship Him?"

140. [When they ask] "Do you believe that Abraham, Ishmael, Isaac, Jacob, and the tribes were Jews or Christians?" say to them, "Who is more wicked than people that hide the testimonies they received from God? God is aware of all that you do."

141. Those people that died before you will receive what they earned. You will receive what you have earned. You will not be called upon to answer for their actions.

142. [When] their foolish people say to you, "Why did they change where they face to pray from the old direction?" [Jerusalem/*Quds* to Mecca], say to them, "The East and West both belong to God. He guides whoever He chooses on the straight path."

143. We made you a balanced nation so that you can be witnesses to other people, and the messenger can witness to you. We changed the direction you face during prayer [*Qibla*] from its old direction as a test to see who was following the messenger and who would turn quickly from faith. It was a hard trial for everyone who was not guided by God. God was not trying to make your [past] worship meaningless. God is kind and merciful to all men.

144. We see you looking to heaven [for guidance], and We will turn you towards a pleasing direction of prayer. Turn your face towards the holy mosque. Wherever you are, just turn towards it. Those who have received the Book know that this

is the truth from their Lord. God is always aware of what they do.

145. Even if you showed the people of the Book all the signs at once, they would not turn towards your direction of prayer. You cannot follow their direction of prayer, and they won't follow each other's. You would commit a clear sin if you began to follow their wishes after the knowledge had been given to you.

146–147. The people of the Book recognize this [him] just as they recognize their own sons. Yet, some of them hide what they know to be the truth. This truth is from your Lord, so do not be one of the doubtful.

148. Everyone has a direction to face towards, so race towards all goodness. God will bring all men together from wherever they are. God has power over everything.

149. No matter where you are, you should turn to face the holy mosque. This is the truth from your Lord. God is aware of everything you do.

150. No matter where you go, you should turn to face the holy mosque. No matter where you are, you should turn to face towards it, so that no man can make accusations against you. Of course, the wicked will accuse you, but do not fear them. Only fear Me, so that I can share my grace with you and give you guidance.

151. We have sent you a messenger chosen from among you. He recites Our revelations, purifying you. He teaches you the Book and wisdom that you didn't know.

152. So remember Me, and I will remember you. Be grateful, and do not reject Me.

153. Oh faithful, seek help through patience and prayer. God is with the patient.

154. Don't call those killed in the way of God dead. They are alive, but you aren't aware of them.

155. While We will test you through fear, hunger, or the loss of your goods, lives, or fruits, [We will continue] to share good news with the patient.

156–157. The people who say, "We belong to God, and to Him we shall return," when faced with hardships, are the ones that God sends blessings and mercy to. They are guided correctly.

158. Safa and Marwa [two mountains in Mecca] are signs of God. So when you are visiting the house or making a pilgrimage to it and pass around the mountains, it is not a sin. Everyone that acts righteously of their own accord will be recognized by God.

159–160. Anyone that hides the signs of God after We revealed them clearly to the people of the Book will be cursed by God and by anyone empowered to curse others. Those who repent and alter their stance by openly declaring the truth will be exempted. I will turn My mercy towards them. I am forgiving and merciful.

161–162. God's curse will be upon people that reject faith and die in a state of disbelief. They earn the curse of the angels and man as well. They will stay within that realm, and their punishment won't be lessened, and they won't be given a break.

163. Your god is the one God, and there is no god except Him, the gracious and merciful one.

164. For those who are wise, the signs are there to see: the creation of the heavens and earth, the night and the day, the ships that sail the waters profiting mankind, the rains that God sends down to bring the earth back to life, the beasts He spread across the earth, the changing winds, and the clouds that obediently sit between heaven and earth.

165. There are some men that worship things as equals to God. They love them in ways they should love only God. The faithful are however more loving to God. If the wicked could only see their future penalty. God is all-powerful, and God will be severe in delivering punishment.

166–167. [One day] those being worshipped will disown their followers. Then they [followers] will see their doom, as their hopes in a protector collapse. They will say, "If we were given one more chance, we would disown them as they have disowned us." God will then show them the results of their deeds, and they won't emerge from the fire.

168–169. Mankind, eat all the lawful and good things on the earth. Do not follow the path of the devil, for he is your enemy. He calls you to be evil and indecent and to speak against God out of ignorance.

170. When they are told to follow God's revelations, they reply, "No, we will follow our father's ways." Why do they do this when their fathers were unwise and lacked guidance?

171. A parable of the faithless: They are like a person that speaks to things that can only hear a shout or a cry. [They are] deaf, dumb, and blind and therefore lack wisdom.

172. Oh faithful, eat all the good things on earth that We provided, and be grateful to God if you truly worship Him.

173. He forbids meat that wasn't slaughtered, blood, pork, and anything that was slaughtered while a name besides God was invoked. If you must eat those things by necessity, then it is not a sin as long as you don't crave it or eat gluttonously. God is forgiving and merciful.

174–176. People that hide God's revelations from the Book or sell them for a small profit are eating nothing but fire. God will not speak to them on resurrection day, and He won't purify them. Their penalty will be grave. These people purchase mistakes instead of guidance, and punishment instead of forgiveness. How boldly they taunt the flames. This is because God revealed the Book in truth. Those who cause disputes about the Book are defiant.

177. Righteousness doesn't come from turning to face the East or West. Righteousness is from belief in God, the last day, the angels, the Book, the messengers; from gifting your wealth out of love for Him, family, orphans, the needy, travelers, and those who ask for it; from freeing slaves, praying and giving to charity regularly, keeping your promises, and being patient when you suffer and panic. Those who do this are sincere. They are fearful of God.

178–179. Oh faithful, follow the law of equal exchange in cases of murder. One freeman for a freeman, one slave for a slave, and one woman for a woman. In cases where a brother partially forgives the murderer, then meet any reasonable demands with a sympathetic payment. This is an improvement from your Lord and a mercy. Anyone that exceeds this limit will face a great penalty. There is life for you in the law of revenge for those wise enough to see and abstain from evil.

180–182. It is ordained that you gift any wealth you have as you near death to your parents and near relatives in a fair manner. This is a duty for the God-fearing. Anyone that changes your will after it's made public is committing a sin. God knows and hears everything. It is not a sin for anyone to correct the distribution of wealth, if they feel the executor is being unfair or not following the wishes of the deceased. God is forgiving and merciful.

183. Oh faithful, you are commanded to fast, just like those before you had to, so you can learn obedience and restraint.

184. You must fast for a set number of days. If you are ill or traveling, you can make up those days later. If you can afford it, you should also feed one needy person. If you choose to feed the hungry out of your own good heart, then it's even better. It is best that you fast. If only you understood.

185. During the month of Ramadan [an important Islamic holy month], the Qur'an was revealed as a guide to man and with clear signs to aid in judgment. Everyone that is home during Ramadan should fast. Exceptions exist for the ill and travelers for them to make up the exact days later. God never wishes to cause you difficulty, but He wants you to fast during the set period to glorify Him for His guidance and to show that you are grateful.

186. When My worshippers ask you about Me, I am always nearby. I listen to every prayer they make to Me. Let them hear My call to them and believe in Me, so they can follow the right path.

187. At night you are allowed to break your fast and have relations with your wives. They are like clothing for you, as you are to them. God knows that you used to do this in secret, so He

extends His mercy to forgive you. So now [at night] you can have intercourse with them, as God allows it, and also eat and drink. Continue the fasting again at the first sign of daylight and continue it until nightfall. Do not touch your wives while you are praying in the mosque. Do not test the limits set by God. God has made His revelations clear to mankind so they can show restraint.

188. Don't squander your wealth improperly among yourselves. Don't use your wealth to bribe judges in order to wrongfully gain another man's wealth.

189. When people ask you questions about new moons, say to them, "They are signs marking the seasons for man and the pilgrimage." The righteous should not enter a house through the back door. The righteous fear God. So enter homes through the proper doors and fear God to be prosperous.

190. Fight [not the term "jihad"] in the way of God against those who fight you. But do not break the laws. God does not love lawbreakers.

191. Kill [the term "jihad" is not used anywhere in this verse] them wherever you find them. Expel them from places they have expelled you, for oppression [treason] is worse than death. Do not fight them near the holy mosque, unless they attack you there. If they fight you, then kill them; it is the punishment for the unbelievers.

192. If they stop, God is often forgiving and merciful.

193. Fight [not the term "jihad"] them until there is no more oppression and religion is for God. If they stop, then let that end the hostilities towards everyone except the oppressors.

194. The sacred month is for sacred events. There is a law of retaliation for prohibited things; so if someone attacks you, then attack them equally. But be obedient to God and know that God is with the righteous.

195. Spend in God's way. Don't use your own hands to toss yourself into ruin. Perform good acts, for God loves the righteous.

196. Complete the pilgrimage [hajj] and visitation to Mecca for the sake of God. If you are unable to do it, then send a sacrificial offering, and do not shave your head until the offering reaches its destination. If you can't shave your head due to illness or injury, then compensate by fasting, feeding the needy, or a sacrificial offering. When you are able to continue the pilgrimage, then make the appropriate offering if you can. If you can't afford it, then fast for three days during the pilgrimage and seven days upon your return, for a total of ten days. These are guidelines for people that don't live in the vicinity of the sacred mosque. Be wary of God and know that God is a strict punisher.

197. The pilgrimage occurs in well-known months. If you begin your pilgrimage in that time, then remember that intercourse, obscenities, or arguing are not allowed. All the goodness you do will be known to God. Bring provisions for the pilgrimage, but know that the best provision for your soul is righteous conduct. Keep your duty to Me, if you are wise.

198. It is not sinful to ask for your Lord's grace. When you all march down from Mount Arafat, remember God near the sacred monument. Remember Him for His guidance to you, because you once were lost.

199. Pass quickly from the place where people start to rush and ask for God's forgiveness. God is forgiving and merciful.

200–202. After you have completed your rituals, celebrate God in a more sincere way than you would praise your forefathers. Some people will ask, "Our Lord, give us [your bounty] is this world!" but they will get no part of it in the hereafter. Some other men say, "Our Lord, give us goodness in this world and the hereafter and protect us from the punishing flames." Those people will be rewarded for what they earned. God is swift to judge.

203. Praise God throughout the scheduled days. If anyone must depart after two days, or if they want to stay longer, it is not a sin if they are acting for righteous reasons. Be wary of God, and understand that everyone will be recalled to Him.

204–206. Some men can impress others with their speeches and even invite God to be a witness to what's in their hearts. In truth, they are the toughest enemies. When they are out of your sight, they seek to make corruption and destroy crops and beasts. God does not like corruption. When they are told to "Fear God," their arrogance drives them to sin even more. Hell is appropriate for them, and it's an evil destination.

207–209. There is another type of man that gives all of his soul to seek God's grace. God is kind to His servants. Oh faithful, be completely submissive, and do not follow the path of Satan, for he is a clear enemy. If you fall backwards after you have received the clear signs [from God], then recall that God is mighty and wise.

210. Are they waiting [to submit] until God appears to them amongst the clouds surrounded by angels? By then they would already have been judged. All matters will end up with God [for judgment].

211. Ask the Israelis how many clear revelations We sent them. God will severely punish anyone that alters the grace of God once it has been revealed to them.

212. The faithless are dazzled by the life in this world, and they mock those who believe. On the day of resurrection, the righteous will sit high above them. God gives His unlimited rewards to whoever He chooses.

213. Mankind was once a single community. Then God sent messengers with good news and warnings. He sent with them the Book of truth to settle all matters that men were arguing about. The men that argued with each other [about the revelations] after they were given clear signs were selfish and envious. Yet God used His grace to guide the [actual] faithful to the truth about their arguments. God guides whoever He chooses on the straight path.

214. Do you think you will enter the Gardens until you have experienced what earlier generations did? They felt adversity and distress and were shaken until the messenger and the faithful cried out, "When will God's help arrive?" God's assistance is surely near.

215. When they ask you how they should spend [charity], say to them, "Whatever wealth you give should go to parents, relatives, orphans, the needy, and travelers." Every act of goodness is known to God.

216. It's written that you must fight [not the term "jihad"], and you should hate it. But sometimes you hate things that are good for you and like things that are bad for you. God knows things that you don't.

217. When they ask you about fighting during the holy month, say to them, "Fighting ["jihad" not used in this verse] then is a most serious offense. But preventing others access to God's way, denying Him, blocking access to the sacred mosque, and

driving people from it are even more outrageous offenses to God. Chaos and/or disbelief are worse than killing. They won't stop fighting you until you reject your religion, if they are able to. Whoever turns away from their religion and dies faithless will find their good deeds won't help them in the hereafter. They will be owners of the fire and will live in there.

218. It is the people that believe, have migrated, and struggled [jihad] in God's way that may share in God's mercy. God is forgiving and merciful.

219–220. When they ask you about alcohol and gambling, say to them, "They are both great sins and a way for men to profit. But the sin is greater than the reward." When they ask you about how much they should they spend [give to charity], say to them, "Give away your surplus." God makes His revelations clear, so that you can think about this life and the hereafter. When they ask you about orphans, tell them, "It's best to help them in all matters, and if you take them into your life, then you are family. God can tell if a man is ruining or helping another. And if God wanted to, He could make your life difficult." He is mighty and wise.

221. Don't marry an idol-worshipping woman until she converts to your faith. A slave who is faithful is better than an alluring idol worshipper. Don't let your girls marry idol worshippers. It's better they marry a faithful slave than an impressive idol

worshipper. The unbelievers are calling you to the flames. Meanwhile, God is calling you through His grace into the Garden and into His mercy. He makes his revelations clear to men, so they can beware.

222. When they ask you about menstruation, tell them, "It is painful and offensive," so stay away from women during menstruation, and afterwards ensure they are clean first. After they are pure, you may have intercourse with them as God has specified. God loves people who look to Him frequently and those who purify themselves.

223. Your wives are a place for you to sew your seeds, so plow your field when you like. But before you do, perform a good act on behalf of your soul and be wary of God. Know that you will meet Him one day. Give good news to the believers.

224. Don't make your promises to God an obstacle to your doing good deeds, being an obedient worshipper, or making peace between men. God knows and hears all things.

225. God won't judge you for anything unintentional in your promises, but He will judge you for the intention in your hearts. God is forgiving and tolerant.

226–227. Those who swear to abstain from their wives must do so for four months [a prelude to divorce]. If they change their minds, then God is forgiving and merciful. If they decide to divorce, then remember that God hears and knows all things.

228. Divorcing women shall remain untouched for three menstrual cycles. If they have faith in God and the last day, then they will not try to hide any child that God has created in their wombs. Husbands have a right to take the women back in that time period if they want a reunion. Women have similar rights to men when it comes to equality, but men have an advantage over women. God is mighty and wise.

229. You may only divorce a woman twice. Then you must either stay together honorably or leave each other on kind terms. Men are not allowed to take back any gifts to their wives, unless they both fear that they cannot be married and keep within God's laws. If they fear that they cannot stay married according to God's laws, then there is no sin attached for any payment she might make to gain her freedom. These are the rules of God, so do not break them. Those who break God's rules are unjust.

230. Once a husband divorces [separates for the third time legally], he can't remarry her until she has married another man and been divorced. Then they can remarry without sin, as long as they think they can stay married within God's laws. These are the rules of God, and He makes them clear to those who are wise.

231. When divorcing a woman, as they reach the end of the specified term, you must either take them back honorably or release them with kindness. Do not take them back just to

hurt them, as it breaks the law. Anyone that does that is harming their own soul. Do not mock God's revelations. Remember that God's grace is upon you and that He sent you the Book and wisdom so that He could guide you. Fear God and remember that God knows all things.

232. When divorced women have waited their specified term, then do not try to prevent her from marrying her husband, if they have chosen to reunite lawfully. This is guidance for those who believe in God and the last day. Doing this will be better for you, and God knows things that you do not.

233. Mothers [that bear children during the divorce] will suckle for two years, if they choose this method. The father must continue to fairly pay for food and clothing. No one should ever have to pay more than they are able. Mothers and fathers cannot be treated unfairly because of the child. The rights of inheritance still attach to the child. If both parties choose to wean the child or to take on a nursemaid, it is not a sin, but ensure she is paid fairly. Fear God and remember that God knows all that you do.

234. Widows should wait [mourn] for four months and ten days. After that period, there is no sin for their actions that are reasonable and honorable. God knows all that you do.

235. It's not a sin for a man to make an offer to marry [a widow] or to hide your feelings of love for her. God knows what's in your hearts. But do not create a secret contract with her and

honorably ask for her marriage. Do not consummate the marriage before the prescribed time period is complete. Remember that God knows what's in your hearts. Be wary of Him and remember that God is forgiving and tolerant.

236. It is not a sin if you divorce a woman before you have touched her or settled upon a dower [monetary obligation from man to woman] for her. But you should give them a nice [departing] gift, according to your wealth. Those who wish to do the right thing should give her a gift of a reasonable amount.

237. If you divorce her before you have touched her but after you set a dower, then you must give her half of the dower. There is an exception if either the woman or her guardian chooses not to take the half-dower. It is more righteous to refuse the money. Remember to be kind to each other. God sees all that you do.

238. Ensure you pray regularly, especially the noon [or afternoon] prayer. Stand before God humbly obedient.

239. If you are in fear, then you may pray standing or in the saddle, but after you reach safety, pray according to God's teachings. He taught you things you did not know.

240–242. You should leave your widows one years' worth of wealth and a home. If they leave the home, it's not a sin for you, because it's within her rights. God is mighty and wise. Your provision for divorced women should be reasonable if you are trying to live righteously. God makes His revelations clear so that you can understand them.

243. Think about the people who left their homes by the thousands and were afraid of death. God said to them, "Die." And then He brought them back to life. God is gracious to mankind, but most of them are ungrateful.

244. Fight [not the term "jihad"] in God's way, and remember that God knows and hears all things.

245. Who is willing to offer God a gift so that God can multiply it? God is able to decrease and increase things. You all will return to Him.

246. Consider the Israeli chiefs after Moses's time who asked a prophet [Samuel], "Will you appoint us a king so that we may fight [the term "jihad" is not used in this verse] in God's way?" He replied to them, "Is it possible that you won't fight when you are commanded to?" The chiefs responded, "Why would we refuse to fight in the way of God after we and our families were driven from our homes?" And yet, when they were commanded to fight, all but a few of them retreated. God is aware of all the sinners.

247. Their prophet told them, "God has appointed Saul as your king." They replied, "How can he be our king when we are better suited to rule, and he is not even wealthy?" The prophet responded, "Because God chose him over you and graced him

with wisdom and stature. God grants His kingdom to anyone He chooses. God is sufficient and knows all things.

248. Then the prophet told them, "A sign of His authority will come in the form of an ark [chest] containing assurances from your Lord and relics from the families of Moses and Aaron. It will be carried by angels, and it will be a clear sign for people who believe.

249. As Saul marched forward with his army, he explained, "God is going to test us at the stream. Those who drink water won't serve with me. Those who don't drink it will serve with me. If you only use your hand to taste it, you are excused." At the river, almost all the men drank. As the remaining faithful crossed the river, they said, "We won't be able to face Goliath and his army." But the ones that truly believed they would one day meet God cried out, "Think of how many times, through God's will, a small force defeated a larger one! God is with the steadfast!"

250. As they were advancing on Goliath's army they prayed, "Lord, give us endurance, make steady our feet, and help us against the unbelievers."

251. And there by God's will, they won a victory, and David killed Goliath. God had gave him wisdom and the title of king. If God had failed to use some men to defeat others, the world would be in chaos. God is kind to His creatures.

252. These are the signs of God. We recite them to you, because you are one of the messengers.

253. We gave some apostles advantages over the other ones. God spoke to some. Some He glorified above others. He gave Jesus, the son of Mary, clear signs and strengthened him with the holy spirit. If God wanted to, He would have willed the next generations not to fight each other after they received the clear proof. But they chose to argue, with some finding faith and others rejecting it. Again, if God willed it they would not have fought, but God does as He chooses.

254. Oh faithful, spend from what We provide you before the day arrives, when you won't be able to bargain, or call a friend, or be saved by intervention. The unbelievers are sinners.

255. God—there is no god but Him—is alive and eternal. He never tires or sleeps. Everything in the heavens and earth belong to Him. No one can intervene without His permission. He knows the future and past of every creature, and they cannot learn wisdom unless He wills it. His throne [kingdom] extends over the heavens and earth, and he never grows weary of protecting them. He is awe-inspiring and supreme.

256. Religion cannot be forced. The right path is clearly marked from the mistaken one. If you reject the evil ones and believe in God, you have taken hold of the handle that never breaks. God knows and hears everything.

257. God is the guardian of the faithful. He brings them out of the dark and into the light. The disbelievers have chosen evil beings as guardians. They will lead them from the light and into the darkness. They will become the permanent inmates of hell.

258. Do you recall the man [Nimrod] that argued with Abraham about his Lord, because God had given him the kingdom? Abraham told him, "My Lord is the One that gives life and death." The man replied, "I can give life and death." Abraham said, "But God causes the sun to rise in the East, so can you cause it to rise from the West?" This confused the arrogant unbeliever. God does not guide the unjust.

259. There is a story of a man that passed by a ruined town and said out loud, "How could God ever bring this dead place back to life?" God, hearing this, caused the man to be dead for one hundred years and then resurrected him. He [God] asked, "How long were you gone?" The man guessed, "Maybe a day or half a day." He [God] replied, No you were gone for one hundred years. Now take a look at your food and drink and see that it didn't spoil, and then look at your donkey. Look at the bones and how we have covered them in flesh. We make you an example for the people." When he saw all the signs clearly, the man said, "I know that God has power over everything."

260. Abraham once said, "My Lord, show me how you resurrect the dead." God replied, "Don't you have faith?" Abraham said, Yes, but I want to reassure myself." God instructed him, "Take four birds and cut them into pieces. Then place them all over the mountain tops and call them back to you. They will swiftly return to you. Know that God is mighty and wise."

261-262. A parable: A man who spends his wealth in the way of God is like one seed of corn. It will grow seven ears and each ear will contain one hundred kernels of corn. God enriches who He chooses. God is caring and He knows everything. People who share their wealth in the way of God, without trying to seek recognition for it or give an insult afterwards, will have a reward with their Lord. They shall not fear or grieve.

263. Kind words followed by forgiveness is a better thing than charitable giving followed by an insult. God is absolute and tolerant.

264. Oh faithful, don't negate your charity by seeking recognition for it or casting insults. Don't be like the men that spend their wealth to be noticed but don't believe in God or the last day. Those men are like a hard stone covered in soil; after a heavy rain the stone is left uncovered. Those men won't earn anything from their deeds. God does not guide the unbelievers.

265. A parable: Those who spend their wealth seeking only to please God and better their souls are like a fertile garden on

high ground. After heavy rains, it will double its harvest yield; but if it doesn't get a rainstorm, then a light shower will maintain it. God sees all that you do.

266. Would any of you be happy if you owned a garden full of date palms and vineyards, with flowing streams and various fruits, and then when you get old and your children are unable to care for you, it is all lost? If it was struck by a tornado-like fire that burns it down? God makes His signs clear to you, so that you may reflect on them.

267. Oh faithful, give charitably from the good things that you have earned or We created on the earth for you. Do not buy bad things and then give them away, when you clearly wouldn't buy them for yourself. Remember that God is absolute and praiseworthy.

268-269. Satan tries to threaten you with poverty and asks you to act improperly. God promises you His forgiveness and rewards. God is caring and wise. He gives wisdom to whoever He chooses. Those who are granted His wisdom receive an amazing benefit. But only the wise will understand it.

270. God is aware of everything you give in charity and all your devotions. The wicked have no helpers.

271. To give to charity publicly is good, but to care for the needy privately is even better. It will help you wash away some of your sins. God knows all that you do.

272. It is not your job [Muhammad] to set men on the right path. God will guide correctly whoever He pleases. Whatever wealth you give benefits your soul if you are [correctly] giving to earn God's grace. Whatever you give will be repaid to you in full. You won't be treated unfairly.

273. Charity is for the needy that are unable to travel the lands to work or trade. Ignorant people don't think they are poor, because of their humility. You can spot them by their behavior, as they won't insistently beg from everyone. God will know of your charity.

274. Those who give away their wealth, either by night or day or in private or openly, will be rewarded by their Lord. They shall not fear or grieve.

275. People who take interest [financially speaking] can only stand like a person that has been touched and damaged by Satan. Those people say that, "Trade is the same as charging interest," but [actually] God allows trade and forbids charging interest. Those who stop charging interest after they are warned by God to stop can keep their previous earnings and put themselves in God's hands for judgment. Those who continue to break this rule will be the eternal tenants of the fire.

276. God does not bless interest charging but will make charities prosper. God doesn't love the ungrateful and wicked.

277. Those who believe, act righteously, regularly pray, and give charitably will find their reward with their Lord. They shall not fear or grieve.

278–280. Oh faithful, be wary of God, and give away what remains of your profits from charging interest, if you are truly believers. If you do not, then you are being warned of a war [not the term "jihad"] against you from God and His messenger. But if you repent, then you can retain your original capital. You won't cause the borrower to lose money, and neither will you. If the borrower is unable to pay you now, then give him more time. Or you can forgive the debt as a form of charity, and that would be best for you, if you only knew it.

[Verse 281 given at Mina during the last *hajj*]

281. Prepare for the day when you will all be brought back to God. Every soul will be paid completely for what it earned, and no one will be judged unfairly.

282. Oh faithful, when you establish a long-term loan, ensure the terms are written down by a trusted clerk. Ensure the clerk writes in the way God taught him. The borrower should dictate the terms and be fearful of his Lord God, ensuring he captures all that he owes in the contract. If he doesn't understand, is weak, or is otherwise unable to explain the terms, then a guardian should.

You will need two male witnesses. If they can't find two, then one man and two women; in case one woman makes a mistake, the other can help her catch it. Witnesses cannot refuse a request to help.

Don't have contempt for having to write down your contracts. Whether it's a big or small amount, a contract is better in God's eyes, is proper evidence, and will ensure no one doubts the transaction. If you do make a deal to exchange merchandise between yourselves that is immediately carried out, there is no sin for not writing out a contract.

Always take a witness when you sell things to one another. Never let harm come to a clerk or a witness. If you harm them, it is a sin. Be wary of your duty to God. God teaches you and knows everything.

283. If you are traveling and can't find someone to write, then you can pay a security deposit to make the deal. If one of you gives the other a deposit, then the others must keep their end of the deal for fear of their Lord. Do not hide any evidence, for if you do, your heart is full of sin. God knows everything you do.

284. Everything in the heavens and on earth belongs to God. Whether you say what is on your mind or try to hide your thoughts, God will judge you for them. He forgives and punishes who He pleases. God has power over all things.

285. The messenger believes what his Lord revealed to him, and so do the faithful. They each believe in God, His angels, His books, and His messengers, [declaring,] "We don't distinguish between any of His messengers. We hear and we obey. We seek your forgiveness, Lord. Our journey returns us to You."

286. God won't place any burden on a soul that it can't handle. It [a soul] earns from its goodness and is punished for its evil ways.

Prayer: "Our Lord, don't condemn us for our mistakes. Our Lord, don't burden us like you did the earlier generations. Our Lord, don't burden us with something we can't bear. Erase our sins and be merciful to us. You are our guardian, so help us against the faithless."

Chapter 88 (chronologically)

Sura 8 (75 verses), Al-Anfal (The Spoils of War)
[references to the Battle of Badr, year 624AD/CE]

1. When they ask you about the spoils of war [not the term "jihad"], say to them, "The spoils of war belong to God and the messenger. So if you are faithful, be dutiful to God, settle your differences, and obey God and His messenger."

2–4. The faithful are people whose heart shudders at the mention of God, and when they hear His revelations spoken, their faith strengthens, and who trust in their Lord. Who pray regularly and spend from what We give them [charitably]. Those who are faithful will honored by their Lord, be forgiven, and have a noble endowment.

5–6. While your Lord caused you to move out of your home with the truth, there were some believers that were reluctant. They argued with you about the truth after it was made clear, as if they were watching something that was driving them towards death.

7–8. When God promised that you would have one of the two enemy formations, you wished that you would face the unarmed group. But God wanted to win with the power of His words and cut off the roots of the unfaithful, so that He could cause truth to win over an arrogant lie, in the face of the faithless opposition.

9–10. When you called on your Lord for help, He replied, "I will aid you with a thousand angels arranged in ranks." God said it to lift your spirits with a message of hope. Victory only comes with God's help. God is mighty and wise.

11. He calmed you with a safe slumber, brought the rains down to purify you and remove the fear of Satan, and strengthened your hearts while steadying your feet.

12–14. Your Lord inspired the angels, saying, "I am with you, so make the faithful stand firm. I will cast fear into the hearts of the unfaithful. Strike above their necks and cut off their fingertips." This was because they opposed God and His messenger. For anyone that opposes God and His messenger there will be a severe punishment, where they will hear, "Taste the punishment; the punishment for the unfaithful is torment by fire."

15–16. My faithful, when you meet the unfaithful in battle, never turn your back to them. Anyone that turns his back in battle, unless it's a tactic of war or to retreat to your unit, will feel the wrath of God and then dwell in hell, that evil destination.

17. You did not kill them, it was God. When you threw [something], it was actually God that threw [it], so that He could give it as a gift to the faithful. God hears and knows all things.

18. God weakens the strategies of the unfaithful.

19. [spoken to the non-Islamic enemy] You asked for judgment, and so you have it. If you stop, it would be best for you. If you renew [the battle], so will We. No matter how large your force is, it will not win. God is on the side of the faithful.

20–21. My faithful, obey God and His messenger, and do not turn away when you hear him. Don't be like the people who say, "We hear you," but are not listening.

22–23. The worst beings in God's sight are the deaf and the dumb, which have no sense. If God had found any goodness in them,

He would have made them hear. But even if He gave them hearing, they would have rejected faith and turned away.

24. My faithful, answer the call of God and His messenger when He calls you to activities that will give you life. Know that God comes between a man and his heart. It is to Him that you will be returned.

25. Beware of a penalty that might not only strike the sinners amongst you, and know that God is severe when He punishes.

26. Remember when you were a small group, believed to be weak in the lands, and afraid that men might kidnap you. He provided refuge for you, strengthened you by providing assistance, and gave you good provisions, so give thanks.

27–29. My faithful, don't betray the trust of God or His messenger, and don't purposely betray other things entrusted to you. Know that your property and children are a trial in life; God holds the true reward. If you obey God, He will give you the ability to know right from wrong, remove any evils you have, and forgive your sins. God has unlimited mercy.

30. [MC] The unfaithful once plotted to jail you, kill you, or expel you. But while they plotted, God also devised, and God is the best planner.

31–33. [MC] When Our messages are revealed to them, they will say, "We have heard it all before. If we wanted to, we could talk like that, because they are just ancient stories." They also say, “God, if this message is truthful, then rain down stones or inflict a great punishment.” God would not send down a penalty while you were among them; nor would He if they were asking for His mercy.

34. [MC] What excuse can they put forth to avoid God’s punishment when they keep men out of the sacred mosque, when they are not its guardians? Only the righteous can be guardians there. But most men don’t understand.

35. [MC] When they pray at the house, it’s just whistling and clapping. “They will taste punishment for their disbelief.”

36. [MC] The unfaithful spend their wealth to keep men from the path of God. If they continue to spend, they will only have regrets. They will be overcome and ushered towards hell . . .

37. so that God can separate the pure from the wicked. He will pile the wicked into a heap and cast them all into hell. They will be the ones who failed.

38. Tell the unbelievers if they turn now, then their past will be forgiven. But if they continue their ways, then they will get the same punishment as those who came before.

39–40. Fight [kill/battle] them until persecution ends and faith is in God alone. If they stop fighting, God will see all that they do. If they refuse to, then know that God is your protector. He is the most excellent patron.

41. Remember that one-fifth of the spoils you take in war are set aside for God, the messenger, close family, orphans, the needy, and travelers. That is, if you believe in God and in the revelations We sent to Our messenger on the day of testing, the day the two armies met [Battle of Badr, 624 AD]. God has power over all things.

[Battle of Badr recounted]

42. Recall that you were on one side of the valley and the enemy on the other, with the caravan below you. Even if you had a plan to meet at a certain time, you would not have made the appointment, so that God could carry out what needed to be done, and those who died and lived would serve as a clear sign. God knows and hears all things.

43. In your dream God showed you the enemy as a small band. If He had shown you they were many, then your side would have faltered and argued over your strategy. But God saved you, because He knows the secrets of men.

44. When the armies met, He made your enemy appear small to you, and He made you appear small to them. This was so God could carry out an action that was already ordained to occur. All affairs are decided by God.

45. Oh faithful, when you face an army stand firm; and remember God so that you can be successful.

46. Obey God and His messenger, and don't argue with each other, so that you won't falter and lose strength. Be patient, for God is on the side of the steadfast.

47. Don't act like men that come out from their homes [for battle] boasting so they can be seen by other men, but actually hinder others from the path of God. God understands what they are doing.

48. Remember that Satan made them think their actions were reasonable and told them, "No man can defeat you today, for I am your guardian." But when the forces came within sight of each other, he [Satan] proclaimed as he fled, "I am no longer with you. I can see what you can't see. I fear God, for God enacts grave punishment!"

49. The hypocrites and men with diseased hearts said, "These men have been deceived by their religion." But whoever puts their trust in God should know that God is the mightiest and wise.

50–51. If only you could see the how the angels take the souls of the unfaithful at death. How they strike their faces and backs, saying, "Taste the punishment of the flames! This is simply because of the deeds you have committed, for God is never unjust to His servants."

52–54. It is like the example of the Pharaoh's people and communities before them. They rejected the revelations of

God, and so God punished them for their sins. God is strong and severe in His punishment. This happened because God never changes any mercy He bestows to a people unless they change what is in their hearts. God knows and hears all things. What were the deeds of the Pharaoh's people and those generations before them? They rejected the signs of their Lord. Therefore, We destroyed them for their sins. We drowned the Pharaoh's people, for they were unjust.

55–56. The most vile creatures in God's eyes are those who reject Him, those who do not believe. They are the ones that break their promises with you every time you make an agreement. They don't fear God.

57. If you face them in battle, defeat them in such a way that those forces behind them will scatter in fear when they hear of it.

58. If you think any group will betray you, then dissolve your agreements [of peace] with them so you are on equal terms. God does not love traitors.

59. Never let the unfaithful think they will be able to defeat you. They cannot escape [His power].

60. Instead strengthen your military forces and warhorses in order to awe the enemies of God, you, and your allies known only to God. Everything you spend in the cause of God will be repaid in a just manner.

61. If your enemy seeks peace, then you should also seek peace and trust in God. He hears and knows everything.

62–63. But if they try to deceive you, know that God is adequate to your needs. He strengthens you with His power and with His faithful. He united the faithful's hearts to a level you could not achieve by spending everything that is on the earth. God could do that, because He is the mightiest and wise.

64. Oh prophet, God is all that you and the following of believers need.

65. Oh prophet, urge the faithful to fight ["al qital," not the term "jihad"]. If you field only twenty steadfast men, then you can defeat two hundred. If you have one hundred, then you can defeat one thousand of the unbelievers for they are people that do not understand.

66. Right now God has eased your task for you because He knows you have a weakness. Therefore, if there are one hundred steadfast men, they can defeat two hundred; and if you field one thousand, then they can overcome two thousand, by God's will. God is on the side of the steadfast.

67–69. It is not fitting for a prophet to take prisoners of war [that can be ransomed] until he has fought and beaten the enemy widely. Don't look for temporary wealth in this life; instead look to the hereafter. God is the mightiest and wise. You would have been severely punished for what you took, except there was an earlier proclamation about it from God. So, for now, enjoy the spoils of war you took that are lawful and good. But be dutiful to God, for God is forgiving and merciful.

70–71. Oh prophet, tell the captives you have taken, "If God finds any goodness in your hearts, He will replace what has been taken from you with something better and will forgive you, for God is forgiving and merciful." But, if any of them are traitorous against you, then know they have already betrayed God, and so you have been given power over them. God is knowledgeable and wise.

72. Know that those who believed, migrated, and struggled [jihad] in the way of God with their wealth and their lives; and also, those people who gave them shelter are now guardians to one another.

But those who were believers but did not migrate, there is no guardian relationship until they migrate. But if they ask for your help for the sake of the religion, you must help them. Unless they are going against people that you have a treaty with. God sees all that you do.

73. Know that the unbelievers are all guardians of one another. So, unless you protect each other, there will be suffering and corruption on the earth.

74. Those who are faithful, migrated, and struggled [jihad] in the way of God; and those who sheltered and aided them are the true believers. They shall gain forgiveness and generous reward.

75. Those who came to accept the faith later, migrated, and struggled [jihad] beside you are your people. But blood relatives have been given inheritance rights previously in the book of God. God knows all things.

Chapter 89 (chronologically)

Sura 3 (200 verses), Al-Imran (The Family of Imran)

1–2. Alif. Lam. Meem. God. There is no god but Him. The eternal and all-sustaining.

3–4. He sent down the Book to you, by revelation, confirming what was sent before. He sent down the Torah and the Gospel previously to guide mankind and provide the criterion of right and wrong. Those who reject the signs of God will suffer severe punishment. God is the mighty Lord of retribution.

5–6. Nothing on earth or in the heavens is hidden from God. He shapes you in the womb according to His wishes. There is no god but Him, the mighty and wise.

7. He sent down the Book to you. The foundation of the Book is the revelations that are clear while others are metaphors. Those with deviant hearts will attempt to mislead people by explaining the metaphors, when they are truly known only to God. Knowledgeable people will say, "We believe in the Book, which is wholly from our Lord." But only the wisest can understand the warnings and messages.

8–9. "Our Lord, don't let our hearts stray now that you have guided us. Give us your mercy, for you are the most forgiving. Our Lord, You will surely gather all mankind together on that day. God never fails to keep His promise."

10–11. The faithless cannot be saved by their wealth or their children in the face of God. They will only be fuel for the fire. It's like the plight of the Pharaoh's people and earlier communities. They rejected the signs, so God punished them for their sins. God is a severe punisher.

12. Say to the faithless, "Soon you will be overtaken and driven into hell. It's an evil resting place."

13. There was a sign for you when the two armies met [at the Battle of Badr]. One was fighting [*tuqtl,* to kill] in the way of God and the other without faith. The faithful saw the enemy as double their size, but God gives His support to whoever He pleases. There is a lesson in this for those who can see it.

14–17. Mankind has been fooled into desiring the joys of this life: the women and children, amassing gold and silver, horses, cattle, and land. These are only the possessions of this world, while being near to God is the best goal. Say to them, "Do you want me to tell you what is better than this [worldly possessions]? The righteous will be near their Lord, living eternally in the Gardens where rivers flow beneath them. They live with pure friends and enjoy the pleasure of God." God knows His best servants. The ones who exclaim, "Lord, we believe! So please forgive our sins and save us from the agony of the flames!" [They are] patient and honest, obedient and charitable, and they pray for forgiveness at dawn.

18. God testifies that there is no god but Him; so do the angels and knowledgeable men. He maintains His creation justly; there is no god but Him, the almighty and wise.

19. The religion is submission to God. Those who received the Book earlier didn't differ from each other until they received knowledge and became envious of each other. God will be swift in His judgment against anyone rejecting the revelations of God.

20. If people argue with you, then say to them, "I have submitted my will to God, and so have the people that follow me." Then ask the people that were previously given the Book and those ignorant of it, "Do you submit?" If they submit, then they are following the right path, but if they reject it, remember your

duty is simply to convey the messages. God sees all His servants.

21–22. Tell those people that reject God's signs, unjustly kill prophets, and kill people that seek justice for mankind about the grave punishment. Their deeds will bring no success in this world or in the hereafter, and they won't have any guardians.

23–25. Have you thought about the people that have been given a part of the Book? They are being invited to the book of God so that it can judge the disputes between them, but a faction of the group opposes the invitation. It's because they believe, "The flames will only touch us for a set number of days." But their invented beliefs have deceived them about religion. Think of how it will be for them on that certain day when We gather all creatures. Each soul will be paid for what it has earned and all will be dealt with justly.

26–27. "Oh God, the master of the kingdom, you give and take sovereignty from whoever you choose. You strengthen and weaken whoever you choose. Your hand is goodness. You have power over all things. You make night turn to day and day turn to night. You turn the dead into life and bring the dead out of the living. You give endless sustenance to whoever you like."

28. The faithful should not take unbelievers to be their allies instead of the faithful, unless you do so as a precaution and are

wary of the [unbelievers]. Anyone that does this will no longer have the guardianship of God. God warns you to beware of God, as everything returns to God in the end.

29–32. Say to them, "Whether you hide things in your hearts or reveal them, God knows everything. He knows everything in the heavens and the earth, and God has power over all things." On the day that every soul is faced with all the good and evil deeds it has done, the souls will wish for a large distance between themselves and that evil. God warns you to beware of Him. God is most kind to those who serve Him. Say to them, "If you love God, then follow me. God will love you and forgive your sins. God is forgiving and merciful." Tell them, "Obey God and His messenger." If they turn their backs, [they will find] that God does not love those who reject faith.

33–34. God chose Adam, Noah, the family of Abraham, and the family of Imran above all other people. They are the offspring of each other. God hears and knows all things.

35. Imran's wife said, "My Lord, I offer to you what is in my womb as an offering. Accept it, for surely you hear and know all.

36. Then she delivered the child and said, "My Lord, I delivered a female child." Of course, God knew what she had delivered. "Lord, a male is not like a female. I have named her Mary,

and I seek your protection for her and her children from Satan the outcast."

37. Her Lord accepted her and caused her to grow up worthy. He entrusted Zachariah to care for her, and whenever he visited her, he would find her supplied with food. Zachariah would ask, "Mary, where does this come from?" She would answer, "It comes from God, who gives without limits to whoever He chooses.

38. And Zachariah then prayed to his Lord, "My lord, please give me pure offspring, for you hear all prayers."

39. The angels called to him as he stood in the sanctuary, "God sends you good news of a son named John [the Baptist], who will bear witness about a word from God. He will be noble and pure, a prophet of the righteous.

40–41. Zachariah asked, "My lord, how can I bear a son, when I am so old and my wife is barren?" The answer, "It will be so. God does as He pleases." He then asked, "My lord, give me a sign." They answered, "The sign will be that you will speak only to other men for three days by signals. Then praise the Lord constantly and glorify Him in the evening and the morning."

42–43. The angels said, "Mary, God has chosen you, purified you, and prefers you above all other women in the world. Mary, worship your Lord obediently; prostrate and bow in prayer."

44. This account is a secret that We are revealing to you [Muhammad] by inspiration, as you were not there when they argued about who would be Mary's guardian.

45. The angels said, "Mary, God sends you good news of a word from Him. His name will be Messiah; Jesus, the son of Mary. To be held in honor in this world and in the hereafter. He will be one of the ones brought closest [to God]."

46. "He will speak to mankind as a child and as an adult. He will be among the righteous."

47. Mary replied, "My Lord, how can I bear a son when no man has touched me?" They said, "It will be so. God creates what He wills. Once He decides on a matter, He only has to say 'Be' and it is so."

48–51. "He will teach him the Book and wisdom, the Torah, and the Gospel [*injeel*, the revelations inspired in Jesus by God]. He will make him a prophet to the children of Israel." He [Jesus] will declare, "I have brought to you a sign from your Lord. I will form a bird out of a lump of clay and breathe life into it. By God's power, it will become a bird. I will heal the blind and leprous and bring the dead back to life through God's will. I will tell you what you can eat and also store in your homes. There are signs here if you are faithful. I verify to you the laws of the Torah sent before me. I will make some things lawful to you that were forbidden previously. I come to you with a sign from your Lord. Be dutiful to God and obey me.

God is my Lord and your Lord. Worship Him; that is the straight path."

52–53. When Jesus noted their lack of faith, he called out, "Who will help me with God's work?" The disciples replied, "We will be God's helpers; we believe in God. We testify that we are those who submit [Muslims]. Lord, we believe in your revelations, and we will follow the messenger. Count us among those who will testify."

54. They [the unbelievers] plotted and schemed, but so did God, and God is the best planner.

55–56. God said, "Jesus, I am going to ascend you to Me and purify you from those who lack faith. I will make your followers superior to the unfaithful, until the resurrection day. Then when you all return to Me, I will decide all the matters that you once disagreed upon. Those who reject the faith, I will punish severely in this life and in the hereafter. They will not have anyone to help them."

57. The faithful that live righteously will be given their full reward by God. God does not love the unjust.

58. What We recite to you are signs and wise reminders [some say *the* wise reminder, meaning the Qur'an].

59. Jesus is similar to Adam in relation to God. He created him from dust and then said, "Be!" and he was [alive].

60–61. This is the truth from God, so do not be a skeptic. If anyone argues with you about this after receiving this knowledge, then say to them, “Let us gather our sons and women with us and then humbly pray for the curse of God upon the liars.”

62. That is a true account. There is no god except God. God is the almighty and wise.

63. If they turn from the message, know that God is fully aware of those who are corrupt.

64. Say to them, “People of the Book, we should come to an agreement. That we will only worship God, that we won’t associate any partners to Him, and that we will not look to any other lords besides God.” And if they reject this, say to them, “You are all witnesses that we are announcing we are ‘those who submit [to God]’ [Muslims or in Qur’anic Arabic *muselmun*].”

65–66. People of the Book, why do you argue about Abraham when the Torah and the Gospel were not revealed until after Abraham’s death. Why don’t you understand? You are people that argue about things you don’t understand. Why do you argue about issues you have no knowledge of? God has this knowledge, and you do not.

67–68. Abraham was not Jewish or a Nazarene [Christian], but he was righteous and submitted himself [to God, Muslim], and he was not a polytheist. The people most like Abraham are those who follow him, this prophet, and those who are faithful. God is the guardian of the faithful.

69. Some people of the Book want to lead you astray. They actually only lead themselves astray, but they are not aware of it.

70–71. People of the Book, why do you reject the signs of God when you are witnesses to them? People of the Book, why do you try to make lies seem true and knowingly hide the truth?

72. Some of the people of the Book will say, "Believe the revelations of the faithful in the morning, but reject it by the evening, so that they may return to their religion."

73–74. "Don't believe anyone that doesn't follow your religion." Say to them, "The only true guidance is that of God. No one can give you revelations like what you have received, and no one can argue with you in front of your Lord." Say to them, "All grace sits in God's hand. He grants it to whoever He wishes. God is generous and knowledgeable." He gives His mercy to whoever He selects. God is the giver of great mercy.

75. There are people of the Book that you could loan a mass of gold to and expect repayment. There are others that you could loan a single coin to and only be repaid after you constantly remind them to. This is because some say, "We are not required to keep our promises to illiterates [the ignorant ones]." They are knowingly attributing lies to God.

76. [It's better for] those who keep their promises and are righteous. God loves the righteous.

77. People that would sell God's covenant and their own promises for a small price will gain nothing in the hereafter. God won't speak or even look at them on the day of judgment, and He won't purify them. They will face a painful penalty.

78. There are some people that distort the Book with their own words. You might think it is actually part of the Book, but it isn't. They say, "This is from God." It is not from God, and they are knowingly lying about God.

79. It seems impossible that a man that is given the Book, wisdom, and the duty of a messenger would say to his followers, "Worship me instead of God." He should rather say, "Be faithful servants of the Lord, because you have studied and taught from the Book."

80. [That man] would not command you to worship angels and prophets as lords and saviors. Would he try to command you stop being faithful after you have submitted [to God/become Muslim, muselmun]?

81. When God made His covenant with the prophets He said, "I give you the Book and wisdom; and when a messenger comes after you that confirms the knowledge you have, will you believe him and aid him? Do you agree with this and accept our covenant as binding? They [the prophets] said, "We

agree." He continued, "Then you and I are witnesses to this agreement."

82. If anyone rejects this, then they are sinners.

83. Are they seeking to follow a religion other than God's? This, after all creatures—willingly or unwillingly, in the heavens and on the earth—have submitted to Him and to Him they will all return?

84. Say to them, "We have faith in God and what God has sent down to us: Abraham, Ishmael, Isaac, Jacob, the tribes [Jacob's offspring], Moses, Jesus, and the other prophets. We do not recognize any differences between any of them, and we submit to Him."

85. Anyone that seeks a religion other than Islam will find that religion is unacceptable, and they will suffer great loss in the hereafter.

86–89. How can God guide people who reject the faith after they have already accepted it, testified that the messenger was real, and seen clear signs? God does not guide the unjust. They have earned the curse of God, His angels, and all mankind. They will dwell in it [hell], and their penalty won't be lessened, nor will they get any relief. Unless they repent and then make amends, because God is often forgiving and merciful.

90–91. But anyone that rejects their faith after submitting [to God] and then grows even more faithless will never have their repentance accepted. They have truly gone astray. And anyone that stops being faithful and dies rejecting faith couldn't have their repentance accepted even if they tried to pay a ransom for their soul worth all the gold on earth. They face a painful punishment and will have no assistance.

92. You can never achieve righteousness until you give freely from what you love. God will know how much you give.

93. All food was legal for the children of Israel, before they received the Torah, except what the Israelis had forbidden themselves [or what Israel/Jacob forbade himself]. Say to them, "If you are honest men, then bring the Torah and read it."

94. Whoever invented any lies against God after [reading] that is a sinner.

95. Say to them, "God speaks the truth. Follow the religion of Abraham, the righteous. He was not a polytheist."

96–97. The first house [sanctuary] for man was the one in Bakkah [in Arabic "Bbka" but interpreted by most as Mecca]. A blessed place and guidance for all people. In it are clear signs, and it's a place where Abraham stood. Whoever enters it is safe. Pilgrimage to the house is a duty men owe to God, for those who can afford the trip. If anyone rejects this duty, then recall that God needs nothing from His creatures.

98–99. Say to them, "People of the Book, why do you reject the revelations of God when God is witnessing all that you do?" "People of the Book, why do you block the faithful from the path of God by trying to make it crooked, even though you know its truth? God is witnessing all that you do."

100. Oh faithful, if you listen to one group of the people of the Book, they will try to make you rejecters of your faith after you have believed.

101. How can you become a disbeliever when you are listening to the revelations of God sent down for you and the messenger is living among you? Those who remain steadfast to God are guided on the right path.

102. Oh faithful, respect God as He requires it, and do not die unless you are in submission [to him/muselmun, Muslims].

103. [Oh faithful,] hold together onto the rope of God and don't divide yourselves [into sects]. Remember God's grace, because you were once enemies, and God made brothers out of you by joining your hearts. And He saved you when you were on the edge of the pit of fire. God sends clear revelations to you so you can be guided correctly.

104. A nation should form from among you that calls for goodness, supports what is right, and forbids what is wrong. They will be successful.

105–107. Don't become like the people that argued and separated into sects after they received clear revelations. They face a grave punishment. On that day when some faces are white and others are blackened, it will be asked of the blackened ones, "Did you reject your faith after you accepted it? Then taste the penalty for your rejection!" Meanwhile, those whose faces are whitened shall dwell eternally in God's mercy.

108. These are the signs of God recited truthfully to you. God does not seek injustice for any of His creatures.

109. Everything in the heavens and on earth belongs to God, and everything returns to God.

110. You are the best nation to come from mankind. You support what is right, forbid what is wrong, and believe in God. It would have been best for the people of the Book to believe. While some of them are faithful, most are sinners.

111. They will not harm you and can only annoy you. If they try to fight you, you will watch them retreat, and no one will help them.

112. Shame befalls them everywhere, unless they are under a covenant from God or a promise from men. They earned God's wrath and have been made impoverished. They have

rejected the signs of God, unlawfully killed the prophets, disobeyed, and were sinful.

113–115. But not all of them are the same. Some people of the Book stand for what is right, recite the revelations all night, and pray [prostrate to God]. They believe in God and the last day, call for righteousness, forbid what is wrong, and actively perform good deeds. They are part of the righteous. The good that they do will be rewarded by God, for He knows who are righteous.

116–117. But those who reject the faith won't be aided by their wealth or children when they face God. They will dwell eternally in the fire. What they spend in this life is similar to a frost destroying the harvest of some people that have hurt their own souls. It isn't God that is unjust to them; they are unjust to themselves.

118–119. Faithful, don't take in confidants from outside your people. They will go to great lengths to ruin you, as they seek your failure. You have heard the hatred in their words, and what they hide in their hearts is worse. We have sent clear signs for those who are wise. You would love them, and even though you believe in all the books [scripture], they don't love you. When you are with them they say, "We are faithful." But, when they are alone, they bite their fingertips in rage. Say to them, "Die from your rage." God knows what men keep secret.

120. When you have good news, they are saddened. When disaster strikes you, they are happy. If you are steadfast and righteous, their schemes cannot harm you. God knows what they are doing.

121. Once you left home in the early morning to position the faithful for battle. God hears and knows all things.

122. Once two of your groups almost retreated in cowardice; but God was their protector. Let all the faithful trust in God.

123. God helped you at the Battle of Badr when you were weak and small. Fulfill your duty to God and be grateful.

124–125. It was then you told the faithful, "Isn't it enough for you that your Lord would send down three thousand angels to help? If you remain steady and righteous, in the event that the enemy attacks you quickly, then your Lord will send down five thousand angels of distinction."

126–129. God sent this message to you to raise your morale and steady your hearts. Victory only comes from God, the mighty and wise. He can cut down a part of the faithless forces or dishonor them, so they will retreat from their mission. You have no say in this matter: whether He gives them mercy or punishes them, for they are sinners. Everything in the heavens and on earth belongs to God. He forgives and punishes who He likes; but God is forgiving and merciful.

130–132. Faithful, do not take [excessive] interest [financial term] that has been doubled or multiplied. Be dutiful to God instead, and you will prosper. Beware of the flames that burn for the unbelievers. Obey God and the messenger, so that you might receive mercy.

133–136. Always seek forgiveness from your Lord and seek the paradise that is more vast than the heavens and the earth and awaits the righteous. [It is for] those who give to others in good times and in bad, who control their anger, and forgive others. God loves those who do good deeds. [It is for] those who ask for forgiveness when they commit a sin, for who can forgive you besides God? For those that don't knowingly continue to commit sins. Forgiveness and an eternal home in the gardens with rivers flowing beneath them is the reward for these people. What an excellent reward for the hard workers.

137–138. Many examples over time occurred before you, so travel the lands and see what happened to those who rejected the truth. There are clear explanations to mankind, guidance and warnings for those who are dutiful [to God].

139. Don't lose heart or grieve; you will overcome others if you are faithful.

140–141. If you are wounded, then be assured: other people have been wounded alike. We share trials among all men, so that God can determine who is faithful and be able to select witnesses from among you. God does not like those who do wrong. This way God can test the faithful and scar ["blight" is exact word] those who don't believe.

142. Do you think that you can enter heaven without God determining who has struggled [those who performed jihad] and who was steadfast?

143. You all wished for death before you ever saw it [firsthand], and now you have seen it.

144. Muhammad is a messenger. Other messengers have died before him. If he dies or is killed, will you run away? If you retreat, you will not harm God at all. But soon God will reward the thankful.

145. No soul can die unless God allows it and it is their time. Anyone desiring the rewards of this life, We will give it. Anyone desiring the reward of the hereafter, We will give it. Soon We will reward the thankful.

146. Many a prophet fought [not "jihad"; the Arabic word used is "q-t-l"] with bands of faithful beside them. They never lost heart toward God's path [not "jihad"] despite the obstacles; they didn't weaken, and they didn't humiliate themselves. God loves the steadfast.

147. They only said, "Our Lord, forgive our sins and excesses, steady our feet, and help us against the faithless."

148. God rewarded them in this life and even greater in the hereafter. God loves the righteous.

149–150. Oh faithful, if you obey the unbelievers, they will make you retreat, and you will be losers. God is your guardian, and He is the best helper.

151. Soon We will place terror in the hearts of the unfaithful for associating partners to God. They had no authority from Him to do this. They will dwell in the fire, and it's an evil place for the unjust.

152. God was keeping His promise to you as you were, by His allowance, about to destroy the enemy, but then you faltered and argued with your orders. You disobeyed when you saw the war spoils that you craved. There are some among you that desire for things in this life and some for the hereafter. He then made you flee from your enemy so He could test you. He forgave you for this, as God is gracious to the faithful.

153. You scurried away, forgetting everyone around you and ignoring the calls of the messenger to come back. God then avenged you with multitudes of pain to teach you not to grieve over what you didn't retrieve or how you felt. God is aware of all you do.

154. He sent you security after the anguish. Some of you He calmed with sleep, while another group was anxious and thought selfishly and ignorantly about God. They [the second group] asked, "Do we have any say in these matters?" Tell them, "The matter belongs completely to God." They are hiding their true thoughts from you. They will say, "If we had

any role [control] in this matter, we would not have been slaughtered here!" Tell them, "Even if you [all] stayed home, those destined to die would have ended up where they were supposed to die. God tests what is in a man's heart, so He can purify it. God knows the secrets in your hearts."

155. Satan alone caused the men to fail and retreat that day the two forces met, due to some evil they committed. Surely God has forgiven them, for God is forgiving and merciful.

156. Oh faithful, don't be like the unbelievers, or God will make you regretful if you talk about your brothers as you travel or fight by saying, "If only they had stayed beside us, they would not have died or been killed." God alone gives life and death, and He knows what you say and do.

157. If you die or are killed serving in God's way, then God's mercy and forgiveness is worth more than you can ever achieve.

158. If you die or are killed, then you will be gathered back to God.

159. God's mercy allowed you to be gentle with them. If you were too harsh, then they would have left you. Pardon their faults, pray for their forgiveness, and talk to them about their conduct. When you are finished, then put your trust in God. God loves people who trust Him.

160. When God assists you, no one can best you. But if He abandons you, then who can help you? The faithful must rely on God.

161. No prophet should ever break their trust, and those who are shown untrustworthy will present their failures on judgment day. Every soul justly receives all that it earns [good or bad].

162–163. Is a man that follows God's will equal to one that earns God's wrath and is destined to dwell in an evil hell? All men are marked by varying grades in God's eyes. God sees what they do.

164. God clearly favored the faithful when He sent a messenger from their people to recite the revelations of God and to purify them. To teach them the Book and wisdom, when earlier they were clearly wrong.

165. [You recoil] when a single struggle faces you, saying "What is this?" although you have delivered twice the misfortune on others. Say to them, "This is because of your own souls." God has power over all things.

166–167. What happened to you on the day the two forces met was according to God's plan, so that He could test the believers and identify the hypocrites. They were told, "Come! Fight [not "jihad"; instead says *quteloo*] in the way of God or defend yourselves!" They replied, "If only we knew how to fight, we would have come." On that day, they were closer to disbelief than faith. They said the opposite of what was in their hearts, but God knows their secret thoughts.

168. [Challenge] those who sat at home safely and then say of others, "If only they had listened to us, they would not have been killed" by asking, "If you are not liars, then save yourselves from death."

169–171. Don't think of the men who were killed [following] the path of God as dead. They are living and being provided for by their Lord. They celebrate their reward from God and celebrating the men that have not arrived to join them yet. They have no more fear and do not grieve. They celebrate the kindness and abundance of God and that God doesn't waste any of the faithful's reward.

172–173. The wounded who still heeded the call of God and the messenger—the righteous and dutiful—will receive a grand reward. Likewise the men whose faith increased when people warned them, "You should be afraid, for a large army is facing you" and replied, "God is all we need! He is an excellent guardian!"

174. They all returned with God's grace and favor and were not harmed. They sought the good graces of God. God is the Lord of infinite grace.

175. Only Satan tries to make men scared of his followers. Don't fear his followers; instead fear Me if you are faithful.

176–178. Don't worry about those who rush into disbelief; they cannot hurt God. God doesn't plan to reward them in the hereafter, and they will suffer severe punishment. Those who choose disbelief at the expense of faith can't hurt God, and they face a great penalty. Don't let the unbelievers think We give them longer lives to improve their souls; We give it instead, so they can sin even more. They face a shameful punishment.

179. God doesn't want to leave the faithful in their current state of being, but He must identify the good and the wicked. He cannot tell you all the secrets of the unknown, so instead He sends messengers to you with knowledge. So believe in God and His messengers. If you are faithful and righteous, you will be rewarded greatly.

180. Don't let the stingy think that hoarding what God has given them from His grace is good for them; it's bad for them. What they withheld will be hung around their necks on resurrection day. God inherits everything from the heavens and the earth. God is aware of what you do.

181–182. God heard them [Medina inhabitants that wouldn't pay to support the battle] sneering, "If we are the rich ones, God must be very poor!" We will record their words and how they unjustly kill prophets, saying to them, "Taste the punishment of the flames for the deeds you committed prior; God is not unjust to His servants."

183–184. To those who say, “God commanded us not to believe any prophets unless they showed us a burning sacrifice,” reply, “Messengers came before me delivering just such a thing. If you are being honest now, then why did you kill them?” If they still reject you, then know that they also rejected previous messengers that showed them clear signs, scriptures, and an enlightening book.

185. Every soul dies. On judgment day, all will be repaid what they earned in full. The ones saved from hell and allowed in paradise will have obtained life’s objective. The comforts of this world are an illusion.

186. You and your possessions will be tested, and the polytheists and people who received the Book prior will say wrong things to you. But the steadfast and righteous are on the best path.

187. Know that God made a covenant with the people who received the Book, and it was supposed to be clear to all men. But they hid it [revelations], and hiding it gained them little. What a despicable bargain they made.

188. Don’t think that people who celebrate what they do and seek praise for it will escape punishment. They face a painful penalty.

189–190. God is the sovereign of heaven and earth and has power over everything. The creation of the heavens and earth and the alternation of night and day are signs for those who can understand.

191–194. All men that celebrate God—when they sit, stand, and lie down, thinking about the creation of heaven and earth—shall pray, "Our Lord, you didn't create this in vain; glory to you! Save us from the punishment of the fire. Our Lord, those you send into the fire are covered in shame. There is no help for sinners. Our Lord, we heard someone calling us to faith saying 'believe in your Lord,' and we believed. Our Lord, forgive our sins, remove our misdeeds, and cause us to die with the righteous. Our Lord, give us what the messengers promised. Do not disgrace us on resurrection day. You never break your promises."

195. The Lord heard and answered them: "The works of any man and woman will be counted, as you are both of one humanity and co-equals [in rewards and accountability]. People who migrated, who were driven from their homes, who were suffering [not "jihad"] in My cause, and those who fought and died [not the word for martyr or "jihad"] will be absolved of their misdeeds and, as a reward from God, will be admitted into the Garden with streams flowing beneath it. God holds the best rewards."

196–197. Don't be misled by the business of the unfaithful, for it's a deception. Their enjoyment is fleeting, but their final destination is hell, an evil place.

198. Those who are dutiful to God shall live eternally in Gardens full of streams. Due to hospitality from God. What God has in store is best for the righteous.

199. Among the people of the Book there are surely some that have faith in God, in the revelations you recite, and in the revelations sent to previous prophets. [Some are] humble towards God and don't sell God's signs for a little profit. They [too] will have a reward near their Lord. God is a swift judge.

200. Oh faithful, be patient, steadfast, alert, and dutiful to God so that you can succeed.

Chapter 90 (chronologically)

Sura 33 (73 verses), Al-Ahzab (The Confederates)

1–3. Prophet, keep your duty to God and don't obey the faithless or hypocrites. God is all-knowing and wise. Follow the revelations of your Lord, for God is aware of all you do. Put your trust in God, for God is a sufficient guide/guardian for you.

4. God did not put two hearts in any one person. He did not make the wives you divorced using that ancient Arab method [*zihar*] into your mothers. He did not make your adopted sons your true sons. Those are all words from your own mouths. God tells you the truth and guides you to the right way.

5. It is better in God's eyes if you call them by their father's names. If you don't know their fathers, then just call them your brothers in faith and your friend. There won't be any sin if you make an unintentional mistake. God is forgiving and merciful.

6. The prophet is more important to the faithful than they are to themselves. His wives are their mothers. God ordains that blood relatives are closer to each other [for inheritance] than other believers and migrants. But you should also treat your close friends fairly according to the Book.

7–8. Recall that We required a pledge from the prophets. From you, Noah, Abraham, Moses, and Jesus, the son of Mary. We required a solemn covenant, so that He could ask for the loyalty of those charged with delivering the truth. He has prepared a grave penalty for the unbelievers.

9–12. Oh faithful, recall when you received God's favor as a group came against you [a battle near Medina—the Battle of the Ditch], and We sent a mighty wind towards them so they couldn't see. God watches all that you do. They came towards you from above and below. As your eyes showed fear, your hearts rose into your throats, and you began to doubt God, it was the moment the faithful were tested and shaken by a severe shock. It's when the hypocrites and those with diseased hearts were saying, "God and His messenger have falsely promised us victory."

13. A group among the faithful called out, "Men of Yathrib [now Medina], you cannot withstand this [assault], so go back!" One group also asked the prophet if they could flee, saying, "Our homes are exposed," but they were not; they just wanted to run away.

14–15. If the flanks had been penetrated by the enemy force and the men were asked to renounce [Islam], then they would have done so with little hesitation, even though they had pledged to God that they would not retreat. Broken promises made to God must be answered for.

16–17. Say to them, "You will not gain from retreating! Even if you escape being killed, you will only know enjoyment for a little while. Who do you think can protect you from God if He chooses to harm or pardon you?" They will not find anyone besides God that can protect and aid them.

18–20. God knows who is trying to hold men back [from battle] and who is saying, "Come follow us" when they actually stay in battle for only a short time, only grudgingly helping you. [You will know them because] when they are overcome with fear, their eyes will appear to faint at the sight of death. Then after the fear passes, they will attack you with their sharp tongues because of their greed. These men are not faithful. God will make their deeds unsuccessful. This is easy for God. These men think that their confederates have not left the battle for good. If their confederates were to advance again, then the men would wish they were out in the desert among the Bedouins [nomadic Arabs] asking them for reports about you. It they were beside you [in battle] they would fight very little.

21. You will find the messenger of God a good role model for anyone that looks to God, hopes for the last day, and praises God frequently.

22–24. When the faithful saw the confederate forces, they said, "This is what God and His messenger promised to us. God and His messenger told us the truth." Their faith and submission increased. The faithful are men that keep their vows to God. Some have already completed their vow, while others are waiting to do so, but they are still just as determined to keep it, so that God can reward the honorable men for their truth. And then punish the hypocrites, if He chooses, or offer them His mercy. God is often forgiving and merciful.

25. God repulsed the unfaithful; despite their rage they gained no advantage. God was able to keep the faithful from feeling the attack. God is strong and mighty.

26–27. The people of the Book that helped the faithless were targeted by God. He took them from their fortresses and put terror in their hearts. Some you took captive and others you killed. He gave you their lands, houses, and wealth, and even land you had not seen before. God has the power to do anything.

28–29. Prophet, say to your wives, "If you only seek life in this world and the shiny things it offers, then tell me. I will pay for your comfortable life and let you leave [divorce] fairly. But if you seek God, His messenger, and a home in the hereafter, then God has prepared your reward for the righteous."

30–31. Wives of the prophet, know that if any of you are guilty of indecent conduct, your punishment will be doubled. This is an easy thing for God. But whoever is obedient to God and His messenger and acts righteously will be given double the reward. We have prepared a generous reward for those women.

32–33. Wives of the prophet, you are not like other women. If you are dutiful to God, then don't be free in your speech, or you might cause those with sick hearts to desire you. Speak only in an honorable way. Stay in your homes, and don't display your fine attire like women used to before in the time of ignorance. Pray and give to charity regularly, and obey God and His messenger. God only seeks to remove all immorality from the members of the household, cleansing you by thorough purification.

34. Remember the revelations of God and His wisdom that is recited in your homes. God understands all subtleties and is aware.

35. God has prepared mercy and a great reward for Muslim men and women: for the faithful, obedient, honest, patient,

humble, charitable men and women that maintain the fast, protect their modesty, and remember God always.

36. Once God and His messenger have made a decision on an issue, faithful men and women should not act against it. Anyone that disobeys God and His messenger is following the wrong path.

37. Recall when you [Muhammad] told someone [Zayd] that had received God's mercy and your blessing, "Keep your wife and be dutiful to God." When you said it, you were hiding something in your heart that God was going to make come true. You were in fear of what the people would think, but you should have feared God instead. When Zayd [the man mentioned above] properly divorced his wife, We married her to you. We did so to show future people that there is no sin for a believer to marry divorcees or adopt their sons as long as the divorce was proper. God's command must be fulfilled.

38–39. The prophet cannot be held responsible for any actions that God has ordained lawful for him. This was the way for the prophets before him, and the commandments of God are absolute. Such as delivering the messages of God and fearing God and only God. God keeps records of everything.

40. Muhammad is not the father of you men, he is the messenger of God and the last of the prophets. God has knowledge of all things.

41–44. Oh faithful, remember God frequently and glorify Him in the mornings and evenings. He and His angels bless you, so that He might bring you from the darkness and into the light. He is full of mercy for the faithful. On the day that they meet Him, they will say to Him, "Peace." He has prepared a generous reward.

45–48. Oh prophet, We sent you as a witness, a bearer of good news, as a warner to summon men to God, with His permission, and as a torch spreading light on earth. Tell the believers the good news about the grace God has prepared for them. [Tell them] not to obey the faithless and hypocrites or listen to their annoying talk; that they should trust in God. God is all they need as a guardian.

49. Oh faithful, if you marry a faithful woman but want to divorce her before you have touched her, then there is no waiting period. Simply provide for her and release her honorably.

50. Oh prophet, We have made lawful for you many options for wives. Legal are those that you have paid a dower for, slaves from among the prisoners of war that God has given you, daughters of your paternal and maternal aunts and uncles that migrated with you. And any faithful woman that gives herself fully to the prophet and that you choose to marry, although these are lawful only for you and not legal for other faithful men. We realize who We have allowed faithful men to take

for their wives among free and slave women, so you are not to blame [for their choices]. God is often forgiving and merciful.

51. You [Muhammad] can reject or select any woman you choose, and there is no sin for inviting back women that you earlier rejected. It's better than letting her be uncomfortable or unhappy, as all of them will be satisfied with what you give them. God knows what's in your hearts, and God is knowledgeable and forgiving.

52. It will not be lawful for you [Muhammad] to take any women from now on or to exchange any wives for prettier ones; your slaves are an exception to this. God is watching over all things.

53. Oh faithful, do not enter any of the prophet's houses for a meal without an invitation, and do not arrive before it's prepared. Arrive when you are invited and leave quickly once you've eaten, without chatting afterwards. That type of behavior is annoying to the prophet, but he is too kind to tell you. God is not ashamed to tell you the truth. When you talk to his women, do so from behind a curtain, as it's better for their purity and yours. It is not right for you to annoy God's messenger, and you should never marry his widows ever. That would be a grievous thing in the eyes of God.

54. God has knowledge of everything, whether you act in public or keep things private.

55. It is not a sin for them [all women or possibly only Muhammad's wives] to interact with their fathers, sons, brothers, nephews, their own women, or slaves. Oh women, fear God, for God is the witness of everything.

56. God and His angels have blessed the prophet, so the faithful should pray for blessings for him and speak to him with respect.

57–58. People that malign God and His messenger are cursed by God in this world and in the hereafter. He has prepared them a disgraceful punishment. Those who malign faithful men and women are guilty of slander, which is a major sin.

59. Prophet, tell your wives, daughters, and other faithful women to cover themselves with outer garments. This will be better so they are recognized and not hassled. God is often forgiving and merciful.

60–62. If the hypocrites, sick-hearted, and troublemakers in the city do not stop, then We will urge you to go against them. After that they will be your neighbors for only a little while longer. They will be cursed and wherever they are found, they will be seized and killed mercilessly. That was God's way in the past, and you won't find any changes in God's practice.

63. When men ask you about the coming hour, tell them, "Only God knows about that day." For all you know, the hour could be soon.

64–68. God has cursed the disbelievers and prepared a blazing fire for them, where they will dwell eternally. They will find no guardian or aid. On the day that their faces are turned over in the flames, they will cry, "If only we had obeyed God and His messenger!" They will continue, "Our Lord, we obeyed our chiefs and great men, and they misled us from the right path. Lord, given those men double the punishment and a mighty curse."

69. Oh faithful, don't be like the ones that slandered Moses. God proved him innocent of their charges, and he was honorable in God's sight.

70–71. Oh faithful, fear God and always speak the truth. He will guide your conduct towards righteousness and forgive your sins. Those who obey God and His messenger will reach the highest success.

72. We offered [total] moral responsibility to the heavens and the earth, but they wisely declined it and were afraid of it [that heavy burden]. But mankind took it. He was foolish and found undeserving.

73. God punishes all hypocrites and polytheists while turning His mercy towards all believers. God is forgiving and merciful.

Chapter 91 (chronologically)

Sura 60 (13 verses), Al-Mumtahana
(The Examination of the Women)

1. My Faithful, don't take My enemies as your friends. Don't offer them affection, as they have rejected the message that you received and have driven the apostle and you from your homes—just because of your faith in God. If you strive on My path and seek My good graces, [don't take them as friends]. If you secretly befriend them, be aware of all you do in public and in secret. Anyone that does this has strayed off the righteous path.

2. They would not befriend you if they were victorious. They would use their hands and tongues to commit evil against you. They want you to become faithless and reject the message.

3. Your family and children won't be able to help you on judgment day. He will judge you separately, and God sees all that you do.

4–5. Look at the excellent example of Abraham and his followers. They told the other people, "We are no longer associated with you or anything you worship other than God. We reject you, as there is now hostility and hatred between us that will last forever, unless you believe in God and God alone. Remember Abraham said to his father, "I will pray for your forgiveness, although I have no power to get that reprieve from God."

[Then the faithful prayed,] "Our Lord, in you we trust and to you we remorsefully turn. You are the end of our journey. Lord, do not use us as a trial for the unfaithful. Forgive us Lord. You are the mighty and wise."

6. This is a great example for you to follow, if you place your faith in God on judgment day. If any reject the message, just know that God is free from wants and worthy of all praise.

7. God might bring friendship between you and your current enemies. God is all-powerful. God is forgiving and merciful.

8. If you are fighting an enemy that is not making war on you based on your religion and did not drive you from your homes, then God does not forbid you from treating them with kindness and fairness. God loves those who are fair.

9. God only forbids you extending friendship to enemies that fight you based on religion and have personally driven you from your home or supported someone who drove you off. Anyone who extends friendship under those circumstances is a sinner.

10. My faithful, if women come to you as refugees, you must examine them. God knows who is faithful. If you determine that she is faithful, then don't send her back to the unfaithful. They can't be lawful wives of the unbelievers, and the unfaithful can't be a lawful husband to them, so send them back their dower. It is not a sin to marry a woman once you

have paid back her dower. Additionally, do not maintain relations with disbelieving women. Get back the dower you paid for her, and let the unfaithful men get back their dowers for women who believe. This is the command of God. He judges between men and is knowledgeable and wise.

11. If any wives leave their men, and their dower is not repaid, then take money from the next military raid to repay those men. Be dutiful, as believers, to God.

12. Prophet, if faithful women come to you to take an oath of allegiance and they swear they won't associate anything in worship to God, steal, commit adultery, kill their children, lie, slander, or disobey your just commands, then receive their allegiance and pray to God for His mercy on them. God is often forgiving and merciful.

13. My faithful, do not make friends with people that God has turned His wrath on. Those people are hopeless about the hereafter, just like the unfaithful are hopeless about those buried in graves.

Chapter 92 (chronologically)

Sura 4 (176 verses), Al-Nisa (Women)

1. Mankind, keep your duties to your Lord. He created you from a single being. From this He created a mate, and from them He widely spread men and women. Be careful of your duty to

God, by whom you claim your familial rights. God is always watching you.

2–3. Ensure orphans retain their property. Don't exchange their valuables with your worthless things or take it for your own property. That is a grave sin. If you don't think you can fairly deal with [female] orphans, then marry other women of your choice, up to four. If you are afraid that you can't be equal to them all, then marry only one or a slave. Then it will be more likely that you are fair.

4. Upon marriage give the woman her dowry. But if she chooses [on her own] to give you a part of it, then you can gladly add it to your wealth.

5. Don't give the mentally weak management of your wealth, if God has given the wealth to you to manage. Feed and clothe them from the profits. Advise them honestly about it.

6. Test orphans at the age of marriage, and if you find they have mature and sound judgment, then give them their property. Don't use their wealth quickly or extravagantly before they reach maturity. Wealthy guardians should not use the orphan's wealth, and poor guardians should spend it only reasonably and justifiably. When you release their property to them, have a witness. God is sufficient for judgment.

7. Whether it is large or small, men and women have a legal share of the wealth left behind by their parents or close relatives.

8.-10 When orphans and the needy are present at the dividing of the inheritance, then share it with them and advise them kindly. When executing a will, treat any orphans the way you would want your own children treated if they became orphaned by you. Be dutiful to God and speak fairly and honestly to them. People who unfairly consume the wealth of an orphan are basically swallowing fire, and soon they will enter the blazing fires.

11. God's inheritance rules for your children: Males receive a portion twice as large as the woman's. If you have only daughters: when it's two or more, they split two-thirds of the total inheritance; if only one daughter, then she gets one-half of the total. For the surviving parents: If there are children, then each gets one-sixth of the total; if they left no children and the parents are sole heirs, the mother receives one-third. But if there are siblings, then the mother receives only one-sixth. All the amounts are determined after the deceased's debts and specific bequeaths are deducted. You do not know which relative has benefitted you the most, so these portions are ordained by God. God is knowing and wise.

12. If you have no children and your wife dies, then your share is one-half, but with children it's one-fourth of what remains

after debts and bequeaths. But if you die with no children, she gets one-fourth, and if you have children, then she gets one-eighth after your bequeaths and debts. If a man or woman dies without parents or children, the siblings inherit what's left after bequeaths and debts are paid. If each one has one sibling, then they get one-sixth each. If it's more than two siblings, then they share one-third, so that everyone gets something. This is ordained by God, and God is knowing and generous.

13–14. These are the limits set by God. Whoever obeys God and His messenger will be allowed to live eternally in the Gardens where the rivers flow beneath. This is the ultimate achievement. Those who disobey God and His messenger and break these limits will enter the fires to dwell eternally. That is a shameful punishment.

15. If any of your women are accused [written as guilty] of indecent behavior [consensus meaning is adultery], then you must find four witnesses. If they testify that the allegations are true, then confine her to her home until she dies or God decrees some other path for her.

16. If two of you [referring to homosexuality] are found guilty of indecent acts, then punish them both. If they repent and adjust [their behavior], then leave them alone. God is sympathetic and merciful.

17. Only people who sin out of ignorance and then quickly repent will be forgiven by God. It is only them that God gives His mercy to. God is knowing and wise.

18. Forgiveness isn't for people that continue to sin until they face death and then cry, "I now repent!" Forgiveness also isn't for those who die rejecting faith. We have prepared a painful punishment for these people.

19. Oh faithful, you are not allowed to inherit women against their will. You cannot treat them harshly so that you can take away any part of the dowry you gave them, except in cases of indecency. You should treat women honorably. Be careful, for if you begin to hate them, you might be hateful towards someone that God uses to bring about much goodness.

20–21. If you plan to replace one wife with another one, then do not keep any part of the dowry you gave her. Would you try to take it by slander and clear sin? How could you take it back after you have been intimate with each other and they have made a solemn promise to you?

22. Never marry any woman that your father once married. What occurred in the past is forgiven, but it was an indecent custom.

23. The following are prohibited from marrying you: mothers, daughters, sisters, aunts, nieces, foster mothers and sisters, mothers-in-law, stepdaughters that were born to wives you have since slept with—if you haven't, then they are legal—the

wives of your biological sons, and two sisters at the same time, although previous marriages are allowed, for God is forgiving and merciful.

24. Additional prohibited marriages include women that are currently married, with an exception for slaves. These are the rules ordained by God. Lawful marriages include all other women, as long as you entice them with gifts from your wealth and desire an honest marriage and not lustful fornication. For women you have already enjoyed, you must now give them the minimum dowry. If you both agree to increase the dowry, after the minimum was accepted, it is not a sin. God is knowing and wise.

25. If you cannot afford to marry a free woman of faith then marry a slave that believes. God understands your faith best. You are equal in faith. Gain the permission of her people and pay the proper dowry. The women should be pure and not be sexually active with boyfriends. After marriage if she commits indecencies, her punishment will be half of a freewoman's. This is allowed for men that fear committing a sin [of unlawful intercourse], but it's best if you remain patient. God is forgiving and merciful.

26. God makes His guidance clear to you with examples from the past and wants to be merciful to you. God is knowing and wise.

27. God wishes to give His mercy to you, while the wicked ones want to take you far astray from what is right.

28. God wants to lighten your load, for man is weak.

29. Oh faithful, don't waste your wealth through vices or illegal means; let there be free and fair trade among you. Do not kill yourselves. God is merciful to you.

30. If you do that unjustly and aggressively, We will throw you in the fire. That is easy for God.

31. If you avoid the worst sins that have been forbidden, We will absolve your remaining sins and allow you to enter the noble gate.

32. Do not covet the gifts that God has given to others, for He gives more to some people. Men and women are rewarded for what they earn. [Instead] ask God for His grace. God is aware of all things.

33. We have arranged shares and heirs for any property left by parents and relatives. Also, share it fairly with people you have made promises to. God is a witness to everything.

34. Men are in charge of and protect women, because God made men stronger and because they support them with their wealth. Therefore, righteous women are obedient to their husbands and guard what God has commanded they protect. If you think women are behaving badly, then by sequential steps, first scold them, then kick them out of bed, then beat

them. If they begin to obey you again, then treat them well. God is the greatest.

35. If you suspect a split between a husband and wife, then appoint one mediator from each side of the family. If they want to stay together, God will rebuild their harmony. God is knowing and aware.

36–38. Serve God and don't associate anything to Him. Be kind to parents, relatives, orphans, the needy, nearby neighbors, your family's neighbors, your companions, travelers, and slaves. God does not love arrogant and boastful people, or those who are cheap and push others to be stingy, or hoard the wealth that God gave them. We have prepared a shameful punishment for the faithless. For those who flaunt their wealth and don't believe in God or the last day have taken Satan for a friend. An evil friend they have.

39. How hard would it have been for them to believe in God and the last day and to have given money out of God's gifts? God knows everything about them.

40. God is never unfair, not even in the least. For any good that is done, God will double it in payment from Himself as a great reward.

41–42. What will it be like when We produce a witness from each community and We bring you [Muhammad] as a witness against these people? On that day, the people who rejected faith and disobeyed the messenger will wish to hide in the earth. Not one secret will be hidden from God.

43. Oh faithful, don't go to prayer while intoxicated until you know what you're saying. Don't go when you are unclean, unless it's from traveling, until you have completely bathed. If you are sick, traveling, used a toilet, or have been with a woman, and you can't find any water, then use dirt. Take some clean sand or dirt and rub it on your faces and hands. God pardons and forgives.

44. Have you noticed those people that were given a part of the Book, when they exchange money for it and hope that you would leave the righteous path?

45. God knows well who your enemies are. God is all the protection you need. God is all the guidance that you need.

46. Some of the Jews move words around to change the meanings. They say, "We hear and we disobey" and "Hear but don't hear anything" and "Listen to us." They twist their tongues and slander religion. It would have been better for them to say, "We hear and obey" and "Listen." God cursed them for their disbelief, but few of them will become faithful.

47. Oh people who have received the Book, believe in Our revelations that confirm what your Book says. Do it before We erase your faces and turn them backwards or curse you

like We cursed the previous Sabbath violators. The command of God must be carried out.

48. God will not forgive anyone for associating partners with Him, but He can choose to forgive anything else and anyone. Associating anything with God is a terrible sin.

49. Have you seen the people that claim that they are pure? Only God can purify. He purifies whomever He chooses, and they will receive perfect justice.

50. Look at how they invent lies against God. That is an obvious sin.

51. Have you seen the people who were given a part of the Book, that believe in superstition and false gods, and then tell the unbelievers that they are taking a better path than the faithful?

52. God has cursed these people. Those that are cursed by God will have no helper.

53. Do they think they own a share of the kingdom [of heaven]? If they did, they wouldn't be able to give anything to mankind.

54. Maybe they are jealous of mankind because of what God has shared from His wealth. We have already given the people of Abraham the Book and wisdom, and given them a mighty kingdom.

55–56. While some of them believed him [Muhammad], others turned away from him. The flames of hell are appropriate for them. We will soon throw those who rejected Our signs in the fire. And as their skins are burned off, We will replace them so the punishment can continue. God is mighty and wise.

57. The faithful and righteous will soon enter Our Gardens where the rivers flow beneath as their eternal home. They will find pure companions there, and We will provide comforting shade.

58. God commands you to pay your debts, and when you decide issues between men that you judge fairly. God cautions you with excellent guidance. God sees and hears all things.

59. Oh faithful, obey God, the messenger, and people given authority among you. If you truly believe in God and the last day, then refer your disputes to God and the messenger. It will be best in the end.

60. Have you seen the people who claim to believe in what was sent to you and others before you, and yet to settle disputes they look to false judges, although they were commanded to reject them? Satan's wish is to lead them far astray.

61–63. When they are told to come towards what God revealed to the messenger, they turn away in disgust. Yet when they earn misfortune by their own actions, they come to you swearing to

God that they were actually seeking harmony and goodness. God knows what is in their hearts, so avoid them, but also warn them, in clear language, about the risk to their souls.

64–65. We sent every messenger with Our permission to be obeyed [by man]. If the people had come to you after sinning to ask for God's forgiveness, and if the messenger had asked forgiveness for them, they would find God forgiving and merciful. But by Lord, they can't find faith until after they ask you to judge a dispute and find themselves satisfied with your verdict. Then they submit completely.

66–68. If We had decreed they must lay down their lives or leave their homes, few would have done it. If they just did what they were told, it would be best, and they would be strengthened [in faith]. We would give them Our greatest reward and guide them on a straight path.

69–70. Whoever obeys God and the messenger are shown the grace of God. They include the prophets, the sincere, the witnesses, and the righteous. What wonderful company. Such is the grace of God, and God knows all.

71. Oh faithful, listen to the warnings and go out in groups or all at once.

72–73. Remember that among you there are men who would like to stay behind. When you are struck by disaster, they will say, "God favored me, as I didn't go with them." Then when you are fortunate, they will say, "I wish that I had been with them so I could have found great success."

74. Those willing to trade this life for a life in the hereafter should fight [not "jihad"] in the way of God. Those who fight [not "jihad"] in the way of God, whether they are killed or are victors, shall soon be given a great reward by Us.

75. What reason do you have for not fighting [not "jihad'] in the way of God? [For] the feeble men, the women, and children? [For] those who call out, "Our Lord, rescue us from this town of oppressors, give us a protector, and a defender"?

76. The faithful fight [not "jihad"] in the way of God. The unbelievers fight [not "jihad"] in the cause of false idols [tyranny]. Fight [not "jihad"] the friends of Satan. Satan's strategy is weak.

77–78. Haven't you noticed the actions of the people that were told to steady their hands, pray regularly, and give to charity? When they were finally ordered to fight [not the term "jihad"], a group of them was more fearful of man than they should be of God. They cried, "Our Lord, why are you ordering us to fight [not "jihad']? Won't you give us a longer break?" Say to them, "The enjoyment of this life is short, but in the hereafter, the righteous will find the best of things. You will not be judged unfairly in the least. Wherever you are, death will find you, even if you are secure in a tower." When something good happens to them, they say, "This is from

God," but when something bad happens to them, they say, "This must be from you [Muhammad]." Reply to them, "Everything is from God." What is their problem? They understand nothing.

79. Everything good that happens is because of God, while everything evil that happens is due to yourself. We sent you as a messenger to man. God is witness to this.

80–81. Whoever obeys the messenger, obeys God. Remember if they turn from you, that We didn't send you to be their guardian. They tell you they are obedient, but at night a group of them leaves to make plans other than what you ordered. God records these nightly plots. Stay away from them and trust in God. God is all you need as a guide.

82. Haven't they studied the Qur'an closely? If it was not a revelation from God, it would be full of inconsistencies.

83. When they hear news that concerns public safety or danger, they broadcast it. If they would take this news to the messenger or to other leaders, then it would be investigated. If it wasn't for the grace of God, almost all of you would be following Satan.

84. Fight [not the term "jihad"] in God's way. You are only truly responsible for yourself, but urge on the faithful. God might restrain the power of the unbelievers. God is the mightiest and strict in punishment.

85. Everyone that takes part in a good act becomes a part of the goodness. But whoever takes part in an evil act will be responsible for that evil. God controls everything.

86. When you are given a kind greeting from another, then return an even more courteous one, or at least an equal greeting. God records even the smallest of actions.

87. God. There is no god except Him. Undoubtedly, He will gather you all on judgment day. Who will keep their promise better than God?

88. How can you have two opinions about the hypocrites? God has sent them back to disbelief for their evil ways. Are some of you thinking of guiding someone that God has led astray? Those God has led astray from the path will remain lost.

89–90. Their wish is that you would reject faith like they have, so you can be faithless like them. So don't take them as friends, until they migrate [from home] in the way of God. If they later turn on you, then seize them and kill them wherever they are. There is one exception for taking friends from them. The ones that are seeking refuge with someone you have a treaty with are acceptable as long as their hearts forbid them from fighting you or their own people. If God had desired, He could have made them strong enough to want to fight you. So if they hold back and offer you peace, then God is blocking you from fighting them. [none of these violent terms are the word "jihad"]

91. There will be some that pretend to want peace from you and their own people. But when they are tempted, they always give in. So if they don't hold back and remain unarmed, then seize them and kill there wherever they are. In that case, We are providing you a clear justification.

92. The faithful may never kill another believer. If it happens by mistake, then there are compensation rules: Free a faithful slave and pay compensation to the family of the deceased, unless they give money as charity. If the victim is from a warring rival group, then free a faithful slave. If the mistaken victim is from a group and you have a treaty with them, pay the family compensation and free a faithful slave. If you cannot afford to follow these rules, then you must fast for two months straight to demonstrate remorse to God. God is knowledgeable and wise.

93. If anyone intentionally kills a believer, then the punishment is eternal damnation to hell. God will curse him and unleash His wrath while preparing a painful penalty.

94. Oh faithful, when you travel [and meet other groups] study them carefully [for belief in God], and don't just brand someone who says to you "peace" as a nonbeliever, saying, "You are not faithful!" When you do this because you want their wealth in this life, you are missing out on the rewards God has for you [in the hereafter]. You were once like him,

and God has given you His favor. Always carefully determine their faith, because God is aware of all you do.

95–96. Those who stay behind safely, unless they are injured, are not at all equal to those who strive [jihad] in the way of God with their wealth and persons. God marks with distinction those who strive [jihad] with their wealth and lives, well above those who sit it out. God has promised all the faithful a good reward, but those who strive [jihad] He will give a greater reward than those who hang back. [Rewards like] special rank, forgiveness, and mercy. God is forgiving and merciful.

97–99. When an angel takes a soul of a person that dies while in a state of sin, they will ask them, "What was your situation [that caused you to be a sinner]?" When the people reply, "We were vulnerable in our lands," the angels will respond, "Didn't God give you enough earth to move away [from evil men]?" Those sinners will reside in hell, and it's an evil destination. There is an exception for those men, women, and children who were actually weak and vulnerable [to sin]. Those who had no power to escape and weren't guided. There is hope that God will forgive them. God often pardons and is forgiving.

100. Whoever migrates in the way of God will find many places to rest and plenty of resources. Those who die as an emigrant for God and His messenger will find his reward with God. God is forgiving and merciful.

101. When you are traveling it is not a sin to shorten your prayers, if you fear unbelievers will attack you. The unbelievers are a clear enemy to you.

102. When people come to pray with you [when in hostile territory], have part of the men pray while the others stand guard. Those praying should stand with you, with their weapons near them. Then have the men change duties. The unbelievers hope that you will be careless with your weapons [security] and baggage, so they can finish you off all at once. It's not your fault if you put down your weapons due to rain or sickness, but always protect yourselves the best you can. God has a shameful punishment for the unbelievers.

103. After prayer ensure you worship God standing, sitting, and lying down. But after the danger has passed, perform a proper prayer sequence. It is ordained for the faithful to pray at fixed times.

104. Do not slow your pursuit of the enemy. If you are suffering, then they are suffering just as much. But you have been given hope by God that they do not have. God is knowing and wise.

105–106. We have sent you a true book so that you can make judgments between men with the knowledge God has given you. Do not be an advocate for traitors instead; pray to God for His forgiveness towards them. God is forgiving and merciful.

107–108. Do not plead for people that deceive their own souls, because God does not love traitors or sinners. They may be able to hide their sins from men, but they cannot hide them from God. He is with them at night when they scheme in a manner that does not please God. God is ever-present around them.

109. You will find yourself pleading for them in this life, but no one will plead on their behalf with God on the day of resurrection.

110–112. If someone sins against their own soul, but then asks God for mercy they will find that God is forgiving and merciful. If anyone sins, it only counts against their own soul. God is knowing and wise. But if someone sins and then accuses an innocent person of the sin, then they are guilty of slander, and that is a clear sin.

113. God's grace kept you from being led astray by a group of men. They don't understand that they can only mislead themselves and that they don't have the power to harm you. God sent down the Book and wisdom to you and taught you things you didn't know. The grace that God gives you is great.

114. During their secret talks, there is little goodness discussed. But if they call for charity, good acts, and peacemaking, then they are seeking God's grace, and We will give them a great reward.

115. Whoever opposes the messenger after they have received the guidance [from God] and doesn't live like a faithful person will be left to wander on the path they have chosen. They will end up in hell, and it's an evil place.

116. God will not forgive anyone that associates a partner to Him. He can forgive whoever He chooses for other sins, but those assigning partners to God have truly made a mistake.

117–121. They worship females [pagan idols were mostly women] instead of Him. They are praying to the rebel Satan that was cursed by God. He told Him [God], "I will lure a portion of mankind to me. I will mislead them, give them evil desires, have them slit their camel's ears, and make them change God's creations." Those who choose Satan as their guardian instead of God will suffer greatly. Satan promises them much and stirs their poor desires, but he is deceiving them. For being fooled, they will live in hell and never escape it.

122. For the faithful that do righteous acts, they will soon enter the Gardens where rivers flow beneath. There they live eternally. This is God's truthful promise. Is anyone more honest than God?

123–124. Despite your hopes or the hopes of the people of the Book, if you commit evil acts, then you will pay for your actions. You won't find any guardians besides God to protect you. And every man and woman that does good deeds and has faith will enter heaven. They won't be judged unfairly at all.

125. Can anyone be more pious in their religion than someone that surrenders their life to God, acts righteously, and follows the tradition of the noble Abraham? God chose Abraham as a friend.

126. God owns everything in the heavens and on earth, and He is everywhere.

127. If people ask your guidance about women, say to them, "God has given you instructions about them. Remember what was recited to you from the Book about female orphans that you don't give the set portion to, yet you still wish to marry them. Remember how to deal with weak children and that you should treat orphans fairly. Every good deed you do is known by God."

128. When a wife thinks that her husband is being cruel or that he has deserted her, there will be no blame on the couple for reaching a settlement, and that is what's best. Men are often controlled by greed. But if you try to be good and show restraint, then God will know what you have done.

129. No matter how hard you try, you will never be equally fair to your wives. But never ignore one completely, leaving her unsure of her situation. If you come to an agreement and show restraint, God is forgiving and merciful.

130. If they separate, God will provide for them both. God is generous and wise.

131. Everything in the heavens and earth belong to God. We have told you and those given the Book before you to be wary of God. But if you deny belief in God, then know that God owns everything in the heavens and on earth and does not want for anything. He is worthy of praise.

132. Everything in the heavens and on earth belongs to God, and God is all the protector you need.

133. If He wanted to, He could destroy mankind and create others. He has the power to do it.

134. If you desire rewards in this life, then you should know that God gives rewards in this life and in the hereafter. God hears and sees everything.

135. Oh faithful, stand up for justice and be a [honest] witness for God. Even if the judgment goes against you, your parents and family, and the rich or poor. God is a better guardian for them all than you. So ignore your desires so you don't deviate from justice, for God is aware of everything you do.

136. Oh faithful, believe in God and His messenger, the revelations He sent to this messenger, and those sent before. Whoever doesn't believe in God, His books, His angels and messenger, and the last day is wandering lost.

137. God will not forgive or provide guidance to people that are faithful and then reject faith, and then start believing and rejecting faith over and over as they become more faithless.

138–139. Tell the hypocrites that there is a painful punishment for people that take unbelievers as friends instead of the faithful. Are they trying to earn their honor? If so, they should understand all honor is for God.

140. In the Book He sent to you, [it says] that when you hear God's revelations being rejected and mocked, you should avoid those people until they change the topic. If you stay and listen, you will be like them. God will gather all the hypocrites and unbelievers in hell.

141. There are some people that wait to side with the stronger side. If God hands you a victory, they ask, "You knew we were on your side, right?" But if instead the unbelievers are successful they say, "When we were your leaders, didn't we protect you from the faithful?" God will provide a judgment about who was correct on the last day. He will not provide the unbelievers a way to defeat the faithful.

142–143. The hypocrites think that they can deceive God, but He is outwitting them. They stand for prayer in a sluggish way, and pray just to be seen by others, while they barely give any remembrance to God. They move allegiance back and forth, never truly belonging to one group or another. Those that God sends astray will never find their way [to God].

144. Oh faithful, do not choose unbelievers as friends instead of the faithful. Are you trying to give God evidence to hold you accountable for?

145–147. The hypocrites will suffer in the deepest depths of the flames, and no one will help them. But those who repent, change their lives, cling tightly to God, and purely have faith in only God may soon be granted the faithful's great reward by God. Why would God punish you if you are grateful and faithful? God sees and knows all things.

148–149. God only wants to hear publicly about man's misconduct from the person that was hurt by their injustice. God hears and knows everything already. It doesn't matter if you are good in public or private, or excuse an evil deed; God is powerful and can forgive sins.

150–151. There are some people that don't believe in God and His messengers; those who make distinctions between God and His messengers, saying they only believe in some of them; and some people are in between these two groups. All of these people are truly faithless, and We have prepared a humiliating punishment for them.

152. But for the faithful who believe in God and His messengers, without being selective about which messengers they believe in, God has prepared rewards. God is forgiving and merciful.

153–154. The people of the Book often ask you to make an actual book descend from the heavens. Remember they asked Moses for a bigger miracle saying, "Let us see God in person." For that sin lightning and thunder shook them. Then they even worshipped a calf after they had seen clear signs [of God]. Yet still We forgave them, and We gave Moses authority over them. As a covenant, We lifted the mount above them, commanded them to enter the gate with humility, and ordered them to follow the rules of the Sabbath. This was a strong covenant between us.

155. They broke their covenant. They rejected the signs of God. They illegally killed prophets. They say they have sealed their hearts [against more revelations from God]. Actually, God has sealed their hearts because of their disbelief. Few of them are truly among the faithful.

156–158. They are also sealed for their rejection of faith and slander against Mary. They claimed, "We killed Jesus, the Messiah and son of Mary." But they only appeared to kill and crucify him. People who believe they killed him are full of doubts about it, and the only proof of it occurring is speculation. It is certain they did not kill him. God raised him up into heaven. God is mighty and wise.

159. Every person of the Book will surely believe in him [some interpret as Jesus and others Muhammad] before their death. On the day of judgment, he will be a witness against them.

160–161. We made many things forbidden to the Jews that were previously allowed [for their actions]. They blocked many people from God's way. They took forbidden interest while money lending. They lied to quickly use up other men's wealth. We have prepared a painful punishment for those who disbelieve.

162. But for those among them that remained grounded in knowledge and for the faithful that accept the revelations We sent you, who establish regular prayer, regularly give to charity, and believe in God and the last day, We have prepared a great reward.

163–165. We have revealed to you what We revealed to Noah and the messengers after him. What we sent to Abraham, Ishmael, Isaac, Jacob and the tribes, Jesus, Job, Aaron, Solomon, and David in the form of the Psalms. We have sent it to messengers that are known to you and to some that you don't know. To Moses We even spoke directly. To all these messengers we gave good news and a warning for mankind, so that no one could argue with God after a messenger appeared. God is wise and mighty.

166. God testifies [to the truth] about what He has sent to you from His own wisdom. The angels are witnesses as well. God is the only witness you need [to have faith].

167. People who reject belief and stop other men from following God's path are lost very far from that path.

168–169. God will never forgive people who don't believe and who commit evil. He will not guide them on any path, unless it leads to eternal hell. This is easy for God [to do].

170. The messenger has brought mankind the truth from your Lord; it would be best that you believe him. If you reject faith, remember that everything in the heavens and on earth belongs to God. God is knowing and wise.

171. People of the Book, do not exaggerate about your religion. Don't say anything about God that isn't true. The Messiah Jesus, the son of Mary, was only a messenger of God, His word bestowed upon Mary, and a spirit from Him. Believe in God and His messengers. It will be better for you if you do not say "trinity." God is only one God. He is glorious and above having a son. Everything in the heavens and the earth belongs to Him. God is all you need for a guardian.

172. The Messiah would never have contempt for being a servant of God, nor would His favorite angels. Those who disapprove of worshipping Him and act arrogantly will be gathered back to Him [for judgment].

173. He will give earned rewards from His great bounty to the faithful who act righteously. He will give a painful penalty to the condescending and proud. They won't find anyone that can protect them except for God.

174. Mankind, you have seen convincing proof from your Lord. We have sent you a pure light.

175. Those who believe in God and cling to Him will soon feel His mercy and grace. He will guide them on a straight path to Him.

176. When they ask you for a legal ruling, say to them, "God has ordained the rules for inheritance and heirs. Men who die with no children but have a sister will award her half of the inheritance. If a woman dies with no children, then her brother takes all of the inheritance. When there are two sisters, they will split two-thirds of the inheritance. If there are brothers and sisters, then the bothers will receive twice the share of the sisters. This is made clear to you by God so that you don't make mistakes. God knows all things.

Chapter 93 (chronologically)

Sura 99 (8 verses), Al-Zalzala (The Earthquake)

1–8. On the day the earth experiences a violent earthquake and throws off her burdens, man will ask what is wrong with her. The Lord will inspire [the earth] to tell her story. Mankind will be sorted into groups and learn about the deeds they performed in life. Even just an atom's weight of good work will be discussed; likewise, an atom's weight of evil shall be shown.

Chapter 94 (chronologically)

Sura 57 (29 verses), Hadid (Iron)

1–6. Let everything in the heavens and on earth glorify God, the mighty and wise. He has dominion over the heavens and the earth. He controls life and death and is all-powerful. He is the first and the last; the known and the unknown; He knows everything. He created the heavens and the earth in six days and then sat upon the throne. He knows everything that enters or leaves the earth and the heavens. He is with you everywhere and knows everything you do. He owns the heavens and earth, and all things return to Him. He turns night to day and day to night and knows what is in every heart.

7–8. Believe in God and His messenger and spend [charitably] from what He allows you to earn. Those who give to charity will have a great reward. Why shouldn't you believe in God while the messenger is inviting you to believe? He has made a covenant with the faithful.

9. He inspires His messengers with clear signs, so they may lead from the dark and into the light. God is full of kindness and mercy.

10. What reason do you have for not spending in the way of God, when God inherits the earth and the heavens? Those who spent and fought [not translated from the Arabic word

"jihad"] before the victory [the return to Mecca] are higher in rank than those who spent and fought after [that event]. God had promised a good reward to everyone, and God knows all that you do.

11. Who would lend God a good loan, so that He can double the worth and [also] receive an excellent reward?

12. One day you will see faithful men and women, with lights running ahead of them and by their right hands [book of deeds in it] hearing, "There is good news for you today. Gardens where rivers flow beneath, and you are immortal. This is the grand achievement!"

13–15. That day the hypocritical men and women will say to the faithful, "Wait for us! Can we borrow your light?" But they will hear, "Go back and look for your own light!" Then a wall will be placed between them and a gate fastened. Within the wall there will be mercy. Outside the wall will be doom. Those outside the wall will cry, "Weren't we with you?" In reply they hear, "Yes but you gave in to temptation, you tried to outlast [us], you doubted, and your desires deceived you until God's promise arrived. The deceiver fooled you about God. Today no ransom can save you or those who rejected God. Your home is in the fire, a final refuge and evil place."

16. Isn't it time for the faithful, with humble hearts, to engage in the remembrance of God and accept the truth of the revelations, so that they don't become like those who received

the Book of scripture before. Their hearts grew hard over time, and many of them are disobedient.

17. You should know that God gives life to the earth after it dies. We have shown you the clear signs so you can understand.

18. Men and women that give to charity, lending God a fair loan, shall have their loan doubled and also receive a noble reward.

19. Those believing in God and His apostles, which are the most sincere and loyal in their Lord's eye, will have their reward and their light. But those who reject God and deny Our signs will reside in hell.

20. Understand that life in this world is just diversion and amusement, pageantry and boasting about your wealth and children. It is like how rain helps vegetation grow, delighting the planters. But soon it withers and turns yellow until it dries and blows away. In the hereafter there is either God's severe punishment or His forgiveness along with His good pleasure. The life of the world is but an illusion.

21. Seek forgiveness from your Lord more than anyone else, and a garden as vast as heaven and earth will be prepared for those who believe in God and His apostles. That is God's grace, and He gives it to whomever he chooses. God is the Lord of infinite grace.

22–24. Every misfortune that happens to earth or your souls is recorded prior in a book, and We cause it to occur. It is easy for God and is so you do not despair about what didn't happen or excessively celebrate your gifts. God does not like arrogant boasting or stingy people that ask others to be ungenerous. No matter how many turn back [on God's path,] God is free from all needs and is praiseworthy.

25. We sent Our messengers with clear signs, the Book, and balance [scales of right and wrong] so that mankind could be just. We sent down iron, a mighty material, and having many uses for men, so that God could secretly observe a test of the men that would be useful to God and His messengers. God is strong and mighty.

26. We sent Noah and Abraham, and We ordained prophethood on their ancestors and gave them the Book. Some of them were righteous, but many of them were wicked.

27. We then sent other messengers, and then We sent Jesus son of Mary and gave him the Gospel. We put mercy and compassion into the hearts of his followers. But they invented monkhood, which We did not ordain for them, as We asked only that man seek God's pleasure. Instead they sought to fulfill it the wrong way. We will give the faithful among them their reward, but many of them are wicked.

28. Oh faithful, be dutiful to God and believe in His messenger, and He will give you a double portion of mercy. He will give you a light to brighten the right path and forgive your past. God is often forgiving and merciful.

29. The people of the Book should know that they have no power over God's grace. God entirely controls His grace and bestows it where He chooses. God is the Lord of infinite grace.

Chapter 95 (chronologically)

Sura 47 (38 verses), Muhammad (Muhammad)

1–3. God will stop the attempts of anyone that disbelieves and turns men from the path of God. But if they believe, commit righteous deeds, and believe in the revelations sent to Muhammad, for it is the truth from their Lord, He will remove their sins and improve their life. This is because the faithless are guided by lies, and the faithful follow the truth from their Lord. This is how God compares men.

4–6. When you meet the unbelievers [on the battlefield], strike
their necks. When you have subdued their force, bind them
[captives]. Later, either set them free or ransom them, until
the war finally ends. That [is God's command], but if God
wished, He could crush them. [But He doesn't] in order to
test you with others [enemies]. Those killed in God's way will
never be forgotten by Him. 5. He will guide them, take care of
their affairs, 6. and admit them into paradise, which He has
told them about.

7–9. Oh faithful, if you help God, He will help you and steady your feet. For the unbelievers, there is damnation, and He will disrupt their works. That is because they hate the revelations of God, so He nullifies their deeds.

10–12. Don't they travel the lands and see the consequences of the evil acts of earlier generations? God utterly destroyed them. Similar fates await the unbelievers. God is the protector of the faithful, while the unbelievers have none. God will admit the faithful and righteous into the Gardens where streams flow beneath. God will send the unbelievers, that enjoy this life like grazing cattle, into the fire.

13. [During migration MC to MD] Think of how many cities that were stronger than these were destroyed by Us for their sins. They were helpless.

14. Is someone that follows clear guidance from their Lord not better than those who conduct evil deeds that please them while they follow their lust?

15. Let Me describe the Garden that is promised to the righteous. There are rivers of pure water, of milk that never spoils, of delicious wine, and of purified honey. There are a variety of fruits and forgiveness from your Lord. Can this paradise be compared to those dwelling eternally in the fire that can drink only boiling water that tears up their bowels?

16–17. Some men will appear to listen to you, but when they leave you, they will ask knowledgeable people, "What is he saying?" God has sealed the hearts of those men, and they follow their own desires. For those who follow the guidance, He will increase their guidance and give them restraint to guard against [evil].

18. Are they just waiting for the [final] hour to suddenly be upon them? The warnings of it have already been sent down. How can they just wait for revelations when it has already been delivered?

19. Know that there is no god but God, and [that you should] ask forgiveness of your sins and the sins of the faithful men and women. God knows the road you will travel and your final destination.

20. The faithful ask, "Why wasn't a chapter sent to us?" But when a chapter with clear decrees is revealed, and fighting is mentioned [the term for combat is used, not jihad/striving], you will see the weak hearts of the men, as some of them will appear to faint in the face of death. Misery is for them.

21. If they obeyed and said a proper phrase [as is expected], when a decision is made, it would be best for them.

22–23. Who are the ones that if put in command would cause corruption and break their ties with their family? They are the ones that God has cursed, making them deaf and blind.

24–26. Won't they reflect upon the recitations [Qur'an], or are their hearts sealed? Those who turn away after they have seen the revelations have been seduced by Satan and given false hopes.

It's because they told the ones who hate God's revelations, "We will obey you in some things." God knows their secrets.

27–28. Awaiting them, when their souls are taken by angels, are beatings to their faces and backs. All because they acted in ways that angered God and hated actions that would please God.

29–30. Those with diseased hearts think their hateful secrets won't be exposed by God? If We chose to, We could show them to you and mark them. But you will know them by the tone of their voice. God knows all you do.

31. We will test you all to see who strives hardest [*mujahedeen*] and is steadfast. We will record and assess the results.

32. People that reject God, turn others from the path of God, and oppose the messenger after he has clearly revealed Our guidance, will not hurt God one bit. He will make their actions unsuccessful.

33. Oh faithful, obey God and obey the messenger so your actions are not in vain.

34. People that reject God, turn others from the path of God, and die as unbelievers will never be forgiven by God.

35. So do not falter nor call for peace when you are winning. God is with you and will not let your actions go unrewarded.

36–38. Life in this world is just for sport and amusement. If you believe and are righteous, He will reward you and not ask for your possessions. If He did ask you for it [wealth], [and should] you be stingy, He would expose your hatred. [If so] you are the ones being called to spend in [supporting?] God's way. Some of you are hoarders. Any who are stingy do so at the risk of your soul. Know that God is free from any wants; and it is you that are in need. If you turn your back on the light, He will replace you with another people much better than you.

Chapter 96 (chronologically)

Sura 13 (43 verses), Al-Rad (The Thunder)

1. Alif. Lam. Meem. Ra. The verses in this Book are the truth sent down to you by your Lord, but most men do not believe it.

2–4. God raised the heavens without any visible supports and presides over it on His throne. He set the sun and moon on their eternal paths. He explains His revelations in detail so that you can be certain of your future meeting with your Lord. He spread the earth and placed mountains and flowing streams upon it. He made every fruit in pairs. He sets the cover of nighttime over the day. In these acts, there are signs for the wise men to see. The earth has diverse patches of land where vineyards, cornfields, and palm trees, all with different root systems, can be irrigated with the same water. We have made some vegetation better to eat than others. These are all signs for those who can understand them.

5–6. If you seek to marvel, then think about this strange question, "When we are but dust, shall we then be created anew?" There are some who deny their lord. They will be chained by the neck and join the others to dwell in the fire. They ask you to bring upon them evil instead of asking for good, even when they have seen the examples of earlier punishments. Your Lord is full of mercy for mankind even though they sin. And your Lord is strict in His punishment.

7. When the unbelievers ask, "Why hasn't our Lord sent us a sign?" Remember that you are simply a messenger and a guide to every person.

8–11. God knows what every woman's womb will bear and the length of her pregnancy. He knows the measurement of every single thing. He knows the visible and the invisible; He is great and noble. It makes no difference whether man speaks aloud or in secret or whether he lurks in the night or moves by day. Every man has angels around him. They guard you by the command of God. God does not change a man's fate until man changes his heart. Know that once God directs His punishment, there is no repelling it, and there is no one that can protect you besides Him.

12–13. He shows you the lightning creating both fear and hope. He creates the rain clouds. The thunder sings His praises along with the awestruck angels. He sends down the thunderbolts to punish who He chooses. And still they argue about God. He is the mighty.

14. He alone merits true prayer. Prayer to any others besides Him is like reaching for water with your hands and hoping it ends up in your mouth, but it never does. The prayers of the faithless will be of no use.

15. Everything in the heavens and earth and their shadows too, willingly or unwillingly, bows only to God in the mornings and evenings.

16. Ask them, "Who is the Lord of the heavens and the earth?" They reply, "God." Ask them, "Do any of you worship guardians other than Him, that have no power to benefit or harm even themselves?" Ask them, "Are the blind equal to those with sight? Are the depths of darkness equal to the light? Have they assigned partners to God that have not created anything like what He created, such that their creations seem alike?" Tell them, "God is the creator of all things. He is the One, the supreme and irresistible."

17. God shows mankind the difference between truth and falsehood. He sends down rains that fill the valleys, and as it washes along, the foam rises to the surface. You can see the impurities rise to the top when ore is heated to make jewelry

and utensils. The filthy foam and scum are thrown out, while the pure things remain on earth for mankind.

18. Those who respond to their Lord's call will be rewarded. Those who do not respond to Him will wish they could trade every treasure they acquired on earth to redeem themselves. The reckoning will be terrible, and they shall dwell in hell, a true bed of misery.

19–24. Is a blind man equal to someone that knows what the Lord has revealed is the truth? Only the wise will heed the warnings. The ones that keep their promises to God, who only unite things that God commands to be joined, who are in awe of their Lord, and who fear a terrible reckoning. Those who are steadfast in seeking the grace of their Lord, who pray regularly, who spend from the wealth they are given openly and privately, and who repel evil with goodness. They will have the eternal home; the Gardens of Eden. They will live among their righteous fathers, wives, and children. The angels will call to them from every gate, "Peace be upon you who were steadfast. This is your wonderful final home!"

25. But for those who break their covenant with God, separate the things that God commanded be joined, and cause corruption in the lands, for them is a curse and a terrible home.

26. God increases or decreases the sustenance of anyone He chooses. While they will rejoice in the life of this world, it is a tiny luxury when compared to the hereafter.

27–29. The disbelievers will ask, "Why didn't our Lord send us a sign?" Tell them, "God sends whoever He chooses astray, but He guides everyone that turns towards Him, those who believe and whose hearts are satisfied by the celebration of God. Undoubtedly the heart finds peace by celebrating God. Those who believe and are righteous in deed are blessed and earn a good destination.

30. We have sent you down among a nation long after many nations have passed away, so that you may recite to them what We inspired in you. When they reject the gracious One, say to them, "He is my Lord. There is no God but Him. I trust in Him and will return to Him."

31. If there was a recitation [Qur'an] that could move mountains, split the earth, or make the dead speak, [it still wouldn't cause the unfaithful to believe]. Know that all decisions are God's. If he chose, He could have guided all humans. Disasters will continue to strike the sinners or near their homes until the promises of God come true. God always keeps His promise.

32. Messengers before you were also ridiculed. But I gave relief to those unbelievers before finally punishing them. My penalty was terrible.

33–35. Can He that watches every soul [be compared to others]? Yet they associate partners to God. Say to them, "Name them! Are you able to tell Him about something He does not already know about the earth?" Their conspiring seems right to the faithless. They have been blocked from the right path, and those that God leads astray are without a guide. There will be a penalty for them in this life, but the hereafter shall be more painful. They will have no protectors against God. The Garden promised to the righteous will have rivers flowing beneath and perpetual food and shade. That will be the reward for the righteous, while the unfaithful will earn the fire.

36. Everyone that We gave the Book to should rejoice for Our revelations. Among you there are clans that reject some of it. Say to them, "I am commanded to worship only God and to never associate a partner to Him. I pray to Him, and I will return to Him."

37. We have revealed to you clear guidance in Arabic. If you follow your desires after you are made aware of this knowledge, then you will have no protector against God.

38–40. We sent messengers before you, and We gave them wives and children. Never were they allowed to reveal a message without God's permission. There is an appointed time for everything. God erases and declares whatever He wishes. He is the source of the Book. Whether We show the entire message to you in your life or take your soul before it's done, your only duty is to ensure the message reaches them. Our duty is the reckoning.

41–42. Don't they see how We gradually reduce the edges of the land? When God commands it, there is no one that can delay it. He is swift in judgment. Those before these also plotted, but God is the master planner who knows every soul's earnings. Soon the unbelievers will know who has earned [heaven].

43. The unfaithful will say, "You are not a messenger." Tell them, "God is a sufficient witness between me, you, and the others that have knowledge of the Book."

Chapter 97 (chronologically)

Sura 55 (78 verses), Al-Rahman (The Merciful)

1–4. The all-merciful has taught the Qur'an. He created mankind and taught him to speak.

5–6. The sun and moon were set on their precise courses. The stars and trees bow [to Him].

7–9. He set the sky on high with proper balance so, that you would not upset it. Therefore maintain just measurements and don't fall short.

10–13. He laid out the earth for His creatures, where fruits, date palms, and also husked grains and scented herbs [are found]. Given this, which of the favors from your Lord will you deny?

14–16. He created man from clay. He created genies from a flame. Which of the favors from your Lord will you deny?

17–18. He is the Lord of the East and West. Which of the favors from your Lord will you deny?

19–21. He unleashed the two oceans to flow until they met each other and placed a barrier between them that they do not pass. Which of the favors from your Lord will you deny?

22–23. From them [oceans] come pearls and coral. Which of the favors from your Lord will you deny?

24–25. His ships sail smooth on the seas, tall like mountains. Which of the favors from your Lord will you deny?

26–28. Everyone on earth is mortal. Yet the face of your Lord, majestic and honorable, is everlasting. Which of the favors from your Lord will you deny?

29–30. He is called upon by every creature in heaven and on earth, so He works daily. Which of the favors from your Lord will you deny?

31–32. Soon We will make time to deal with both of you. Which of the favors from your Lord will you deny?

33–34. Genies and mankind, if you have the power to pass through the barriers of heaven and earth, you should do it. But you won't pass through without [Our] authority. Which of the favors from your Lord will you deny?

35–36. One day, flames and smoke will be sent towards you, and you won't be able to escape. Which of the favors from your Lord will you deny?

37–38. When the sky is split apart and turns red like a hide, which of the favors from your Lord will you deny?

39–40. That day, no man or genie will be asked about their sins. Which of the favors from your Lord will you deny?

41–42. The guilty will bear marks and will be grabbed by their hair and feet. Which of the favors from your Lord will you deny?

43–45. This is the hell that the guilty denied [existed]. They shall move between it [hell] and boiling waters. Which of the favors from your Lord will you deny?

46–53. But for the ones that feared the day of judgment standing before their Lord, there will instead be two Gardens. Which of the favors from your Lord will you deny? Both will contain various trees. Which of the favors from your Lord will you deny? They will have two flowing fountains. Which of the favors from your Lord will you deny? There will be two pairs of every fruit. Which of the favors from your Lord will you deny?

54–59. They will recline on beds embossed with silk, with the fruits close by. Which of the favors from your Lord will you deny? There will be modest ones there that have never been touched by anyone. Which of the favors from your Lord will you deny? Their beauty is like rubies and corals. Which of the favors from your Lord will you deny?

60–61. Could there be any other reward for goodness than more goodness? Which of the favors from your Lord will you deny?

62–69. There will be an additional two Gardens as well. Which of the favors from your Lord will you deny? They will be dark green in color. Which of the favors from your Lord will you deny? They will both have two gushing springs. Which of the favors from your Lord will you deny? Then more fruits, date palms, and pomegranates. Which of the favors from your Lord will you deny?

70–77. They will contain good and beautiful ones. Which of the favors from your Lord will you deny? The seductive ones will be guarded in their pavilions. Which of the favors from your Lord will you deny? No one will have ever touched them. Which of the favors from your Lord will you deny? There reclining on green carpets and fine carpets. Which of the favors from your Lord will you deny?

78. Blessed is the name of your Lord, mighty and glorious.

Chapter 98 (chronologically)

Sura 76 (31 verses), Al-Insan (Man)

1–2. Do you know that there is a long time period in which mankind is not worthy of mention? We created man from a drop of mixed fluids so that We may test him. We gave him hearing and sight.

3–4. We showed man the way, whether he is grateful or not. For the unbelievers, We prepared chains, shackles, and a fire.

5–6. Meanwhile the righteous will drink from a cup [wine] mixed with camphor. There is a fountain amply flowing where the worshippers of God drink.

7–10. These people fulfill their vows and fear the day when evil is widespread. They feed the poor, orphans, and prisoners out of love for Him. They say, "We feed you out of regard for God and seek neither reward nor your thanks. We only fear the day of wrath from our Lord."

11–14. God will save them from the evil that day and reward them with comfort and joy. For their steadfastness, He will place them in the Garden in silken clothes where they rest on couches. No more excessive sun or cold. The shade will hang close above them, and bunches of fruit will be in easy reach.

15–19. They will pass around silver pitchers and crystal goblets, a crystal clear silver. The drink will be dispensed in precise measurement. The drinks will be mixed with ginger. There is a fountain there named *Salsabil.* Drinks will be served by perpetual youths that look like pearls scattered about.

20–22. When you look around, you will see happiness and a great kingdom. They will wear green embroidered silk clothes and silver bracelets. Their Lord will give them pure drinks and they will hear, "This is reward in recognition of your effort [not the term 'jihad']."

23–26. We sent you the recitation [Qur'an], revealed in stages. So be patient in submission to your Lord's command and do not obey any sinners around you. Remember the name of your Lord at morning and evening. Pray to Him for a part of the night and worship Him all night.

27–28. Those who love this fleeting lifetime have forgotten the day that is to come. We created them and made them sturdy. But when We choose, We can replace them with others.

29–31. This is a reminder that anyone that chooses to can take the path straight to their Lord. But you cannot choose the path unless God wishes it so. God is knowledgeable and wise. He gives mercy to whomever He chooses. For the sinners, He has prepared a painful punishment.

Chapter 99 (chronologically)

Sura 65 (12 verses), Al-Talaq (The Divorce)

1. My prophet, when men divorce women they must calculate the correct waiting period and divorce them at the appropriate time period, being dutiful to God your Lord. Do not let men throw them out or let them leave the house on their own unless they have committed a very severe indecency. This is the law commanded by God, and anyone who disobeys God's law harms their soul. You never know God's plan, and He may bring you into a new situation.

2–3. Once women complete the waiting period, then either keep them honorably or release them honorably. Choose two fair men to serve as witnesses for God's sake. If you believe in the last day and in God, this is the advised way. Whoever is wary of God will be shown a way forward by Him. He will provide a path you couldn't predict. Whoever trusts God will be satisfied, for God keeps his promise. God has a plan for everything.

4. If your wife has aged out of menstrual cycles, or in case you are in doubt, the prescribed waiting period is three months. It's the same time period for those who have not yet started menstruation. For pregnant women, the period ends after birth. For those dutiful to God, He will make these dealings easier.

5. That is the command of God. He sent it to you, so whoever is dutiful to God shall have their sins forgiven and receive an enlarged reward.

6. Let them [women awaiting divorce] live with you, according to your income, and don't make life hard on them to drive them out. If they are pregnant, then sustain them until they deliver the child. If they continue to suckle the child, then pay them reasonable and fair wages. If you two can't get along, have another woman provide nourishment.

7. The wealthy men should spend according to their income, but the man that has modest means should spend from what God has given him. God doesn't place a burden on anyone that requires more than what He has provided for them. After a difficulty, God will provide relief.

8–9. Remember how many communities defied the commands of God and His apostles. They were called to account, and We delivered a severe punishment. They tasted the evil consequences of their sins, and it led to their ruin.

10–11. God has prepared for a severe punishment for them, so be dutiful to God. For those who possess wisdom and are faithful, God has already sent you a message. His apostle recites the clear signs of God so He can bring those who are faithful and righteous from the darkness and into the light. Whoever has faith in God and commits righteous deeds shall be admitted by Him into the Gardens with flowing streams to live forever. God has promised to them an excellent endowment.

12. God created the seven heavens and the earth [and planets]. His command descends through them so that all may understand that God has power over all things and that God is knowledgeable of all things.

Chapter 100 (chronologically)

Sura 98 (8 verses), Al-Bayyinah (The Proof/Evidence)

1–3. Those "people of the Book" [Jews, Christians, etc.] and the polytheists that rejected the message were not going to leave their old worship until they saw some clear evidence. Like a messenger from God reciting holy scriptures that were absolutely correct.

4. The people of the Book did not have differences until after they received clear evidence.

5. All that has been commanded to them is to worship God, be sincere in worship as righteous men, maintain prayers, and pay a charity tax. That summarizes the correct religion.

6. The unbelievers among the people of the Book and the polytheists will dwell in the fires of hell. They are the worst beings.

7–8. People who are faithful and righteous in deed are the best of all beings. Their reward is to dwell forever near God in the Gardens of Eden with water flowing. God is pleased with them, and they are likewise pleased. That's what awaits those who fear their Lord.

Chapter 101 (chronologically)

Sura 59 (24 verses), Al-Hashr (The Banishment [of a Jewish tribe from Medina])

1. Everything in the heavens and on earth glorifies God, the almighty and wise.

2. He made the unbelievers who were among the "people of the Book" leave their homes when the banishment began. You didn't think they would leave, and they thought their fortress would protect them from God. But the wrath of God came at them from an unexpected direction and put terror in their hearts. They destroyed their own quarters with their own hands and the hands of the faithful. Heed this warning if you have eyes to see it.

3–4. If God hadn't banished them, He certainly would have punished them in this lifetime. In the hereafter, they will be tormented in the fire. That is because they oppose God and His messenger. Anyone that resists God will be punished severely by Him.

5. Whether you cut down a palm tree or left it standing it was God's choice, so that He could shame the disobedient.

6–7. God bestowed their [the banished] spoils on His messenger, and you didn't have to charge by horse or camel to get it. God gives His messenger authority over whoever He chooses. God has power over all things. The spoils that God gave to His messenger, from the population of the villages, belongs to God, His messenger, his relatives, orphans, the needy, and travelers. That way it won't just be handed to the wealthy among you. So take what the messenger distributes to you and leave alone what he denies you. Be dutiful to God's commands, for He is a severe punisher.

8–10. Other shares go to the unfortunate migrants that were banished from their homes and lost their property too but sought God's mercy and provisions and aided God and His messenger, for they are loyal. Yet more shares go to those older inhabitants that adopted the faith and accepted you migrants [from Mecca]. Though they were poor, they didn't covet any of the spoils being given to the migrants. These people that are not greedy are those that will be successful. The final share goes to those who arrived later [to the faith], saying, "Lord, forgive us and our brothers that came before us to the faith. Don't put any anger in our hearts towards those who believe. Lord, You are kind and merciful."

11–12. Did you hear the hypocrites tell their unbelieving brothers, who were "people of the Book," "If you are banished we will go with you, we will never obey anyone that's against you, and if you have to fight we will stand with you." But God as a witness, they are liars. If they are banished they will not leave with them, if they are attacked they won't help them, and if they do stand beside them they will retreat and be of no help.

13–15. They fear you [Muslim warriors] more than God, because your enemy doesn't understand. They won't take battle as a unit with you unless they are in forts or behind walls. Their strength is great and you would think they are united, but their hearts are divided, because they have no wisdom. Just like the men before them, they will face the evil of their decisions and in the afterlife face a severe punishment.

16–17. Satan deceives them by telling them to reject God. After they reject God he [Satan] tells them, "I won't have anything to do with you now because I fear God the Lord of the worlds." The result for both of them is the eternal fire. That is the repayment for evildoers.

18–19. My faithful, be dutiful to God. Let every soul think about his actions being recorded for tomorrow. Be reminded of God and know that God is aware of everything you do. Don't be like the people that forgot God, for He caused them to forget their own souls. They are the sinners.

20. The inhabitants of the fire are not equal to the companions in the Garden. The companions of the Garden are successful people.

21. If We had set down this Qur'an [recitation] on a mountain, you would have seen it humbled as it crumbled in fear of God. We create these metaphors for men so they can reflect.

22–24. He is God, and there is no god except Him. He knows all things both public and private. He is most forgiving and most merciful. He is God and there is no god except Him, the sovereign, the holy, the perfect, the guardian, the mightiest, the irresistible, and the supreme. Glorified is God above all things that they associate with Him. He is God, the creator, the designer, the shaper. All the best names belong to Him. Everything in the heavens and the earth glorifies Him. He is the almighty and the wisest.

Chapter 102 (chronologically)

Sura 24 (64 verses), Al-Noor (The Light)

1. We have sent down this chapter containing laws as a clear sign so that you may take warning.

2. Men and women guilty of adultery [or fornication/illegal sexual intercourse] should be lashed one hundred strokes. Don't be moved by compassion and fail to carry out God's

will. If you are faithful and believe in the last day, then gather other believers to witness the punishment.

3. Men and women guilty of adultery must marry other adulterers or unbelievers. Its forbidden for believers to marry them.

4–5. If anyone accuses an honorable woman of adultery and can't provide four witnesses to the act, then they should be struck eighty lashes. Never trust them to testify again, as they are sinners, unless they repent and act righteously later, because God is forgiving and merciful.

6–7. If any man accuses his wife but has no witnesses, then he shall swear four oaths to God that he is telling the truth and a fifth oath that he will incur God's wrath if he is lying.

8–9. The woman can avoid punishment if she also swears four oaths to God that the husband is lying and then swear a fifth oath to God that she will incur His wrath if the husband is not lying.

10. If it weren't for God's grace and mercy towards you, as He is pleasant and wise, [you would be ruined].

11. There is a group among you that created this slander [against the prophet's wife]. Don't think of it as a bad thing for all of you, for it's actually good. Every single man is punished only for what he earns in sin. The one who leads the group will have a painful penalty.

12–13. When the faithful men and women heard of the slander, why didn't they think better of their friend and say, "That is clearly a lie." Why didn't they produce four witnesses to prove [the statement]? Because they don't have four witnesses, they are liars before God.

14–15. Only by the grace and mercy of God towards you, in this world and the hereafter, have you avoided a grave punishment for what you have said. When you formed it [the lie] on your tongues and spoke about something without knowledge of the truth, you thought it a small matter; but to God is was most serious.

16–17. When you first heard it why didn't you say, "It is not right for us to speak of this. Glory be to God, this is a lie." If you are faithful, God cautions you to never repeat this action.

18–20. God makes clear revelations for you, and God is knowledgeable and wise. For those who like to see slander spread among the believers there will be a grave punishment in this life and in the hereafter. God knows all things and you do not. [You escape ruin] only because of the grace and mercy of God on you. God is full of compassion and mercy.

21. Oh faithful, do not follow Satan's footsteps. Those who do should know that Satan commands you to be indecent and sin. If it were not for God's mercy and grace none of you could ever be pure. God purifies who He chooses, and God hears and knows all.

22. None of the wealthy should fail to help their family, the needy, and the migrants on God's path; instead they should forgive and pardon them. Don't you seek God's forgiveness? God is forgiving and merciful.

23–25. Anyone who slanders honorable women who are faithful but careless will be cursed in this life and in the hereafter. They will earn a great penalty when their own tongues, hands, and feet will testify about their past. God will pay them for what they have earned, and they will realize that God is the bringer of truth.

26. Vile men and women are for each other. While good men and women belong together, and they are not stained by what people say about them. They receive forgiveness and honorable provisions.

27–29. Oh faithful, be warned that before you enter another person's home, you should announce yourself and upon receiving permission salute them. If no one is home, then don't enter until you get permission. If you are asked to go away, then do so, for your own soul. God knows all that you do. It is not however a sin if you enter an uninhabited home if it can be of use to you. Again, God knows what you do in public and private.

30. Tell the faithful men to avoid looking [at forbidden things] and dress modestly. That will make them purer, and God knows all that they do.

31. Tell the faithful women to avoid looking [at forbidden things] and to dress modestly. They should not display their adornments [like jewelry] except for what is outside their clothes. They should cover their bosom with a scarf and only show their adornments to their husbands, either father, all sons and nephews, their women [unspecified as to who], slave girls, male servants that lack sexual desire, and innocent children. Also they should not stamp their feet to make their hidden ornaments jingle, drawing attention to them. Gather towards God repentantly, my faithful, so you can be successful.

32. Marry those around you that are single and the pious male and female slaves. If they are poor, God will enrich them. God is generous and knowledgeable.

33. Those who cannot afford marriage should remain virtuous until God graces them the means to do so. If any slave seeks release papers, then sign them and if they are good people, then give them some money from the wealth God gave you. Don't force your female slaves into prostitution, if they want to remain honorable, just so you can gain [enjoy] more things in life. But if anyone does force them, surely God is forgiving and merciful.

34. We have sent down revelations making clear the examples of generations that passed before you as a warning to those who fear God.

35. God is the light of the heavens and the earth. A parable about His light: There is a niche with a lamp in it. The lamp is enclosed by glass, like a glittering star. It's lit by a blessed olive tree, that is neither eastern or western, and its oil nearly lights up without the touch of a flame. Light upon light. God guides whomever he chooses to his light. God creates parables for men, and God knows all things.

36–38. In houses that God ordained to be created to honor Him, let Him be glorified in the morning and evening by men that won't let daily work distract them from remembering God, saying prayers, and giving to charity. They do this so that God may reward them for their best deeds and give even more to them from His bounty. God gives endlessly to whom He chooses.

39–40. The deeds of the unbelievers are like a mirage in the desert. The thirsty men think they see water, but when they arrive at it they find none; instead they find God and are paid back in full what they earned. God is quick in His reckoning. [The deeds of the unbelievers are] also like the darkness of the deep ocean, where wave upon wave collect. Where man holds out his hand and hardly sees it. There is no light for those that God doesn't bestow it upon.

41. Can't you see that God is praised by every being in heaven and on earth? Like the birds in flight? Everything knows how to worship, and God is aware of what they are doing.

42. God has dominion over the earth and the heavens, and to God all return.

43. Can't you see that God moves the clouds, gathering them to make the rains? He sends mountain-sized clouds of hail to strike and spares who He chooses. The flash of His lightning will nearly blind you.

44. God causes the night and the day. This is a lesson for the wise.

45. God created every animal from water. Some move on their stomachs, some on two legs, and others on four legs. God creates what He chooses, for God has power over everything.

46. We have sent down clear signs, and God guides who He chooses to the straight path.

47. Some will say, "We believe in God and the messenger, and we obey," but then they turn from Him. They are not true believers.

48–50. When all are called to God and His messenger so that He can judge them, a group will decline to come forward. If they had been righteous, they would have come forward willingly. Do they have a disease in their hearts? Do they have doubts or fears that God and His messenger will treat them unfairly? In reality those men are unjust.

51–52. As for the believers, when they are called to God and His messenger so they can be judged, they only say, "We hear you and we obey." They are the ones that will be prosperous. Those who obey God and His messenger, fear God, and act righteously will achieve the most.

53–54. To those who swear solemn oaths to God that they will follow any command, say, "Save your oaths and actually be truly obedient. God knows everything you do." Tell them, "Obey God and the messenger. But if you turn back, then know that he [the messenger] is only responsible for his duty, and you for your own duties. If you obey him, you will be on the right path. The messenger's duty is simply to deliver the revelations.

55. God has promised the faithful and righteous that He will make them the rulers of the earth, will firmly establish their religion, and will exchange their fear with safety and peace of mind. "They will serve Me and will not associate any partners to Me. From now forward, those who reject the faith are being rebellious and wicked."

56–57. Establish prayer, give to charity, and obey the messenger, so that you may receive mercy. Never think that the unfaithful can escape on the earth. They will reside in the flames, an evil destination.

58–59. Oh faithful, ensure your slaves and prepubescent children ask permission to see you during three of your private moments each day: before the morning prayer, when you disrobe during the noonday heat, and after your late-night prayer. There is no sin for either of you during other times of the day when you all are attending to your duties. God makes clear signs for you; God is knowledgeable and wise. Also, once children reach puberty, they must ask permission. God makes His signs for you clear. God is knowledgeable and wise.

60. There is no sin for women past childbearing age or not seeking marriage that remove their outer garments as long as they don't display any ornaments; but it's best that they refrain. God hears and knows all things.

61. There is no blame upon the lame, blind, ill, nor you for eating in your own homes or the homes of your parents, siblings, aunts, or uncles. Likewise, for homes that you possess keys for or the home of a close friend. There is no issue whether you eat with others or alone. Remember as you enter houses to salute each other with a greeting from God. God makes all His signs clear so you can understand them.

62. The faithful believe in God and His messenger. When you are with him on a common activity, then ensure you ask permission to depart before you leave. The faithful who believe in God and His messenger will always ask for permission, and when they do grant it to them while asking God for their forgiveness. God is often forgiving and merciful.

63. Do not call out to the messenger like you would other people. God knows who is trying to slip away using a flimsy excuse.

Beware those who defy the messenger's orders to avoid a difficult time, for they will receive a great punishment.

64. You can be sure that God has dominion over everything in the heavens and on earth. He knows all about you, and on the day that you return to Him, He will tell you the truth about yourself. God knows all things.

Chapter 103 (chronologically)

Sura 22 (78 verses), Al-Hajj (The Pilgrimage)

1–4. Mankind, fear your Lord, because the earthquake of the hour will be grave. On that day, you will see nursing mothers distracted from their children; those that are pregnant will immediately deliver; and mankind will seem drunk. The wrath of God will be dreadful. Yet amongst men are some that argue about God without any knowledge. They follow every stubborn devil. It has been decreed that whoever takes him [Satan] as a friend will be led astray and be guided to the punishment of the flames.

5–7. Mankind, if you have doubts about the resurrection, then remember that We created you from dust, transforming you into sperm, then a clot, then a lump of flesh, so that We could make a clear sign to you. We leave you in the womb for a set period, and then We bring you out as infants. We let you grow until you reach maturity. Some We call home while young, and others age until they are feeble of body and mind. You can see that after the earth is barren We send down the rains to bring it back to life, so that every kind of thing can flourish. All of this is because God is the truth who gives life to the dead and has the power to do anything. Know that the hour will certainly come, and without a doubt God will resurrect the dead from their graves.

8–10. There are men among you that argue about God although they are ignorant, lack guidance, and are without a book of enlightenment. They turn away in arrogance in order to lead men away from the path of God. They will have disgrace in this life, and on the day of resurrection We will make them feel the punishment of the flames. They will hear, "This is for your own misdeeds, because God is never unjust to His servants."

11–13. There are some men that serve God as long as it's useful to them. If they experience good events, they are content with Him. But when they are faced with a trial, they turn from Him. The latter fail in this world and in the hereafter. What a terrible loss. They call on others besides God, that can neither help them nor harm them. They are making a grave error. They call on someone that is more likely to harm them than profit them, an evil patron and companion.

14. God allows those who are faithful and righteous in deeds to enter the Gardens with streams flowing below them. God does as He wishes.

15. If anyone thinks that God will not help him [Muhammad] in this world and in the hereafter, then they should tie a rope to the ceiling and hang. See if that action will take away what angers you.

16. We have sent down clear revelations and explained that God guides who He chooses.

17. On judgment day God will decide amongst those who are faithful, the Jews [the Zion], the Sabians, the Christians [Nazarenes], the Magi, and the polytheists. God is witness to everything.

18. Did you notice that everything bows to God; all that's in the heavens and the earth, the sun, moon, stars; the hills, trees, animals, and many from mankind? There are many that are due to receive their doom. Whoever God chooses to disgrace cannot be made honorable by anyone, for God does as He wishes.

19–22. There are two groups arguing about their Lord. The ones that do not believe will wear clothes cut from fire and have boiling water poured on their heads. The fluid will melt their intestines and skin, and they will be punished with iron rods.

Every time they try to seek relief from the pain they will be shoved back in hearing, "Taste the penalty of the flames."

23–24. God will allow those who believe and conduct righteous deeds into the Gardens where rivers flow beneath. They will be adorned in gold and pearl bracelets and clothes of silk. They have been guided to the purest of speech and along the path to the glorious One.

25. The unbelievers will receive Our most painful punishment. It's for those who kept men away from the way of God and out of the sacred mosque that We opened to all mankind, for the native and the visitor. Any who enter there for unjust reasons will join the unbelievers.

26. Remember that We told Abraham where to place the [sacred] house, saying, "Do not associate any partners to Me and sanctify My house for all worshippers, whether they pass around it, or stand, bow, and prostrate themselves to the ground."

27–28. Announce to mankind the need for pilgrimage [hajj]. They will come to you on foot and on the backs of thin camels from remote places. They can then witness their benefits. They should mention the name of God on certain days over the cattle that He has provided them for sacrifice. Eat from it and feed the needy.

29. Have them complete the prescribed traditions, perform their vows, and circle around the ancient [or free] house.

30–31. That [shall be done], and whoever honors the commands of God will be purer in the sight of his Lord. During the pilgrimage, cattle are the approved food along with exceptions told to you. Avoid the unholy idols and telling lies. Be true to your faith to God, and do not associate any partners to Him. For people who associate partners to God are like those that have fallen from heaven and been snatched by birds or winds and taken to a distant place.

32. That [shall be done] and know that those who honor the signs of God do so because of their devoted hearts.

33–35. You may benefit from them [animals] until a set time when they should be sacrificed near the ancient house. We created rituals for sacrifice for every nation, so they can honor the name of God above the cattle We gave them. Know that God is one God; submit to Him, and share the good news with those who humble themselves. To those whose hearts tremble at the mention of God. Who are patient and steadfast under trial, who pray regularly, and spend from what We gave them towards charity.

36–37. The sacrificial camels that We made for you are a symbol of goodness from God. Mention the name of God over them as you prepare the slaughter, and once they are carved on their sides then eat them and feed the needy. We made such animals to serve you so you may be grateful. Neither their blood nor flesh reaches God but instead your devotion does. He made them subservient to you so you can use them to glorify God for sharing His guidance with you. Tell other righteous men the good news.

38. God defends the faithful. God does not love ungrateful traitors.

39. Those who have been attacked ["jihad" is not used here] are permitted [to fight], because they have been wronged. God is able to help them.

40. For those who were driven from their homes unjustly for simply saying, "Our Lord is God." If it had not been for God using one group of men to stop another, then mankind would have destroyed the monasteries, churches, synagogues, and mosques—places where the name of God is mentioned often. God helps those who help Him. God is strong and mighty.

41. [God defends] those who, if we give them power, would pray regularly, give to charity, instruct kindness, and forbid sins. God decides every affair.

42–45. If they reject you, [know that] the people before rejected their prophets. The people of Noah, Ad and Thamud, Abraham and Lot, the Midians and Moses. But I allowed the unbelievers some relief before I punished them. My rejection of them was terrible. We destroyed so many communities as they sinned; tumbling in their roofs, their wells are idle today and places empty.

46–48. Don't people travel the lands so that their hearts can learn, eyes see, and ears hear? It's not that their eyes are blind but rather their hearts. And still they ask you to speed up the arrival of their punishment! God will never break His promise. But know that one day in the presence of your Lord is like a thousand years in your time. How many towns did I give relief to while they sinned? But in the end I punished them, as everything returns to Me.

49–50. Say to them, "Mankind, I am simply a messenger to you." For the faithful and righteous there is mercy and generous provisions.

51. And those who oppose Our signs will be inmates in the fire.

52. [Recited between MC and MD] Every prophet We sent before you, when he recited Our message, was interfered with by Satan. But God will abolish anything that Satan proposes. God will establish His revelations. God is knowledgeable and wise.

53. [between MC and MD] He [God] will make those proposals from Satan a trial for men whose hearts are diseased and hardened. For those wrongdoers are in opposition [to the truth].

54. [between MC and MD] Let those who have received this knowledge know that it is the truth from your Lord. You may believe in it and submit your hearts humbly to Him. God guides the faithful onto the right path.

55. [between MC and MD] Those who reject the faith will be in constant doubt until the hour comes suddenly or they are overtaken by destruction.

56–57. On that day God will hold all sovereignty. He will judge between men. Those who were faithful and righteous will enter the blissful Gardens. Those who rejected the faith and Our revelations await a humiliating doom.

58. Those who migrate in the way of God and who are killed or die shall have a substantial provision from God. God bestows the best provisions.

59. He will allow them to enter a place that is very pleasing. God is knowledgeable and generous.

60. And anyone that retaliates equal to the injury they have been given and then is attacked again will be helped by God. God pardons and forgives.

61. God turns night into day and day into night. God hears and sees all things.

62. God is real. Whoever they invoke instead of God is a lie. God sits on high and is the greatest.

63–66. Haven't you seen how God sends down rains and causes the earth to turn green? God knows all things and is aware. Everything in the heavens and on earth belongs to God. He wants for nothing and should be praised. Can't you see that God has made everything on earth to serve you? The ships sailing through the waters at His command? The skies can only fall on the earth by His command. God is kind and merciful to mankind. He gave you life, causes you to die, and will give you life again. Mankind is surely ungrateful.

67. We gave every people rituals they were supposed to perform. Don't let them argue with you about these matters. Summon them to your Lord. You are following the right path.

68–69. If they do argue with you, then say, "God knows all that you do. God will judge amongst you on the day of resurrection about all the things you disagree on."

70. Don't you know that God is aware of everything in the heavens and earth? It is all recorded in a book; it is easy for God.

71. Those who worship anything besides God and have not been delivered any authority by Him to do so and have no knowledge of it will not have any helper for their sin.

72. When they hear our clear messages recited, you will notice unbelievers with the denial on their faces, as if they are ready to attack the messenger. Say to those people, "Do I need to

tell you about something even worse? [Maybe] the fires of hell? God promises it to the unfaithful, and it is an evil destination."

73–76. Mankind, hear this parable. Those you worship besides God cannot even create a mere fly, even if you gathered them all together for the creation. And if a fly ever took anything away from those you worship, they wouldn't have enough power to take it back from the fly. Those who seek them and those who are sought are both feeble. They do not give God His rightful high regard. God is strong, the almighty. God chooses His messengers from among the angels and men. God hears and sees all things. God knows the future and the past, and to God all things are returned.

77. Oh faithful, bow down and prostrate in worship to your Lord. Do good so that you may prosper.

78. Strive [jihad] for the sake of God, a struggle [jihad] that is worthy of Him. He has chosen you, and the religion He created for you has no obstacles; it's the faith of your father Abraham. He named you Muslims, earlier [in scripture] and in this [revelation], so that the messenger can witness to you and you can witness to mankind. Establish regular prayer, give to charity, and hold steady to God. He is your patron. A blessed protector and excellent helper.

Chapter 104 (chronologically)

Sura 63 (11 verses), Al-Munafiqun (The Hypocrites)

1. When the hypocrites speak to you, they say, "We swear that you are indeed God's messenger." But, God knows that you are His true messenger, and God swears that the hypocrites are liars.

2–3. They use their oaths as shields for their sins and turn men away from the ways of God. They committed evil acts because they once believed and then rejected the message. So their hearts were sealed, and they could never understand.

4. When you see them, they are pleasing, so when they speak, people listen. They are like logs propped on a wall. They think every cry is directed against them. They are your enemies, so be wary. The curse of God is on them. Look how they are straying from the truth.

5–6. When someone says, "Listen, God's messenger will pray for your forgiveness," they turn their faces, and you can see their arrogance. It doesn't matter if you pray for their forgiveness or not; God will never forgive them. God does not guide the sinners.

7–8. They are the ones that say, "Don't spend any money with those who follow God's messenger until they desert him." But the hypocrites don't understand; all the treasures of the heavens and earth belong to God. They say, "When we return to the city, the mighty will expel the weak." But the hypocrites don't know that might belongs to God and His messenger and the faithful.

9–11. Oh faithful, never let your wealth or children distract you from your duties to God. Those who forget will lose. Spend the wealth that We provided you before you die. Or else you might ask, "My Lord, why didn't you give me a little more time so I could give my wealth to charity and join the righteous." God will grant reprieve to no soul, for when your time is up you are finished. God is well informed of what you do.

Chapter 105 (chronologically)

Sura 58 (22 verses), Al-Mujadila (The Pleading Woman)

1. God heard the plea of the woman that complained to you [Muhammad] about her husband. God always hears the arguments between people, for He sees and hears all things.

2. Any man that tries to divorce his wife by saying she is acting like your mother should know they are not your mother. Only people who gave birth to you can be your mother. These people are using hateful language and lies. Luckily God is able to forgive sins and is merciful.

3–4. If you have divorced your wife by saying she is acting like a mother and you want to remarry her; then you have to free a slave before you can touch each other. This is the rule, and God is watching all you do. If you can't afford to free one slave, then you must fast for two consecutive months before you touch each other. If you can't do that, then you must feed sixty needy people to prove your faith to God and His messenger. These are the laws of God, and if you reject them there will be a severe punishment.

5. People who oppose God and His messenger will be humiliated like those before. We have sent down clear signs. The unbelievers will have a shameful punishment.

6. God will resurrect all beings and show them the record of their deeds. God will have judged its value, and although some may have forgotten, God has witnessed all things.

7. Didn't you notice that God knows all the things that occur in the heavens and the earth? There are no secrets between three people because He is the fourth, no secrets between five because He is the sixth. No matter the number, He is with them everywhere they go. On that day, He will tell them about their conduct. God knows everything.

8. Didn't you see those who were forbidden from holding secret talks doing what was forbidden? They talk secretly of sins and rebellion and disobeying the messenger. When they approach you, they greet you in a way that God does not and then ask

themselves, "Why doesn't God punish us for those words?" Hell will be all they deserve, and they will burn in that evil place.

9. Oh faithful, when you talk in secret do not speak of crimes and revolt and disobeying the messenger. Talk instead about righteousness and piety and fear of God, He who will resurrect you.

10. Conspiracies are inspired by the devil to harm the faithful. He cannot harm them in any way unless God allows it. The faithful put their trust in God.

11. Oh faithful, if you are asked to make room in the assembly, then make room, for God will provide it for you. When you are told to rise, then rise. God will lift those who are faithful and those who are wisest to higher heights. God is well informed about what you do.

12–13. Oh faithful, before you meet with the messenger in private, give something to charity beforehand. It will be best for you and is purer behavior. If you cannot afford to, God is forgiving and merciful. If you are afraid about giving money to charity before your private talks, then don't be. God forgives you. At least pray regularly, be charitable, and obey God and His messenger. Know that God is aware of all you do.

14–17. Think about the people who befriend those that God's wrath is upon. They are not on either person's side, and yet they knowingly lie. God has a severe punishment for them, for they are evil. They use their promises to hide their sins and block men from the straight path of God. They have earned a humiliating punishment. Their wealth and children will not protect them from God. They are destined for the fire.

18–19. On the day that God resurrects them for judgment, they will swear to God like they swore to mankind. They will think they are safe, but they are liars. Satan has gained control of them, making them forget to honor God. They are comrades of Satan. The followers of Satan will perish.

20–21. Those who oppose God and His messenger will be humiliated. God has said, "My messengers and I will prevail." God is the strongest and is mighty.

22. On the last day, you will not see any of the faithful helping anyone that resists God and His messenger, even if it's their own father, son, or brother, or their family. God had written faith into their hearts and empowered them with His own spirit. He will invite them into the Gardens where rivers flow beneath them to live forever. God will be happy with them and vice versa. They align with God, and the party of God will be successful.

Chapter 106 (chronologically)

Sura 49 (18 verses), Al-Hujraat (The Apartments)

1–5. Oh faithful, don't let yourself get ahead of God and His messenger. Be dutiful to God, for He hears and knows all. Oh faithful, don't raise your voices louder than the prophets or shout at him while speaking, as if you were talking to one another. Or your deeds may all be in vain and you won't know it. People who lower their voice in the presence of God's messenger have hearts that God has found righteous. They will receive mercy and a great reward. But most of the people who shout out to you [Muhammad] from inside their apartments have no sense. It would have been better for them to show patience and let you come to them. God is forgiving and merciful.

6. Oh faithful, if a reckless person brings you news, you should verify it. Otherwise you might unknowingly cause harm to others and later regret your decision.

7–8. Remember that God's messenger is among you. If he followed all your desires [in governing], you would all be in big trouble. [Fortunately,] God has inspired you towards faith, making it appealing to your hearts. He made you hate disbelief, wickedness, and disobedience. This describes the righteous people. It's a grace and favor from God. God is knowledgeable and wise.

9–10. If two groups of the faithful begin to fight, then make peace between them. If one of the groups during the fighting severely breaks the rules [Islamic rules of war], then take the side of the victim until the wicked side complies with God's commands. If they comply, then you should make peace between them fairly. God loves people who are fair and seek justice. All the faithful are in one brotherhood, so seek to bring peace and reconciliation between your brothers. Be dutiful to God so that you might receive His mercy.

11. Oh faithful, don't let men pick on one another; the victim might be the better person. Don't let women laugh at one another; she also may be the better person. Don't slander each other or use nicknames as an insult. It is very wicked to call a brother by an evil name once he becomes faithful. Those who don't regret this are sinning.

12. Oh faithful, try not to be suspicious; in some cases, suspicion is a sin. Don't spy on each other, and don't reveal a man's private information behind his back [backbiting]. Would any of you want to eat the flesh off his dead brother? No, you would hate it. Be dutiful to God, for He is forgiving and merciful.

13. Mankind, We created you from a single male and female and then made you into nations and tribes so you might identify each other [easily identify families]. The most honorable

among you is seen as the most righteous by God. God knows all things and is fully aware.

14. The Bedouins [desert Arabs] say, "We have faith." Say to them, "You do not have faith yet, so you should say 'We have embraced Islam.' For faith has still not entered your hearts. But if you obey God and His messenger, He will not withhold any reward for your deeds." God is forgiving and merciful.

15. Only the faithful people believe in God and His messengers and have never doubted. They have strived [jihad] with their wealth and their body in the way of God. They are the sincere followers.

16. Say to them, "Are you the one that should tell God about your religion? God knows everything about the heavens and the earth and is aware of all things."

17–18. When they act like they did the messenger a favor by surrendering to Him, say to them, "Don't count your submission as a favor to me; instead, know that God has done you a favor. He has led you to the truth if you are sincere." Remember God knows all the secrets of the heavens and the earth, and God knows better than anyone what you do.

Chapter 107 (chronologically)

Sura 66 (12 verses), Al-Tahrim (The Forbidding)

1. Prophet, why do you forbid yourself from enjoying things God commanded are allowed in order to please your wives? God is often forgiving and merciful.

2. God has ordained that you [Muslims] can dissolve your contracts, and God is your master. He is knowledgeable and wise.

3–4. There was a time that the prophet confided in one of his wives. Then she told another wife, and God, [overhearing it] told him [Muhammad] about part of what He heard. When the prophet told the first wife, she asked, "Who told you this?" He replied, "The all-knowing and all-aware told me, and if you both turn to God regretfully [it will best for you], then your heart's desire is [forgiveness]. But if you both unite, siding against him [Muhammad], then know that God is his guardian, and Gabriel and every righteous faithful being and also the angels are on his side."

5. If he divorces you, maybe God will give him wives even better than you all. [Maybe] wives, whether previously married or virgins, who are submissive [to God], faithful, obedient, repentant, sincere worshippers, and who fast [sometimes translated as "take pilgrimage"].

6–7. Oh faithful, save yourself and your family from the flames where men and stones act as fuel. Where strong and severe angels guard you and precisely execute what He commands them. They will say to you, "You unbelievers need not make excuses on this day, for you are being repaid for what you did."

8. Oh faithful, turn to God sincerely in hopes that your Lord will forgive your sins and show you into the Gardens where the rivers flow. On that day, God will not humiliate the prophet or his followers. Their light [reputations/souls] will arrive before them, and by their right [hands] they will say, "Lord, perfect our lights [our beings] and forgive us. You are able to do all things.

9. Oh prophet, strive [jihad] against the unbelievers and hypocrites and be stern. Their destination is hell, an evil ending.

10. God showed an example for the unbelievers in the wives of Noah and Lot. They were under two of our righteous servants and betrayed them. Their husbands didn't assist them as they faced God, and they were told, "Enter the fire with the others."

11. Another example God shows the faithful is the Pharaoh's wife. She said, "My Lord, build me a mansion next to you in the Garden and save me from Pharaoh's evil conduct and these evil people."

12. Also there is Mary [whose father isn't named in the Bible], the daughter of Imran [often believed to be Amram of Old Testament], who was a virgin. We breathed into her some of Our spirit. She accepted the messages of her Lord and His scriptures and was an obedient servant.

Chapter 108 (chronologically)

Sura 64 (18 verses), Al-Taghabun
(The Determination of Losses and Gains)

1–4. Everything in the heavens and on earth glorifies God. He is sovereign and is owed all praise. He has power over everything. He created you, and while some are unbelievers and others are believers, He sees all that you do. He created the heavens and the earth perfectly, has shaped you and made you beautiful, and back to Him do we journey. He knows everything in the heavens and on earth, including what you hide and what you say publicly. God knows all the secrets in men's hearts.

5–6. Haven't you heard of the people who rejected faith before you? They felt the severe consequences for their actions. They sustained a painful punishment. It was because when their messengers brought them clear signs, they would say, "How can mere mortals guide us?" They rejected the messages and turned their backs. But God is self-sufficient and doesn't need mankind; He is worthy of praise.

7–8. When the unbelievers say they won't be resurrected, say to them, "By my Lord, you will be raised again and then told the truth about everything you did. It will be easy for God." Have faith in God and His messenger and in the light We sent down. God knows well everything you do.

9–10. On the day that He assembles all of you, there will be mutual loss and gain among you. For those who are faithful and righteous, He will remove your sins, and He will send you into the Garden where rivers flow beneath to live forever. It will be the greatest achievement. Meanwhile those who reject faith and rejected Our revelations will enter the fire and live there—an evil destination.

11–13. No evil events occur without God's permission. Whoever believes in God receives His guidance in their heart. God knows all things. Obey God and His messenger. Know that if you reject Our messenger, his only duty is to clearly proclaim Our revelations. God; there is no god except Him. Let the faithful put their trust in God.

14–15. Oh faithful, beware that even among your wives and children there can be an enemy to you. But even if you forgive, ignore, and cover up [their faults], God is forgiving and merciful. Your wealth and your children are merely a trial for you. In the presence of God is the greatest of rewards.

16–18. Be dutiful to God the best you can. Listen and obey, and give to charity to benefit your own soul. Those who can be saved from their own greed will achieve prosperity. If you set aside a sizeable loan for God, He will double it for you and forgive you. God is appreciative and forgiving—knowledgeable of the known and unknown, mighty and wise.

Chapter 109 (chronologically)

Sura 61 (14 verses), Al-Saff (The Ranks)

1. Everything that is in the heavens and on earth glorifies God. He is mighty and wise.

2–3. Oh faithful, why do you say things that you don't actually do? God hates people that don't do as they say.

4. God truly loves those who fight [not translated from the word "jihad"] in His way in ranks, like they are a solid structure.

5. Recall when Moses told his people, "Why are you tormenting me when you know I am the messenger from God?" Later, when they did evil deeds, God sent their hearts astray. God does not guide people who are disobedient [to God].

6. Recall when Jesus, the son of Mary, said, "Children of Israel, I am the messenger of God, sent to confirm the Torah's laws and tell you the good news about another messenger that will

come after me. He will be called Ahmad." But after he showed them clear signs, they said, "This is only sorcery."

7–9. Who can be more wrong than someone who creates a lie against God while he is being invited to Islam? God does not guide unjust people. They intend to extinguish God's light with their mouths, but God will perfect His light despite the unbeliever's opposition. He sent His messenger with guidance and the religion of truth so that he can proclaim it over all religion, even though the polytheists oppose it.

10. Oh faithful, shall I show you a bargain that can save you from a painful punishment?

11. If you believe in God and His messenger and strive [jihad] in the way of God with your wealth and your souls it would be best for you. If you only knew.

12. He will forgive your sins and admit you to the Gardens where rivers flow beneath you. There will be beautiful mansions in the Garden of Eden. That is the supreme triumph.

13. One more favor, which you will love, will be assistance from God and a speedy victory. So tell the good news to the faithful.

14. Oh faithful, be God's helpers. Jesus, the son of Mary, once asked his disciples, "Who will be my helpers for God?" The disciples replied, "We are God's helpers." But when some of the Israelis [tribe of Israel] became faithful, and another group

disbelieved. We gave strength to the faithful and they prevailed.

Chapter 110 (chronologically)

Sura 62 (11 verses), Jumuah (Friday/Gathering)

1–4. Everything in the heavens and on earth glorifies God, the sovereign, holy, mighty, and wise One. He sent a messenger from among them to the uneducated people to recite His revelations. The messenger purified them and instructed them in scripture and knowledge. Before Him they were clearly unguided. He also did this for others who haven't submitted yet. He is the mighty and wise. This shows the grace of God. He gives it to who He chooses. God has infinite grace.

5. The people entrusted with the laws of Moses but who failed to keep their obligations are similar to an ass that is carrying many books [but can't understand them]. People who reject the messages of God are an evil image. God does not guide people who are unjust.

6. Say to them, "Oh Jews, if you think that you are favored by God above other people, then you should ask for death, unless you are lying."

7. They will never ask for death because of the deeds they have committed. God knows who commits evil.

8. Say to them, "The death you are avoiding will eventually overcome you. Then you will be sent back to He who knows all your secret and public details, and He will tell you the truth about what you did."

9–10. Oh faithful, when you hear the call to prayer on Friday, stop your business and move quickly towards remembrance of God. If you are wise, you know this is what's best for you. After prayer disperse throughout the lands and work to secure the bounty of God. Praise God often so that you may be prosperous.

11. When men spot some merchandise or sport, they run to it, leaving you standing alone. Say to those people, "The rewards of God are better than any merchandise or sport. God is the best provider."

Chapter 111 (chronologically)

Sura 48 (29 verses), Al-Fath (The Victory)

1–3. We have granted you [Muhammad] a clear victory; may God forgive your sins past and future, continue His blessings on you, and guide you on the straight path, and may God assist you with His might.

4–6. He gives the hearts of the faithful reassurance so they may perfect their faith. God has dominion over everything in the heavens and on earth. God is knowledgeable and wise. He is able to absolve faithful men and women of their sins and allow them into the Garden with streams flowing in them to stay for eternity. That is God's ultimate success. He is also able to punish the hypocritical and polytheist men and women who hold evil thoughts about God. They will receive a reverse of fortune, for the wrath of God is upon them. He has cursed them and readied hell for them, and it's an evil place.

7. God has dominion over everything in the heavens and on earth. God is knowledgeable and wise.

8–9. We have sent you a messenger to witness, bear good news, and to warn [mankind] so that you may believe in God and His messenger. So you may assist and honor Him and glorify Him in the morning and evening.

10. Those who swear an oath to you [Muhammad] are swearing allegiance only to God, and the hand of God will be above their heads. Should anyone break their oath, they do so at the risk of their soul. Whoever fulfills their promise to God shall receive a great reward from Him.

11–12. The Bedouins [desert Arabs] who stayed behind [during the migration or battles] now say to you [when they arrive], "We were very busy looking after our wealth and our families, so will you ask for forgiveness for us?" They are saying something they don't really mean. Reply to them, "If God intends to harm you or help you, who can possibly intervene? Don't worry; God is aware of everything you do." You thought that the messenger and the faithful would never return to their families, and that pleased you. That was an evil thought, and you are a wicked people.

13. For anyone that does not believe in God and His messenger, We have prepared a blazing fire.

14. God has dominion over everything in the heavens and on earth. He can forgive and punish whoever He wishes, but God is forgiving and merciful.

15. When you prepare to march off to capture spoils of war and those [Bedouins/desert Arabs] who stayed behind ask you, "Please take us with you," they are seeking to change God's rules. Reply to them, "You cannot come with us. God has decreed it." They will respond by saying, "You are jealous of us." They don't understand much.

16. Tell the Bedouins that stayed behind, "You will be called to face a band of strong warriors, and they will embrace Islam or you will fight them. If you obey God, He will reward you. But if you turn back like you did before, He will punish you severely."

17. If you are blind, lame, or sick or you obey God and His messenger; He will send you into the Gardens where streams flow. He will severely punish whoever turns back.

18–19. God was pleased with the faithful that swore allegiance to you beneath the tree. He knew what was in their hearts, so He steeled them [for battle] and rewarded them with an impending victory, where they would capture many spoils of war. God is mighty and wise.

20. God promises that you will acquire many spoils of war, and He brought you a rapid victory by holding back the hands of the opposing army. This may be taken as a sign for the faithful, and may He guide you on a righteous path.

21. Other gains exist that you haven't taken yet. But God has thought about them, and God is able to do anything.

22–23. When the unbelievers fight you, they will retreat and have no protectors or aid. That is the way approved by God and how it occurred in the past. There will be no changes in the paths approved by God.

24. He restrained the hands of your enemy and also your hands in the valley of Mecca after He awarded you a victory over them. God sees all that you do.

25. They [the enemy] are the ones who rejected the revelations, blocked you from the sacred mosque, and kept the sacrificial animals from reaching their destination. [You were held back at that moment] to avoid the risk of trampling the anonymous faithful men and women among them, for which you would have been blamed. Because God can give His mercy to whomever He likes. Had those faithful people been separated

[from the unfaithful enemy], We would have punished the unbelievers severely.

26. The unbelievers' hearts were full of arrogance, the arrogance born of ignorance, so God sent down calming reassurance to His messenger and the faithful. This allowed them to use self-restraint, and they were worthy of the calming gift. God is aware of all things.

27. God will fulfill the vision of His messenger. You shall enter the sacred mosque, God willing, with hair shaved and cut and without fear. He knew what you did not, and He granted you an impending victory.

28. God is a sufficient witness that He sent His messenger with guidance, and the religion of truth, to proclaim it over all religions.

29. Muhammad is the messenger of God. The faithful with him are strong in the face of unbelievers, but merciful towards each other. You can see them bowing and prostrating [in prayer], seeking God's mercy and approval. Their foreheads bear the mark of constant prayer [where they touch the ground]. There is a similar story in the Torah and Gospel. A seed sends up its shoots, then it strengthens as it thickens, and finally it stands firm, delighting the planter. This makes the unbelievers angry at them. God has promised the faithful and righteous forgiveness and a great reward.

Chapter 112 (chronologically)

Sura 5 (120 verses), Al-Maida (The Table)

1. Oh faithful, keep all your promises. Except for those noted here, all four-footed livestock are permitted for food. When starting the pilgrimage, eating wild game is forbidden. God ordains laws that please Him.

2. Oh faithful, don't disrespect God's symbols, the sacred month, any animals or animal's decorations brought to sacrifice, or any people moving towards the sanctuary. Once you have ended the pilgrimage, you may hunt again. Don't let your hatred of the people that once blocked you from the sacred mosque cause you to sin [against them]. Be helpful to each other, so you can be righteous and pure. Don't join or help others in sin or hatred. Be wary of God, for God gives severe penalties.

3. [Given from Arafat on the last hajj] Forbidden foods include animals that died before proper slaughter, blood, pork, sacrificial animals offered to anyone besides God, animals killed by strangulation or beating, animals dying from a fall or goring, animals partially eaten by wild beasts unless you were able to purify it before death, and anything sacrificed on stone altars. Also, dividing meat by raffling arrows [a game of chance] is prohibited. People that are forced by hunger to eat

[unlawful foods] without intentionally sinning should remember that God is forgiving and merciful.

At this point in time the unbelievers have given up hope on your religion. Do not fear them; fear Me. I have now perfected your religion for you, completed My blessing on you, and chosen Islam as your religion.

4. When they ask you what [food] is allowed, tell them, "All good things are lawful. Wild game caught by your hunting animals and birds can be eaten once you have mentioned God's name over it. Be dutiful to God, for God gives justice swiftly.

5. From now on all good things are legal for you. All foods made lawful to people receiving the Book are legal for you. It's legal for you to marry virtuous women, both believers and people of the Book, after you have paid their dowry if they are seeking an honorable marriage. [Do not take women] simply seeking fornication or to have mistresses. Anyone that rejects their faith will continue to work in vain and in the hereafter; they will be among the lost [souls].

6. Oh faithful, before you pray, wash your faces, your hands and arms up to your elbow, wipe your heads, and wash your feet up to your ankles [with water]. If you are in a state of uncleanliness, then [completely] bathe. If you can't find any water and are sick, traveling, just used a toilet, or had sexual intercourse, then use dirt to at least rub your hands and face.

God isn't trying to place a burden on you, He wants to make you clean and give His grace to you, so you can be grateful.

7. Remember God's grace and the covenant that He and you ratified when you told Him, "We hear and we obey." Be dutiful to God, for God knows your secret thoughts.

8. Oh faithful, be steadfast, supporting justice for God's sake. Don't let others' hatred cause you to be unjust. It is your duty to be fair. Obey your duties to God. God knows all you do.

9–10. God promises a great reward to the faithful and righteous. Hell awaits those who reject faith and Our signs.

11. Oh faithful, recall feeling God's grace when some men attempted to raise their hands toward you but He didn't let them touch you. Be wary of God, and put all your trust in God.

12. God previously made a covenant with the sons of Israel and created 12 chiefs among them. God told them, "I am with you. Establish prayers, practice charity, believe in My messengers—honor and aid them, and give God a good loan. I will absolve your sins and allow you into the Garden where rivers flow beneath you. But after this [covenant], if anyone loses their faith they have truly gone off the right path.

13. But they broke their covenant, so We cursed them and hardened their hearts. They now change the words in, and have forgotten parts of, Our message. Except for a few of

them, they are constantly revealing their betrayals. Nevertheless, look past their sins and forgive them. God loves people who are good to others.

14. We also made a covenant with those who say they are Christians [*nasaree*]. But they have forgotten part of Our message to them. So We have created hatred and hostility among them that will last until the resurrection. Then God will tell them what they have done.

15–16. People of the Book, Our messenger has clarified for you things that you used to hide in your book or pass over. A light from God and a clear book have been given to you. With them God guides those seeking His good graces on a path to peace. He leads them out of the dark and into the light, guiding them on a straight path.

17. Some unbelievers say, "God is the Messiah, the son of Mary." Say to them, "Who has the power to stop God, if He wishes to destroy the Messiah, son of Mary, his mother, and everyone on earth?" God is the king of everything in the heavens and on earth. He creates what He chooses. God has power over all things.

18. When the Jews and Christians say, "We are God's children and His beloved ones." Reply to them, "Then why does He punish you for your sins? You are merely humans that He created. He forgives and punishes whoever He chooses,

everything in the heavens and earth are in His kingdom, and everything returns to Him in the end."

19. People of the Book, Our messenger has come to you clarifying revelations for you, after a long absence of Our prophets on earth, so that you cannot say, "No one came to give us the good news and warn us away from evil." Now a messenger has brought you the good news and warned you. God has power over everything.

20–21. Moses told his people, "Recall God's grace upon us when He sent prophets among you, made you kings, and gave you something that no other people had. My people, enter the holy land that God ordained for you. Do not turn back on Him or you will be lost."

22. They responded to Moses, "There are strong people in this land, and we will not enter until they have left."

23. Two God-fearing men stepped forward who had been touched by God's grace and said, "Charge them at the gate, for once inside you will be victorious. If you are faithful, then put your trust in God."

24. The people responded again, "Moses, we will not enter the lands until they leave. You go and your Lord can go fight them, but we will sit right here."

25–26. He [Moses] said, "My Lord, I only have power over my brother and I; please separate us from these unjust people."

He [his Lord] replied, "They are now forbidden from this land for forty years. They will now wander the earth. Do not mourn for these evildoers.

27–29. Tell them the true story of the two sons of Adam. Each of them offered a sacrifice, but it was accepted by only one of them. One said, "I will kill you." The other replied, "God accepts sacrifice only from the truly God-fearing. Even as you reach out your hand to kill me, I won't try to kill you. I fear God, the Lord of the worlds. I intend for you to earn a place in hell by sinning against me along with your other sins. That is what evil men earn."

30–31. But the first brother's soul led him to murder his brother. He killed him and became one of the lost. God then sent a crow to scratch at the ground and show him how to hide the dead body. He [the murderer] spoke: "Have I become as low as this raven that I must bury my brother's body." He was then filled with regret.

32. Because of this incident, We made a decree for the Israeli tribe that if any of them kill a person [unjustly], except for cases of capital punishment for murderers or corruption, then it will be as if they killed every human being. On the other hand, if anyone saves just one life, then it will be as if they saved all of humanity. And even though we sent Our messengers with clear signs to these earlier generations, some

of them still acted beyond the limits [set by God] all over the land.

33–34. The punishment for anyone that wages war [not the Arabic term "jihad"] against God and His messengers and spreads corruption on earth is either death, crucifixion, having their opposite hands and feet cut off, or banishment. That will be their punishment [humiliation] in this world, and then in the hereafter they earn a heavier penalty. 34. There is an exception for those who repent before they are captured. God is often forgiving and merciful.

35. Oh faithful, be respectful of God. Seek the course towards Him. Strive [jihad] on His path so that you may be successful.

36–37. People who reject faith can collect everything of worth on earth and multiply it by two, but when they try to pay their way out of punishment on resurrection day, it won't be accepted [as payment]. They face a painful penalty. They will wish they could leave the flames, but they won't get out. Theirs is an enduring punishment.

38–39. For male and female thieves, the punishment is to cut off their hands. This serves as an example of punishment for that crime from God. God is mighty and wise. If the thief repents for the crime and reforms, then God will forgive them. God is forgiving and merciful.

40. Don't you know that God owns the kingdom of the heavens and the earth? He punishes and forgives whoever He chooses. God has power over everything.

41. Messenger, do not grieve for people that are racing towards disbelief. Not the ones who say, "We are faithful" with their words but deny faith in their hearts. Not the Jews who are eavesdropping, to either tell lies about you or to tell other people what you are saying. They use the words out of context [for instance] saying, "If you are given this, then take it. But if you are not given this, be wary."

Whoever God wishes to be misled cannot be helped by anyone. No one can [has power to] go against God. There are people that God does not want to purify in this life. There is a grave punishment for them in the hereafter.

42–43. [Some] listen to lies and are hungry for the forbidden. If they come before you [for legal guidance], then you can hear them or refuse to get involved. If you decline to give judgment, [don't worry,] they cannot harm you. If you do judge between them, then be fair. God loves those who judge fairly. Why do they come to you for judgments when they already have the Torah containing God's guidance? Despite having this they turn their backs. They are not truly faithful.

44. We revealed the Torah that contains guidance and light. It was used by the prophets who submitted [to God] to judge the Jewish people. It was also used by rabbis and priests who

were entrusted to preserve the Book of God and bear witness about it. Do not fear men; instead fear Me, and don't sell my revelations for a cheap price. Anyone who renders judgment without using what God revealed is an unbeliever.

45. In it [the Torah] We set forth the following [guidance]: "A life for a life; eye for an eye, nose for a nose, ear for an ear, tooth for a tooth, and retaliation for wounds." Anyone can attempt to atone for their sins by acts of charity. Anyone who renders judgment without using what God revealed is unjust.

46. After them We sent Jesus [*bai-eesi*] the son of Mary, who confirmed the laws sent before him in the Torah. We sent him the Gospel, containing guidance and light. It confirmed the Torah and serves as guidance and advice for those dutiful to God.

47. Now have the people following the Gospel, judge [their cases] by what God has [recently] revealed. Anyone who renders judgment without using what God revealed is unjust.

48. We sent you this true Book that confirms the revelations before it; keep it safe. Judge between men by the laws revealed by God. Don't give in to their desires where it differs from the truth revealed to you. In every community, We created a code of law and a path. If God had wished, He could have just made mankind one community. Instead He needed to test you based on what He gave [each of] you. So compete with each other in trying to do good deeds. To God you all will

return, and He will explain all the things that you argued about.

49. Judge between men by the law God revealed, and don't give in to their desires. Beware of their attempts to lure you from God's revelations. If they reject you, you can be sure that God wants to punish them. There are many unjust men.

50. Maybe they are seeking the old justice from the ignorant times. Who can give better justice to the faithful than God?

51. Oh faithful, do not make Jews and Christians your friends or guardians [also translated as "parents"]. They are friends to each other. Anyone that desires them for friendship is one of them. God does not guide the unjust.

52–53. You can see the disease in their hearts as they seek them [Jews and Christians] out, as they say, "We are afraid a catastrophe will ruin us." Maybe God will give you [Muhammad] victory or act upon them Himself. Then the faithful will repent for their secret desires. The faithful will ask you, "Aren't these the men that swore to God they were with you?" Their [those seeking friendship] plans will have failed, and they will become lost.

54. Oh faithful, if any among you reject your faith, know that God will soon create a community that He will love. They will love Him, be humble to the faithful, and be stern towards the unfaithful as they strive [jihad] in the way of God. They

will not fear any criticism from their detractors. Such is the grace of God; He can give it to whoever He chooses. God is complete and knows everything.

55–56. Your only guardians are God, His messengers, and your fellow believers. Those who pray regularly, are charitable, and bow in prayer. Those who take God, His messenger, and the faithful as their guardians should know that party of God will triumph.

57–58. Oh faithful, don't make friends with people who mock your religion, whether they were previously given the Book or they are unfaithful. Instead be wary of God if you are faithful. Those who mock you when you are saying the call to prayer are ignorant people.

59. Say to them, "People of the Book, why do you criticize us? Is there any other reason besides our belief in God and belief in the revelations that have come to us, and that were previously sent to you? Maybe you are the disobedient ones?"

60. Say to them, "Let me explain a revenge from God that is worse than this. The people who are cursed by God and feel his wrath. Those who are transformed into apes and pigs and who worship idols. They are in a worse situation and have strayed far from the right path [of God]."

61–63. Some people come to you, saying, "We believe!" But actually, they came before you as unbelievers and left you the same.

God knows what they are hiding. You have seen many of them sinning and cheating as much as they can, taking illegal gains. What they do is evil. Why don't their rabbis and legal scholars forbid them from their evil speech and illegal gains? They are clearly committing sins.

64. The Jews say, "God's hands are tied." It is their hands that are truly tied, and they are cursed for what they say. God's hands are outstretched. He gives [as much and as often] as He likes. The revelations you receive from God, only seem to make many of them become more rebellious and more faithless. We have created animosity and hatred between them that endures until judgment day. Whenever they start a war, God stops it, yet still they try to cause trouble on the earth. God does not love the troublemakers.

65–66. If the people of the Book had been faithful and righteous, then We would have forgiven their sins and allowed them into paradise. If they had followed the Torah, the Gospel, and the revelations sent by their Lord, they would have enjoyed complete nourishment. There is a righteous group among them, but many of them are on an evil path.

67. Messenger, recite the revelations that your Lord sent to you. If you do not, then you have not [fulfilled your mission to] conveyed His message. God will protect you from mankind. God does not guide the unbelievers.

68. Say to them, "People of the Book, you are not on solid ground unless you observe the Torah, the Gospel, and the revelations sent from your Lord." Many of them will become more rebellious and unfaithful by the revelations that were given to you by your Lord. Do not worry about the faithless.

69. The faithful, the Jews, the Sabians, and the Christians that believe in God and the last day and are righteous will not fear or grieve.

70–71. We took a covenant from the Israelis and sent apostles to them. Whenever messengers brought them a message they didn't like, they would label some of them liars and kill the others. They thought there was no [possible] punishment, so they became as the deaf and blind. Even after God gave them mercy, many of them again acted deaf and blind. God sees all they do.

72. There are unbelievers that say, "God is the Messiah born to Mary." But the Messiah said, "Israelis, worship God, my Lord and your Lord." Those who ascribe partners to God will be forbidden from entering paradise by God. They shall reside in hell. The unjust will not have a guardian.

73–74. Unbelievers say, "God is one part of a trinity." There [surely] is no god except the one God. The faithless that do not renounce this statement will face a great punishment. Why don't they turn to God and ask His forgiveness? God is forgiving and merciful.

75. Mary's son, the Messiah, was only a messenger [apostle]. There were many messengers that died before him. Mary was an honest woman, and both of them had to eat food. See how We have made past signs more clear for people, and still they turn from the truth.

76. Ask them, "Instead of God, why do you worship something that cannot harm you or help you, when God knows and hears everything?"

77. Say to them, "People of the Book, don't go beyond the proper limits of your religion. Don't follow the false ways of the generations before you; they misled themselves and many people from the correct path."

78–79. David and Jesus, the son of Mary, spoke curses to the faithless among the Israelis for their disobedience and sins. They failed to forbid each other from being wicked. What they did was evil.

80–81. You now see many of them becoming friends with the unbelievers. This act is surely recorded against their souls [in heaven]. God is unhappy with them for this, and they will face torment in the hereafter. If they believed in God, the prophet, and the revelations, they would never choose them [the unfaithful] as friends. But most of them are sinners.

82–84. You will find that the people most hostile towards the faithful are the Jews and polytheists. You will also find that the friendliest towards the faithful are the ones that say, "We are Christians." They have priests and monks with them and are not arrogant. When they hear the revelations received by the messenger, you see them become tearful. They recognize the truth and say, "Our Lord, we believe, so list us among the witnesses. What reason is there for us not to believe in God and the truth revealed to us, when we desperately hope our Lord will allow us to join the righteous?"

85–86. Because of what they said, God rewarded them with an eternal home among the Gardens where streams flowed beneath them. That is the reward for the righteous. But those who are faithless and reject Our signs will enter hell.

87–88. Faithful, don't make laws forbidding things that God has ordained good for you. And don't break the laws, for God doesn't love sinners. Eat from what God provides as lawful and good, but be dutiful to God, in whom you believe.

89. God won't punish you for unintentionally breaking promises, but He will punish you for deliberately breaking your oath [to God]. To atone for this sin, feed ten needy people with the average meal you give your family, clothe them, or free a slave. If you cannot do any of these acts, then fast for three days. That is the compensation for breaking oaths, but it's best to keep your promises. This is how God makes His signs clear to you, so you can be grateful.

90–91. Oh faithful, wine, gambling, stone monuments, and divining arrows are a disgrace and come from Satan. Shun these things so you can be successful. With wine and gambling, Satan seeks to insert hatred among you, to keep you from remembering God, and to make you forget to pray. Won't you abstain from them?

92. Obey God, obey the messenger, and be wary. If you turn away, you should know it's only Our messenger's duty to recite the message clearly.

93. The faithful and righteous will not be blamed for anything they have eaten in the past. As long as they remember their duty to God, believe, and do good deeds. Continue to remember your duty to God and be faithful. Continue to remember your duty to God and be righteous. God loves the righteous.

94–95. Oh faithful, God will test you when you are hunting [wild] game with your hands and spears. He can then know who fears Him secretly. Those who sin after this will earn a painful punishment. Oh faithful, don't kill game on pilgrimage. If you kill game intentionally, then atone by bringing a domestic animal as offering to the Kaaba. It should be judged equivalent to the game by two men. Or to atone you can feed the needy, or fast equal to the animal. This is so the sinner can feel the consequences of their action. God has forgiven all these types of sins in your past, but if anyone resumes this activity God will punish them. God is the mighty avenger.

96. Wildlife from the sea and its food is permitted for you and the travelers, but wild game on land is forbidden on pilgrimage. Be wary of God, to whom you will all return.

97. God made the Kaaba, the sacred house, secure and beneficial for mankind; the same for the holy month and the offering of garlands. Know that God is aware of everything in the heavens and on earth. God knows everything.

98. Know that God punishes severely and that God is also forgiving and merciful.

99. The apostle's duty is simply to recite the message. God knows what you do in public and in private.

100–102. Say to them, "Evil and good things are not equal, and the richness of evil will attract you." For those who understand, be wary of God so that you can be successful. Oh faithful, don't question things that will trouble you if they are revealed. If you do ask while the Qur'an is being revealed, then you will be answered. God will forgive this, for God is forgiving and patient. People before you asked these questions and then lost their faith.

103. God did not invent superstitions about slitting camel ears, allowing camels to avoid work, sacrificing idols for livestock

twin births. These were lies against God created by unbelievers. Most of them are unwise.

104. When some are told, “Come believe in God’s revelations and the messenger,” they reply, “We are satisfied following our fathers’ ways.” How can this be when their fathers had no knowledge and no guidance?

105. Oh faithful, take care of your own souls. The unguided people cannot harm those who are correctly guided. To God you will all return, and He will recount everything you did before.

106–108. Oh faithful, when death is near choose two faithful witnesses to create your will [pass on your wealth]. If you are traveling, take two other [non-Muslim] men as witness. Choose them after prayers and ask them to vow to God, “We will not seek to gain from this, even if it passes to [our] relatives. We won’t hide this testimony before God, for that would be sinful.” If you find these two men have been guilty of sinning [perjury], then choose two others that are near the family and make them vow to God, “We are more truthful than those two men and have not sinned, for that would make us evildoers.” This method ensures that your testimony will be passed truthfully, as men would fear that others would be selected to become witnesses after them. Fear God and listen to Him. God does not guide evil people.

109. One day God will gather all the messengers and ask them, “What responses did you receive from mankind?” They will

reply, "We do not know. Only you know what's in a man's heart."

110. God will talk to Jesus, saying, "Jesus, son of Mary, do you remember when I gave My blessings to you and your mother? When I inspired you with the holy spirit so you could speak to mankind as a child and an adult? That I taught you the Book and wisdom, then the Torah and Gospel. When, with my permission, you made a clay bird and breathed life into it, healed the blind, cured the lepers, and raised the dead? When I kept the Israelis from harming you when you showed them clear signs, as the unfaithful sneered, 'This is only magic.'?"

111. I inspired the disciples to have faith in Me and My messenger. They said, "We believe and testify that we are in submission." [Muslims, muselmun]

112–113. The disciples asked, "Jesus, son of Mary, can your Lord send down to us foods from heaven?" Jesus replied, "Be wary of God if you are faithful." They responded, "We seek to eat the food so we can be satisfied that you have spoken the truth, and so we can witness a miracle."

114–115. Jesus, son of Mary, said, "God our Lord, send us a meal from heaven. It will be a feast for the earliest and later disciples and a sign from you. Grant us sustenance, for you are great sustainer." God replied, "I will send one, but if any of you reject faith after this, I will inflict a punishment on them like I have never done before."

116. God will ask [of Jesus], "Jesus, son of Mary, did you tell mankind, 'Worship me and my mother as gods beside God.'?" He [Jesus] will reply, "Glory to you. I had no right to say that, so I never could have. If I had said that, you would have known it. You know what's in my heart, and I don't know what's in yours. You know all that is secret."

117–118. "I [Jesus] only told them what you commanded me to say: 'Worship God, your Lord and mine.' I served as a witness to them, and after you took me up, you watched over them. You are a witness to all things. They are your servants, should you choose to punish them. And you may choose to forgive them, as surely you are mighty and wise."

119. God will reply, "Today the truth will benefit the honest men. They will eternally have Gardens with rivers flowing beneath them. God is pleased with them, and they are pleased with God. This is the greatest success."

120. God is the king of all that is in the heavens and on earth. He is able to do anything.

Chapter 113 (chronologically)

Sura 9 (129 verses), Al-Tawbah (The Atonement/Repentance)

1–2. [A statement of] immunity from God and His messenger towards the polytheists that you have made a treaty with: [permission] to travel across the lands for four months, but acknowledge that you cannot escape from God, and God will disgrace the faithless.

3–4. [This is] an announcement from God and His messenger that on the day of the greater pilgrimage, God and His messenger will dissolve all previous treaties with polytheists. It would be best if you repent, but if you reject the message, know that you cannot escape God. There is a painful punishment for those who won't believe, except for any polytheists that you [Muslims] have made a treaty with. As long as they have not failed you in any way or aided any of your enemies. Therefore, fulfill your treaty to them until its term ends. God loves those who keep their duty to Him.

5. Now, once the sacred months have passed, you should kill the polytheists wherever you find them. Capture them, surround them, and wait in ambush for them. If they repent, establish prayer, and give regularly to charity, then let them pass. God is forgiving and merciful.

6. If any of the polytheists ask you for protection, then grant it, so they can hear the word of God. Escort them to a safe place. Do this because they are an ignorant people.

7–8. How can a treaty, made before God and His messenger, be allowed with any polytheists besides the ones that you made an alliance with near the sacred mosque? [Because] as long as they keep their word, you must keep your word. God loves people that are steadfast in their duty. How [can there be a treaty] when you know that if they gain the upper hand, they will not treat you as a friend or honor their oaths? They try to please you with nice words while their hearts are hateful to you. Most of them are wicked.

9–10. They sold the signs of God for a small profit, and many of them block men from His way. They have committed evil deeds. They don't respect friendship or promises to the faithful. They are grave sinners.

11. But if they repent, establish prayer, and give to charity regularly, then they are your religious brothers in faith. We explain Our signs in detail for those willing to understand.

12. Now if they break their promises after the treaty and scorn your religion, then fight [not the term "jihad"] the leaders of the unfaithful. Because they do not keep their word, maybe they will stop.

13. Won't you fight [not the term "jihad"] the people that broke their promises, plotted to expel the messenger, and attacked you first? Do you fear them? It is God you should fear, if you are truly faithful.

14–15. Fight them [not the term "jihad"] and God will use your hands to punish and humiliate them. This will help you to beat them and strengthen [heal] the hearts of the faithful. It will remove the rage from their hearts. God gives mercy to who He chooses. God is knowing and wise.

16. Do you think you are safe? As if God doesn't know who among you struggled [jihad]? [That He] doesn't know who made friends with those who were not God, His messenger, or other faithful? God is aware of everything you do.

17. It is not [proper] for the polytheists to tend to God's mosques as they are testifying against their own souls for their disbelief. Their deeds would be in vain, and they will still dwell in the flames.

18. God's mosques shall be maintained only by people who believe in God and the last day, pray and give to charity regularly, and fear only God. Hopefully they are people on the right path.

19. Do you think that giving water to the pilgrims or maintaining the holy mosque has the same [value] as believing in God and the last day and struggling [jihad] in the way of God? They are not comparable to God. God does not guide the wicked.

20–22. Those who are faithful, have migrated, and struggle in the way of God with their wealth and their lives have greater worth to God. They will be successful. Their Lord gives them good news of His mercy, His pleasure, and the Gardens they will live in eternally. The greatest of all rewards is in God's presence.

23. Oh faithful, don't take your fathers and brothers for your friends if they desire faithlessness more than faith. Anyone that takes them as friends is doing wrong.

24. Say to them, "If you feel that your fathers, brothers, wives, tribe, wealth, possible business losses, or homes are more beloved by you than God, His messenger, and striving in His way [jihad], then wait until God passes judgment [on you]. God does not guide the wicked."

25–26. God helped you in many situations. On that day at Hunayn [battle fought in 630AD/CE], you were impressed by your own strength in numbers, but they didn't help you. Instead the lands, though vast, became narrow to you, and you retreated. But God sent down reassurances to His messenger and the faithful. He sent down unseen forces and punished the unfaithful. That is how He repays the faithless.

27. God will then share His mercy with whomever He chooses. God is forgiving and merciful.

28. Oh faithful, the polytheists are unclean. So, after this year, don't let them approach the holy mosque. If you are afraid of poverty, God will soon enrich you if He chooses. God is knowing and wise.

29. Fight [not the term "jihad"] people who were given the Book yet do not believe in God or the last day, fail to forbid things that have been forbidden by God and His messenger, or

acknowledge the true religion until they readily pay the tax for being non-Muslim and are subdued.

30. The Jews say that Ezra is the son of God, and the Christians [Nazarenes] say that the Messiah is the son of God. These words are from their own mouths, based on what the unbelievers before them used to say. May God destroy them. They are deluded.

31. They treat their scribes and monks like they are lords beside God. They also treat the Messiah, the son of Mary, as such, although he commanded them to serve only one God. There is no god except God. He is too glorious to have any partners associated with Him.

32. They are trying to extinguish the light of God with their words, but God will perfect His light, no matter how much the unbelievers oppose it.

33. He sent His messenger with guidance and the true religion, so that no matter how much the polytheists oppose, it might prevail over all other religions.

34–35. Oh faithful, there are many rabbis and monks that wrongly consume man's wealth and block them from the way of God. Warn those who hoard gold and silver instead of spending it in God's way of their grave penalty. The day that they will be burned by the hellfire and branded on their foreheads, sides, and backs, they will be told, "This is what you hoarded for yourselves. Now taste what you have hoarded."

36. God ordained that there would be twelve months [in a year] when He created the heavens and the earth. Four of them are sacred; that is the correct religious view. Do not sin during those months. Fight [not the term "jihad"] against all the polytheists as they fight against all of you. Remember that God sides with the righteous.

37. Postponing [or moving sacred months around] is an act of disbelief for those being misled. They make this legal one year and forbidden in the next, so they can adjust the number of God's sacred months each year and make sacred months normal. They think this evil act is correct. God does not guide the faithless.

38. Oh faithful, what is wrong with you? Why do you cling strongly to the earth when you are asked to "Go forward [not the term "jihad"] in the way of God"? Do you prefer this life to the hereafter? The comforts of this life are nothing compared to the hereafter.

39. If you do not go forward, He will punish you with a grave penalty and then put others in your place. You cannot harm Him at all. God has power over everything.

40. Whether you help him [or not] God has already helped him [Muhammad]. When the faithless drove him out and he had

only one companion. When the two were in a cave and he told his companion, "Do not fear, for God is with us." When God sent him composure and strengthened him with unseen forces. He made the unbelievers' words falter while raising the word of God to the highest. God is mighty and wise.

41. Go forward, lightly or heavily, and strive [jihad] with your wealth and lives in God's way. If you only knew what was best for you.

42. If they had seen an easy gain or a short journey, they would have followed you [Muhammad], but the distance looked long to them. And yet they swear by God, "If we could have, we certainly would have gone with you." They harm their own souls, for God knows they are lying.

43. May God forgive you. Why did you allow them to stay behind? You could see who was being truthful and who was lying.

44. Those who believe in God and the last day would never ask you to be exempt from struggling [jihad] with their wealth and their lives. God knows who do their duty [to Him].

45. Those asking you for an exemption do not believe in God and the last day. Their hearts are doubtful, so they hesitate.

46. If they had intended to travel, they would have surely prepared. But, God was against them traveling out, so He

made them hold back, saying, “Sit here with the sluggish ones.”

47–48. Had they traveled with you, it would not have strengthened you. They would have spread rumors and caused disagreements. There are spies among you, but God knows who is evil. Earlier [these people] tried to cause dissent and make things more difficult for you. That was until the truth arrived and the commandments of God were made clear, despite how much they opposed it.

49–50. There are some among them that say, “Give me an exemption, so I am not put in a predicament [about following him or not].” They are already being tested. Hell surrounds the disbelievers [always]. When things are going well for you they are grieving; but when you face hardship they gleefully say, “We are glad we took precautions.”

51. Say to them, “Nothing can happen to us that isn’t willed by God. He is our protector.” Let all the believers put their trust in God.

52. Say to them, “Are you waiting for anything besides one of the two best things? We also wait to see if God will send His punishment by His own hand or our own hands. We will wait with you.”

53–54. Say to them, “Whether you pay willingly or unwillingly, it [contributions] will not be accepted from you, for you are wicked people." The reasons their contributions are rejected are: they don't believe in God and His messenger, they only pray half-heartedly, and they make payments reluctantly.

55–57. Don't let their wealth or sons impress you. God plans to punish them with those very things in this life and take their souls while they are unbelievers. They swear to God that they are with you [believers], but they are not. They are afraid. If they could find a refuge, a cave, or a place to hide, they would quickly run to it.

58–60. There are some men that slander you about the distribution of charity donations. When they are given some of it, they are happy. If they are not, they are angry. They should be content with what God and His messenger gives them, saying, "God is enough for us. God and His messenger will share of His bounty soon. We turn our hopes to God." Charities are for the poor and needy, for charity officials, for enticing followers, for freeing captives, for debtors, for the cause of God, and for the travelers. This is God's ordinance. God is knowing and wise.

61–63. There are men who aggravate the prophet by saying, "He is just an ear [believes everything he hears]." Say to them, "An ear that listens to what's best for you. He believes in God, trusts the faithful, and is compassionate to those who believe." Those who aggravate the messenger face a painful punishment. They swear by God they will please you

[Muslims] but they should aim to please God and His messenger if they are truly believers. Don't they know that those in opposition to God and His messenger will dwell in the fires of hell? That is the ultimate disgrace.

64–66. The hypocrites fear that a new chapter [of revelations, a new sura] will arrive exposing what is truly in their hearts. Say to them, "Keep mocking this; God will reveal what you fear." If you do question them [about mocking you], they will say, "We are just joking around." Say to them, "Was it about God, His revelations, and His messenger you were mocking? Do not make excuses! You rejected the faith after you accepted it." If We forgive some of you, We will punish others for their sins.

67–68. Male and female hypocrites are all the same. They enable evil and forbid what is right, and they withhold payments. They have forgotten God, so He has forgotten them. The hypocrites are disobedient and sinful. God promises both male and female hypocrites and the unbelievers the fires of hell. There they will dwell, and it is appropriate for them. God has cursed them with this eternal penalty.

69. This is like an earlier group of people, although they were stronger, wealthier, and had more children. They enjoyed their life's circumstances like you do. They engaged in idle talk like you do. Their works were all in vain, on earth and in the hereafter. They were lost.

70. Haven't the stories of earlier generations reached them? The people of Noah, Ad, Thamud, Abraham, Midian, and the cities that were overthrown? They all received messengers with clear signs. God didn't treat them with injustice, they were unjust to their own souls.

71–72. The faithful men and women are supporters of one another. They enable what is right and forbid evil, pray and give to charity regularly, and obey God and His messenger. God will have mercy on them. God is mighty and wise. God has promised the faithful men and women eternal happiness in fine dwellings, in the Garden of Eden where rivers flow beneath them. But the greatest of all blessings is God's acceptance.

73. Oh prophet, strive [jihad] against the faithless and hypocrites. Be firm with them. Their ultimate place is hell, that evil destination.

74. They swear by God that they do no wrong, but they utter words of disbelief, and they renounce their faith after they have submitted. They plotted schemes [against you] that they couldn't carry out. They have no excuse for scheming, as God and His messenger enriched them from His bounty. It would be best if they repented, but if they return [to their evil] God will punish them severely in this life and the hereafter. There will be no one on earth that can protect them.

75–77. Some people pledged to God that if He shared His bounty, then they would give to charity and become righteous. But after He gave to them, they hoarded it and broke their pledge. Therefore, He placed hypocrisy in their hearts that would last until the day they returned to Him. This was for breaking their word to God and lying.

78. Don't they know that God knows their thoughts and their secret conversations? God knows all hidden things.

79. [There are] people who slander and ridicule the faithful for giving freely to charity and even the believers that have nothing to give except their hard work. God will ridicule them in return, and they will pay a great penalty.

80. It does not matter if you [Muhammad] ask for their forgiveness. Even if you ask seventy times, God will not forgive them. They have rejected God and His messenger, and God does not guide the wicked.

81. Behind the messenger of God's back, those who stayed behind [from an expedition] were happy to sit it out. They didn't want to strive [jihad] with their wealth and lives in the way of God. They advised, "Don't go out in this heat." Reply to them, "The fires of hell are more intense than this heat." If only they could understand.

82. Let them laugh for now, for they will cry later for the repayment they have earned.

83. If God brings you back in contact with any of these people, and they ask you if they can travel with you now, tell them, "You can never travel with me or fight [not the term "jihad"] any enemies with me. You were content before to sit it out, so now you stay behind with the stragglers."

84. Do not pray for these people when they die or visit their grave. They rejected God and His messenger and died in a state of wickedness.

85. Don't be impressed by their wealth and sons. God plans to punish them with these things in this life and make them perish while they are unbelievers.

86–87. When a chapter is revealed that asks men to believe in God and strive [jihad] beside His messenger, the wealthy men will ask for an exemption, saying, "Let us stay behind with those who sit at home." They are happy to stay with those who are left behind, because their hearts are sealed, and they don't even know it.

88. The messenger and the faithful that strive [jihad] like him with all their wealth and their lives are bound for good things. They will be successful.

89. God has prepared Gardens for them where rivers flow, and there they will dwell. This is the greatest achievement.

90. There were Bedouin Arabs that made excuses and claimed exemptions [from jihad] and also those who lied to God and

His messenger and who sat at home. A painful punishment awaits the unbelievers among them.

91. It is not the fault of the weak, sick, or poor who can't give [to the cause], as long as they keep their duty to God and His messenger. There are no grounds for blaming those who are righteous. God is forgiving and merciful.

92. There is also no fault in the men that came to you [faithful] and asked for an animal to ride [when you had none to give/sell]. When you told them, "I cannot provide you an animal," they turned away with tears of sorrow, for they could not give to the cause.

93. There is blame only for the ones that are wealthy and still ask for an exemption to stay at home. They prefer to stay with the others. God has sealed their hearts so they don't realize it.

94. When you return home, these men will start making excuses, so tell them, "Keep your excuses, for we won't believe them. God has told us the truth about you. God and His messenger see your actions. You will one day be brought before the One that knows what is public and private, and He will show you what you did."

95. They will promise in God's name, upon your return, that you should leave them alone. So leave them alone. They are impure, and they will dwell in hell, as payment for what they earned.

96. They will swear that you can be accepting of them. But if even if you can, God will not accept this disobedient bunch.

97–98. The desert Arabs are the most unfaithful and hypocritical. They are also most likely to be ignorant of the decrees that God sent down to His messenger. God is knowing and wise. Some of the desert Arabs think of their payments as a fine [punishment], and they are hoping for disaster to overcome you. The real disaster will harm their fortunes. God hears and knows everything.

99. But some of the desert Arabs believe in God and the last day. They think of their payments as sacred gifts that bring them closer to God and as a way to obtain the messenger's prayers. It is an acceptable offering, and God will extend His mercy to them. God is forgiving and merciful.

100. God is very pleased with the first followers [the vanguard] that migrated from their homes, those who aided them the [*ansar*], and those who followed them virtuously. Of course, they are pleased with God, who has prepared them Gardens where rivers flow beneath where they will dwell eternally. This is the supreme achievement.

101. Certain desert Arabs are hypocrites. Some citizens of Medina are stubborn hypocrites and thought you don't know them. We do. We shall punish them twice and then send them towards a grave penalty.

102. There are some people that have admitted their sins. They have confused righteous acts with evil ones. Maybe God will be merciful to them. For God is forgiving and merciful.

103. Take from their wealth some charitable funds, so you may purify them and then pray on their behalf. Your prayers are a relief for them. God hears and knows everything.

104. Don't they know that God is the One who accepts His followers' repentance, their charitable gifts, and that God is sympathetic and merciful?

105. Say to them, "Continue working so that God, His messenger, and the faithful can observe your actions. Soon you will return to the One who knows everything that is public and private. He will show you truthfully what you did.

106. There are others who also await God's decree. He will either punish them or extend His mercy. God is knowing and wise.

107–108. There are people that hold [take/join] a mosque for those that once warred against God and His messenger. They are unbelievers and seek to cause harm and disunity among the faithful. If you ask them their purpose, they will swear they have good intentions. God testifies that they are liars. So do not stand to pray there! You should instead pray in a mosque that was built on devotion from the beginning. There you will find men who seek to purify themselves. God loves those seeking purity.

109–110. Who is better? The man that lays a foundation based on duty to God and His grace or one that lays his foundation on the edge of a crumbling bank? A bank that is crumbling into hell and will take him with it. God does not guide the wicked. The [latter's] building foundation will always be a source of doubt in their hearts, until their hearts are torn to pieces. God is knowing and wise.

111–112. God has purchased the faithful's souls and possessions in exchange for paradise. They fight in the way of God, kill and are killed [none of those words are translated from "jihad"]. It's a promise from Him in the Torah, Gospel, and the Qur'an. Who keeps their promise better than God? Celebrate the bargain you have made with Him. It is a great achievement. [Celebrating are] those who are repentant, serve and praise Him, fast, bow and prostrate in prayer, call for goodness and forbid evil, and follow the laws set by God. Give the good news to the faithful!

113–114. It's not proper for the prophet or the faithful to pray for the forgiveness of polytheists, once it's clear that they are hellbound. Even if they are your relatives. When Abraham prayed for his father's forgiveness, it was only to keep a promise he made him. But once it was clear that his father was an enemy of God, he cut ties with him. Abraham was kind-hearted and patient.

115–116. God never leads anyone astray, once He has begun guiding them, until He makes clear to them what should be avoided. God knows all things. God is the sovereign of the heavens and the earth. He gives life and takes it. There is no protector except God.

117–118. God surely gave His mercy to the prophet, the migrants, and those people who supported them in their hour of need, when some of their hearts were weak. He is compassionate and merciful. His mercy also helped the three that were left behind [from an expedition]. They found themselves with no options and felt their souls were in jeopardy. They realized there was no escape from God, and their only refuge was in Him. His compassion was so they could become remorseful. God is the most compassionate and merciful.

119. Oh faithful, mind your duty to God and side with the honorable ones.

120–121. It is not right for the citizens of Medina or the desert Arabs among them to avoid serving with the messenger of God. They shouldn't place their own lives above his [Muhammad's]. No righteous deeds will be recorded in their ledger if they never experienced thirst, fatigue, or hunger serving the way of God. Or if they fail to take any steps that anger the faithless or gain any ground against an enemy. God doesn't waste the rewards for the virtuous [on those who don't earn it]. If they pay anything, small or large [for the cause], or navigate a valley, it is written down as a credit. God will repay them for the best things they did.

122. It doesn't make sense for all the faithful to leave together. Parts of every group can go out and study religion, so they can give warnings to their people when they return, so they are made aware.

123. Oh faithful, fight the unbelievers that are near to you and be harsh to them. Remember that God is with those who are dutiful to Him.

124–125. Every time a chapter is revealed, there are people who ask, "Who has become more faithful because of this?" But those who believe will have their faith increased and celebrate. Meanwhile those with diseased hearts will only have their wickedness doubled, and they will die as unbelievers.

126–127. Can't they see that every year they are tested once or twice? And still they are not regretful and don't learn from it. Every time a chapter is being revealed, they look at each other and ask, "Does anyone see anyone watching us?" and then walk away rejecting it. God turns the hearts of those who do not understand away from the lights.

128. [MC] A messenger has been chosen from among you. He worries about your souls, is very concerned for you, and is compassionate and merciful to the faithful.

129. [MC] If they turn away from you [Muhammad], then say to them, "God is all I need. There is no god but Him. I have put my trust in Him. He is the Lord on the supreme throne."

Chapter 114 (chronologically)

Sura 110 (3 verses), Al-Nasr (Assistance)

[Verse 3 from Mina on the last hajj]

1–3. When God's assistance and victory arrive, and you see crowds
of people entering God's religion, [3.] then celebrate the tributes
of your Lord and ask His forgiveness. He is always ready to
show mercy.

Section 2.

Analysis

This short analysis section is aimed at explaining what the contents of the Qur'an actually are compared to the myths and stereotypes about the contents. I have chosen the topics listed based on word repetitiveness in the text and the questions I get from my audiences about key topics.

As the three charts show, most of the topics and key words in the Qur'an are not what people usually assume based on what they have heard or read. More important, when you look at these graphics, notice how infrequently some of the most commonly used (or misused) words from the Qur'an are actually mentioned.

These are very close estimates about how often a word or concept appears in the Qur'an. Large numbers have been rounded, while smaller numbers are more precise. These charts are made using simple word searches of my English interpretation. The numbers will vary based on other interpretations and were designed to give the reader a visual sense of the contents of this text.

Word cloud of key topics and concepts in the Qur'an

Note: The graphic is based on a simple word search of key topics in this English interpretation. The top five topics in every ten-chapter grouping were used to create a word cloud for the entire book based on topic popularity throughout the Qur'an. This graphic is focused on concepts, although some proper names far outweighed the concepts in their grouping.

Comparison of major Qur'anic categories and topics

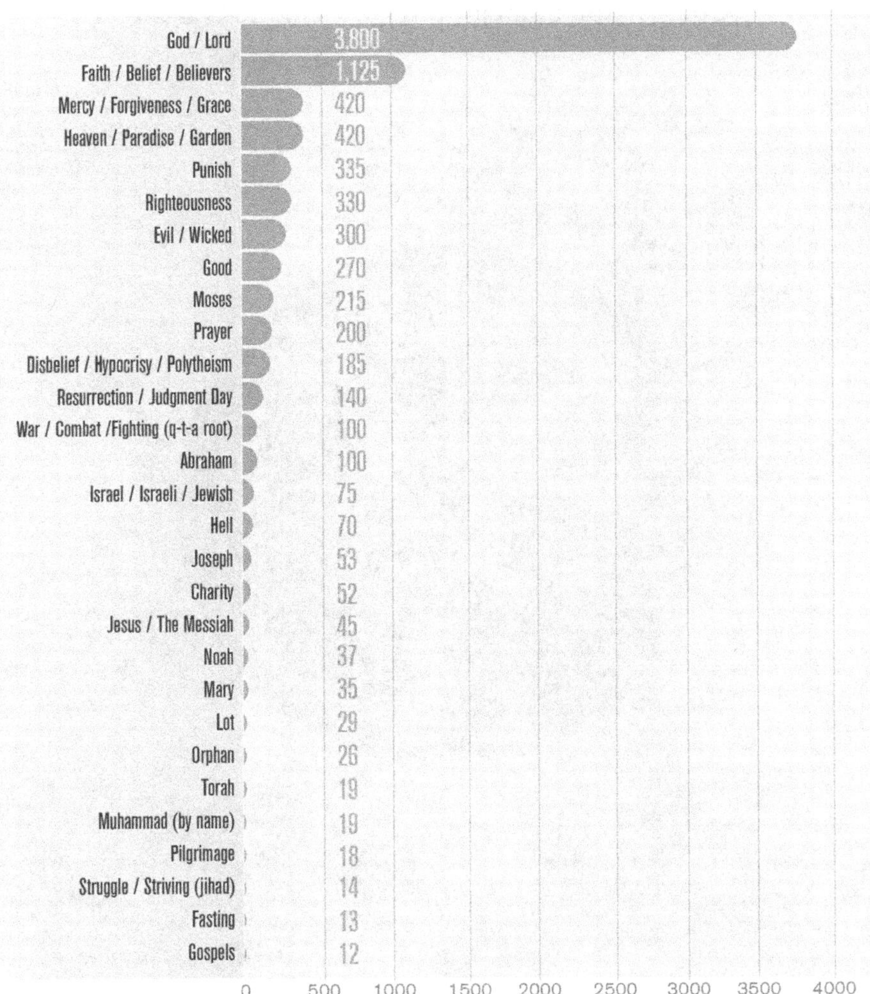

Note: A word search of this interpretation reveals the number of mentions of these topics.

Comparison of major categories in the Qur'an

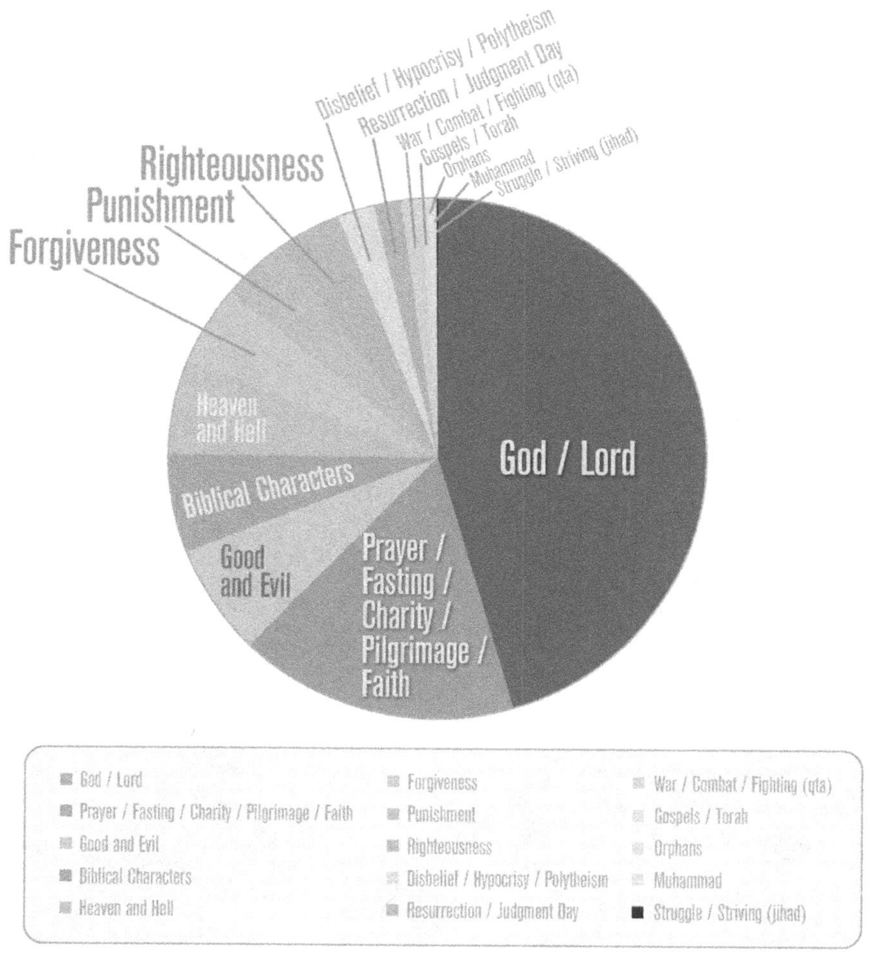

Note: This comparison allows readers to easily compare how much of the Qur'an is focused on some topics of interest to students of Islam.

Sources

Primary Sources

missionislam.com/quran/revealationorder.htm.

bombaxo.com/chronsurs.html.

qran.org/q-chrono.htm.

quran.com.

tanzil.net/docs/revelation_order.

oxfordislamicstudies.com/article/opr/t236/e0661.

Al Hilali, Muhammad and Khan, Muhammad. Interpretation of the Meanings of The Noble Qur'an in the English Language. Riyadh, Saudi Arabia: Darussalam, 1996.

Esposito, John. *Islam: The Straight Path*. New York: Oxford University Press, 2005.

Farah, Caesar. *Islam: Beliefs and Observances*. New York: Barrons, 2003.

Haleem, M.A.S. Abdel. *The Qur'an: English Translation with Parallel*

Arabic Text. New York: Oxford University Press, 2010.

Khalidi, Tarif. *The Quran: A New Translation*. London: Penguin Classics, 2008.

Pickthall, Muhammad. *The Holy Qur'an: Transliteration in Roman Script and English Translation with Arabic Text*. Various editions and publishers.

Qara'i, Ali Quli. *Holy Qur'an: Phrase by Phrase English Translation,* trans. Ali Quli Qara'i Elmhurst, NY: Tahrike Tarsile Qur'an, 2005.

Sahih International Qur'an. https://quran.com.

Shakir, Muhammad. *The Qur'an: Arabic Text and English Translation*. New York: Tahrike Tarsile Qur'an, 1993.

Tahir-ul-Qadri, Dr. Muhammad, *The Glorious Qur'an: English Translation*. London: Minhaj-ul-Quran Publications, 2014.

Yusuf Ali, Abdullah. *The Meaning of the Holy Qur'an*. Beltsville, MD: Amana Publications, 2001.

Supplemental Resources

Abu Khalil, Dr. Shauqi. *Atlas of the Qur'an, Places. Nations. Landmarks*. Riyadh, Saudi Arabia: Dar-us-Salam, 2003.

Algar, Hamid. *Wahhabism: A Critical Essay*. Oneonta, NY: Islamic Publications International, 2002.

Aslan, Reza. *No God but God: The Origins, Evolution, and Future of Islam*. New York: Random House, 2005.

Belt, Don. *The World of Islam*. Washington, DC: National Geographic, 2001.

Bergensen, Albert, ed. *The Sayyid Qutb Reader: Selected Writings on Politics, Religion, and Society*. New York: Routledge, 2008.

Cleveland, William. *A History of the Modern Middle East*. Boulder: Westview Press, 2004.

Dar rah Haqq's Board of Writers. *A Glance at the Life of the Holy Prophet of Islam*. Dubai, UAE: Green Gold General Trading, 2002.

Embassy of Saudi Arabia. *Understanding Islam and the Muslims*. Washington, DC, 1989.

Hafez, Mohammed. *Why Muslims Rebel: Repression and Resistance in the Islamic World*. Boulder: Lynne Rienner Publishers, 2004.

Hourani, Albert. *A History of the Arab Peoples*. New York: Warner Books, 1991.

Howk, Jason Criss. "Lions in the Path of Stability," thesis. Naval Postgraduate School, Monterey, CA, 2008.

Ibrahim, I. A. *A Brief Illustrated Guide to Understanding Islam*. Houston: Darussalam, 1997.

Kadhim, Abbas. "Politics and Theology of Imami Shia in Baghdad in the 5th. AH/11th. AD Century." PhD diss., University of California, Berkeley, 2005.

Malone, Joseph. *The Western Lands of Western Asia*. Englewood Cliffs, NJ: Prentice Hall, 1973.

Muhammad Ali (Maulana). *A Manual of Hadith*. Dublin, OH: Ahmadiyya Anujman Ishaat Islam Lahore USA, 1941.

Musavilari, Mujtaba. *Lessons on Islamic Doctrine*. Dubai, UAE: Green Gold General Trading, 2002.

Nasr, Vali. *The Shia Revival.* London W. W. Norton, 2006.

Rogerson, Barnaby. *The Heir of Muhammad: Islam's First Century and the Origins of the Sunni-Shia Split.* New York: The Overlook Press, 2008.

Russell, James, Editor. *Critical Issues Facing the Middle East.* New York: Palgrave, 2006.

Said, Edward. *Orientalism.* New York: Random House, 1978.

Shahrastani, Muhammad. *Muslim Sects and Divisions.* London: Kegan Paul International, 1984.

Tabataba'i, Mohammad. *Islamic Teachings, An Overview.* Dubai, UAE: Green Gold General Trading, 2002.

University of Leeds Qur'an tool. http://www.comp.leeds.ac.uk/nora/html/64-1.html.

Yuksel, al-Shaiban, Nefeh. *Quran, A Reformist Translation.* Brainbow Press, 2010.

Personal Resources

Field notes from Malone Fellowship in Islamic and Arabic Studies trip to the Sultanate of Oman.

Notes from Dr. Abbas Kadhim's Islam course and numerous other Middle Eastern–focused courses at the Naval Postgraduate School, Monterey, CA.

Notes from NCUSAR National Conferences, 2006–2016.

Conversations with Najibullah Sahak, MD; Abbas Kadhim, PhD; and John Duke Anthony, PhD.

Lessons from assisting the Afghan National Government develop their Reintegration, Reconciliation and Peace Program, August 2009–June 2010.

Notes from 18 months of interfaith dialogues given to predominantly non-Muslim audiences in the United States, 2015–2017.

Index A

(Subentries are listed by chronological chapter.
Locators are given by chapter, verse, and page number.
For example, 50:30 (138) indicates chapter 50, verse 30, page 138.)

Index of Commandments or Rules from God:

Index B

(Subentries are listed by chronological chapter.
Locators are given by chapter, verse, and page number.
For example, 50:30 (138) indicates chapter 50, verse 30, page 138.)

Index of Notable Passages and Controversial Topics in the Qur'an

About the Author

Jason Criss Howk is an author, public speaker, adjunct lecturer, and advisor. He focuses on Islam, foreign policy, national security, leadership, and strategy. He retired after 23 years in the U.S. Army operating on joint, interagency, and multinational teams conducting defense, diplomacy, education, and intelligence missions. He holds an MA in Middle East & South Asia Security Studies from the Naval Postgraduate School, studied Dari and Arabic at the Defense Language Institute, and has focused his career on the broader Middle East and the Islamic World. He is a Malone Fellow in Arab and Islamic Studies and a former term member on the Council on Foreign Relations.

During his career, Jason served as an assistant and advisor to three General officers involved with the Afghanistan war. He assisted Karl Eikenberry when he served in Kabul leading the U.S. effort to build the new Afghan National Army and to orchestrate the U.S. and UN led Afghanistan Security Sector Reform (SSR) program. He later assisted Stan McChrystal while he was evaluating and developing the new Afghan War strategy. Finally, Jason assisted Sir Graeme Lamb as he partnered with the Afghan government to develop an internationally supported Afghanistan Peace and Reconciliation process. In all these positions and in many others Jason worked directly with Muslim colleagues from Middle Eastern and South Asian nations and dozens of military and diplomatic officers from the international community.

Jason served on the FAO Journal of International Affairs editorial board, authored a monograph about the development of the International Security Sector Reform Program in Afghanistan, and authored a thesis/book about the Sultanate of Oman (later translated into Arabic). He has written for numerous publications and worked with various media outlets. He is a writer-in-residence at Weymouth and a member of the George C. Marshall Foundation. Jason earned a governmental success medal from Afghanistan and has been honored with the Legion of Merit and two Bronze Star Medals, among other awards, from the U.S. Government. In his spare time he mentors young adults seeking careers in foreign policy and national security.

He is currently leading interfaith dialogues across the United States to educate people about the differences among the religion of Islam, the concept of Islamism as a political ideology, and the deadly ideology followed by the modern global network of violent radical Islamist groups. His aim is to increase interreligious understanding and promote peaceful coexistence.

Follow Jason at Dispatches from Pinehurst (website and Facebook) and @jason_c_howk (Twitter).

The pens have stopped writing and the papers have dried.

—Imam Abu `Isa Muhammad at-Tirmidhi

50:38 Earth

5:51 Jews & christians

28:15-16 moses

CPSIA information can be obtained
at www.ICGtesting.com
Printed in the USA
BVHW070403231020
591513BV00007B/956